FIELD-MARSHAL SIR H. H. WILSON, BT., G.C.B., D.S.O.
COLONEL 1915–1922.

Printed and bound by Antony Rowe Ltd, Eastbourne

THE HISTORY OF THE FIRST SEVEN BATTALIONS
THE ROYAL IRISH RIFLES
(*Now The Royal Ulster Rifles*)

EX LIBRIS

For Private Circulation only.]

THE HISTORY OF
THE FIRST SEVEN BATTALIONS

The Royal Irish Rifles
(Now The Royal Ulster Rifles)

IN THE GREAT WAR

Vol. II

By
CYRIL FALLS
Formerly Captain, General Staff, 36th (Ulster) Division

Printed for the Regimental Committee by
GALE & POLDEN LTD., WELLINGTON WORKS, ALDERSHOT
1925

FOREWORD

THIS History has been written with the object of filling in the gap that existed, in the historical record of the Regiment, between the narrative of events up to the year 1912—which was so carefully compiled by the late Lieut.-Colonel Laurie—and the story of the deeds of the 36th (Ulster) Division, which has been well told by Captain Falls.

When, during the war, in various divisions and at various times, I saw battalions of the Royal Irish Rifles, I had, of course, no idea that in the future I should have the honour of becoming Colonel of so distinguished a regiment. But even so, I have very special recollections of the gallant deeds performed by the 6th Battalion under my command and under my own eyes on the Gallipoli Peninsula, and by the 2nd Battalion in my Corps at the Battle of Messines; also of the soldierly bearing of the 7th Battalion as it paraded for my inspection and marched past me on the market square at Bailleul in 1917. *Of the Special Reserve Battalions their fate was to remain at home, but they may rightly share in the glory, for it was to them that their sister battalions overseas turned to replace their casualties.* They performed their duty right well. And when I read the stirring words of my old friend and fellow campaigner, Major-General Sir Wilkinson Bird, the account that his Battalion gave of itself under his exceptionally gallant and capable leadership in the early days of 1914, and the brilliant record of the 1st Battalion, I feel more than ever proud—as a North of Ireland man who has done all his regimental soldiering in Irish regiments—to think that I should have been chosen as the successor to our late Colonel, Field-Marshal Sir Henry Wilson. Would that he were still with us to write this Foreword. How proud he would have been to read such a record of his Regiment, in which his interest was so intense. But the fact that he was our Colonel is ever with us, and the example of his career as a soldier and that of General Bird, coupled with this story of the Regiment in the Great War, cannot fail to ensure that the history of the Royal Ulster Rifles of the future will be as glorious as that of the 83rd and 86th Foot and Royal Irish Rifles in the past.

We owe a great debt of thanks to Captain Falls and Captain Whitfeld for this admirable narrative.

Alex Godley
General

Colonel, Royal Ulster Rifles.

BRITISH ARMY OF THE RHINE,
April 14th, 1924.

AUTHOR'S PREFACE

THIS record, the inception of which was due to Lieut.-Colonel H. R. Charley, C.B.E., then Commanding the 1st Battalion, is chiefly compiled from the official War Diaries of the battalions concerned, and of their brigades and divisions. I have to acknowledge information from private diaries which has supplemented these, in particular the very valuable diaries of Major-General Sir W. D. Bird, K.B.E., C.B., C.M.G., D.S.O., Captain G. H. P. Whitfeld, M.C., and Father Gill, S.J., formerly Roman Catholic Chaplain to the 2nd Battalion. To Captain Whitfeld, who has carried out all the correspondence, and given me all the assistance possible, I am particularly indebted, and, so far as the result is of value, the Regiment also. I desire also to thank Major A. F. Becke, late R.A., in charge of Maps, Historical Section (Military Branch) Committee of Imperial Defence, for his kindly help with regard to sketch maps, and Mr. H. Burge, the draughtsman, for his good work on them.

I am indebted to the War Office for their permission to reproduce the official maps. I also acknowledge the courtesy of the History Committee of the 36th (Ulster) Division in supplying maps.

This volume, though concerned only with the Great War, is a continuation of Volume I of the Regimental History by the late Lieut.-Colonel G. B. Laurie, published at the beginning of 1914. There is little to be said of the short and uneventful period between the publication of the latter and the order for mobilization.

The 1st Battalion was in India, at the point where Colonel Laurie left its future. On October 28th, 1912, he himself was promoted Lieutenant-Colonel, and assumed command of the Battalion; Lieut.-Colonel W. E. O'Leary being placed on the half-pay list. On December 7th, 1913, the Battalion, less " C " and " F " Companies, left Kamptee for Aden, where it remained, as will be seen, till considerably after the outbreak of war.

The 2nd Battalion was left at Tidworth, and it made no further move till it received the order for mobilization. Lieut.-Colonel J. Hamilton Bell, the Commanding Officer, went on half-pay early in 1913, and was succeeded in September by Lieut.-Colonel W. D. Bird, late the Queen's Royal Regiment (West Surrey).

On March 14th, 1914, General Wilmot Bradford, Colonel of the Royal Irish Rifles, died at Bournemouth, at the great age of ninety-nine years. Sir H. H. Wilson, his successor, was not appointed till November 11th, 1914.

CONTENTS

BOOK I: 1914

CHAPTER I
	PAGE
I. The Outbreak of War	1
II. The Battle of Mons	3
III. The Battle of Le Cateau	6
IV. The Retreat	8

CHAPTER II
I. The Marne and the Advance to the Aisne	11
II. The Battle of the Aisne	13
III. The Battle of La Bassée	16

CHAPTER III
I. Formation of the 6th and 7th Battalions	20
II. The 1st Battalion returns from Aden	21
III. The 2nd Battalion in the Salient and before Wytschaete	22

BOOK II: 1915

CHAPTER I
I. The 2nd Battalion in early 1915	26
II. The Battle of Neuve Chapelle	27
III. The Attack at Fromelles	31

CHAPTER II
I. Trench Warfare: The 1st Battalion	34
II. The First Attack on Bellewaarde	34
III. The 2nd Battalion in the Salient	37

CHAPTER III
I. The Second Attack on Bellewaarde	39
II. The Action of Bois Grenier	42

CHAPTER IV
I. Winter, 1915: The 1st Battalion	46
II. Winter, 1915: The 2nd Battalion	47
III. The 7th Battalion	48

CHAPTER V
I. The Suvla Bay Scheme	50
II. The Battle of Sari Bair	51
III. The Move to Salonika	53
IV. The Actions of Kosturino and Retreat on Salonika	54
V. The Move to Rendina Gorge	55

BOOK III: 1916

CHAPTER I

	PAGE
I. January—June, 1916: The 1st Battalion	58
II. 2nd Battalion's Raid at Le Touquet	60
III. 2nd Battalion in Mine Warfare near Arras	61
IV. The 7th Battalion and the April Gas Attacks	64

CHAPTER II

I. The Battle of Albert: 1st Battalion	66
II. The Battle of Albert: 2nd Battalion	68
III. The Battle of Bazentin Ridge	70
IV. Trench Warfare on the Somme	71
V. The Battle of Ginchy	72
VI. The 1st Battalion at Loos	75

CHAPTER III

I. The Battle of the Ancre Heights	76
II. The 1st Battalion in Attack on Misty Trench	77
III. The 2nd Battalion at Ploegsteert	79
IV. The 7th Battalion in Flanders	80

CHAPTER IV

I. The 6th Battalion's Life in Macedonia	81
II. Operations in the Struma Valley and Capture of Jenikoj	84
III. The Affair of Barakli-Jama'a	85

CHAPTER V

I. The 3rd, 4th and 5th Battalions	87
II. The Rebellion of Easter Week in Ireland	88

BOOK IV: 1917

CHAPTER I

I. The German Retreat to the Hindenburg Line	91
II. The 2nd Battalion in Early 1917	94
III. The 7th Battalion in Early 1917	95

CHAPTER II.

I. The Battle of Messines, 1917: The 2nd Battalion	97
II. The Battle of Messines, 1917: The 7th Battalion	99
III. The Battle of Pilckem Ridge	100
IV. The Capture of Westhoek	103
V. The Battle of Langemarck: The 1st Battalion	106
VI. The Battle of Langemarck: The 7th Battalion	108

CHAPTER III.

I. Autumn, 1917: The 1st Battalion	111
II. Autumn, 1917: The 2nd Battalion	112
III. Autumn, 1917: The End of the 7th Battalion	113

CHAPTER IV

		PAGE
I. The Battle of Cambrai: The Tank Attack	...	115
II. The Capture of Bourlon Wood: The 2nd Battalion at Mœuvres	...	117
III. The German Counter-Attacks	...	118
IV. The Second Battle of Passchendaele	...	120

CHAPTER V

I. The Struma Valley	...	122
II. The Evacuation of the Struma Valley	...	124
III. The Move to Palestine	...	125
IV. The Third Battle of Gaza	...	126

BOOK V

CHAPTER I

I. January—March, 1918	...	131
II. The Actions of Tell 'Asur	...	132
III. The End of the 6th Battalion	...	134

CHAPTER II

I. Early 1918	...	136
II. The Battle of St. Quentin	...	139
III. The Actions at the Somme Crossings	...	142
IV. The Battle of Rosières	...	143
V. The End of the Retreat	...	144

CHAPTER III

I. The Move to Flanders	...	146
II. Withdrawal in the Salient	...	147
III. In Line at Bailleul	...	149
IV. The German Retirement	...	150

CHAPTER IV

I. The Battle of Ypres, 1918	...	153
II. The Battle of Courtrai	...	155
Conclusion	...	160

APPENDICES

I. List of Honours and Rewards issued to Officers belonging to the first seven Battalions of the Royal Irish Rifles for Services in the Great War, 1914-19	...	167
II. List of Decorations awarded to Warrant Officers, Non-Commissioned Officers and Men of the first seven Battalions of the Royal Irish Rifles for Services in the Great War, 1914-19	...	174
III. Roll of Honour: Officers	...	182
Roll of Honour: Other Ranks	...	185
IV. Number of Other Ranks who proceeded as Reinforcements from the Special Reserve Battalions—3rd, 4th, 5th Battalions Royal Irish Rifles, during the Great War, 1914-18	...	186
V. Title of the Regiment	...	186
VI. List of Battle Honours and Committee	...	187
VII. Regimental Committee on Battle Honours for the Great War	...	188

ILLUSTRATIONS

FIELD-MARSHAL SIR H. H. WILSON, BT., G.C.B., D.S.O., COLONEL 1915–1922 *Frontispiece*

FACING PAGE

THE ULSTER DIVISION MEMORIAL AT THIEPVAL, FRANCE 70
MEMORIAL TABLET IN THE ROYAL MILITARY COLLEGE CHAPEL, SANDHURST 182

MAPS AND SKETCHES

FACING PAGE

THE BATTLE OF MONS	6
THE BATTLE OF LE CATEAU	8
THE BATTLE OF THE AISNE	16
THE BATTLE OF LA BASSÉE	18
THE BATTLE OF NEUVE CHAPELLE	30
THE FIRST ATTACK ON BELLEWAARDE	36
THE SECOND ATTACK ON BELLEWAARDE	42
THE BATTLE OF SARI BAIR	52
THE BATTLE OF THE SOMME	70
THE ATTACK AT GINCHY	74
THE NORTHERN BATTLEFIELD OF THE SOMME	94
THE BATTLE OF MESSINES, 1917	100
THE BATTLES OF YPRES, 1917	110
THE BATTLE OF CAMBRAI, 1917	118
THE SALONIKA THEATRE	126
JUDEA	134
THE BATTLE OF ST. QUENTIN	140
THE RETREAT OF MARCH, 1918	144
THE FINAL ADVANCES, 1918	160

INTRODUCTION

A REGIMENT is a large family. No member of a family has, I suppose, a soul so small as to deaden all sense of interest in tales of his ancestors. But when, as in our case, the family is great and its record second to none, the story of illustrious deeds can surely never fail to awaken a thrill of pride, an impulse of emulation.

All the fine qualities that belong to race and are developed in training—the fire and resilience of the Southern Irish, the firmness of their northern brothers, for we were Irish before we became Ulster, and to a small extent the coolness of the English and the lively courage of the men of Jersey—are blazoned in the pages of Captain Falls' narrative of the deeds of our family.

Obedience, which the greatest of all soldiers has assured us is to be accounted in war above every other quality, and endurance shine out in the story of the Retreat from Mons. Steadfastness and self-sacrifice are displayed in the long trial of trench warfare in the clinging mud of Flanders; in the bitter, bloody protracted battles of the Western Front; in the fierce striving to go forward on the rock-bound coastline of Gallipoli; in the fever-stricken areas of Salonika; and in the ardent training for these harsh tests that took place in the home lands. Swift, timely daring is exhibited on every stricken field; and men march in the spirit of crusaders over the holy hills of Palestine.

The history of our first seven battalions indeed shows war in every one of its aspects. War was once described as glorious for the "pride, pomp, and circumstance" that made "ambition virtue." War is still glorious, but its glory is decked in the austerer dress of suffering. In place of pomp have come the dread responsibility of commanders, and the equally heavy charge that is laid on those in the lower ranks; for to each in his own particular work are entrusted, at one time or another, the lives of all his comrades. We are now shown, instead of pride, the long, rugged struggle upward against enemy forces that had been prepared during years of plodding endeavour; and we see in strong contrast to the vaulting ambition of our enemies the romance of the final victory.

It is such tales as this that cannot fail to teach the love of right because it is the right, and all the high thoughts that go to make a man.

W. D. Bird
Major General

THE ROYAL IRISH RIFLES IN THE GREAT WAR

BOOK I: 1914.

CHAPTER I

I.—THE OUTBREAK OF WAR.

IT was at 7 p.m., on August 4th, 1914, that the British Ambassador handed to the German Foreign Minister Sir Edward Grey's ultimatum on the subject of Belgian neutrality. No formal reply to that ultimatum was tendered, and, automatically, by 12 midnight there was a state of war between the two countries. The British mobilization had been delayed as long as possible, in order not to jeopardize the last efforts for peace. It was not till 6 p.m. on the afternoon of the 4th that the 2nd Battalion the Royal Irish Rifles, at Tidworth, received orders to mobilize. Earlier that day German advanced guards had already crossed the Belgian frontier, and artillery had opened fire upon the forts of Liège. By August 9th the mobilization of the 2nd Battalion was complete, and it was ready for its move with the Expeditionary Force to France. Meanwhile the Reserve Battalions had also mobilized. The 3rd Battalion (Antrim) was undergoing its annual training at Kinnegar Camp, Holywood. On the order for mobilization being received, training was suspended, the regular establishment returning to Belfast that same night. Upon it fell the duty of receiving the reservists as they rejoined. On the 6th a draft of 224 was despatched to the 2nd Battalion at Tidworth. On the 8th the 3rd Battalion moved from Belfast to Dublin, being quartered for a few days at Ship Street Barracks, and then in Portobello Barracks. The 4th Battalion (Royal North Down) mobilized at Newtownards on August 5th, moving next day to Palace Barracks, Holywood, whence detachments proceeded for coast defence duties to Bangor, Donaghadee, Belfast, and Greypoint Battery. Over five hundred ex-soldiers and recruits joined in August. The 5th Battalion (Royal South Down) was mobilized on August 8th, and for a short time accommodated in the Ulster Hall, Belfast, later being moved to Victoria Barracks. The Foreign Service Battalion, the 1st, passed the first two months of the war quietly enough at Aden, large parties working on the Aden defences. Detachments were sent to escort prizes to Bombay during this period.

The British Expeditionary Force to cross the Channel and take up its position on the left of the French line was to consist of two infantry corps and one cavalry division. The II Corps, to the command of which General Sir H. Smith-Dorrien succeeded on the sudden death of General Sir J. Grierson, consisted of the 3rd and 5th Divisions. The 3rd Division, commanded by Major-General Sir H. Hamilton—a name that had assuredly ranked among those of the greatest British commanders in the war but for its owner's untimely death—consisted, as to infantry, of the 7th, 8th and 9th Infantry Brigades. In the 7th Brigade, which was commanded by Brigadier-General McCracken, was the 2nd Royal Irish Rifles ; the other battalions being the 2nd South Lancashire Regiment, the 3rd Worcestershire Regiment, and the 1st Wiltshire Regiment. The 2nd Royal Irish Rifles was commanded by Lieutenant-Colonel W. D. Bird.

The passage and concentration of the Expeditionary Force will always be remembered in military annals by reason of its swiftness, smoothness and secrecy. Not one in a thousand of the inhabitants of this country knew anything about it till the official announcement that it had been accomplished. All the accounts of it are the baldest and shortest statements of moves, simply because from start to finish it was carried out without hitch. That dealing with the 2nd Royal Irish Rifles is no exception. On the afternoon of August 13th the Battalion left Tidworth for Southampton, in two trains. The first half sailed on the *Ennisfallen* at 8 p.m., reaching Havre at 5 a.m. next morning, and disembarking at Rouen in the evening. The second half-battalion, embarking on the *Sarnia*, did not sail till 4.30 a.m. on the 14th, but was nevertheless at Rouen over an hour in advance of the first half. The Battalion marched to a camp at Mont. St. Aigan, three miles from the quays of Rouen. As some faint foretaste of the conditions to be prevalent for the next four years, a thunderstorm, with torrents of rain, turned the camping-ground into liquid mud that night, and rain fell all the following day.

However, the Battalion was not to be here for long. On the morning of the 16th it entrained at Rouen, and was carried to Aulnoye, a village east of the great Forest of Mormal, where it billeted in a factory. Next morning it marched to Marbaix, five miles farther south. Here it remained for two days, during which route marches were carried out, moving on to St. Hilaire, on the outskirts of Avesnes, on the 20th. It was still, it will be seen, a long way from the position upon which the British Army was to meet the enemy, the Condé—Mons Canal. No officer or man in its ranks, it may safely be said, knew anything of what progress the war was making. None can have known, when in the afternoon of the 20th the Battalion marched through Avesnes, to be " shown off " to the townsmen, and was greeted with wild enthusiasm, that at that very moment the Germans were making a triumphal entry into Brussels, and, away to the east, had reached the banks of the Meuse. But they had not long to wait before the real business of the campaign began. On the 21st the 3rd Division marched north, starting at 4 a.m., the 7th Brigade billeting the night at Feignies, near Maubeuge. The march was not excessively long, about eighteen miles, but the heat at midday was very great, and the roads were dusty. The troops were much fatigued by the time they reached their billets. The following morning the march was resumed at 7.17 a.m. There was a long halt at Quévy-le-Petit, and by about 1 p.m. the Battalion was at Ciply, an industrial village two miles south of Mons. The heat at midday had again severely tried the troops, the atmosphere being particularly close and sultry. At Ciply was concentrated the whole of the 7th Brigade, except the 2nd South Lancashire, which was at Frameries, a town of 12,000 inhabitants, a couple of miles farther west. Later in the afternoon a company of the 2nd Royal Irish Rifles was sent to Nouvelles, the next village east of Ciply, on outpost duty.

II.—THE BATTLE OF MONS.

The country in which the troops found themselves was as ugly as the ugliest corner of Durham. Mons is the centre of a great coal-field, and an important railway junction. West and south-west is a nest of towns, Jemappes, Quaregnon, St. Ghislain, Paturages, Frameries, La Bouverie, each with ten thousand inhabitants and upward, the boundary of each being hard to discover, so thickly powdered is the plain with miners' cottages and high slag-heaps about pit-heads. The only good defensive position, when time for preparation is not available, is the line of the Condé Canal, and it was along this that the II Corps took up its position on the evening of August 22nd. The 3rd Division was on the right, with an outpost line from Villers-St. Ghislain on the Mons—Binche road, through Nimy, on the Canal north of Mons, to the Mariette bridge, four and a half miles west of the town. The 8th Brigade was on the right, the 9th on the left, the 7th in reserve in the positions mentioned.

At 6 a.m. on the 23rd, while his battalion was standing to arms, Lieut.-Colonel Bird was sent for by Brigadier-General McCracken, commanding the 7th Brigade, and rode with him and his Brigade Major into Harmignies. General McCracken pointed out to him a line along an undulating plain, from the village up to but excluding a high bluff a mile north of it, upon which he was to entrench. The Battalion was moving to this position when it encountered troops of the 4th (Guards) Brigade, from whom Colonel Bird learnt that they were to take his place and that he was to move back to the cross-roads east of Nouvelles. This point was reached at 11.30 a.m., and arms were piled. An hour later the Cavalry Squadron* of the 3rd Division passed through, reporting that it had lost heavily and that the enemy was advancing. Then came an officer of the 2nd Royal Scots, with orders that the Royal Irish Rifles was to relieve that battalion at the bluff which Colonel Bird had seen in the morning. This position was reached at 2.30 p.m.

Of what had happened during the morning, Colonel Bird and his officers were completely unaware. Indeed, it would seem that during the early open warfare of the campaign, battalion commanders were rarely able to form any appreciation of the general situation, or knew the intentions of the command. On the troops of the I Corps coming into line on the right, the outpost position of the 3rd Division on that flank had been withdrawn to this bluff, north of Harmignies station. Thence it ran round Mons, by St. Symphorien to the bridge at Obourg, through Nimy to Mariette. The 7th Brigade, less the 2nd Royal Irish Rifles, was in reserve, preparing a defensive position from Nouvelles to about the third kilometre-stone on the Mons—Frameries road. From about eleven o'clock onwards heavy attacks had been launched by the enemy on the sharp salient of the canal-line north of Mons, and had been repulsed with great loss, the German masses offering extraordinary targets to the rapid fire of the 8th Brigade. Eventually, however, the Germans having crossed the canal east of Obourg, the line of the 3rd Division was withdrawn to the south of Mons, the 9th Brigade now prolonging the line of the 7th, from north of Frameries. It will be seen that thus at 3 p.m., by the time this withdrawal was complete, the line of the 7th Brigade had become the main line of resistance, and that the 2nd Royal Irish Rifles was separated from its own Brigade.

Colonel Bird found a company of the 2nd Royal Scots extended along the bluff, the remainder of the battalion being on the Mons—Harmignies road in rear. He

* 15th Hussars.

extended two of his companies, " C " and " D," on its right, put his machine guns into position to flank the line of the Royal Scots along the Mons road, holding his remaining two companies in the cutting, where the road to Harmignies wound its way up the bluff. The position was by no means ideal, but was as good as was likely to be found. In any case trenches had already been half dug. The machine guns and the flanking company had an excellent field of fire, up to 2,000 yards, but on the rest of the front held by the two battalions the field of fire was poor, there being dead ground from 1,500 to 300 yards.

At 4 p.m. the German batteries opened fire, and it was seen that an attack was developing. Lieut.-Colonel McMicking, commanding the 2nd Royal Scots, then asked for Colonel Bird's reserve companies, stating that he did not think he could hold his position without them. They were accordingly sent to him. Hardly were they in position when the men of the Battalion saw for the first time the grey waves advancing.

Heavy losses were inflicted on the enemy at long range, but owing to the nature of the ground, which has been described, he could not be prevented from pressing up to within 300 yards, the general sight-line of the position. According to the modern German theories, it should have been easy to rush the defence from this point. But these theories had not taken into account the musketry training of the little professional British Army, which had been developed to a perfection unknown among continental short-service levies. As the Germans came forward, such a blast of rapid fire burst forth all along the line as pinned them to the ground or drove them back to cover. The artillery fire was heavy, but the shrapnel was bursting high, and did not cause serious loss or inconvenience. The first attack had been a complete failure.

Between 5 and 5.30 p.m. the position was reinforced by the 2nd Grenadier Guards and 1st Irish Guards of the 4th (Guards) Brigade, troops of which brigade had, doubtless owing to contradictory orders, played a game of hide-and-seek with the Royal Irish Rifles that morning. A fresh attack was launched by the enemy after 6 o'clock, and again ended with the triumph of British rapid fire. Then fell quiet. In Colonel Bird's belief the enemy had fallen back to cook, leaving an outpost line in front of the British position at this point. The light of his fires could be seen. The Royal Irish Rifles had four men killed and a few wounded in the action. The 8th and 9th Brigades of their Division, which had borne the brunt of the fighting, had suffered somewhat severe losses.

In the first day's fighting the II Corps had merely been forced to withdraw to a second line of defence from its dangerous salient round Mons. It had experienced no real difficulty in checking the enemy. The men were weary, but their opponents had been at least as highly tried, as they knew. They must have felt that in such conditions they could resist almost indefinitely, and there was general surprise when the order came for a retirement. But at 5 p.m. the British Commander-in-Chief had learnt that the Fifth French Army on his right was in retirement, and that he himself was being attacked by the whole of the German First Army, of four corps. With his left in imminent danger of being turned, with a gap on his right, with a force at least twice his own upon his front, there was no choice between immediate retreat and eventual annihilation.

It appears to have been the intention of Major-General Hamilton that the 2nd Royal Irish Rifles should rejoin its brigade upon the line Nouvelles—Ciply—Frameries, as, between 8 and 8.30 p.m., Colonel Bird received orders to withdraw at 10. But Brigadier-

General Doran, commanding the 8th Brigade, told him that he must remain upon the bluff till the troops of that brigade had withdrawn, and that this would probably be accomplished by midnight. It was, however, actually 2 a.m. on the 24th before the Battalion was able to go, its retirement being covered by the troops of the 4th (Guards) Brigade. By 5 a.m. it was at the place from which it had advanced, the cross-roads east of Nouvelles. Had the Commanding Officer known it, he was not far from the 1st Wiltshire of his brigade, but in the grey dawn, with all roads choked by the transport and throngs of refugees from this densely-populated area, he was unable to find any trace of the latter. Large columns were moving down the Mons—Maubeuge road. A staff officer of the 3rd Division stated that the 7th Brigade was to the west. The Battalion therefore cut across the retreating columns. His men being very fatigued, Colonel Bird ordered them to discard their packs.

As a matter of fact, he was upon an entirely different line of retreat from that of his brigade, which, after beating off heavy German attacks in the early hours of the morning, received orders at 6.45 a.m. to retire upon Bavai. Discovering his mistake, Colonel Bird decided to strike across country. His first-line transport, which had been at Nouvelles, was swept on with the general stream into Maubeuge, and was not recovered for several days. The Battalion marched by a field-track into Quévy-le-Petit, and thence along the lane from that village to Blairegnies. Taisnières was reached at 3 p.m., and the Battalion halted for a meal. It then moved into Bavai, where the rest of the 7th Brigade was met at 5 p.m. The whole Brigade then marched out on the Valenciennes road to the hamlet of Le Plat de Bois, and bivouacked for the night. Food had been dumped there, and the troops were able to enjoy some rest behind the shelter of their outposts.

At 5 a.m. on the morning of the 25th orders were issued by the 7th Brigade which announced that the 3rd Division was continuing its retirement in a south-westerly direction, in two columns, with the 7th Brigade acting as rearguard. Outposts were withdrawn at 8 a.m. and the retreat began. There was no sign of the enemy save for a few horsemen, but General McCracken learnt shortly afterwards that Valenciennes had fallen. The column was accordingly closed up, the 2nd Royal Irish Rifles acting as rearguard. The Battalion left Le Quesnoy, marching along the Solesmes road, at 3.30 p.m., considerably in rear of the Brigade, owing to an order to wait for a section of howitzers. It had rejoined the latter less than twenty-four hours previously. Now it was to be cut off from it once again.

About 4 p.m. an intelligent despatch rider, passing along the column, showed Colonel Bird a message addressed to the 3rd Division to the effect that there were " two columns of the enemy close behind and one or two cavalry regiments, with artillery and infantry, moving on Le Quesnoy." At the same time he received a message from Lieut.-Colonel Pitman, commanding the 11th Hussars, that he would hold on as long as possible in Le Quesnoy, but did not expect to be able to check the enemy for long. Colonel Bird continued his march, and reached Romeries, where he had been promised relief, at 5.30 p.m. Here he was checked by artillery crossing his front, and, while he halted, the village was shelled with shrapnel. Clearly the enemy was close at hand. From the cross-roads, 400 yards east of Solesmes, he saw the village in flames. He was in the midst of British cavalry, which knew nothing of his brigade, and of the latter he could find no trace. As a fact, it had been heavily engaged on the plateau north-west of Solesmes, had fought a rearguard action south of the village, and was retiring upon Caudry. Two mounted officers, sent into Solesmes, failed to find it. It is doubtful if Colonel Bird, even had he known its whereabouts and direction, could have crossed the Selle River, so swift had been the German advance here. He had to fall back somewhere, and he decided that at Le Cateau he was most likely to get orders and information. The Battalion marched with General Briggs's Cavalry Brigade by the shortest route, through Amerval, picking up on the way the 41st Battery, R.F.A. (42nd Brigade : 3rd Divisional Artillery). At Le Cateau a telephone message was sent to the II Corps, which ordered the Battalion to march to Reumont and take the battery with it. It reached this village at 2 a.m. on the 26th, reporting to the 5th Division. Not even there did it have a rest, for it received orders to march to Maurois, as an escort to the Supply Column, it having been reported that there were enemy patrols about. He arrived at Maurois at 4 a.m., where the Battalion had three and a half hours' rest. The Staff of the 5th Division had stated that the retreat would continue, and the Battalion waited for troops to pass through. It had marched forty-five miles in forty-eight hours, after a previous day in action.

III.—THE BATTLE OF LE CATEAU.

The morning of August 26th was an eventful one in the history of British arms. Sir John French, distrusting the roads of the Forest of Mormal, which, it has since been generally agreed, would have been good enough to have borne at least the traffic of one division and were actually used by troops of the German First Army in pursuit, had divided his two corps, sending Sir Douglas Haig to the east of it and Sir Horace Smith-Dorrien to the west. It was the latter who was the more severely pressed by Von Kluck. The commander of the II Corps had issued orders overnight for the resumption of the retreat at 7 a.m., when he learnt that, so far as the 3rd Division at least was concerned, it would be impossible to move by that hour. He knew his men were dog-tired, that his rearguards had been greatly delayed. In these circumstances he decided that it would be impossible to continue his retirement without first turning upon the enemy and striking hard. That decision has since been severely criticized by his Commander-in-Chief, but the balance of competent military opinion appears to be that not only was it inevitable but that in the main, as it was put into effect by the admirable troops under his command, its results were satisfactory.

The general line of the 3rd Division on the morning of the 26th was Troisvilles–Audencourt—Caudry. On its right flank was the 5th Division, on its left the newly arrived 4th Division of the III Corps, which had come up the previous afternoon. It was disposed with the 9th Brigade from Troisvilles to a point half a mile east of Audencourt, the 8th Brigade about that village, and the 7th Brigade (less the 2nd Royal Irish Rifles) holding Caudry, which formed a pronounced salient in the line. The 7th Brigade had the 1st Wiltshire on the right, on the high ground north-east of the town, the 2nd South Lancashire on Hill 129, north of it, and the 3rd Worcestershire defending the north-west outskirts. There appears to have been a gap between this battalion and the right of the 4th Division at Beauvois. There had been some preparations for defence between Troisvilles and Caudry the previous evening and during the night.

The 2nd Royal Irish Rifles had a meal in Maurois and, as has been stated, three and a half hours' rest. At 7 a.m. it received orders to march to Bertry, a large village or small town a mile and a half to the north-west. Passing Sir H. Smith-Dorrien's headquarters, Colonel Bird was complimented by him on the appearance of the Battalion. A staff officer of the II Corps led it to a position south of Caudry and ordered Colonel Bird to

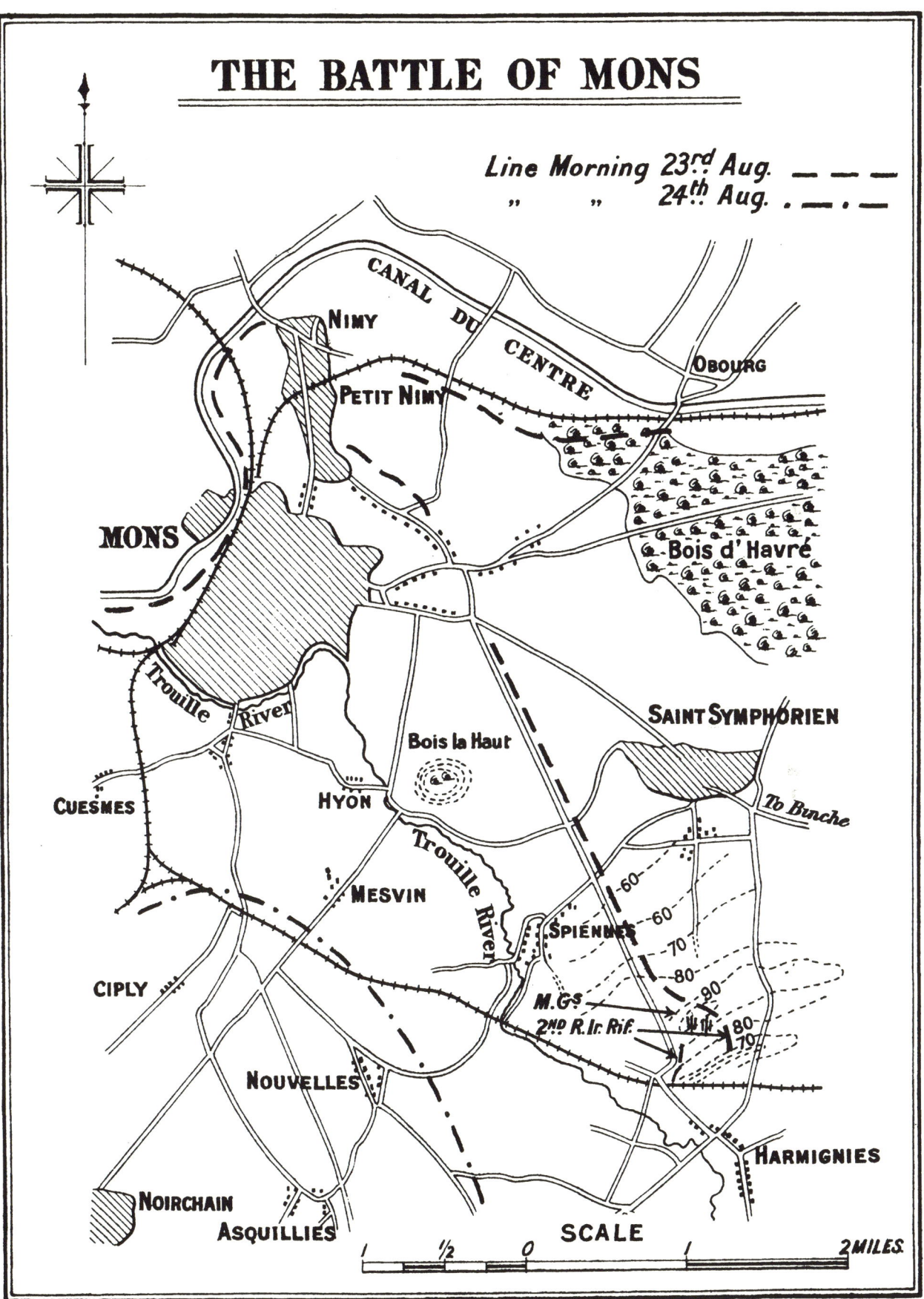

form a second line of defence to his brigade. In front the battle was now raging. The full weight of the German attack was not upon the front of the 3rd Division, for Von Kluck was seeking to turn both flanks of the greatly inferior force with which Sir H. Smith-Dorrien was barring his path, but the 7th Brigade at least, upon the Caudry salient, was in the thick of the fight, had beaten off one heavy assault, and was now under bombardment preluding a second. The information received was that the enemy would probably break through and that it was the Battalion's task to stop him. The Battalion dug itself in hastily on the high ground north of Montigny, from a stud farm a mile from that village on the Audencourt road to the Caudry—Clary road. With it was still the 41st Battery, R.F.A.

At 8.30 a.m. the line in Caudry was stiffened by two weak companies of the Royal Irish Regiment, which took up position along the railway cutting east of the village, where both the Wiltshire on the right and the Worcestershire on the left were involved in heavy fighting. " B " Company and half " A," 2nd Royal Irish Rifles, under Captain Master, were ordered forward into the market square in reserve. Heavily shelled here, this detachment moved forward to the northern edge of the town to escape the bombardment, and took up a position on the right of the Worcestershire. About noon some of the troops of the 7th Brigade began to fall back through the village, and it appears that the enemy may have penetrated its northern outskirts, but the position was speedily restored with the aid of a half-company sent up by Colonel Bird. Thereafter was a short lull, but at 1.40 p.m. the bombardment burst out with renewed violence, fresh artillery having doubtless been deployed by the advancing Germans. Under its pressure the troops of the 7th Brigade retired from the village. The 3rd Worcestershire came into line on the left of the 2nd Royal Irish Rifles ; both battalions prepared to prevent the enemy from debouching from the village. A counter-attack by the Worcestershire reached the southern houses.

At 3 p.m. Colonel Bird saw Major-General Hamilton, who ordered him to take command of the 7th Brigade, Brigadier-General McCracken having been stunned by a shell, and to clear the village of Germans. Directly the General had gone the commander of the 2nd Royal Irish Rifles received an order to retire. Fortunately he did not obey it, and a few minutes later the General returned and cancelled it, stating that the Welch and Royal Fusiliers would be sent to him for an attack on Caudry. What had happened was that the line of the 5th Division on the right had been broken by the overwhelming pressure of Kluck's turning movement, and the II Corps had issued an order that the 3rd Division was to retire in conformity with it, from the right. A short time afterwards Lieut.-Colonel Maurice, of the II Corps staff, rode up to say that the Division was to withdraw. Colonel Bird, who had been rejoined by his detachment, still held his ground, though the disquieting news reached him that Ligny, behind his left flank, was in the hands of the enemy. Then Major-General Hamilton, certainly the guardian angel of his division in this battle and throughout the retreat, came up once more and ordered him to withdraw the troops still in Caudry, covering their retirement with his battalion and two batteries, the 41st and another.

By 4.30 p.m. Caudry was almost clear, though the companies of the Royal Irish, still in the railway cutting, did not receive an order to withdraw and remained in position. By this time the Battalion was in a situation as ugly as can well be imagined. To right and left of it the line was broken. The troops that had been defending Audencourt fell back downhill in some confusion on the right. Had German cavalry been handled with boldness and promptitude, there might have been a disaster. For a further twenty minutes Colonel Bird and his battalion waited alone, the 41st Battery shelling the high ground between Caudry and Audencourt. They must have expected at every moment to distinguish the Germans advancing over the crest, but none came. Then Colonel Bird got his Divisional Commander's permission to withdraw, and marched back in driving rain *via* Serain to Beaurevoir, where he arrived at midnight, rejoining the 7th Brigade. The losses of the Battalion in the day's fighting were 5 officers (Major H. R. Charley, Lieutenant and Quartermaster Clark, 2nd-Lieutenants Mathews, Donaldson, and Finlay) wounded, 29 other ranks wounded, and 60 killed or missing.

The Battle of Le Cateau was certainly that in which British troops were most heavily outnumbered by the enemy in the Western Front up to the time of the German offensive of 1918. It can scarcely be doubted that it was of great importance in the checking of the German plan of campaign. The II Corps lost heavily, but the enemy must have had considerably greater losses. A fair proportion of the British casualties were in prisoners, but these prisoners had very faithfully served before they were captured. They consisted of detachments scattered about the front which did not receive the order to retire, and by remaining in position hindered the Germans from following up the retreat, and probably kept them in uncertainty as to whether the British were really gone. But splendid as was the British defence, high as was the toll they took of the enemy, it is pretty clear that the German First Army missed, late in the afternoon, such a chance of winning a great victory as seldom occurred in the Western Theatre of War.

IV.—The Retreat.

The 2nd Royal Irish Rifles had no long repose at Beaurevoir, nor indeed was long repose possible in its present situation. The Brigade continued its march at 2 a.m. on August 27th to a point north of Hargicourt, where the column had from three to four hours' rest, according to the position of battalions in it. No supplies had been received, but the men collected what they could from the civil population. About noon it was reported that the German advanced guards were approaching, and the Brigade moved on, the 2nd Royal Irish Rifles now acting as rearguard with one company of the Worcestershire and four batteries. At Vendelles Colonel Bird was met by an officer of the 4th Division (on the left of the 3rd, as it will be remembered), who stated that it was being hard pressed and asked for assistance. Colonel Bird then marched down to the hamlet of Soyécourt, where he sent a message of the 4th Division. After an hour's wait, at 4.30 p.m., he received a message from General Snow's staff to the effect that he was to remain where he was till nightfall, after which "his detachment would be broken up and he would be at liberty to rejoin his division." But again that division's good genius, Major-General Hamilton, appeared on the scene and told him "he had better make it nightfall now" and move on into Vermand. Here the Battalion once again rejoined its brigade, after some trouble in making its way through streets choked with transport. After a few hours' halt and a meal came another night march of from ten to twelve miles to Ham, where the Somme was crossed. Three and a half years afterwards the Battalion was to cross the river at almost the same point, in the course of the second and final "advance on Paris."

South of Ham there was another rest of about four hours. Then, at about 10 a.m. on August 28th, the Battalion marched down the shadeless national road, through

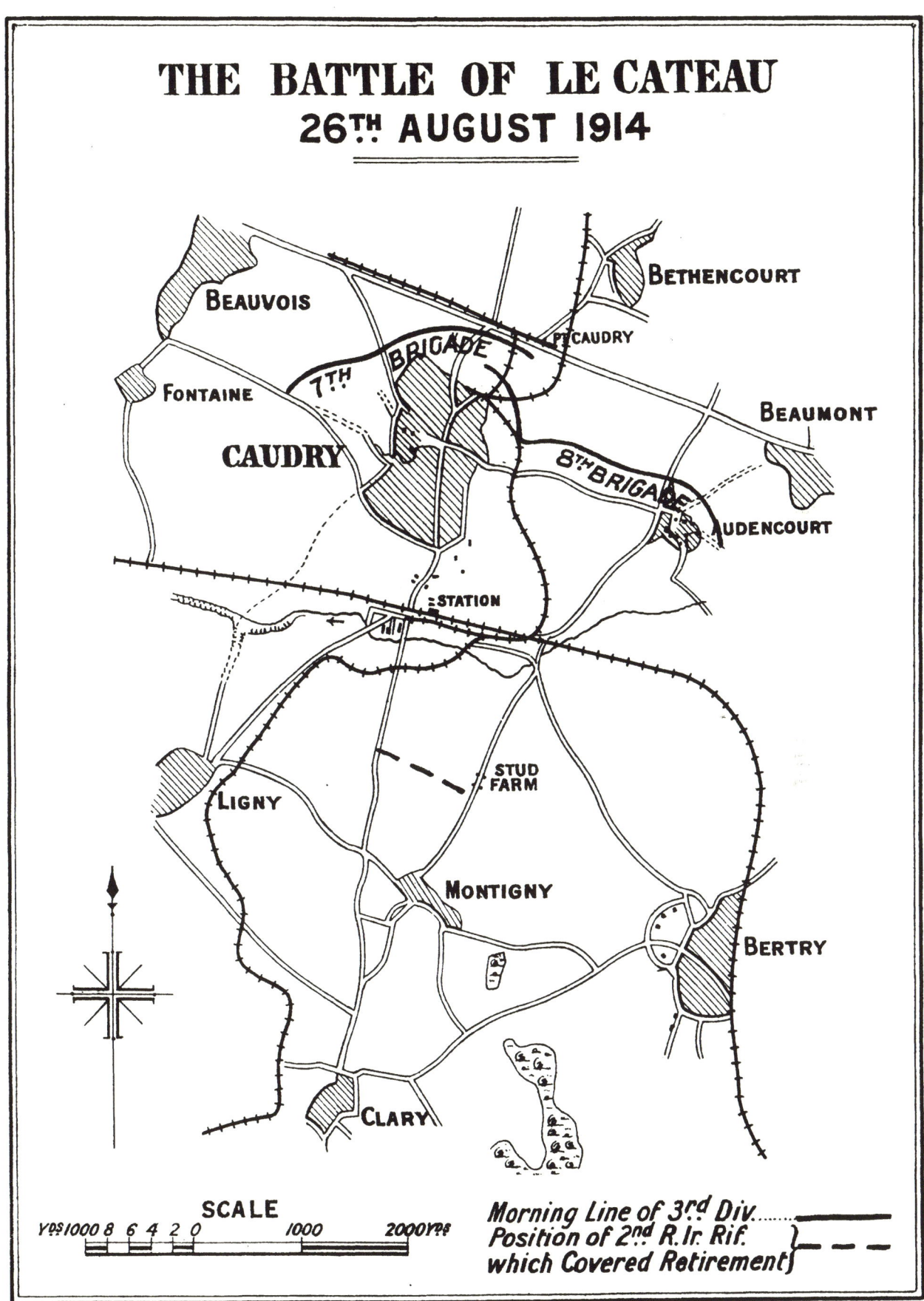

Guiscard, to Tarlefesse, a suburb of Noyon. It passed within three miles of the position, west of Cugny, upon which, in March, 1918, it was to make its magnificent stand against the German onrush, when not a man escaped to tell the tale. It was a blazing hot day, and the troops, dazed with heat and fatigue, took five hours to cover twelve miles. But at the end of their journey there awaited them the first real rest they had known since Mons, for they were allowed to remain in their billets till noon on the 29th. The pressure upon the British Army had been eased, it being now far to the south of its neighbour, the Fifth French Army, which that morning gained an important success at Guise. Moreover, on its left flank had appeared troops of the new Sixth French Army, then in process of hasty formation, with which Von Kluck had been engaged.

At 1 p.m. on the 29th the 7th Brigade took up a position in the great forest northeast of Noyon, several square miles in extent, known as the Bois d'Antrecourt. The 2nd Royal Irish Rifles was on the left, in touch with the 8th Brigade on the Guiscard—Noyon road. Colonel Bird was considerably disquieted by the situation. It appeared to him that if dusk caught his battalion in the maze of the forest, traversed by rides not easy to identify from the map even in daylight, it would be well-nigh impossible to get out before morning light. He suggested to his Brigadier that, if the retreat was to continue, it was desirable that the Battalion should be withdrawn before dusk. Otherwise it was likely to be trapped. There was no touch as yet with the enemy, but Uhlans on patrol had been seen in the distance. Permission to withdraw was refused.

Colonel Bird then made inquiries for reliable guides, and found two *gardes forestiers*, who declared they knew the paths by night and agreed to lead the Battalion out when the time came. This was not till after midnight. Then was a strange spectacle, two long files of men moving in the darkness like snakes through the trees, each man holding the coat or the rifle of his predecessor, in front of each file one of the French keepers, and the Commanding Officer with a candle in his hand. The mist which often rises from the valley of the Oise grew thicker and thicker till by the time they were clear of the forest it formed a dense cloud, in which they would have been more completely lost than amid the trees. But their excellent guides led them to the river-bank and across the bridge at Varesnes, just before it was blown up. The Battalion rejoined the Brigade, now acting as rearguard to the Division, at Pontoise, and on the morning and afternoon of the 30th carried out a long march *via* Blérancourt to Vic-sur-Aisne. It is highly probable that it owed its salvation to the presence of mind of its Commanding Officer and the good qualities of the guides he had found for it. At Vic-sur-Aisne there was a sorely needed night of repose.

The march of the next day, the 31st, was again long and carried out under trying conditions. The noonday heat was again intense. Some of the men were almost at their last gasp from fatigue. The men of the Battalion, however, seem to have marched in wonderful fashion, and no such trouble is reported as some others experienced. That day's march, to Coyelles, which was reached at 4 p.m., was of about fifteen miles, but in the latter part of it there was some shade. The British Army was entering now the beautiful forest-country, birthplace of the French nation, known as the Ile de France. The reader knows what was to follow. The troops did not know it, and they can have had a very hazy idea of what had already happened. August was at an end, but the retreat was not. Still day by day came those terrible marches—back, always back. They could not understand it. But the new scheme, admirably evolved by the French

Commander-in-Chief from the wreckage of his old, was maturing. There were to be but a few more days of retirement.

On the morning of September 1st the Battalion marched at 8 a.m., in rear of the 7th Brigade. From Vauciennes to Lévignen it followed the main Paris road. To the west the 5th Division was withdrawing through Crépy-en-Valois, and there was a halt for some hours in case it might be necessary to fight a covering action. At 4.30 p.m. the march was resumed, the Battalion now at the head of its brigade. It bivouacked that night at Villers-St. Genest, marched again at 4.30 a.m. to Pringy, which was reached at noon. Both the 1st and 2nd had been hot days, and the troops were considerably distressed, but there was a good rest at Pringy. The Battalion moved out at 3 a.m. on the 3rd to the hamlet of La Marche, and took up a rearguard position, as it was reported that the enemy was not more than three or four miles away, north of St. Soupplets. The rest of the Brigade being clear, it moved on at 10 a.m. as rearguard, crossing the Marne at Meaux, the bridge being immediately afterwards destroyed. At Sancy it bivouacked for the night, and remained there the whole of the 4th, " A " and " C " Companies forming an outpost screen round the hamlet of Vaucourtois from dusk until the 7th Brigade was again well on its way southward. The Battalion then followed on, marching *via* Crécy, when yet another river, the Grand Morin, was crossed, to the neighbourhood of La Motte Farm, when it again bivouacked on the morning of the 5th, being now relieved from outpost duty. Here it received its first reinforcement, which had arrived from St. Nazaire.

The great retreat was at an end. That very day the French Sixth Army, to the north, had driven Von Kluck's advanced troops across the Thérouanne stream. That very day General Joffre had informed Sir John French that he was about to turn and strike back. On the following morning was to open one of the most vital conflicts in the world's history, the Battle of the Marne.

CHAPTER II

I.—The Marne and the Advance to the Aisne.

The Battalion in the fate of which we are interested played no important part in the Battle of the Marne, but a short account of the situation is necessary to the understanding of the events that follow. About August 30th the Commander of the First German Army, Von Kluck, had begun to bend his course south-eastwards, and had gradually sheered off Paris. This has often been represented as the German " error of the Marne," but it must be remembered that a wide and widening gap separated the First Army from the Second, and that a march upon Paris would have been for the former an isolated operation. Not that such a consideration appears to have been uppermost in the mind of the very resolute soldier who commanded it. On the contrary, the movement was offensive. Kluck was seeking to carry out the German plan, in spirit if not in letter, and to roll up the enemy's left flank. Paris could wait a while. A great victory was of far greater importance. Kluck thought he saw the chance of striking a decisive blow by his left-handed wheel. What force he could spare he left to watch Paris, believing he could easily strengthen it if necessary. Meanwhile the French Sixth Army, under General Maunoury, which had already been in action, but had withdrawn for final constitution, was ready to play its essential part in Joffre's counterstroke. On the morning of the 5th it reached Dammartin, and during the day became engaged with the enemy's flanking corps, that which had been posted by Kluck precisely with the object of checking a diversion from Paris. As Frederick the Great remarked, we should all be fine soldiers if we knew as much before a battle as we did afterwards. It seems clear to-day that the Battle of the Marne would have resulted in a far more complete French victory, with results far more damaging to the enemy, had Maunoury been allowed by his immediate superior, General Galliéni, the Governor of Paris, to hold off for another twenty-four hours and allow Von Kluck to be definitely committed to his encircling movement before he disclosed his position. Before midnight Von Kluck had issued orders for one corps to recross the Marne to meet the new danger.

The British Army had orders to attack in a north-easterly direction on the morning of September 6th. From right to left it had in line the I Corps, the II Corps, and the III Corps, the last-named now consisting of the 4th Division and 19th Infantry Brigade. The II Corps in the centre was now to direct its right upon La Houssaye and its left on Villeneuve. Its advance was to be covered by the 3rd and 5th Cavalry Brigades under Brigadier-General H. Gough.

At 5 a.m. the 7th Brigade moved forward, at first back upon its old tracks, past the Obelisk in the Forêt de Crécy to Faremoutiers. The 1st Wiltshire in the van saw some fighting, the 2nd Royal Irish Rifles none. Like a flame set to oil, the spirits of the troops had leapt up. At last, at long last, they were going forward once more. They had not fully understood the retreat; they certainly did not understand the advance. Their officers at least knew they had been pursued by an army containing at least four corps. Where were those corps now? How was it that no more than advanced guards were in action and that the columns could go forward without deploying? The true explanation was that they had struck a " pocket." Von Kluck that night withdrew a second corps to meet Maunoury on the Ourcq. The line of the enemy upon the British front was filled chiefly with cavalry.

On the morning of the 7th the 1st Wiltshire was attacked by a couple of squadrons of dismounted cavalry, which it beat off with ease. Then the march was resumed. At Coulommiers, where the Grand Morin was crossed, the 2nd Royal Irish Rifles got its second reinforcement under 2nd-Lieutenant Magenniss. At Les Petites Aulnois half the Battalion billeted, the remainder bivouacking. When the advance continued on the 8th it was in the van of its brigade, but had the 8th Brigade in front of it. This brigade had to fight hard before it could win its way across the Marne. It captured 300 prisoners, two machine guns, and two motor lorries. A few wounded Germans were picked up by the Battalion on its march to Bussières, and a few more were found in the village.

On the 9th the 7th Brigade was again in reserve, and the Royal Irish Rifles marched in the centre of its column. Then was a long halt near Nanteuil, but the troops of the Brigade were not called upon to support the fighting going on in front. Seen after dusk, the Brigade was in Bézu, a village seven miles west by south of Château-Thierry. That day, though once again the men knew it not, had been of the highest importance to the Allied cause. That day the obstinate Kluck, who had been desperately interlocked with Maunoury, found he had to go. His colleague Bülow, in command of the Second Army, was already in retreat. The British, pressing forward upon their comparatively lightly defended front, were threatening Kluck's left flank—his left rear indeed—in a fashion that could no longer be disregarded. Had the progress of the British III Corps been as swift as that of the II Corps on its right, the threat would have been even more dangerous. By the afternoon the whole German right wing was moving back to the Aisne.

On September 10th the Battalion marched *via* Veuilly and Chézy to the hamlet of Montemafroy, a distance of some fifteen miles, and went into billets, the advanced guard of the Division on this day taking over 120 prisoners. A few stragglers were taken by the Royal Irish Rifles. All day long the Battalion passed deserted German bivouacs, all littered with empty wine-bottles, of which also every village garden had its pile. Next day the Brigade was advanced guard to the 3rd Division, and Colonel Bird commanded the vanguard, consisting of his battalion, the Cyclist Company, artillery, and a section of sappers. No enemy was encountered, as, marching by Neuilly–St. Front over the Ourcq, where the bridges were standing, the leading troops passed through Oulchy-la-Ville to Grand Rozoy. Rain fell in the afternoon, but the Battalion was then already under cover, save for a proportion on outpost duty. In one officer's diary it is recorded that his luncheon on arrival at Grand Rozoy consisted of duck, fruit, red wine, and bread —greatest luxury of all in those days of ration biscuit.

The heat had been trying enough. The troops were now to experience wet for a change. On September 12th the Battalion had a late start in rear of the 7th Brigade, which in turn was in rear of the 3rd Division. At 11 it began to rain very heavily, and did not cease all day. They marched *via* Les Crouttes and Maast-et-Violaine to a poor hamlet called Cerseuil in a sort of coomb running down to the River Vesle. A few lucky ones got into houses; the rest sought the shelter of caves, from which the fires they lit to dry themselves smoked them out into the rain. Ahead of their brigade the 9th Brigade had had a fight before it was allowed across the river at Braisne, and had captured sixty prisoners. They were close to the Aisne now.

II.—THE BATTLE OF THE AISNE.

On Sunday, the 13th, they moved forward at 7 a.m., but got no farther than Braisne, a matter of three miles, where they bivouacked in a field and remained that night. Ahead there was more fighting, and one explanation of the slow progress had been the heavy shell-fire on the roads, which had checked the leading troops. The 8th Brigade had crossed the Aisne at Vailly during the afternoon, as had troops of the other two British corps and of the French armies on either flank. By 2 a.m. on the 14th the 9th Brigade also was across. The plateau north of the river was a position naturally strong, but none realized that it was that upon which the enemy had decided to make his supreme stand, nor that within a day or two the war of movement was to come to an end upon this front.

At an early hour on the 14th the 8th Brigade was heavily engaged, and was forced to give some ground. At 5 a.m. the 7th Brigade moved forward. The Royal Irish Rifles had received four sets of orders during the night, being told to be prepared to march first at 3.30 a.m., then at 5 a.m., then at 7 or 8 a.m., before the eventual hour at which it moved was sent. In heavy rain the Brigade moved to a covered position in the woodlands east of Chassémy, which was reached at 7.30 a.m. The orders were that it should move forward, the 2nd Royal Irish Rifles following the 1st Wiltshire, cross the river by the engineers' bridge at Vailly, and move up as an advanced guard through the brigades on the other side. But the day of advanced guards was over for a while. Eventually, the German artillery fire upon the new bridge being very heavy, the 1st Wiltshire was ordered to turn right-handed along a cart-road through the woods and make for the destroyed railway bridge about a mile east of Vailly, beside which a foot-bridge, a single plank in breadth, had been hastily constructed. Colonel Bird was given command of the two battalions. But all was going by no means to plan, for as the head of the Wiltshire approached the bridge the men saw the Lincolns of the 9th Brigade withdrawing across it. Evidently there was somewhat serious trouble up in front.

The Wiltshire was at once ordered to cross, which it did, under heavy shell-fire, suffering a certain number of casualties. On the other side it took up a covering position. Then came the turn of the Royal Irish Rifles. As the head of its column approached the bridge, it likewise suffered, Captain Gifford and Lieutenant Cowley being wounded here. It was an uncomfortable performance, this passage of a wide, swollen river on a crazy plank, with shrapnel bursting overhead and shells plumping into the water below, but it was accomplished with singularly small loss. Directly "D" Company was across, it was moved up on the left of the Wiltshire, which had driven back the enemy at Rouge Maison, a big château a mile north of Vailly. "A" Company followed, and took post on its left. As soon as the Battalion was across, the Lincolns were ordered to return by the way they had come. Another officer casualty of the Battalion was Captain Soutry, "A" Company, slightly wounded.

Hardly were the platoons of the Battalion in position when they were strongly attacked by bodies of the enemy moving downhill. They succeeded, however, in holding their ground, checking the enemy by rifle fire. Colonel Bird was even able to spare one company, which he moved temporarily to the support of the 9th Brigade, heavily engaged on his left. By 8 p.m. the 3rd Worcestershire was across, and the worst of the danger was over. The enemy made another attack in the darkness, but it was half-hearted and was easily beaten off. Before this "D" Company had had a very unpleasant experience, having been shelled out of its position by our own artillery and compelled to withdraw its line. By nightfall the 3rd Division held high ground in a semi-circle about Vailly, the 7th Brigade being on the left, with its right (1st Wiltshire) on the Ostel road. The 2nd Royal Irish Rifles was due south of Rouge Maison.

September 15th was a most unlucky day for the Battalion. On Colonel Bird's arrival at daybreak in the front line, his second-in-command, Major Spedding, pointed out to him German trenches in a little hollow 700 yards to their front, and told him that he had ordered "D" Company twenty minutes before to advance to the edge of the wood, about halfway between them, and hold it. The commanding officer saw no harm in this, but felt a little nervous lest the company, now lost to sight in the trees, should become involved in a premature attack. On the other hand, as "D" Company had not come into action, it was possible the Germans had retired. He accordingly ordered "A" Company to move forward with all possible caution on its right to support it in case of need. Almost immediately, to his horror, "A" Company began to attack, advancing by rushes upon the enemy trenches, meeting heavy machine-gun fire. What had happened was that the company commander had seen "D" Company on his left advance upon the German trench, and had conceived it to be his duty also to attack to support it. "D" Company did actually capture a section of the German trench, but was driven out by a prompt counter-attack, and the original line was taken up. In this abortive action 2nd-Lieutenants Swaine and Magennis were killed, Captains Bowen-Colthurst, Durant, and Lieutenants Peebles and Varwell wounded. The total casualties were not far short of 150, chiefly wounded. The ugly day, with ceaseless wet adding to other miseries, ended in alarms, and a rattle of musketry along the front caused by the reports of German attacks which were probably no more than the movements of patrols. It had been disappointing. The 3rd Division had been ready for a new advance in co-operation with the 2nd on its right, but by now it had been decided that there could be no new attack that day. It was intended to continue the advance both on the 16th and 17th, but as a fact there was thereafter no serious attempt to go forward on the British front. The centre of interest was shifting northward, where the rival turning movements known as the "race to the sea" were preparing. For the British all chance was gone with the arrival of strong German reinforcements on their front, while they were completely outgunned by the siege howitzers which the enemy was hastening forward.

The 16th was devoted to preparations for a rumoured counter-attack, which did not develop. Once again it poured all day, and the condition of the troops was wretched in the extreme. Thursday, the 17th, dawned fine after a night of shell-fire. All about the Battalion's trenches large shell-craters were discovered in the morning, but casualties had been very light. More rain fell in the afternoon. Next day brought no change beyond increasing shell-fire. But the enemy had not resigned himself. At noon on the 19th there was a heavy bombardment, which died down only to burst out with renewed vigour at 5 p.m. There was no support from our artillery, which could not fire across the Aisne. An hour later the enemy launched a heavy attack upon the 1st Wiltshire, which speedily spread to the front of the Royal Irish Rifles. Colonel Bird, Captain Becher, the Adjutant, Lieutenant Dillon, and Lieutenant Cowley (already hit once), were wounded, and there were heavy casualties among the men. For a time things looked ugly, and two platoons of the Worcesters were thrown in to support the Battalion's line. In the end the attack died down in the darkness. Once again the rapid fire of the " Old Army " had prevailed. Colonel Bird lay throughout the action in a cave in the quarry held by the Battalion, listening to the noise of the fight. At one period some men rushed in, but were led back into action. Then there was a sudden silence, and Colonel Bird wondered if his men had been beaten. A voice called, " Are we downhearted ?" A roar of " No !" made answer. All was well.

The loss of Colonel Bird, who was severely hurt, was a very serious one for his battalion. Sagacious, determined, and swift of decision, he had brought it through some very tight places in the past kaleidoscopic month. Its debt to him was high. Major Daunt was left in command of the Battalion.

On the 20th was another German attack, in which Captain Becher was wounded a second time, and finally evacuated. " Both machine guns," says the Diary, rather pathetically, " were put out of action." Captain Goodman led up supports of the Worcestershire, which turned the enemy's right. Once again straight shooting checked the enemy, who remained quiet for over twenty-four hours, trying again at dusk next evening. He got no good of it, and having beaten him off, the Battalion was relieved in the early hours of the 22nd by the Leicesters, of the 16th Brigade, and marched back to the village of Augy for a rest, which, it will be admitted, did not come before its time. It is noted by the Brigade Diary as a novelty worth recording that " telephone lines were left in position." To those who did not arrive in the field before the stabilization of trench warfare the phrase has a curious sound.

Comfortable billets were a delight after the shelling and the sodden banks of the Aisne. The Battalion had them for three days, doing some digging on rear lines the while, but that hurt no one. Then it took its turn farther forward, moving up to Chassémy in support, and on the 27th was dragged from its slumbers by a false alarm that the enemy was crossing the bridge at Condé, the one point for many miles either way where his defence touched the bank of the Aisne. On the last day of the month it withdrew, not this time to its former billets at Augy, but to the neighbouring village of Couvrelles. On October 1st it marched south by night to Grand Rozoy, through which it had advanced to the Aisne three weeks earlier.

The reasons which induced Sir John French to apply to General Joffre to relieve him on the Aisne are well known, and need only be briefly recapitulated. The battle upon this front had ended in stalemate. On the other hand, it was in full swing up to the north, and he was anxious about the Channel ports, and that his forces should take part in their defence if they were threatened. Moreover, there were now three French armies on his left, across the lines of communication of which his own passed through Paris. The Battalion saw nothing of the relief, which was a good piece of staff-work on both sides, and was kept hidden from the enemy. For the first day or two it knew only that it was marching away from the scene of action.

On the night of the 2nd the 7th Brigade marched via Billy-sur-Ourcq and Chouy to Noroy, getting into billets at 1.30 a.m., five hours after the start, which was good marching seeing that the distance was fifteen miles. There, as usual, it spent the day in billets, moving at night through the Forêt Dominial de Retz and the hamlet of Coyolles, old acquaintance of the retreat, on the skirts of Villers-Cotterets, to Vaunoise. Thence forward, on the 4th, to Verberies, and next night over the Oise by the bridge of boats at Port Salut to the station of Longueil Ste. Marie, where the Battalion entrained at 2 a.m. on the 6th. After halts at Amiens and Pont Remy, where the officers bought such luxuries as butter, the train reached Noyelles at 4.30 p.m., and there the Battalion passed the night in comfort.

III.—The Battle of La Bassée.

At once the Division was moved up to meet the enemy, the Battalion having two marches, which brought it to Hesdin, and then being packed into motor-buses and taken to Floringhem, when it took up an outpost line. After billeting on the night of the 10th in Pernes, it marched next day to Hinges, and the day after to La Couture, where French cavalry was engaged with the enemy.

The Battle of La Bassée is an action which has been largely overlooked by the general public. It is overshadowed by the still more tremendous fighting which developed farther north. But it is a most critical moment in " the race to the sea." Its results were disappointing, for with a shade of luck it would have succeeded at least in the consolidation of the Aubers Ridge, which would have had an important influence upon the future campaign on the new British front. The three British corps were being directed, the II on La Bassée, the III upon Armentières, the I upon Ypres. The II Corps was to drive the enemy, not yet assembled in any considerable strength, from La Bassée and press on to Lille. The 3rd Division had deployed along the Aire Canal, its right on Hinges, where it was in touch with the 5th Division. On its left was the French Cavalry Corps of General Conneau, which was also forming a screen in front, and had detachments, already hard pressed, in La Couture and Richebourg St. Vaast. The orders issued by the Division at half-past two in the afternoon were for the 8th Brigade, on the left, to advance in the direction of Herlies, on the Aubers Ridge, and the 7th to move into La Couture. The movement was to be a right wheel of the left flank to turn the flank of the enemy engaged with the 5th Division. Hardly had the 2nd South Lancashire entered La Couture when the enemy in his turn attacked. Company by company, the 2nd Royal Irish Rifles was drawn in. The attack was beaten off, the Battalion having few casualties, among them Captain Master killed and Major Goodman, Captain Smyth, and 2nd-Lieutenant Fitzgerald (Leinster Regiment) wounded. The 8th Brigade had been held up, and was still at Vieille Chapelle.

At dawn on the 13th the wheel began in earnest, the Battalion advancing on the left of its brigade line. The enemy, consisting of dismounted cavalry and the Jäger battalions attached to German cavalry divisions—admirable troops—fought desperately, and every foot of the advance was contested. By half-past twelve the 3rd Worcestershire had Richebourg St. Vaast, from which the French posts had been driven, with the 2nd South Lancashire on its left. Then came the 2nd Royal Irish Rifles, which had reached the cross-roads of Croix Barbée, but was held up by machine-gun fire from houses just beyond. From this position it was withdrawn for the artillery to shell the village, moving up again after the bombardment. Here Lieutenant Whitfeld was killed and Lieutenant Heron wounded.

On the 14th there was a pause in the advance, due to enemy counter-attacks and possibly to the death of the 3rd Division's able and popular commander, Major-General Hubert Hamilton, a grievous loss to the British Army. But at 2 p.m. on the 15th, after a bombardment lasting all the morning, the wheel continued. The 2nd Royal Irish Rifles, in touch with the 8th Brigade on the left, poured through Croix Barbée and reached the main Estaires—La Bassée road at Rouge Croix. Not many casualties were suffered in this day's advance, at the end of which the troops dug hasty

THE BATTLE OF THE AISNE
Advance and Position in Firing Line of
2nd Royal Irish Rifles marked red.

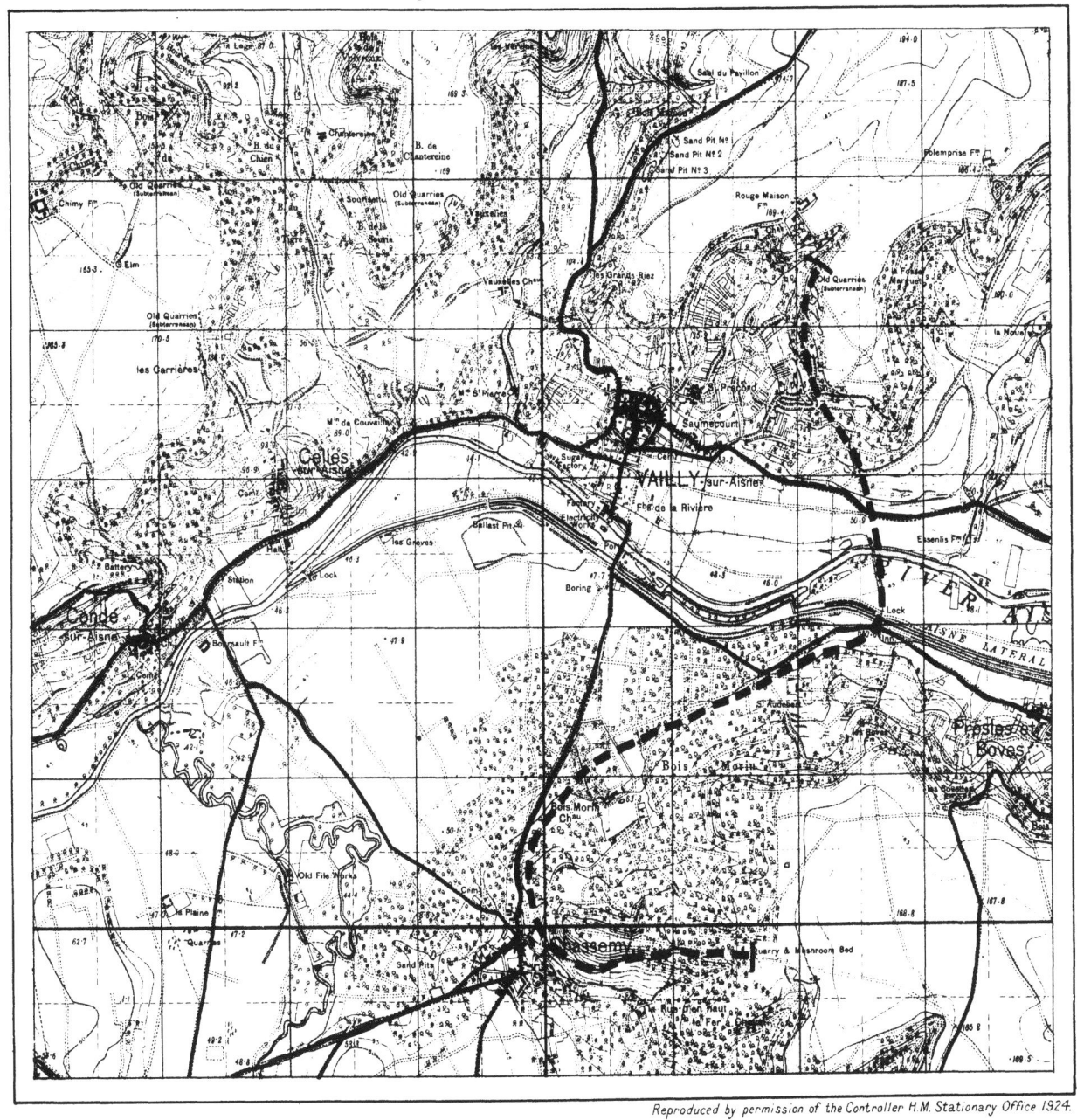

entrenchments and pushed forward a line of outposts. October 16th dawned in fog, which considerably hampered the advance. Pivoting on the 2nd South Lancashire, the Royal Irish Rifles swung its left well clear of the main road, and, feeling its way forward in the mist, halted at 11.30 a.m. on the Neuve Chapelle—Fauquissart road. Then, at 2 p.m., the Battalion went forward again. The Des Layes stream was crossed, and by night its line ran from the north-east corner of the Bois du Biez, in touch with the 2nd South Lancashire. This battalion was relieved by the 1st Wiltshire at dark.

The 17th was perhaps the most successful day of the battle, but it was also that which saw the arrival of heavy German reinforcements. The 9th Brigade, which had come up in place of the 8th, drove the enemy out of Aubers, while the French cavalry on its left took Fromelles. The Royal Irish Rifles took Haut Pommereau, on the slopes of the Aubers Ridge. Then for a moment German resistance seemed to crack. Pressing forward in irresistible fashion, the 9th Brigade took Herlies, beyond the ridge's crest, with the bayonet. But before it had been taken, large bodies of the enemy had been seen moving down from Fournes to La Bassée. It was evident that hotter work was preparing.

In the early hours of the 18th the Battalion was relieved by the 2nd K.O.Y.L.I., and moved to Pont Logy, where it had a few hours' rest, being brought back in the evening to east of the Bois du Biez. That day marked the first serious check to the turning movement, an attack upon the village of Illies by the K.O.Y.L.I. being beaten off. It was, in fact, the turning point of the battle, though Le Pilly was captured next morning, when further efforts of the 7th Brigade to force its way into Illies were unavailing. At night the Battalion again relieved the K.O.Y.L.I. on its outskirts. On the right was the 1st Wiltshire; on the left, the Lincolns, of the 8th Brigade.

The 20th saw the German reserves thrown in with a vengeance in counter-attacks all along the front. The 7th Brigade by afternoon had all its battalions in line, but it held its ground. At night the Battalion was ordered to fall back on Halpegarbe, leaving " C " Company to hold its old position till it was entrenched on the morning of the 21st. That day was desperate fighting, though little of its weight fell upon the Royal Irish Rifles. Under cover of the mist, the Germans penetrated the front of the South Lancashire, on the right of the Brigade line, which was restored by a counter-attack of the 3rd Worcestershire and Royal West Kent. Away to the left the Germans had retaken Le Pilly. The 7th Brigade was obliged to make another slight withdrawal at night.

On the 22nd the battalion of Chasseurs Alpins holding Fromelles was forced out of the village. It was evident that the enemy, at the beginning in an inferiority, was now in a considerable superiority. The commander of the II Corps therefore ordered a further withdrawal at midnight. The 2nd Royal Irish Rifles found itself told off to hold the village of Neuve Chapelle. Three companies dug trenches round the eastern skirts, while the fourth was held in reserve in the school. On the left the line of the 8th Brigade was echeloned back, which constituted a serious weakness. The Battalion's patrols were greeted with volleys of musketry from the 8th Brigade front whenever they ventured too near during the night.

The 24th passed quietly till about dusk, though the Battalion's position in Neuve Chapelle was particularly unpleasant, as the village was the principal target for heavy German artillery about La Bassée. Under this fire, which caused a good deal of loss, the men worked hard in improving the position. Two field guns had been dug into the first line trench, of which, however, one had its recoil spring broken and was put out of action. Then about 5 p.m., after a heavy bombardment, the Germans attacked Neuve Chapelle. It was a wild evening of volleys fired at the flashes of the enemy's fire or at dim figures distinguished in the darkness, with ever and anon a momentary break-through, men meeting with shouts and oaths on the wet, slippery ground, thrusting at one another with bayonets. For an hour the affair was doubtful. Then gradually the enemy was shaken off, and by 6 p.m. the attack was definitely repulsed. It had been a fine exhibition of obstinate courage and endurance. Heavy losses had been inflicted on the enemy, to judge by the noise of the wounded in front of our lines, as the Diary grimly remarks. Those who have heard that sound remember it.

But, unfortunately, the enemy had captured some houses on the left flank, from which, working down before light, he took the left part of the Battalion's trench and its remaining field gun. The remains of " B " Company in reserve, three-fourths of which had gone forward to replace casualties, with a platoon of the Lincolns, made a most gallant counter-attack and retook the trench. And then came another taste of the maddening ill-luck that dogged the whole action. Our own artillery, ill informed as to the position, shelled our men out of this portion of the trench. The Battalion still clung to Neuve Chapelle, but it was now in grievous case. In the last two days it had lost Captains Reynolds and Kennedy and Lieutenant Rea killed, and Lieutenants Lowry and Lavelle wounded. Major Daunt had already been wounded, and the command devolved upon Captain C. S. Dixon, who had not more than four or five officers left with his thinned companies. Two of these, " A " and " C," were moved back to Richebourg St. Vaast for a short rest on the morning of the 26th. This was the blackest day of all. An enemy attack swept into the village from the north-east corner. " B " and " D " Companies were simply swallowed up, Lieutenants Finlay and Innes-Cross, the only officers with them, and every soul in their ranks, being reported missing. About 6.30 p.m. a counter-attack reoccupied half the village, and the rest of the Battalion, hastily summoned from Richebourg, took its place in the line. South-east of the village their splendid colleagues of the Wiltshire had clung to their trenches even when the enemy was behind them.

On the morning of the 27th the enemy turned the left flank of the Battalion. After terrible fighting from house to house, in which little groups were caught by the oncoming enemy like rocks flooded by a rising tide, Captain Dixon withdrew his handful to the western outskirts in an effort to save his brigade's flank. The battle had become at this point what the soldier aptly calls a " dog fight," a wild fury of rush and counter-rush. By evening there was half a battalion of the 47th Sikhs, hastily moved up, Lincolns, Northumberland Fusiliers, Royal Fusiliers, remnants of the South Lancashire, and French Cyclists sent by General Conneau, clinging to the western edge of Neuve Chapelle, now in flames. And then at last, after ten days' fighting, the last remnants of the Battalion were moved back to Richebourg St. Vaast. Captain Davis had been killed, Lieutenants Mulcahy-Morgan and Jonsson were wounded and missing. The body that retired to Richebourg consisted of two officers and forty-six men.

It saw nothing of the bitter fighting on the morrow, when fresh attacks by Indians, French, and odd units of the 3rd and 5th Divisions, with regiments of the 2nd Cavalry Brigade, fought their way once more through Neuve Chapelle. On the 29th it was withdrawn to La Couture, and the 7th Brigade was finally relieved by the Lahore Division. On the 30th it withdrew to Doulieu, and on the last day of the month the whole of the 7th Brigade marched to Merris.

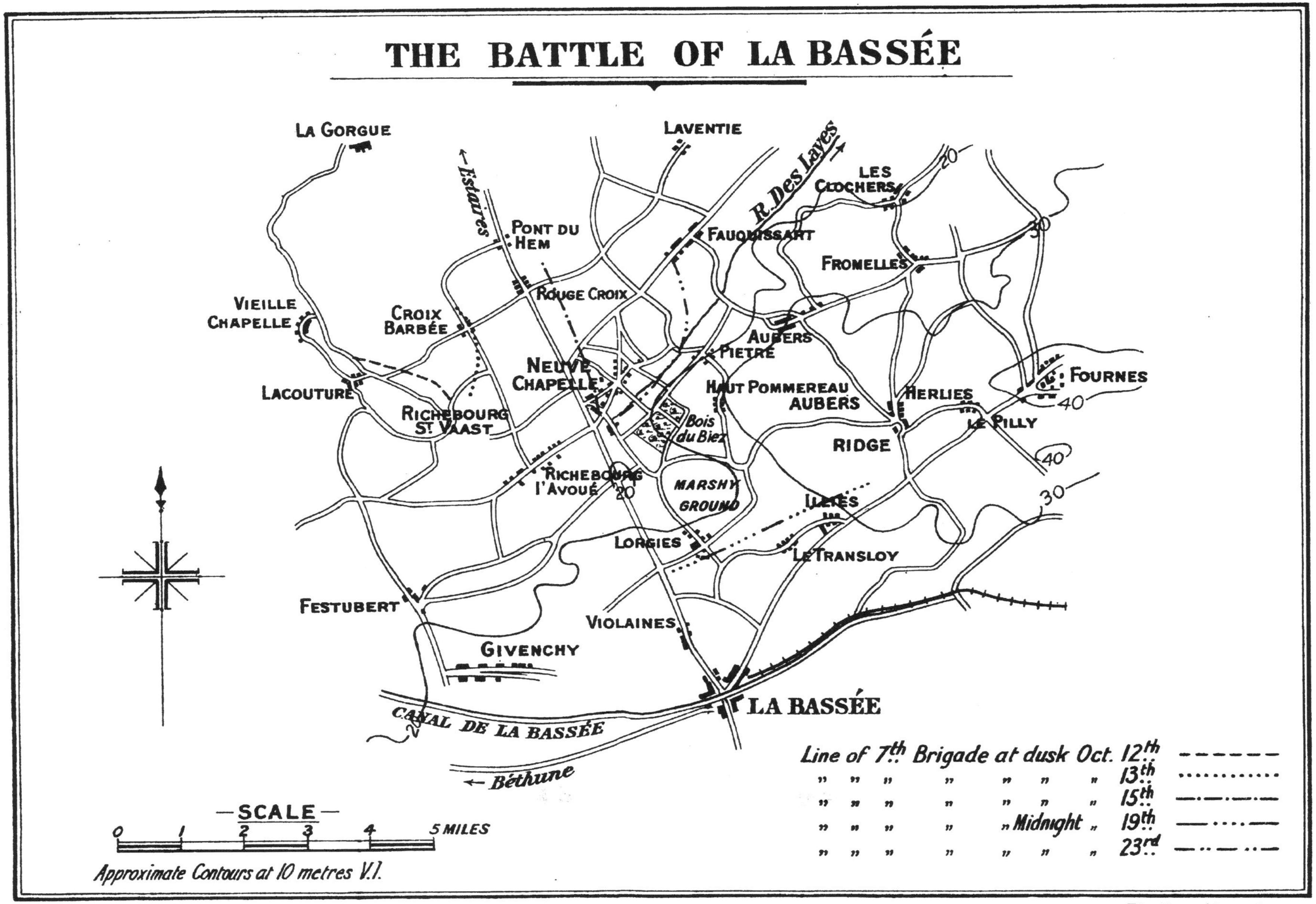

Facing page 18

The Royal Ulster Rifles.

The II Corps had—though, as has been said, the fact has not fully been realized—met very much the same experience as the I Corps at Ypres. The difference, which caused the fighting farther north to be even more terrible, was that there the Germans continued their effort longer and threw in greater forces. But, like Sir Douglas Haig, Sir Horace Smith-Dorrien had taken the offensive and then found himself turned to a desperate effort to hold off greatly superior forces seeking a break-through. Neuve Chapelle was eventually lost, and it wanted a very costly battle next year to retake it. But by that time the crisis was past. The British line had held. The nation has recognized its debt to the men of Ypres. It is time it should understand that it owed the safety of the Channel ports no less to those who, in those horrible mauls amid the burning ruins of Neuve Chapelle, stood and died that the enemy might not pass.

CHAPTER III

I.—FORMATION OF 6TH AND 7TH BATTALIONS.

WHILE the " Old Army " was dying in Flanders, while the 2nd Battalion as it originally existed was passing away in the flat country about La Bassée, while the Reserve battalions were hastily drilling men to fill the terrible gaps in its ranks, two new battalions were formed to take their places in the new armies which, under Lord Kitchener's inspiration, were turning these islands into an armed camp. The 6th (Service) Battalion Royal Irish Rifles was the first to be formed and the first in the field. It was in the 29th Brigade of the 10th (Irish) Division. It was formed in Dublin, at Wellington Barracks, in the last ten days of August, 1914, the other battalions in the Brigade being the 5th Royal Irish, the 5th Connaught Rangers, and the 6th Leinster Regiment. In September it moved to Fermoy for a month's training, returning to Dublin, to the Royal Barracks, in October. Four months were passed in the city. The 10th Division, being intended for early service overseas, was on the whole better treated in the matter of equipment than the other Irish Divisions, the 16th and the 36th (Ulster), then in training in the country. February, March and April saw the 29th Brigade at the Curragh, a period of field work succeeding one upon " the square." At the end of April it was transferred to New Park Camp, in Hackwood Park, Basingstoke. There training became intensive, musketry being carried out at Aldershot. On May 28th H.M. the King, and on June 1st Lord Kitchener, reviewed the 10th Division in Hackwood Park. On July 6th the 6th Royal Irish Rifles left Basingstoke for embarkation at Liverpool, its destination being in the first place Alexandria, and then the Gallipoli Peninsula.

The 7th (Service) Battalion Royal Irish Rifles, formed in Belfast in September, 1914, was in the 48th Brigade, 16th (Irish) Division. It spent practically the first year of its existence at Mallow, Co. Cork, and Ballyvonare Camp, where it had excellent training-ground in the Ballyhoura Mountains. Recruiting was none too rapid even in those days for this, the second of the three Irish Divisions, and the Battalion was glad to receive a company of Jerseymen, 6 officers and 225 other ranks, in March, 1915. These men belonged to the Jersey Militia, and were well trained. As fifty per cent of them spoke French, it can easily be imagined that they were useful in France, where they sang French songs on the march, to the astonishment of the country-folk.

From mid-June to mid-August, 1915, the Battalion was under canvas at Ballyhooley, on the banks of the Blackwater, near Lord Listowel's seat. It was very fit and well trained when, in September, 1915, it left Ireland for Aldershot. Being at the heart of military life meant that it had many inspections to undergo in the succeeding weeks. On December 2nd the 16th Division was inspected by H.M. the Queen, and before it left the country Cardinal Bourne gave an impressive address to the Roman Catholics, who were in a great majority.

On December 19th the Battalion entrained at Farnborough for Southampton, disembarking next day at Havre and going into camp.

II.—THE 1ST BATTALION RETURNS FROM ADEN.

Meanwhile, from all corners of the Empire the regular troops on foreign service were moving homeward. On September 27th the 1st Battalion, at Aden, embarked on the *Delaware*—strength, 19 officers and 990 other ranks—and on October 22nd arrived at Liverpool. It was at once entrained to Hursley Park, where the new 8th Division, to complete the IV Corps, the 7th Division of which was already in France, was concentrating. The Battalion formed part of the 25th Infantry Brigade, with the 2nd Rifle Brigade, 2nd Lincolnshire, and 2nd Royal Berkshire. A draft of 200 non-commissioned officers and riflemen from the 3rd Battalion awaited it, whose first work was to learn to use the short service rifle, with which they were unacquainted. The Battalion had the strong points and the weak to be associated with troops returning to this country from service in the East. Its general training was splendid. On the other hand, the long stay at Aden, the month on ship-board, the change in temperature, lowered its marching qualities below those of a home service battalion.

It was given small time for acclimatization. At 6 p.m. on November 5th it embarked on the *Anglo-Canadian* at Southampton, landed at Havre, and moved into camp. At 9 p.m. on the 9th it entrained, moving *via* Rouen, Abbeville, Calais, St. Omer and Hazebrouck to Strazeele, a zigzag journey which took the best part of twenty-four hours. The 8th Division had orders to relieve the Lahore Division in the Laventie area, near the scenes of the 2nd Battalion's bitter fighting. The Battalion moved first to billets at Neuf Berquin, on the night of the 11th, which are described as "very pleasant"; and, indeed, in early days the villages of that area were comfortable enough. On the night of the 14th it had quarters less pleasant, in Laventie, and the following evening took over its first line of trenches from the 59th Rifles, the 15th Sikhs, and a company of the Manchester Regiment.

The trenches were situated two thousand yards north-east of the village of Fauquissart. The front line consisted of a series of scattered posts. They were mere scratchings in the ground, but already flooded. At the end of twenty-four hours there was an outcry that rifles were clogged, and insistent demand for paraffin and old socks to clean them. The Battalion might have had its initiation upon a wilder front—in the Salient, for example; it could not have been sent to one more comfortless. The line had not yet really settled down after the shock at La Bassée, and daring German snipers often crept through gaps and fired upon men in the posts from the rear. But the wet was the worst enemy. "Trench feet," as a result of which the sufferer's feet and ankles became swollen and discoloured till they looked like lumps of raw meat, speedily took toll of the Battalion. Men wrapped their legs in straw, tied sandbags round them, rubbed them with whale oil when that became available, but the evil was never really fought down till the beginning of 1915, when rubber thigh-boots arrived in large quantities.

As soon as things settled down, the system was one of three-day tours in the trenches, with three days in billets alternatively in brigade reserve at Fort d'Esquin and divisional reserve at Laventie. Enemy snipers caused serious losses in the early days, probably half the Battalion's casualty list of 41 for the month of November. Next month two good marksmen per platoon were chosen as company sharpshooters, to keep down the German snipers. It was found that they succeeded admirably in this task, and that casualties from sniping were greatly diminished. On the afternoon of December 18th the 23rd Brigade attacked Neuve Chapelle and captured the enemy front line, but was bombed out next day with considerable loss. Then came the curious "Christmas truce," about which there was at the time so much talk and, it may be said, so much exaggeration.

On Christmas Eve Germans came out of their trenches and shouted that they would not fire on Christmas Day if we did not. Some of the riflemen went forward into "No Man's Land" and talked with the enemy, many of whom spoke English well. They looked big and clean, and were evidently highly optimistic, for they declared the war would be over in three weeks, being just about two hundred weeks out in their calculation. The General Officer Commanding 8th Division did not object to refraining from shooting, but ordered that the Germans were not to be trusted nor allowed near our trench. And on Christmas Day our men, though they walked about in the open, kept near their own parapets, and warned away the Germans who ventured near. The latter danced gaily, shouted "Merry Christmas," and made suggestions that the truce might last another day. This was sternly refused, and they were told they must be under cover by midnight. The whole affair was rather mysterious. The German infantrymen were simple enough, but it was thought curious that they had been able to guarantee the night before that there should be no firing by their artillery.

Next night a deserter to the Kensington Rifles, which was attached to the 25th Brigade, announced that there would be an attack at 12.15 a.m. As a result, the Royal Irish Rifles, just relieved, was hurriedly marched to La Flinque, where it passed an uncomfortable night. The Diary expresses sincere regret that the Battalion was unable to lay hands upon the deserter who had raised the false alarm.

The year ended with conferences upon the subject that was become far the most pressing for the troops. Drainage in a country where the ground frequently did not fall a yard in a mile would always have its limitations. It could never make trenches in the ordinary sense possible. So for such trenches a substitute must be found. "Come out of the ground" was the new motto of the Division, and its new policy defence behind breastworks. For the rest, the period had been one of experiment in minor projectiles for trench warfare. Trench mortars—"made locally," as the Diary remarks simply—had been employed with indifferent results against the enemy's mortars, which had not been made locally, but had come from Essen. Rifle grenades, of a sort, had been issued. A stick hand-grenade had been the subject of experiment. But most use had been made of the ration jampot bomb, with a four-second fuse—another "local" appliance, manufactured by the Royal Engineers. The history of the British bombs is a chequered one. The iron "orange" followed the "jampot" in 1915, and was not a great improvement upon it. Next came the "lemon," or Mills, a well-made bomb, the finest weapon imaginable when used as a rifle grenade with a short steel rod secured to it, but as a hand-propelled weapon too heavy for any but men of exceptional physique. A few "egg-bombs," copied from the Germans, were issued towards the end of the war. We went on experimenting till we produced the ideal hand grenade, which was ready for use soon after the Armistice.*

III.—THE 2ND BATTALION IN THE SALIENT AND BEFORE WYTSCHAETE.

The 2nd Battalion, battered and reduced to a shadow by the La Bassée fighting, was left moving northward to take a hand in the still more terrible fighting in the Salient,

* Casualties of 1st Battalion to end of 1914 were: Captain B. Allgood killed, and 102 casualties in other ranks, four-fifths wounded.

which had reached its height on October 31st. On November 1st, when the Battalion marched to Locre, Messines and Wytschaete had been lost. Then came a lull in the battle, if such a term can be applied to a period of stupendous cannonading. Then, on the night of the 5th, the Battalion entered the line east of Hooge and south of Heronthage Château in relief of troops of the 7th Division, which had lost three-fourths of its strength in the recent struggle. The fighting strength of the Battalion was about 250. Next day saw it attacked, but holding its ground. Lieutenant Eldred was wounded, and there were 17 other casualties. On the 8th it was withdrawn to the support line, and on the 10th brought back to the front.

Wednesday, November 11th, was the day of the memorable attack astride the Menin road by the Prussian Guard*, one of the most famous events in the history of the war, to which a touch of the romance that had fled from these battlefields of blood, mud and iron was brought back by these magnificent troops executing a few steps of the *parade-schritt* before they advanced to the assault. The attack by these few regiments of picked men struck all imaginations, but it is not so generally recognized that it was part of an attack all along the line by some six army corps. The right of the Guard appears to have been directed on the north corner of Nonne Bosschen Wood, their left just about the Battalion's left flank, south of Heronthage Château. The attack was preceded by the heaviest bombardment the British Army had suffered. To north of the road the British line was broken by the weight of that disciplined shock. Upon the road itself and south of it it was repulsed with terrible slaughter. Once again straight, cool shooting by the survivors of the cannonade won the day, and the best troops in Germany, led by the sons of its proudest houses, were heaped upon the ground. Then on the left came those splendid counter-attacks which closed the momentary breech.

From the moment the first attack died down the enemy had been massing troops in the woods opposite the Battalion, which were evidently intended for exploitation—to go through to Ypres. At dusk a fresh attack was launched. But the sting of the German valour of that morning was gone. The men who stood up to their battered parapets and fired, coolly as ever, at the dimly seen figures characterized the new assault as "half-hearted," and so it was, judged by the standard of what had gone before. After it was over the Battalion was withdrawn to support. Its casualties for the day were 15 killed, 10 wounded, and 19 missing—over a quarter of its present fighting strength, for it now numbered no more than 130 all ranks in the line. But once again its pitiful remnant had proved of what quality was its spirit.

On the 14th, when the last sparks of the battle were fanned to a new flame, the Battalion was at Hooge, in reserve. On the 16th it was ordered to send up 1 officer and 30 men to reinforce the line of the West Kent, and next day 1 officer and 50 men to reinforce that of the K.O.S.Bs. Both these battalions were involved in the heavy attack of the 17th, and both killed an extraordinary number of the enemy, who pressed forward with the greatest bravery, being dropped in many cases within a few yards of the trench. There is no record of the work of the riflemen who were sent to their aid, of whom, indeed, very few survived, but we may feel sure that they played their part in that defence which makes adjectives a mockery. When all was over and the Battalion arrived at Westoutre, it was exactly 40 strong. It had been cut to pieces in one action, had received a few reinforcements, had been hurried north to take part in a still fiercer battle, and had again been cut to pieces. On November 21st there arrived Captains

* Officially known as the Battle of Nonne Bosschen.

Chatterton and McLoughlin and Lieutenant Norman with a draft of 463 non-commissioned officers and men, which turned it into a fighting force once more. Next month it was to receive further drafts totalling nearly 350, under Major Festing, and Captain Becher, recovered from his wound on the Aisne, and Captain Burgoyne. It was a battalion again at full strength, but it was a new battalion. Save for transport and unemployed men, there can have been hardly a soul in the ranks who had survived three months of war. There was, among its large drafts, a sprinkling of men who had been lightly hit at Mons or had gone sick in the early days, but no more than a sprinkling. To all intents it was a new force. Its lot was worse than that of some of its colleagues, but not much. For we must remember that, but for the units in later formations such as the 8th and 29th Divisions, the infantry of the " Old Army " died in 1914. Such few battalions as kept any proportion of the regular soldiers were to lose them a few months later, in the Second Battle of Ypres.

Nevertheless, just as the scanty remnant of that " Old Army " was to be the leaven for the formation of the new, so in each individual battalion there remained a few—a single subaltern, perhaps, three or four non-commissioned officers—who remembered the peculiar spirit and traditions and how they had been given effect. That old spirit, those old traditions, did not die. They lived and were renewed again and again. It would be absurd to pretend that any reconstituted battalion of the Regular Army could ever equal its old self that had been in musketry. The old training in that respect was unique in the military world, not to be acquired in six months or a year. But most of the Regular battalions did manage, with the aid of their boys from Sandhurst, to cling to *something*, which only the very best battalions of the New Army ever acquired, and the old Regular divisions were always, up to the last day of the war, among the best troops in the Army. As for the 2nd Royal Irish Rifles, it was to prove in its sacrifices at Bellewaarde, in its brilliant actions at La Boisselle, Messines and the Westhoek Ridge—the last three decisive successes in days when such were few—how fiercely its spirit survived, how excellently it adapted itself to new and undreamed of conditions of warfare.

After November 21st, when it received the large draft mentioned above, half a battalion in itself, it was to have a few days for rest and reorganization. On the 25th Major J. W. Alston arrived and took over the command. On the 27th it moved from Westoutre to Locre. On the 30th it took over a new line before Wytschaete.

Here the situation was almost as it was to remain till the Battle of Messines, two and a half years later, but fighting had not died down, nor had the elaborate trench systems on both sides come into being. The position held by the Battalion lay between the Kemmel—Wytschaete road and the other road which branches from it at Maedelstede Farm, curves northward, and then runs roughly parallel with it, past Rossignol Wood, to the main road from Neuve Eglise to Ypres. The German line ran almost exactly through the junction between these two roads at Maedelstede Farm, the British some hundred and fifty yards away. Communication trenches or shelters there were practically none, and the front-line trench was a ditch which had frequently three feet of water in it. Here also in later days, when the folly of digging into such soil had been recognized, breastworks took the place of trenches, and the Messines sector became even in winter, except in the bottom of the Douve Valley, by no means the worst upon the British front, and in summer a really " comfortable " line, so far as lines were ever comfortable. Now, in the Flanders winter, it was incredibly vile. One advantage, however, it had to men who had come from the shambles of Neuve Chapelle and Hooge. Shell-fire was light, casualties amounting to not more than one or two a day. But, as has been explained, there were very few here who had seen either of those horrors, and the new drafts must have felt that this was evil enough. One loss the Battalion had in Captain Whelan, which well illustrated the chances of warfare. He had survived all the shelling at Hooge, being left in command of the scanty remnant of survivors, and now was killed upon the quietest of fronts.

On December 14th the front lost its quietude and flamed up once more for a couple of days, when the 8th Brigade attacked the Petit Bois.* Things went well at first, and forty prisoners were taken by the Royal Scots, who entered the wood; but the force, and still more the artillery behind it, was inadequate for the capture and retention of such a position, and eventually the attack was abandoned. The Battalion saw nothing of it, but stood to arms in the rain outside the billets at Locre, returning to the line next night, when the 7th Brigade relieved the other two of the Division. Christmas Day was spent in the trenches. The " Christmas truce " which was experienced by the 1st Battalion at Fauquissart and reached its zenith at Ploegsteert Wood, does not appear to have extended so far north as this, or at any rate only in very modified form.

So the year 1914 passed out in a period of comparative quiet, but in conditions of horrible discomfort and suffering, while each side was accumulating more munitions and assembling fresh forces. How our men lived and died in those days was almost unknown at home, for their indomitable courage extended to their letters and made light of evils almost unendurable. Wives and parents were not to be " worried " by hearing of the worst, and the terms " rotten hole " or " filthy place " or " warm spot," which the slang of the day would have applied equally to uncomfortable seaside lodgings or a period of rush-work in a factory, did not reveal much, nor were intended to. It was well perhaps that private individuals were spared the knowledge of how those dear to them lived ; but it was a national calamity that the nation was allowed to go on believing that all was well, or more or less so, while its sons were suffering and dying—suffering more and dying in far greater numbers than needs were—for lack of the resources and the appliances with which the enemy who faced them was equipped.

* Officially known as the Attack on Wytschaete.

BOOK II: 1915

CHAPTER I

I.—THE 2ND BATTALION IN EARLY 1915.

THE 2nd Battalion had an all too lively existence in the five months of 1914. It was not again to go into action till the first Bellewaarde battle in the summer. As a fact, there was no fighting on a large scale till the Battle of Neuve Chapelle in March, and that the Battalion missed. In the west, indeed, there was a temporary lull. We heard much of the German superiority in munitions, and that superiority had been only too obvious at Ypres. But it seems certain that just at the beginning of 1915 the Germans also experienced a temporary shortage of shells. Moreover, in the east, Germany's new-found hero, Hindenburg, was attacking the Russians, and certain troops from France and Belgium were sent to his assistance.

The early part of 1915, then, was passed in routine trench warfare before Wytschaete, with billets at Locre, Westoutre, or Dranoutre. The trenches were being gradually improved, but they were still far from being comfortable even in the sense in which the word can be applied to trenches. However, the line was quiet, and casualties for the most part light. Gradually the Battalion " found itself " once more.

In March it was fortunate enough to escape participation in an ugly, abortive and costly little action, an attempt by its brigade to capture the Spanbroek Hill, a piece of high ground in the enemy's front line which gave him a certain amount of observation. The attack, probably intended to prevent reliefs while Neuve Chapelle was being fought, was carried out by the 1st Wiltshire and 3rd Worcestershire on March 12th, the 2nd Royal Irish Rifles moving up to Lindenhoek in support, to be called in if needs were. It was a misty day, and the operation, set for the morning, had to be postponed till the afternoon. The artillery preparation had been quite insufficient, and the men were simply mown down by the enemy's fire as they showed themselves. A few of the Worcestershire actually entered the enemy's front-line trench, but they were a mere handful, who could not hold their ground. Looking back on the affair, with the knowledge of later days, one is inclined to say that failure was far less expensive than success would have been. The Battalion returned after dark to its billets without having been employed or suffering any casualties from shell-fire.

At the end of the month the 7th Brigade moved back to the southern side of the Salient, the northern half of which was now held by the French. On the 29th the Battalion entered the trenches between Voormezeele and St. Eloi, which had just been the scene of further fighting, its billets being in the village of La Clytte. All three brigades of the 3rd Division were soon in line here, the 7th being in the centre, with the 9th on its left. Next came the 5th Division, opposite the notorious Hill 60.

On April 15th the Battalion lost its popular commanding officer, Major J. W. Alston, a sniper's bullet aimed at his periscope being deflected by a sandbag, and killing him instantly. He was buried two days later in the churchyard at Dickebusch. On the evening of his funeral the 5th Division, after blowing a series of mines, captured Hill 60, and for the next three days there was the fiercest hand-to-hand fighting amid the craters and shell-holes of its tortured surface.

Hardly was that affair over than there occurred the most horrible event of the war, ghastly in itself and in its effect up to the day of the Armistice, the gas attack which began the Second Battle of Ypres. This was on the morning of April 23rd. The effect of the gas did not extend to this part of the front. A few men complained of smarting eyes—nothing more. But there was, as may be imagined, much excitement as the battle raged to northward, and some uneasiness as stories leaked out of this terrible new form of warfare. Within a few days the first primitive masks, made by women in Calais and other base towns, were issued. The German artillery fire increased, and there was an outbreak of bombing by aeroplanes, another terrible but legitimate form of warfare, then in its infancy. On April 26th five bombs were dropped on Canada Huts, Dickebusch, where the Battalion was resting out of the line, causing seventeen casualties. But the bombs of those days were comparatively small, and none of those hit was killed.

On May 5th the Germans retook Hill 60, using gas again. Most of the trenches on either side of the hill were immediately regained by counter-attack, but not the high ground itself. The casualties of the British had been very heavy, and two battalions of the 7th Brigade—the 2nd Royal Irish Rifles, and 2nd South Lancashire—were put at the disposal of the 5th Division. On the 6th the Battalion was ordered to march to a point north of Hill 60 and relieve the Bedfords of the 13th Brigade. The relief was carried out amidst considerable confusion. The guides led the Battalion from the ill-famed Shrapnel Corner, on the Ypres—Wytschaete road, along the side of the Zillebeke Lake, in single file, amid falling shells, by a path littered with the wounded and gassed, whose stretcher-bearers had been forced to set them down for a few moments' rest to their aching arms. Having lost their way more than once, they reached Dormy House, the Battalion headquarters, at 1.30 a.m. on the 7th. And for 2.30 a.m. a bombing attack to clear a communication trench held by the enemy had been planned. Father Gill, the Battalion's chaplain, who describes the relief, states that he saw the scheme on the back of an envelope. The men were not in position till ten minutes before that hour, utterly wearied already. Moreover, the barricade, which was supposed to have been mined, did not " go up," and the bombers were met by heavy fire from it. The attack failed with heavy loss, Captain Burgoyne and Lieutenant Leask being wounded, and of other ranks 9 killed and 16 wounded.

Next day there was further violent fighting at Hooge in which the Battalion was involved only to the extent of some bomb-throwing. It lost Captain V. Gilliland killed, 2nd-Lieutenant G. W. Webb wounded, and had 12 other casualties. On the 12th it was relieved and returned to its brigade, moving to its old billets at La Clytte. The remainder of the month was passed in the old Kemmel—Wytschaete area, which seemed a paradise after the Salient.

II.—The Battle of Neuve Chapelle.

The 2nd had a long start of its sister battalion in service and sacrifice, but in the early part of 1915 the 1st was to go a long way towards catching it up. It likewise began the year quietly. The building of the new breastworks was its chief task, made difficult by the vigilance of German snipers. Owing to the cold and wet of the line from 50 to 75 per cent. of the Battalion holding it was accommodated in the ruined houses of the Rue Tilleloy, whence it could quickly reinforce in case of danger. The Battalion had three days in line, three in brigade reserve, and three in divisional reserve, at Laventie—no comfortable refuge. The town was repeatedly shelled, particularly on nights of relief, of which the enemy always had accurate knowledge, possibly from overhearing telephone conversations, possibly through spies. Leave was now regular, though the allowance was small. A shortage mentioned by Major Edwards, the quartermaster, was only less serious—that of rum. On mornings in that sodden line it took all the strength of that spirit to bring to life again men numbed, stiff, and in a sort of miserable coma from the cold and wet of the night.

So passed January and February, with about 60 casualties. Then, on March 1st, the Battalion moved back out of this filthy area to the decent little town of Estaires. Here began a week's hard training, mostly of a physical nature, to set up again bodies cramped by the trenches; running over ploughed fields, route marching, Swedish drill. Blocking parties, to hold points in captured trenches, were trained. It was evident that something new was being prepared. That was, in fact, the Battle of Neuve Chapelle.

Neuve Chapelle was a new type of battle, which was for long to be the model for the attacks of trench warfare. A great concentration of artillery was obtained to crush out all resistance in front before the infantry attack was launched. Its objective was the Aubers Ridge, for which there had been a struggle so fierce in the previous winter, the capture of which might eventually involve the German evacuation of Lille. The attack was to be carried out by the IV Corps and the Indian Corps. The village of Neuve Chapelle itself was to be assaulted by the 8th Division and the Meerut Division on its right; the 25th Brigade, on the former's right, attacking from the centre cross-roads of the village to the north-eastern angle of the well-known triangle of roads in the northern half. The first objective, to be captured by the 2nd Royal Berkshire on the right, and the 2nd Lincolnshire on the left, was a German system of two main lines of trenches defending the village. These were to be bombarded for thirty-five minutes, then assaulted. Meanwhile, the artillery was to lift on to the rear defences, which were not numerous, and the village itself, for half an hour; and then the supporting battalions, the 2nd Rifle Brigade on the right, directed mainly upon the church, with its left on the southern angle of the Triangle, and the 1st Royal Irish Rifles on the left, were to pass through. And so the Battalion found itself ordered to attack over the very ground on which the men of the 2nd had struggled and died.

At 3.45 a.m. on March 10th the Battalion assembled in an orchard 600 yards north of Pont Logy. At 7.30 the intense bombardment opened. It was such as no British troops had yet witnessed, certainly not upon their enemy's trenches. The German trenches seemed to be blown to pieces, and their high built parapets crumbled away in a few moments. At 8.5 the Lincolns charged, and took their objective easily. Behind them many men of the 1st Royal Irish Rifles, instead of waiting at their parapet, pressed forward to the German front line.

Then at 8.35 the Battalion advanced on the second objective. It was its first battle, and it was in high fettle. It was magnificently trained, with a comparative sprinkling of reservists in the ranks and a few men who had been in action with the 2nd Battalion at Mons. The days of walking behind a creeping barrage were not yet come, and the Riflemen swept forward at the double, " A " and " B " Companies in the van. As they passed through the Lincolns, who cheered them, Captain Graham was blowing long blasts on a French postman's horn, and shouting hunting holloas. The main street of the village, which formed the western side of the Triangle, was reached in five minutes, but the leading troops had to be withdrawn a hundred yards as 6-inch howitzers were firing on it till 9 a.m. At that hour they had the whole of the Triangle and the château grounds east of its southern angle. They had captured 30 prisoners and had had very few casualties. By their fire they inflicted considerable casualties on the enemy retiring towards the Bois du Biez.

On their right flank they were in touch with the Rifle Brigade, but their left was at this time in air, and two platoons under Captain Galwey had to be swung back along the northern side of the Triangle before touch could be obtained with the 23rd Brigade, which had found more difficulty in advancing, having been held up by uncut wire and having suffered heavy casualties. On their own front there was now not a German in sight, and they were able to complete their entrenchments without a shot being fired at them. Lieutenant-Colonel Laurie sent back a message suggesting that he should swing round to the left to aid the 23rd Brigade, but was refused permission to do so. Eventually this brigade fought its way up into line. But invaluable time had been lost. The chance of a "break-through," that will-o'-the-wisp of the first years of the war, had actually appeared, but did not remain long when it was not taken. The Battalion remained all the afternoon in this position, while fresh attacks, which met with bitter opposition, were launched to north and south. At 9 a.m. on the 11th it was relieved by troops of the 24th Brigade and withdrawn to the old German trenches.

On this day the attack was held up all along the line. Here and there a few yards were won, but German reserves were up now in force, and their counter-attacks were delivered with all the dash and bravery of fresh and first-class troops. The attacks of the Dehra Dun and 24th Brigades, on the front with which we are immediately concerned, were a failure. The German shell-fire was now very heavy, and the Riflemen got no sleep that night in their trenches. At 3 a.m. on the 12th the Battalion received orders to move forward for a new attack.

The 25th Brigade was now to cross the Des Layes stream and advance to the Pietre road beyond it which skirts the Bois du Biez. It was to attack with its right upon the road from Neuve Chapelle to the wood, and its left just north of the château, captured by the 1st Royal Irish Rifles. This battalion was to attack on the left, and was to advance from the trench it had itself dug after its successful assault two days earlier. On its right was to be the 2nd Rifle Brigade.

There was considerable confusion and misunderstanding with regard to this new attack. Orders at 3 a.m. were that it should be launched at 4.45. At 4 a.m. came a message postponing it till 10. But at 10.5 no bombardment had begun, and it was put off till noon, in hopes that the fog would lift by then. The fog did lift, but unfortunately the Battalion had moved at 9 a.m. to the Orchards of the Triangle, and here it came under heavy shell-fire, and suffered serious casualties. When the bombardment opened at noon it moved forward to the "jumping-off" trench, in which were the men of the West Yorks, who had relieved it the previous morning. Crossing the open, it came under heavy fire, and many a man dropped before ever he reached our front line.

The diary of the 25th Brigade describes the bombardment as "ineffective." The fact that the Battalion was harassed by musketry fire while that bombardment was upon the German trenches is proof only too sound that the statement was true. It has since been made clear that at Neuve Chapelle we grasped at more than we could reach. There had been accumulated ammunition enough for a remarkable bombardment, but after the first day, when it was every whit as important as before the launch of the attack, it was impossible to repeat the artillery preparation on anything like the original scale. This made it impossible to shake the German defence sufficiently to give any subsequent assault a fair chance of success.

The Battalion was disposed upon a two-company frontage—" C " on the right, " D " on the left, supported respectively by " A " and " B." When the order was given to advance, then burst such a murderous machine-gun and rifle fire that almost every man who exposed himself was instantly shot down. Alone the left half of " D " Company ever really " got going," most gallantly led by Lieutenants Hutchinson and Laing. Both these officers and practically every man following them were killed within half a minute. It appeared then to Colonel Laurie that further attempts to go forward would be madness, and he ordered the line to stand fast.

After the first attempt had so woefully failed General Lowry-Cole, commanding the Brigade, came up to the church to organize a fresh one. But he came to the conclusion, after an examination of the ground, that another frontal attack would be fruitless, and made a request that the advance should at least be postponed till dark, when he thought some ground might be won. At 4 p.m. he received orders to attack and take the position " at all costs." Colonel Laurie now arranged to attack in four successive lines, " B," " C," " A," and " D " Companies, in that order. The new bombardment of half an hour was likewise quite ineffective. When the moment came for the advance, at 5.15 p.m., every man that tried to go forward was knocked over at once. Five minutes later Major Baker, moving down the trench to find out why the attack was hanging fire, came upon Colonel Laurie, dead. He came to the same decision as that of his late commanding officer in the earlier affair. It was sheer waste of life to send men into that zone of bullets. He ordered the advance to stop. That night the 25th Brigade was informed that all along the front the ground held was to be consolidated. The action, so far as the British were concerned, was at an end.

That night and all next day the Battalion held the trenches in the château garden, under heavy shell-fire, during which it lost its adjutant, Captain Wright. In the evening it was relieved by the 2nd Lincolnshire, and a weary remnant withdrew to the old German front-line trenches, where it remained another twenty-four hours, before moving back to the old British breastworks. Even then it was not on its way to that rest which came generally to troops that had been in a great attack and suffered serious loss. On the 16th the men, tired, dirty, and dazed, tramped back through Neuve Chapelle to relieve the 2nd Lincolnshire in the front line, which they found " littered with German and British dead." They spent three days clearing these shambles, burying many of the Germans by turning old trenches inward. Then, on the 20th, they were relieved again, and got as far back as Rouge Croix, and on the 24th to La Gorgue. They finished the month in divisional reserve at Fleurbaix.

The Battalion's losses had been very heavy. Besides its colonel and adjutant, 7 officers—Captains Biscoe and Colles, Lieutenants Hutchinson, Burges, and Barrington, 2nd-Lieutenants Laing and Gilmore—had been killed, and 9 wounded*. The losses in other ranks were 106 killed, 270 wounded, and 15 missing. It had, indeed, been a cruel initiation. The original attack had been inspiring, gallantly carried out, with no

* Wounded : Major H. C. Wright, Captains L. Rodney, A. O'Sullivan, F. Graham, A. Galwey, Lieutenants R. F. Gavin, G. G. Adely, 2nd-Lieutenant D. F. Hubert.

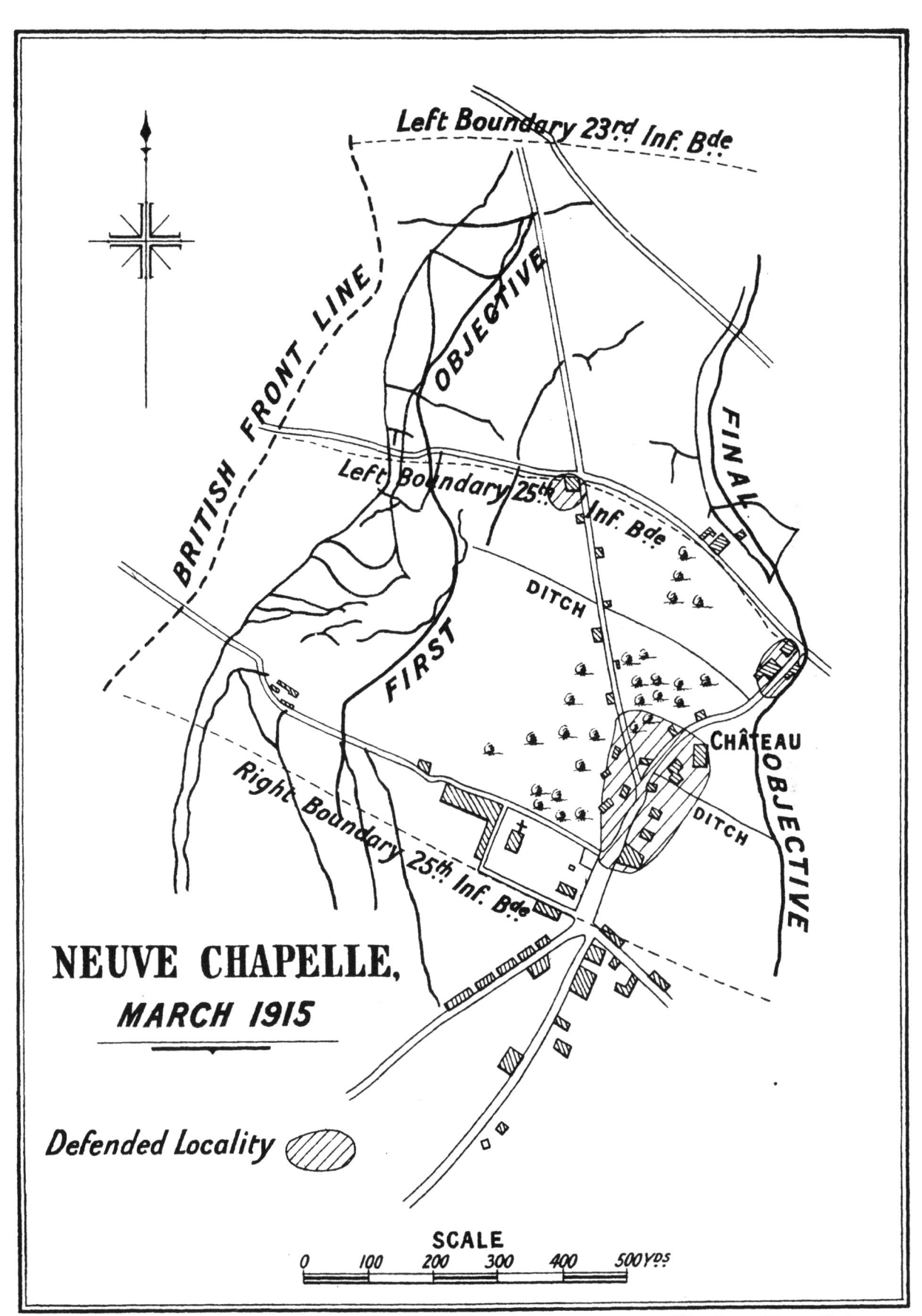

NEUVE CHAPELLE, MARCH 1915

more than reasonable loss, and entirely successful. Then the men had been asked twice, on the same day, to achieve the impossible. The Battle of Neuve Chapelle, for them, as for everyone engaged on it, had ended in grievous disappointment. Our losses had probably been considerably higher than those of the enemy, and what we had to show for them was of small value.

III.—THE ATTACK AT FROMELLES.

April was a month relatively quiet for the Battalion. During the early days it received drafts totalling three officers and over a hundred other ranks, half of whom were returned sick and wounded. On the 17th, when in divisional reserve, it was inspected by the Commander-in-Chief, Field-Marshal Sir John French, being drawn up on three sides of a square at Bac St. Maur. He congratulated the commanding officer, Major Clinton Baker, on the gallantry displayed at Neuve Chapelle, and alluded to the great loss of the Battalion in the death of Colonel Laurie. Speaking to the men, he remarked how high a proportion of officers had been killed. The officers, he said, were always ready to go first. So long as they were followed as they had been at Neuve Chapelle, he had no doubts of ultimate victory.

On the 27th the Battalion had the pleasure of taking over the position held by it before the late battle, " F " lines. The breastworks here had been made by it and the 2nd Lincolnshire, and that good work was now repaid by the comfort of the best line hitherto.* It was soon brought to an end by yet another attempt to take the Aubers Ridge, in concert with the great French attack at Souchez. This attempt was made in two separate attacks, known respectively as the Battles of Fromelles and Festubert, of which we are concerned here only with the former, the most complete reverse with which the British arms had yet been met.

The task of the 8th Division was to break through the enemy's lines in the neighbourhood of Rouges Bancs, south of the Des Layes stream, and gain a position, from the old line in the neighbourhood of La Cordonnerie Farm, through Fromelles and Le Clercq. It was to attack with the 24th Brigade on the right and the 25th on the left, the dividing line being the Sailly—Fromelles road. The 25th Brigade was to attack with the 2nd Rifle Brigade on the right and the 1st Royal Irish Rifles on the left. The task of these battalions was the capture of the front system of trenches, and of the road behind them running from Rouges Bancs towards Fromelles. Thereafter the other battalions were to pass through to a second objective, some 500 yards beyond, astride the Fromelles road. Subsequently an attack, in which the 23rd Brigade was to be employed was to be made on Fromelles.

It is difficult to believe that it was ever seriously hoped to capture the Aubers Ridge, now far better defended than at the time of Neuve Chapelle, after a wire-cutting bombardment lasting a quarter of an hour. In this connection it may be noted that the total number of 18-pounders on the IV Corps' front was 72, while the 13-pounders, of which there were 42, could hardly be considered adequate weapons to prepare an attack upon a fortified position. With heavy howitzers the British were, for those days, fairly well equipped, but a mere quarter-of-an-hour's bombardment by such inadequate weight of artillery meant that almost inevitably there would be great sections of wire uncut. Two mines were to be exploded in the enemy's front line at the hour of the assault, which, it was hoped, would do much to demoralize the defence.

* Casualties for April, 32. Captain W. Lanyon killed, Lieutenant McIlwaine and 2nd-Lieutenant Soulby wounded.

At 2 a.m. on May 9th the Brigade was formed up, the Battalion at La Cordonnerie Farm. At 5 a.m. the first bombardment opened. The wire, at any rate of the front line, appeared to be fairly well cut upon the immediate front, and German retaliation was not at first heavy. At 5.40 a.m., the hour of the assault, "C" and "D" Companies advanced in lines of platoons at thirty paces. Despite considerable fire from the left flank the men went forward with an irresistible rush, broke through the enemy's battered front-line trenches, and at one point reached the Fromelles road, just where it turns sharply southward toward that village. Unfortunately the 13th London, attached to the brigade, which had the task of covering the Riflemen's left flank, was unable to advance beyond the mine-craters in the German front line. As a result, directly the artillery fire lifted, German machine guns came into action on the left flank in great numbers. "C" and "D" Companies, following the leading mass in similar formation, met with frightful losses, and made practically no headway. Two platoons, one on the right under the Commanding Officer, one on the left under the Regimental Sergeant-Major, advanced obliquely to check the cross fire, but both were beaten back with heavy casualties.

The men of the leading companies who had reached the Fromelles road were speedily reduced to a handful. There were Germans not only on their left flank, but between them and the 2nd Rifle Brigade, which had got most of its objective. From the double flanking fire men were dropping at every moment. But they had a task to fulfil, to hold their ground till the battalions for the second objective passed through. With magnificent determination, the little remnant clung to its position. The hour came, but no supports appeared. Though they did not know it, the 2nd Lincolnshire and 2nd Royal Berkshire found themselves unable to get forward through that storm of fire, few even reaching the German front-line trench. They waited half an hour beyond the appointed time; then decided to fall back to the German front line, as no effective reply could be made to the enemy's fire, and another half-hour would have seen the whole party destroyed. At 7 a.m. what was left of them did so, placing themselves under Lieut.-Colonel Stephens, commanding the Rifle Brigade, which had withdrawn to the same line. And there all day long they held their ground.

Meanwhile their Brigadier had come up to the breastworks, to find the whole attack at a standstill. All forward movement had ceased soon after 6 a.m. The ground between the lines was swept by fire. The front British line was choked with men in great confusion, successive lines of the supporting battalions having come up with the rear lines of those in the lead, which had failed to advance. He ordered forward two companies of the Lincolnshire to support the Rifle Brigade. Almost immediately afterwards, in checking a retirement (in which he was successful), he was mortally wounded.

At 2 p.m. an attempt to sap out along the dyke bordering the Sailly—Fromelles road proved unsuccessful; nor could any further aid be given to Colonel Stephens, who with 200 men, which included perhaps 50 of the Royal Irish Rifles, fought it out all that afternoon. At 7.50 p.m. a heavy German counter-attack was repulsed, captured machine guns being used with great effect. It was hoped to cling on all night, as fresh attacks were to be launched in the morning, but it might not be. The final counter-attack came upon the front and both flanks. The machine guns fought to the last, causing heavy losses to the Germans, but at 3 a.m. on the 10th they were driven out and withdrew to the British breastwork. Later that morning the remains of the Battalion withdrew to billets at Bac St. Maur.

THE LOSSES AT FROMELLES

The party from the German lines had been brought in by the Regimental Sergeant-Major, there being no officers left. In fact, of the 23 who went into action, every officer was hit, over two-thirds being killed or missing. The following were killed :—Lieut.-Colonel O. C. Baker, Major A. H. Festing, Captain A. M. O'Sullivan, Lieutenants R. A. Finlay and R. L. Neill, 2nd-Lieutenants C. G. Dixon, A. McLoughlin, A. W. Bourke, O. B. Macausland, D. Hamilton ; Lieutenants La Nauze and J. S. Martin, 2nd-Lieutenant L. A. Dickenson were reported wounded and missing ; 2nd-Lieutenant C. E. Windus missing. Nine were wounded ; Captains C. C. Tee and C. J. Newport, Lieutenants G. Gartlan, G. M. New, R. Soulby, G. A. Coey, H. P. Parkes, A. Hellmers, S. E. B. Millar, of whom the two last died subsequently. Of the other ranks, 44 were reported killed, 207 wounded, and 203 missing ; almost all those in the last category being either killed or wounded. The total casualties were thus 477 out of about 600 who had gone into the attack ; a far heavier proportion than at Neuve Chapelle, when the Battalion had been up to strength, with far less to show for it.

This was, in fact, a far worse action to look back upon than that other. A success such as that gained by the Battalion on the first day at Neuve Chapelle, however heavy the losses, leaves some inspiration of victory to counterbalance the shock which the survivors experience. But a butchery such as Fromelles, when men are mown down and nothing is won, has no such brighter side. It was a memory entirely evil.

The bravery displayed had been of the very highest standard, and no expressions that can be applied to it would appear other than weak. To hold the position meant almost certain death, and the position had been held for half an hour after the time fixed for the arrival of the supports. The splendid devotion of the officers is only too apparent. Neuve Chapelle had not brought the 1st Battalion to the state of the 2nd, when a new one had to be created, with transport and employed as practically the sole basis, but it had not long to wait before it met that fate. It was now no more than a shadow, to be built up anew by new officers. The lessons in the superiority of defence over offence were dearly learned in those early days, for their cost was something which could never be replaced.

After a week in Bac St. Maur the Battalion moved back to Estaires. Between the Battle of Fromelles and the end of May there arrived Major A. D. N. Merriman, who took over command on the 17th, 15 other officers and about 250 other ranks. On the last day of the month it returned to the line in the Neuve Chapelle area. Indeed, it was fated not to move far from that melancholy village, where it had first arrived in November, 1914, except for a month's training and rest at Hazebrouck, till March, 1916.

This record concerns itself little with events outside the Regiment's life, but in the history of an Irish regiment it would be wrong to pass from the Battle of Fromelles without reference to the Brigadier under which the 1st Battalion fought, who there lost his life. Brigadier-General A. W. G. Lowry-Cole, C.B., D.S.O., bore a name distinguished in our annals by that other Brigadier-General Lowry-Cole who won fame so great in the Peninsula, and is commemorated by the well-known monument on Fort Hill, Enniskillen. As the report of the 8th Division points out, his death, which would have been at any time a serious loss to the British Army, was calamitous in occurring at the crisis of the action. He was a commander who always desired to see the conditions for himself during a battle, and his character and personality had a strong influence. Very vigorous and determined when there was chance of success, he was quick to perceive when there was not. Had his wise advice been taken at Neuve Chapelle, a great many lives would have been saved.

CHAPTER II

I.—TRENCH WARFARE: THE 1ST BATTALION.

FOR a month the 1st Battalion remained holding the same line, with three days in the breastworks, three days in either Bac St. Maur, as brigade reserve, or Estaires, as divisional reserve. On the 17th a new commander, Lieut.-Colonel R. Daunt, who had commanded the 2nd Battalion, arrived. At the end of the month there was a short "sideslip" northward, to the Fleurbaix trenches, neither better nor worse than the rest of this front. With the summer that front had improved vastly, and the men, accustomed to far worse, found existence endurable. It is indeed remarkable how healthy were the front-line troops in summer in France, at a period when those in the East were suffering torture and prostrated by dysentery. The evils of overcrowding, which at any earlier period would have produced epidemics, were overcome by greatly improved sanitation and inoculation. Save for the influenza epidemic of 1918, which was world-wide, our armies enjoyed almost complete freedom from illness in the summer months.

There is little of interest recorded in the diaries for this period, save that further large drafts were received in the month of August. It was a period when men's minds were turned largely to improving the conditions under which they lived. The men who at Fromelles had seen the excellent bombproofs in the German trenches set themselves to imitate them. Water stored in petrol-tins saved needless carrying-parties. Officers' messes, not only out of the trenches but in them, were enabled to recover some of their old traditions of comfort and well-cooked food. Experiments with weapons continued, and various kinds of bomb-throwers were tried. Of the bomb-catapult the Brigade Diary complacently records that it was tried "with fair success"; that is to say, of the first six bombs slung by it, three fell *near* the German trench, and three *into* our own front-line trench. They were thrown out with blasphemy before they exploded, and the incident treated as all in the day's work. None of these weapons ever proved a great success, excepting always the Mills rifle grenade. There must be many besides the present writer who can never hear without a shiver the name of the "West spring gun," which arrived a little after this period. It is hard to conceive anything more perturbing than to see one's missile, a Mills bomb with the safety-pin out, instead of proceeding in a graceful curve towards the enemy's trenches, shoot straight up in air above one's head, and to wonder, as one wallowed in the trench bottom, whether it would explode like shrapnel in air, or after it had landed between one's shoulder-blades. One new weapon, however—an experiment like the rest, but an enormously successful one—did begin to arrive this summer in twos and threes. This was the Stokes light trench mortar, an admirable weapon, which was to be employed at the Battle of Loos and the contemporaneous actions. Casualties were very light for three months, and appears to have included one officer only, Lieutenant E. Dent, wounded.

II.—THE FIRST ATTACK ON BELLEWAARDE.

The record of the 2nd Battalion has been carried up to the end of May, when it was in the Vierstraat area. On June 1st Major G. M. Morris, Devonshire Regiment, took over command from Captain Becher. Two days later it was relieved and returned once more to the Salient, of which, indeed, it was to see all too much in the course of its career. The Battalion marched to bivouacs south of the Poperinghe—Vlamertinghe road, and for the next week sent parties varying from 200 to 400 to carry forward barbed wire for the defence of the Salient. On June 5th the 7th Brigade relieved the 3rd Cavalry Division in the line at Hooge, with three battalions, the 4th South Lancashire, the Worcestershire, and the 1st Wiltshire, in line from right to left; with the Honourable Artillery Company, which had for some time been attached, in support at the Ramparts; and the 2nd Royal Irish Rifles in reserve. On the 9th the Battalion relieved the Worcestershire west of Hooge.

The British line at this period was in a curious position. From Hooge it followed the Menin road to near Birr cross-roads, then turned off at right-angles, running north, in front of Cambridge Road, to the Ypres—Roulers railway. The German position, though a salient within a salient, was strong, naturally as well as artificially, rising to a slight ridge, which in that flat country was dignified by the name of the Bellewaarde Spur, which name it took from the Bellewaarde Lake, a sheet of water some twelve acres in extent, with two large wooded islands upon it, lying south of the high ground. The British command decided that an attempt to nip off this minor salient, establishing a line which would run generally from Hooge, along the western side of the lake, across the Bellewaarde Spur, to a point in the Ypres—Roulers railway a little in advance of the old position, would be worth while.

The main attack was to be carried out by the 9th Infantry Brigade, which was to assault the German trenches from the south corner of Y Wood to the north of Railway Wood. On its right the 1st Wiltshire was to support it by attacking the German front-line trench from the Y Wood to the Menin road, and cover its right flank. The other four battalions then in the 7th Brigade—4th South Lancashire, 3rd Worcestershire, 2nd Royal Irish Rifles, and H.A.C. (its own battalion, the 2nd South Lancashire, being detached at this time)—were to be in reserve west of Cambridge Road, to move forward as soon as the attack was launched and occupy the British front-line trenches. The preliminary bombardment was to be considerable, as it was easy even in those days of scarcity to mass a formidable concentration upon a front so relatively small. It was to last from 2.50 a.m. on June 16th till 4.15 a.m., with three short pauses. At the latter hour the infantry was to attack.

On June 11th the Battalion had a troublesome relief at Hooge, being forced to leave behind " B " Company and some men of " C ", who were unable to get clear by daylight. Then, after three nights' rest in bivouac, it paraded at 5.30 p.m. on the 15th and marched up to assembly trenches between Wittepoort Farm and the Ypres—Roulers railway. Its strength going into action was 21 officers and 630 other ranks. Our bombardment had been most effective, and when it lifted off the first objective, the 9th Brigade, with the 1st Wiltshire on the right, easily took it, the latter capturing 60 prisoners. All reports agree that the advance was very much quicker than in previous actions of this nature, and that the organization was caught unawares by the speed with which the men moved and the breakdown of the defence. Our troops were shelled by our own artillery upon the second objective, and had to be withdrawn, which caused confusion. Owing to a thick mist, the forward observing officers of the artillery could see nothing. Finally, the line of the German front trench, through Y Wood and Railway Wood, was taken up, though several small bodies held on farther forward, one in the neighbourhood of Bellewaarde Farm.

The 2nd Royal Irish Rifles had been ordered to support the left flank of the 9th Brigade and consolidate the German first line south of the Ypres—Roulers railway. Unfortunately, two companies, "C" and "D," carried away by their enthusiasm, advanced to the third line, and had to be reorganized and brought back to their proper position. "B" Company never got up. As it moved forward it was very heavily shelled in enfilade, lost forty of its leading ranks, and had to be withdrawn, somewhat shaken.

At about 11 a.m. the General Officer Commanding 7th Brigade came up to the front to attempt reorganization. He found in the German front trench portions of no less than nine battalions of the 7th and 9th Brigades, mixed up and crowded, the communication trenches leading to it choked with dead and wounded, and all telephone wires cut. The Germans were bombarding our front line very heavily. While sorting out the various units, he received orders to launch a new attack to take the final objective at 3.30 p.m. He pointed out that it was impossible for commanding officers to reach their units, and that owing to the mist no detailed objectives for close support could be given to the artillery. The orders for attack were repeated, and the assault was allotted to the 3rd Worcestershire and 2nd Royal Irish Rifles. At 3.35 p.m., five minutes after the hour fixed, there came a message postponing it till 3.50. This certainly never reached the troops, who had only the lifting of the bombardment, not easy to distinguish on the instant, to tell them when to advance. Only those who have experienced it can realize how confusing and demoralizing are last-moment postponements of this nature. Men before an attack are taut-strung—strung to nigh breaking-point—and if the waiting period be unduly prolonged, a slackening is the lesser of two evils. A rupture is the more serious.

Nevertheless this attack was launched with the greatest dash and pressed with the greatest devotion by " C " and " D " Companies, led by Captain Farran and Lieutenant Eales. In this almost hopeless affair the men showed courage equalling their record in any of their actions before or afterwards. Pounded all day by heavy artillery, they had remained cool, steady and unshaken. Now they went forward with unimpaired vigour, after thirty hours without sleep and twelve under fire. But the odds were too great. They might have passed through the frontal fire; that from the flank, from the railway-line, swept away the advance, and the survivors, weary, dazed and angry, fell back to the German front trench. " A " Company meanwhile, on the extreme left flank, worked hard at consolidation. Their bombers kept the Germans in check, and at midnight they handed over their trench intact to the Royal Scots, of the 8th Brigade. The Battalion was not clear till 2 a.m. on the 17th.

The net result of the first Battle of Bellewaarde was the gain of 250 yards upon a front of 800 yards, over 200 prisoners, and 3 machine guns. Heavy losses were doubtless inflicted on the enemy, but probably not more than half our own, which numbered about 3,800 killed, wounded and missing. Of these the 2nd Royal Irish Rifles lost 2 officers killed, 2 wounded and missing, and 9 wounded.* The casualties in other ranks were about 300. The tactics appear to have been crude. Thus, between 4 and 5 p.m. two new battalions, belonging to the 42nd Brigade of the 14th Division, were pushed up into the captured German front line, where the congestion of

* Killed : 2nd-Lieutenants F. C. Joy and J. McIntosh. Wounded and missing : Captain E. C. Farran, 2nd-Lieutenant E. B. Kertland (R. Irish Fusiliers). Wounded: Captain C. M. L. Becher, Lieutenants W. Howard, D. Anderson, 2nd-Lieutenants E. J. Hoare, J. G. Bland, R. L. Vance (R. Irish Fusiliers), T. J. Considine (R. Dublin Fusiliers), C. H. Wale, A. A. Raymond.

1ST ATTACK ON BELLEWAARDE, 16TH JUNE 1915

Facing page 36

The Royal Ulster Rifles.

troops was already serious. This congestion resulted in a high proportion of the loss occurring after all was over, for the heaviest German bombardment of all occurred between 7 and 8.30 p.m., during which period it was estimated that from eighty to a hundred shells a minute fell upon the front of the 7th Brigade. The severest losses among the closely packed men took place during this time.

III.—The 2nd Battalion in the Salient.

On June 23rd Major E. M. Morris left to command a battalion of the King's Own. Major H. R. Goodman, who had joined immediately after the action of Bellewaarde, held command for one day, being succeeded by Major G. A. Weir. The Battalion had the fortune to escape another hopeless action on the 22nd, when the 1st Wiltshire attacked the enemy's works north-west of Hooge, while the 42nd Brigade of the 14th Division attacked strong points north-east of Railway Wood. These operations ended in complete failure.

On July 1st, after a rest in bivouac in the Brandhoek area, the Battalion returned to line, relieving the 1st Wiltshire in the trenches near Hooge, now battered out of recognition by the terrific bombardments to which they had been subjected. It is during this time in the line that the Diary first makes mention of gas shell, from the effects of which one man died. The Battalion was relieved on the 5th, and returned to its bivouac to find a draft of almost two hundred other ranks awaiting it. The fury of the Salient was now slightly diminished, and when the weather was fine existence out of the line was not unbearable. When it rained, however, the ground about the camps speedily became a quagmire, even in summer. There had not yet sprung up the enormous number of hutments which subsequently appeared between Ypres and Poperinghe. The majority of the troops when out of the line lived at this period in tents or, in some cases, in small canvas shelters, which were indifferent accommodation in wet weather upon the wettest soil in Europe. The trenches, however, meant at this time almost inconceivable hardship and discomfort, especially when the 7th Brigade exchanged Hooge for St. Eloi, where there was constant mining. The men of the Royal Irish Rifles and their comrades in the Brigade soon learned that they had, nevertheless, to congratulate themselves upon the exchange. On the 30th of the month the Germans attacked at Hooge, using liquid fire, and succeeded in capturing the British position in its immediate vicinity.

On August 1st one unlucky shell killed 2nd-Lieutenants W. E. Andrews and A. A. Raymond, with two other ranks, severely wounding Lieutenant D. Kirkpatrick, the artillery forward observation officer, and two men. The incident is described by Father Gill, the Battalion's chaplain, in his diary. He knew there was to be some registration fire that afternoon, and was anxious to see it. But when he reached the front-line trench he found a whole group of officers with periscopes.

"Taught by the death of Major Alston," he writes, "I had a strong objection to being one of a large party showing periscopes. I therefore gave out my newspapers and returned to our headquarters. I had not been gone ten minutes when the group was shelled. . . . I fear that many casualties during the war were due to a want of care in small things. . . . Sometimes, of course, there was nothing for it but to take risks, but very frequently a little care would have saved valuable lives." The statement is undoubtedly true. Many a fine life was indeed thrown away in this fashion to no useful end.

On August 11th the Battalion moved to another part of the front, taking over the line running through Wieltje, always one of the worst sections of the Salient. Here, on the 15th, it had a very successful patrol action. A party under Lieutenant Moss met with a hostile patrol out in " No Man's Land," and, after a short fight, killed two and captured one. On our side there were no casualties.

Meanwhile, on August 9th, Hooge had been retaken by the 6th Division. On the 24th the 7th Brigade returned to this, its old battle-ground, taking over the line with the 1st Wiltshire and 2nd South Lancashire. An extraordinary change had taken place since they had last seen the village. Then it had, indeed, been a complete ruin, but one where at least a few feet of the houses still stood. Now the houses had completely disappeared. On the following night the two battalions in line were ordered to work their way forward to the old stables of Hooge Château. They reported after some time that they thought they were upon the ground, but could not be altogether sure, since little trace of the buildings remained. On the night of the 28th the 2nd Royal Irish Rifles relieved the 1st Wiltshire and at once commenced hard work upon the consolidation of the new Stables position. The weather had now taken a turn for the worse. The cross-country tracks became all but impassable, and it used to take almost the whole of the summer's night to carry out reliefs. The trenches were in a terrible state, and littered with the refuse of recent battles. A notable feature of the position was the famous " Hooge Crater," caused by the explosion of a great mine. It was some sixty yards across and upwards of forty feet deep. In its flanks there were dug-outs in two tiers. The château was now no more than a wall a few feet high, but even at that it was the best-preserved building of the locality. At this time also the back-area bivouacs were given up for dug-outs along the canal bank at Ypres, so that the Battalion may be said to have passed its time under continuous shell-fire. There was, however, a certain amount of comfort about these dug-outs, and the casualties to troops occupying them were always relatively small. When, at the end of the month of August, the Battalion went back to bivouacs, this time in the neighbourhood of Dickebusch, no one was gratified by the change.

A letter from the commanding officer, Lieutenant-Colonel G. A. Weir, is illuminating on the subject of casualties. He took over command, as has been stated, on June 24th, immediately after the first action of Bellewaarde. From then till the second action of Bellewaarde was exactly three months, of what was called " ordinary trench warfare." And, he states, during that period, every officer present when he joined, save the Adjutant and the Quartermaster, became a casualty, and none but these two was with it when the Battalion went into the latter fight. It must, of course, be taken into consideration that the Battalion was very low in officer strength when he arrived. The circumstances, however, were not uncommon, and give some idea of the wastage in a section of the front under unremitting shell-fire, and of the difficulties experienced in maintaining a continuity of tradition in any given unit.*

---

*During this period there were killed: Captain Williams, Lieutenant W. E. Morton, 2nd-Lieutenants W. E. Andrews and A. A. Raymond. Wounded: Lieutenant C. Wakefield, 2nd-Lieutenant H. Seth-Smith. About a dozen officers were evacuated suffering from various forms of trench sickness.

CHAPTER III

I.—THE SECOND ATTACK ON BELLEWAARDE

A CHANGE had come over the conceptions of military commanders as to the requirements of victory. It was obvious that in the present conditions defence was beating attack. And it was now the enemy that was on the defensive, and, therefore, having the better of the matter. But it was impossible for the Allies to wait upon the Western Front till the Germans put the Russians out of action and brought to bear upon them in France superior forces. General Joffre decided, therefore, to make an attempt to defeat them by breaking through their lines, and winning an opportunity to manœuvre upon open ground. The meaning of all the lessons learnt hitherto was clear. The attack must be upon a wide front, and must be supported by a great mass of artillery. This was now available to the French. The area east of Rheims was chosen for the venture, and the assault entrusted to General de Castelnau. We are not here concerned with its result, except to say that it failed to achieve all that had been hoped from it, though inflicting a heavy blow upon the enemy.

It was not to be a solitary attack. At the same time two others, each greater than any action of trench warfare hitherto, were to be made by British and French, north and south of Lens, a very important railway junction; the former against the line Lens—La Bassée, the latter against the dominating Vimy Ridge. Neither, as in the case of the greater Champagne offensive, achieved more than a limited success, but the British attack at Loos came very near to being a great victory, and gave the German command a serious fright. These northern offensives had their definite objectives, but had at least in part the subsidiary motive of pinning down German reserves and preventing them being moved down to Champagne. The attack at Loos, in its turn, was to be supported by a whole series of subsidiary actions, to prevent the enemy withdrawing reserves from other parts of the British front. In these actions both the 1st and 2nd Battalions Royal Irish Rifles were engaged, the former comparatively near the main scene of action, at Bois Grenier, the latter on its old fighting-ground of Hooge and the Bellewaarde Lake. As we left the 2nd Battalion at Hooge, we may take its action first. Both attacks, like the three great Battles of Champagne, Artois, and Loos, took place on September 25th.

The month opened with a tremendous bombardment of Hooge, which the Battalion missed, as it was in rest at the time. On the 12th the 7th Brigade was relieved and moved back to Brandhoek. Parties amounting to 400 nightly had to go up in motor-buses to work behind the line, but no man's turn came more than once, and a very pleasant holiday was enjoyed in fine weather. Football matches were played between battalions, and the Brigade was able to get full value from the 3rd Division's Horse Show. On the 18th the Brigade returned to the line, which, as if a match had been set to a powder-barrel, suddenly burst out into a succession of fierce bombardments and counter-bombardments. The Royal Irish Rifles remained out till the eve of the attack.

The V Corps was attacking between the Menin road and the Roulers railway. The 2nd Royal Irish Rifles was to be on the left flank of its division, and its objective was the southern half of the western shore of Bellewaarde Lake and an imaginary continuation of this 200 yards farther south. Its advance, from the present British line covering Hooge, was to be, therefore, in a north-easterly direction. On its right was to be the 2nd South Lancashire, and on its left the 15th Shropshire Light Infantry of the 14th Division. The attack was to be made by two companies—" B " on the right, and " D " on the left, with one, " C," in support, to occupy our front line after it was launched, and " A " in reserve. The final objective was distant not more than from 400 to 500 yards. The assault was to be preceded by an intense bombardment beginning at 3.50 a.m. Four mines were to be exploded along the whole front of attack ; the first pair at 4.19 a.m., the second pair half a minute later. The explosion of the latter pair was to be the signal for the assault.

At 7.10 p.m. on the 24th the Battalion paraded, and marched up to Hooge, relieving the H.A.C. Headquarters were in a dug-out under the Menin road, west of the site of the destroyed village. Five minutes before the bombardment ceased the two attacking companies moved out of their trenches and deployed opposite the position to be attacked. Each was in two lines, two platoons in first and two in second, the latter being just in front of the British parapet. Six sections of bombers and two machine guns accompanied the assaulting troops. The reader who does not know his Ypres can have small conception of the conditions under foot, and many suppose that, since summer was not yet over, the " going " was fairly sound. It cannot be too often insisted upon in the accounts of battles in the Salient that even in summer, even in dry weather, the hole made by a shell was brimful of water in a very short time. In this case there had been considerable rainfall recently, which meant that, even for those who avoided stepping into shell-holes, each footstep sank inches at least into the mud of the churned ground. The so-called " rush " of the assault was in such cases often a very slow movement indeed. And here the opposing trenches were divided by 200 yards of this foul and adhesive clay.

The two companies went forward, and at once came under heavy machine-gun fire. Perhaps half of those making up the first line dropped, killed or wounded, before the German front line was reached. But nothing could check the spirit of the survivors. On the greater part of their front they entered the German first-line trench, killing any survivors of the bombardment that were in it. But on the extreme flanks no entry could be made, mainly on account of the amount of barbed wire which remained uncut by the bombardment. On their right the men of the South Lancashire twice took the German front line, but were in each case driven out by the barrage fire of the enemy's artillery upon his own trench. Farther east, beyond the Stables, the advance was completely held up by uncut wire.

Crossing the German front-line trench the gallant remnant of the attackers pressed on and reached the second line. But they reached it without their sole hope of maintaining themselves, their bombing sections, of which there were no survivors. So often was this the case in attacks at this time and the following year on the Somme, that there is little room for doubt that the Germans fired particularly on the men with canvas buckets in their hands. Immediately the German bombers counter-attacked, and a desperate, one-sided struggle began. Meanwhile " C " Company had moved forward to support the attack. There is no mention of the fact in official reports, but the Commanding Officer states that the company " broke loose," seeing the plight of its comrades, and went forward to their aid without orders. But now the conditions were even more impossible than during the first assault, for the British artillery had lifted off the front line, and there was nothing to check the German machine guns on the flanks, which had not been penetrated. It is stated that very few men of " C " Company ever reached the German trench. Those who did found there a mere handful of the other two companies, which had been obliged to fall back from the second line before a shower of bombs, to which they could make no reply. At 6 a.m. a few of our men could still be seen in the enemy's trench, but thereafter there was no sign of them, though it is possible that a few held out considerably later. " A " Company had been moved up meanwhile into the British front line, and it was with great difficulty that the men were prevented from going over to support, upon what would have been an entirely hopeless venture.

A new attack was contemplated by the 3rd Division, and a further bombardment fixed for 12.15 p.m. At noon, however, this was cancelled, so that the artillery could give all the aid possible to the troops of the 14th Division on the left. These troops had already taken Bellewaarde Farm, and had made strenuous efforts to work down and clear the left flank of the Royal Irish Rifles, but had been twice driven back by a German flanking barrage. At 3.40 p.m. the Corps Commander decided to consolidate the ground already won. His resources were inadequate to further attacks, and there was already a serious shortage of grenades in front line, and great difficulty in replenishing dumps from the rear through the heavy German barrage. The attack of the 8th Brigade, after a good start, had also failed.

" No Man's Land " was full of dead and wounded, and so swept by fire that it was all but impossible to bring in the latter during daylight. Many of them crept into shell-holes to protect themselves, plugged and bound up their hurts as best they might, to crawl back to our trenches when dusk fell, or be picked up by the stretcher-bearers if life still remained in their bodies. The Battalion was relieved by the 1st Wiltshire that night. The relief was a very slow affair, in the mud and still-continuing shell-fire, and after it was over there was the thronged Menin road to be negotiated by the weary men. The Battalion was not back in camp till 6 a.m. on the 26th.

The losses of the 7th Brigade were 23 officers and 706 other ranks killed, wounded, and missing, about a third being in the last category. And of these casualties to its brigade, the 2nd Royal Irish Rifles suffered almost precisely half. Its total losses were 15 officers and 316 other ranks killed, wounded, and missing. The officer casualties were: Killed, Lieutenant A. La Touche, 2nd-Lieutenants W. L. Orr, J. G. Caruth, M. Ross ; wounded, Captains W. Cupples (R. Innis. Fus.), H. N. Young (R. Innis. Fus.), Lieutenants T. H. Ivey, G. W. Calverley, J. R. Tuckett; wounded and missing, Captains H. G. C. Perry-Ayscough (Connaught Rangers), W. P. O'Lone, R. F. Gavin, 2nd-Lieutenant K. Ross ; missing, Lieutenant F. H. Bethel (Connaught Rangers). 2nd-Lieutenant S. Bell, slightly wounded, remained at duty. Heavily as the Battalion suffered, the holding action had been fought at comparatively light cost where its brigade was concerned.

Every witness of this battle, official or private, emphasizes the gallantry of the men of the Battalion and their extraordinary good spirits. The men " fought like tigers," in the phrase of their Commanding Officer, in a hopeless attempt. Had the creeping barrage of the following year been in operation, it would have had some slight chance of success, though even then it would have been an affair of greatest difficulty. As it was, the German machine guns practically held up the attack before it reached their wire, largely uncut. They were the sacrifice to aid the greater venture farther south, and they gave themselves without stint. After such actions, however well troops had fought, there was generally needed a long period before they regained their spirits, but in this case the Battalion threw off the effects of its evil experiences within a few days. And much was demanded of it, for after no more than four days' rest it was moved up again to the line, this time about a mile and a half south of Hooge, in Armagh Wood, and actually remained in the trenches from October 1st to October 12th. Before re-entering the trenches, it had been inspected by the Corps Commander, General Allenby, who spoke in terms of the highest praise of the men's gallantry and dash, telling them that though they had not succeeded in the particular object in view, their sacrifices had been invaluable. They had contained and occupied a large number of German troops and, above all, German guns, which would otherwise have been used against the British or French in their other great attacks. This assault upon an almost impregnable position would rank as one of the greatest achievements of the war. They had added new credit to the already illustrious name, not only of the 2nd Battalion, but to the whole Regiment of the Royal Irish Rifles.

On October 11th, Lieut.-Colonel G. A. Weir, who had commanded the Battalion with great vigour and done a great deal for the comfort of the men, left them, with the good wishes of all, to command the 84th Brigade. He was succeeded by Major L. C. Sprague, Royal Irish Rifles.

II.—The Action of Bois Grenier.

The 1st Battalion was still in the flat country between Armentières and La Bassée Canal, the only front it had known or was to know till the opening of the Somme battle. Between Neuve Chapelle and Fauquissart there now lay the Indian Corps. North of it was a New Army Division, the 20th, then the 8th Division, then the 27th. The attack to be carried out by the 25th Brigade, of the 8th Division, had a similar object to the attack at Hooge, and two others, by the Indians north of Neuve Chapelle and the 2nd Division at Givenchy; that is to say, it was designed purely to pin down German reserves and serve as a diversion from the affair at Loos. But it was perhaps on the smallest scale of any of the holding actions. All that was hoped from it at best was the capture of the German front-line trench upon a front of about 1,200 yards, after which it was intended to join it up to the existing British line. The fact that on either flank, at Well Farm on the right and opposite Fort Bridoux on the left, the British line jutted out into a small salient gave reason to the scheme. In order to allow of the consolidation of the front line, when taken, the second was also to be captured, and the troops withdrawn as soon as the front had been put into a state of defence.

Besides Corner Fort, which faced Well Farm, and Fort Bridoux, there was a very strong position in the German lines, about midway between these two, called The Angle. It was shaped somewhat like a human nose. Just north of it was a work known as The Lozenge. The plan of attack was that these three positions, Corner Fort, The Angle, and Fort Bridoux, were to be assaulted; the first by the 2nd Rifle Brigade, the second by the 2nd Royal Berkshire, and the third by the 2nd Lincolnshire. These positions captured, the troops were to work along the front-line trench and join hands, while bombers fought their way down the communication trenches to the second line and established blocks. On the extreme left of the attack were to be two companies of the 1st Royal Irish Rifles, " C " and " D." They were supplied with a Stokes gun, a great novelty in those days, smoke-candles, eight catapults, and a thousand smoke-bombs,

2ND ATTACK ON BELLEWAARDE, 25TH SEPT 1915

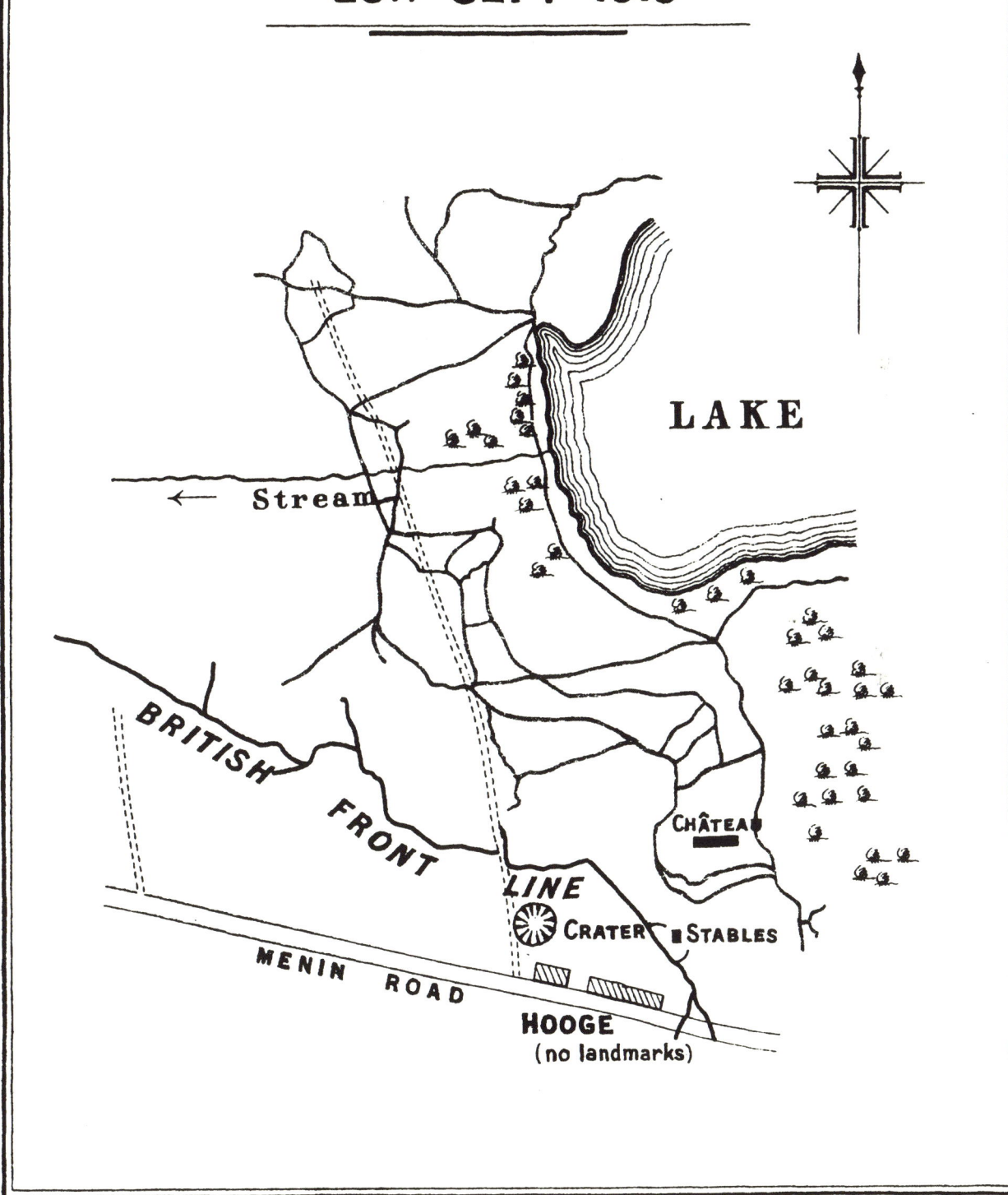

to create a smoke screen on the left flank of the attack, north of Fort Bridoux. Upon their front an 18-pounder gun had also been brought into the trench to support the attack. The assault was preceded by an artillery bombardment over four days. A new feature was that red flags were to be carried to mark the position of the bombers and advanced infantry. These were found in subsequent battles of trench warfare to be most useful, but only if they were displayed in front or on the extreme flanks, and nowhere else. If any infantryman in the German trench, whatever his position, displayed a flag, even though there might be other troops in front of him, the result was frequently that these troops were shelled by our own artillery. On this occasion there does not seem to have been in the Brigade Orders sufficient insistence upon this most important point. Two mines were to be exploded: one at Corner Fort at the moment of the assault, and another shallower one at Fort Bridoux *after* the wave had gone over. This latter was to be blown in " No Man's Land," very narrow at this point, and its object was to form the basis of a communication trench.

At 3.30 a.m. on September 25th the Brigade formed up in the darkness. " A " and " B " Companies of the Royal Irish Rifles were in position on the Rue des Layes, about 900 yards in rear of the front-line companies. These last suffered a minor catastrophe just before " zero," a Stokes shell exploding and setting all their smoke bombs on fire, besides causing some loss. Owing to this misfortune it was impossible to screen the left flank of the Lincolns, as had been planned.

At 4.30 a.m. the infantry charged with splendid dash. On the right, Corner Fort was captured at once. In the centre, the companies of the Royal Berkshire captured the front-line trench at The Lozenge, but below it, at The Angle, were beaten back by heavy machine-gun fire. On the left, the Lincolns took Fort Bridoux and penetrated to the second line. This, however, was full of Germans, who fought stoutly, and a long-drawn battle of bombs followed. At 6 a.m. the bombers of " C " Company of the Royal Irish Rifles were sent to their aid, chiefly for carrying work. Second-Lieutenant Wallace, on entering the German trenches, found that the men of the Lincolns were being outranged by the enemy bombers. He bethought him of the catapults, returned to his own company and fetched one, and with it did some excellent work holding off German counter-attacks. By 8 a.m. the men of the Lincolnshire and Royal Berkshire were in touch, and the German front-line trench was held from The Lozenge to Fort Bridoux. The former battalion, however, was in trouble, and the two reserve companies of the Royal Irish Rifles were moved up into the British front line in its rear.

At 10 a.m. Major Merriman led across two platoons of " A " Company to Fort Bridoux. The second line was still full of Germans, and the fire was heavy. All the morning the fight raged, the Germans, heavily reinforced, counter-attacking time after time. As in so many actions, their bombers were outranging our men, and towards noon the supply of bombs began to fail; that is to say, they could not be got across " No Man's Land " in sufficient numbers. The mine opposite Fort Bridoux, of which much had been hoped, had been a comparative failure, not having broken deeply enough into the ground, and proved small aid to communication. At 1 a.m. came a particularly heavy counter-attack, which drove the men of the Lincolnshire from Fort Bridoux and recaptured the front-line trench for 100 yards south and west of it. Eventually the Battalion was compelled to withdraw, the men of the Royal Irish retiring with it. Major Merriman was wounded in superintending the withdrawal.

The 2nd Royal Berkshire was now " pinched out " from both flanks, and was also compelled to retire. On the right of the attack the men of the 2nd Rifle Brigade had done very well—as, indeed, this fine battalion always did. They had established themselves firmly at Corner Fort, beaten off a series of counter-attacks, and were about to make a big effort to link up with the 2nd Royal Berkshire when the latter were forced to go. They remained in the German lines till 4 p.m., and were then withdrawn in good order to our lines. In fact, along the whole front the withdrawals were conducted coolly and deliberately.

This last fact is proved by an inspection of the 25th Brigade's casualties. High as these were, they pay tribute to the conduct of the operation. The killed amounted to 14 officers and 141 other ranks, the wounded to 19 officers and 866 other ranks, the missing to 5 officers and 114 other ranks. Now, obviously a great proportion of the wounds occurred in the enemy's lines; while of the missing, it may be taken for granted, so comparatively small are the numbers, that the greater proportion were killed. The meaning of the figures is therefore clear. The attacking force was able to carry back to its own trenches practically all its wounded. That is clear proof that there was no rout and that the enemy was held in check to the last. So the operation, though unsuccessful in obtaining that which was its immediate objective, was well conducted. It must also have had considerable value. From Bois Grenier to the northern flank of the Loos offensive was not much over twelve miles, and the country behind the German lines was well served by lateral roads and railways. So hard pressed was the enemy at Loos that doubtless he would have been glad to move down, by road or rail, regiments, or even single battalions, to a front which showed signs of cracking. Instead he was compelled to reinforce strongly his line opposite Bois Grenier with his local reserves. The action had there achieved its purpose.

It had had many difficulties with which to contend. Mist and rain made observation almost impossible. Observers in our lines were unable to see our troops in the enemy's, and it was very difficult to give the latter adequate artillery support after the first assault. The multiplicity of bombs, with which the British were at that period experimenting, which the troops on this occasion took with them into action proved a snare. The men became muddled with all the different types, in the use of which they were not fully trained. It is reported that in many cases they forgot, in the heat of the action, the differences between the various sorts, and some which had to be lighted with a fusee were thrown unlighted. In any case, bombs of this nature were never satisfactory in wet weather. The attack itself had been pressed with great bravery by all the troops concerned, and had inflicted heavy loss upon the enemy.

At 4 p.m. on the afternoon of the 25th, at the time of the withdrawal of the 2nd Rifle Brigade from the region of Corner Fort, the two companies of the Royal Irish Rifles which had been moved up into the trenches of the Lincolns were withdrawn to their original position in the Rue des Layes. Their casualties had not been serious. "C" and "D" Companies remained in the breastwork. On the 30th the Battalion was relieved and withdrew to rest at Pont Mortier.* On October 4th it was inspected by the commander of the III Corps, Lieutenant-General Sir William Pulteney. It then returned to the usual routine of trench warfare, still in the neighbourhood of Bois Grenier.

Meanwhile, at the end of the month of September, the Loos battle had died down, leaving in the minds of the British a sense of bitter disappointment, and in that of the

* The Battalion's casualties were: Killed, 2nd-Lieutenant R. H. Andrews and 11 other ranks; wounded, Major A. D. N. Merriman, 2nd-Lieutenant J. H. Butler, and 76 other ranks; missing, 15 other ranks.

enemy one of proportionate relief. Upon its small front, with its capture of 3,000 prisoners, it had at one moment come closer to complete success than the attack of General de Castelnau upon its great front, and its 25,000 prisoners. But reserves had not been ready to hand at the moment they were needed, and a great initial advantage had not been followed up. The worst of it was that this was not an effort of a sort that could be made every day. We had lost 45,000 men and had expended all the carefully hoarded reserves of munitions. We should have to lie quiet for a while. Some fighting went on at Loos, and one great German counter-attack was routed, but in the main there ensued a period of quietude. To our soldiers in the trenches it must have appeared as if the end of the war were farther off than ever ; nor were they wrong in their surmise. However, they accepted the conditions with equanimity and good temper characteristic of them. So long as the rations arrived regularly, they would go on fighting till the sky fell in, and just as well in a losing as in a winning battle. Indeed, the latter phrase had small meaning to men who were never prepared to admit that they were beaten.

CHAPTER IV

I.—Winter, 1915: the 1st Battalion.

The winter months of 1915, October, November and December, were on the whole quiet upon the British front, except that Loos was lively throughout the first of them. But they were important. During this period more and more New Army Divisions were arriving in the country and learning their work by attachment to veteran troops in the trenches. Where the 1st and 2nd Battalions, Royal Irish Rifles, are concerned, there are no operations of any importance to record.

Till nearly the end of November the former continued to carry out the normal round of trenches and billets. Then came a very welcome relief. On the 25th the Battalion marched with its brigade *via* La Motte and Morbecque to Sercus. It was now in General Headquarters reserve, and about to enjoy a long period of rest and training. Till December 20th it remained at Sercus. Training was given particularly to those who in the complications of modern war were beginning to be known as "specialists." Under brigade arrangements there were special classes for machine gunners, signallers, bombers, trench-mortar personnel, and also for non-commissioned officers. Games and sports of every kind were also instituted, and the men speedily began to show the results of the pleasant change. Not least valuable was the moral tonic of returning, if only for a while, to civilization and unspoiled country from the abomination of desolation near the line.

Afterwards the whole Division had three days' training for open warfare—practically the old "manœuvres" of days before the war—in a special training area established south-west of Aire. The Battalion had some long marches and much hard work, billeting each night in different villages. It returned to Sercus on the 23rd, and there passed Christmas—a very happy occasion when it chanced to fall when troops were out of the line, as can easily be guessed. It did not go back to the line till January 6th, when it took over trenches upon its old front, opposite Rouges Bancs. It had been out of the line for six weeks, a piece of good fortune which did not very often come the way of infantry in France, and, though the rest had come in winter, it had been very much appreciated and had very good results.

One occurrence of the period may be mentioned, though it did not closely affect the 1st Royal Irish Rifles. The 8th Division lost one of its regular Brigades, the 24th, and received in exchange one of the New Army, the 70th. Late in October the 2nd Lincolnshire and 2nd Rifle Brigade were transferred to this Brigade, and in exchange the 11th Sherwood Foresters and 8th K.O.Y.L.I. joined the 25th Brigade. The 25th Brigade then consisted of these two New Army battalions and of its original battalions, the 1st Royal Irish Rifles and 2nd Royal Berkshire. The attachment lasted a couple of weeks only, when the two regular battalions returned to the 25th Brigade. The 70th Brigade, however, became an integral part of the 8th Division; henceforth consisting of the 23rd, the 25th, and the 70th.

II.—WINTER, 1915: THE 2ND BATTALION.

The transfer of brigades had taken place in accordance with the decision of the Higher Command to add a regular brigade to each division of the New Army, in exchange for one of its own brigades. As has been shown, the scheme did not affect the 1st Battalion. It was different with the 2nd, at Ypres. On October 9th it was learnt that the 7th Brigade was to be transferred to the 25th Division of the New Army. On the 12th the Battalion was relieved by the H.A.C. (which left the 7th Brigade, in which it had done excellent service, from that date). On the 14th the divisional commander, General Haldane, came to say good-bye, speaking highly of the conduct of the troops in the affair of Bellewaarde. In the afternoon the Battalion marched back to a tent camp west of Poperinghe. It was the farthest point from the line which it had reached that year, and that line the Salient!

The parting from the 3rd Division, with its glorious record at Mons and Le Cateau, its memories of the desperate confusion at La Bassée, its great achievements of dogged fighting in the Salient, was naturally a sad moment. In the late war, divisional *esprit de corps* became almost as important as regimental, and it was most unfortunate when it had to be broken on occasions such as these. In this case the Battalion was to leave not only its old division, but its old brigade. On the 16th it marched to Merris, where Sir Charles Fergusson welcomed the troops back into his, the II, Corps. On the 24th it was inspected by Major-General Sir B. Doran, commanding the 25th Division. Next day it moved on to Bailleul, and the next to Le Bizet, a village on the Franco-Belgian frontier near Armentières, considerably damaged by shell-fire and partially evacuated by its inhabitants. And on this date it was transferred to the 74th Brigade, now consisting of the 2nd Royal Irish Rifles, 11th Lancashire Fusiliers, 9th Loyal North Lancashire, and 13th Cheshire. It was torn from its ancient roots with a vengeance. However, it had come to a division which was to win a high reputation and take high rank among those of the New Army, which was to have a remarkable proportion of successful actions in the course of its career. The day following the Battalion moved up to the line at Le Touquet, companies moving at half-hour intervals in that open country. The new trenches marked an extraordinary change from those of Ypres. They were very quiet, and casualties were kept very low. The chief enemy was the wet, in a land lying for the most part only between 40 feet and 60 feet above sea-level; whereas that of the Ypres Salient had been all over 100 feet, and in places considerably more. However, as this placid front was lightly held, it was generally possible to find comparatively sound ground for the posts. The discomfort, apart altogether from the shelling, was considerably less than in the Salient. Tours in the line were generally of six days' duration.

There is little to be recorded for the month of November. During its course the Battalion lost Captain O'Lone, killed visiting a listening-post at night, and its very popular medical officer, killed with his sergeant by a shell while tending a wounded man in the trenches. On the 19th the Battalion was inspected by Mr. John Redmond, who had come out to visit Irish troops in France. His speech is thus summarized by Father Gill: "He was glad to meet a regiment which contained men of every creed from so many different parts of Ireland, especially the North. They were now brothers-in-arms, and he was sure their harmony and unity in the great cause in which they were fighting was a happy omen of the relations which would exist between all in Ireland after the war." Alas! Mr. Redmond's prophecy has been falsified by events. "Seeing that the regiment," adds Father Gill, " is in great part from the North of Ireland, and contains many Protestants, the reception of Mr. Redmond was very remarkable." He was loudly cheered by the men. But all, whatever their creed, could appreciate the attitude of Mr. Redmond in the war, and none of those who fought in it can recall his memory without admiration.

In December the weather grew wetter and the trenches more waterlogged. The worst, in the very bottom of the Lys Valley, had to be abandoned altogether. Redoubts were, with much trouble, built in rear of them. Those that were held were now often knee-deep in water. On the 22nd there was a considerable bombardment of Armentières and the trenches, but the Battalion suffered no casualties. It was relieved on the night of Christmas Eve, when there had been a considerable amount of machine-gun and rifle fire, to discourage the enemy from attempting to institute another " Christmas truce " like that of the preceding year, against which there were strict orders. In any case, since the gas attacks of the spring, the British rank and file were much less disposed to fraternization.

The day passed quietly, with the usual ceremonies, and as much good cheer as could be collected, at Le Bizet. No one had any particular case for optimism, yet good spirits were the rule, and the men did not let the war spoil their appetites. They were, as Mr. Kipling writes of the Irish Guards on the same occasion, " in merciful ignorance that those of them who survived would attend three more such festivals." Still more merciful was the ignorance which kept them from knowing how great a number should not survive. They had little to show for all the miseries and sacrifices they had endured since last they had celebrated Christmas ; only the knowledge that they had given of their best, and—their best friend—the power that remained with them to laugh in the face of adversity.

III.—THE 7TH BATTALION.

We must now turn to a new legion, one of the New Army battalions, the 7th. As has already been recorded, it was in the 48th Infantry Brigade, the other battalions in which were the 8th and 9th Royal Dublin Fusiliers and the 9th Royal Munster Fusiliers.

On December 19th the 7th Battalion left Blackdown for Southampton. It embarked at 4.30 p.m., and arrived at Havre at 7.30 a.m. next morning. It missed—fortunately, perhaps, for its early impressions of France—the usual night in a rest camp, and entrained that evening for Fouguereuil, in the coal-mining area. " A " and " B " Companies marched to Noeux-les-Mines, and " C " and " D " to Houchin. These villages of the mining country were incredibly ugly, but scenic beauty was not the first demand of troops in war-time, and they had compensations. Noeux-les-Mines, in particular, was, whatever officers might think of it, one of the most favoured billets in France from the point of view of the rank and file. It had, to begin with, the best bathing facilities on the western front—the hot baths attached to the mines. It was liberally supplied with *estaminets* and eating-houses, where eggs and fried potatoes could be obtained, with other more dubious attractions.

From the 23rd onwards the 48th Brigade was attached to the 1st Division for instruction. The first Christmas on active service came and went before the Battalion had seen the front line, or in any way " found its feet." On the 29th " A " and " B " Companies moved up to Philosophe, to the old British front and support lines, where they had graduated instruction in the holding of trenches.

We have now brought to the front three of the four Regular or Service battalions of the Royal Irish Rifles with which we are here concerned, the other nine being in the 36th (Ulster) Division, which by the end of 1915 had been three months in France ; so that by this time the Regiment had twelve battalions upon the Western Front. We now have to turn to another battalion, the only one which saw service in the East. This is, in some respects, the most interesting of all, since it fought in three different theatres of war.

CHAPTER V

I.—THE SUVLA BAY SCHEME.

ON July 7th, 1915, the 6th Battalion Royal Irish Rifles (less transport), consisting of 27 officers, 1 medical officer, and 912 other ranks, embarked on the *Transylvania*, and sailed from Liverpool at 5 p.m. On the 11th Gibraltar was touched, and on the 14th the transport coaled at Malta, where officers and warrant officers were allowed ashore, sailing next morning. Alexandria was reached on the afternoon of the 17th, and quitted twenty-four hours later. On the 21st Mudros Harbour was entered, the Battalion disembarking next day and moving into bivouac. It spent a week upon the hot, barren, fly-plagued island of Lemnos.

Space does not permit, nor is there necessity for, more than a few words to outline the position on the Gallipoli Peninsula, reached as a result of a landing which ranks as one of the greatest feats in the history of war and of the fierce fighting of June and July. As a result of all that heroic struggle, we still held no more than the southern and western fringes of the Peninsula. On the south-eastern flank the height of Achi Baba still loomed up unconquerable. On the south-western we were touching Krithia, but had not got it. Twelve miles northward along the western coast the Australians and New Zealanders were established on the Sari Bair Plateau, nearly a thousand feet in height, though they held no more than its western fringe and were far from the highest ground. Sir Ian Hamilton, having now been strongly reinforced, to the extent of three divisions of the New Army and two of Territorials, was about to make an attempt on a great scale to capture the Dardanelles defences on the European side. Frontal attacks from the toe of the Peninsula no longer offered a chance of success, and the advance which he planned against Achi Baba was in the nature of a feint. The real attack was to be to northward. The Anzac Corps was to complete the capture of the great Sari Bair Plateau, including Rhododendron Hill and Koja Chemen Tepe. Meanwhile the 10th Division (less one brigade) and the 11th Division were to land on their left, within or just south of the semi-circular Suvla Bay, where no offensive was expected by the Turks, and reasonably light resistance might be reckoned upon, to push forward as rapidly as possible, link up with the left of the Anzacs, and capture the Anafarta Heights, backed up by the 53rd and 54th Territorial Divisions, which would land afterwards. If they should succeed in this operation, the main Turkish position farther south would be completely turned and the Peninsula would be virtually ours. It was in many respects a brilliant plan, but the calls it made upon totally inexperienced troops were very high, and this factor proved its undoing.

In the coming battle the 29th Brigade, in which was our battalion, was not to go into action under its own division, but under the orders of General Godley, who commanded the Anzac left, with a miscellaneous force consisting of the New Zealand and Australian Division, the 13th Division, the 29th Brigade, and the 29th Indian Brigade. For the first day's operations, the objectives of which were the hills of Chunuk Bair and Koja Chemen Tepe, it was to be in reserve.

II.—THE BATTLE OF SARI BAIR.

On the afternoon of August 5th the 29th Brigade sailed from Mudros, the 6th Royal Irish Rifles being in the *Partridge* with Brigade Headquarters and the 72nd Field Company, Royal Engineers. By midnight the Battalion had disembarked, by means of lighters, at Watson's Pier, Anzac Cove, and moved into bivouacs in Shrapnel Gulley, one of the narrow clefts in the hills running down to the shore. Here it remained the following day, drawing bombs and sandbags for the battle. Fighting had begun in the afternoon down at the toe of the Peninsula, while that night, after dusk, the force of General Godley had begun a preliminary advance, which had resulted before dawn in the capture of the ridges known as the Table Tops and most of Bauchop's Hill. On their right, during the afternoon of the 6th, the Australians of General Birdwood's Anzac Corps had taken the Lone Pine Plateau. The Suvla landing, too, took place during the night, and by midnight there was firing all along the coast. The Battalion was heavily shelled in its valley, suffering several casaulties, and at midnight moved to another, known as Rest Gulley.

On the 7th General Godley's force made a very fine attack, capturing Rhododendron Ridge, but could not get their objectives of Chunuk Bair and Koja Chemen Tepe in face of fierce resistance and tremendous heat. The Battalion remained all day in Rest Gulley. Next morning the southern edge of Chunuk Bair was carried after the most desperate fighting, through which men moved up the stony, baked slope, practically without cover, in face of terrible fire. At 9.30 a.m. that morning, the 10th Hampshire* and 6th Royal Irish Rifles moved out of their camp, the former leading, and marched towards the Sari Bair Plateau, halting at midday and continuing the march after dusk. The Hampshire came into line north of Rhododendron Ridge at 4 a.m. on the 9th and deployed. The 6th Royal Irish Rifles deployed on its left. The men were already somewhat fatigued. The march in the darkness across this country of scrub and rock had been very difficult, particularly the crossing of the gorge known as Aghyl Dere. The two battalions, with two of the 13th Division, formed the centre column which was to assault the main height of Chunuk Bair.

At 8 a.m. two companies of the Hampshire, with two machine guns, attacked the 270-metre contour on Chunuk Bair, in conjunction with the general advance of the morning's programme. They met with very heavy machine-gun fire, and got no closer than 300 yards to the crest, having suffered heavy casualties. Here they entrenched. The Royal Irish Rifles, on their left, was then ordered to make good " L " Ridge, one of the innumerable spurs of Chunuk Bair, which it is hard to locate precisely on the indifferent maps of the Peninsula. In this, its first action, the men of the Battalion went forward with great dash in face of heavy fire, beneath a sun already blazing hot, across steadily rising ground. Almost all was won, but not the position upon the desired " L " Ridge. Two hundred and fifty yards short of it the Battalion was driven to ground and dug itself in. There it remained all night. Its position was dangerous, the left flank being in air, and the men suffered agonies from thirst. General Godley's attack had not got all its objectives, but it had got enough to have made a success of its venture if the Suvla force had come anywhere near its programme. But here mistakes, indecision, lack of training, had been fatal to the whole scheme, which had fallen hopelessly behind its time-table. Moreover, it had not diverted Turkish reinforcements from the front opposite General Godley.

* This Battalion had replaced the 5th Royal Irish Regiment in the 29th Brigade.

During the night the tired men managed to scrape out a shallow trench, but it was a poor defence against what followed. At 4.30 a.m. on the morning of the 10th came a tremendous Turkish counter-attack, delivered by fresh troops, upon our position on Chunuk Bair. It was preceded by a bombardment which caused very heavy casualties. Then the Turks came on, wave upon wave, with the utmost bravery, heedless of the heavy loss caused by our fire. Fierce fighting developed all along the line, and both battalions of the 29th Brigade stood their position well. But the losses increased, especially those of officers. The Turk at his best is as good a soldier as there is in Europe, and only those who fought at Gallipoli saw him quite at his best during the late war. He certainly was at this point to-day. With wild courage, his infantry came forward again and again to the assault. The Battalion clung to its position for an hour and a half. It is possible that the same men with six months' experience of war would never have left it. But for raw troops the test was too high. Not, however, till almost all the officers were casualties did the line break, and then the troops were rallied by the three or four who survived, and took up a line 800 yards behind the old position. In a very short period the Battalion had had 3 officers and 42 other ranks killed, 18 officers and 274 other ranks wounded, and 38 other ranks missing. These figures represent a much higher proportion than is realized till it is explained that all battalions of the 28th Brigade had embarked at Mudros at a strength of 25 officers and 750 other ranks, so as to have some trained reinforcements at hand. The counter-attack had had dangerous moments, but it was finally checked, largely by the fire of the ships' guns, though we had lost what ground we had held on Chunuk Bair. When the Battalion was relieved next day and moved to rest in a gorge north of Bauchop's Hill, it was not 300 strong. The other battalions had all suffered severely, and the Brigadier and his staff were all casualties. As for the Battalion, its commanding officer, Lieut.-Colonel E. C. Bradford, and its two Majors, H. J. Morphy and A. L. Wilford, were wounded. Its first reinforcement from Mudros arrived next day, and Captain R. de R. Rose assumed command.

From the 11th to the 16th the Battalion remained in close support, suffering agonies from lack of water and plagued by flies. On the latter date it was ordered to march to Anzac Cove, to work as a beach party unloading stores, its strength being now 8 officers and 429 other ranks. On the 19th the Battalion sent 200 other ranks, under Lieutenants Millar and Parsons, to reinforce the 8th Battalion Australian Infantry at Lone Pine. It did not take part in the local offensives of the 21st and 27th, in which the 5th Connaught Rangers and 10th Hampshire distinguished themselves.*

All through September it remained at its navvies' work, under conditions of which the words " hardship " and " discomfort " afford no adequate picture. It received large drafts from home, over four hundred all told, and was once again something like a battalion in strength; but what chance had it of becoming a battalion in any other particular? Casualties from shell-fire were, though the beaches were constantly shelled, very light, but there were many cases of dysentery.

Meanwhile, all round the Gallipoli Peninsula there was stalemate. The last great *coup* had been attempted and had failed. And it was evident that a great new offensive was being prepared against Serbia, which had so soundly trounced the first made by Austria. Now, however, the conditions were wholly different. There were German troops to stiffen the Austrians, and one of the greatest of German soldiers, Mackensen,

* The Actions of Hill 60.

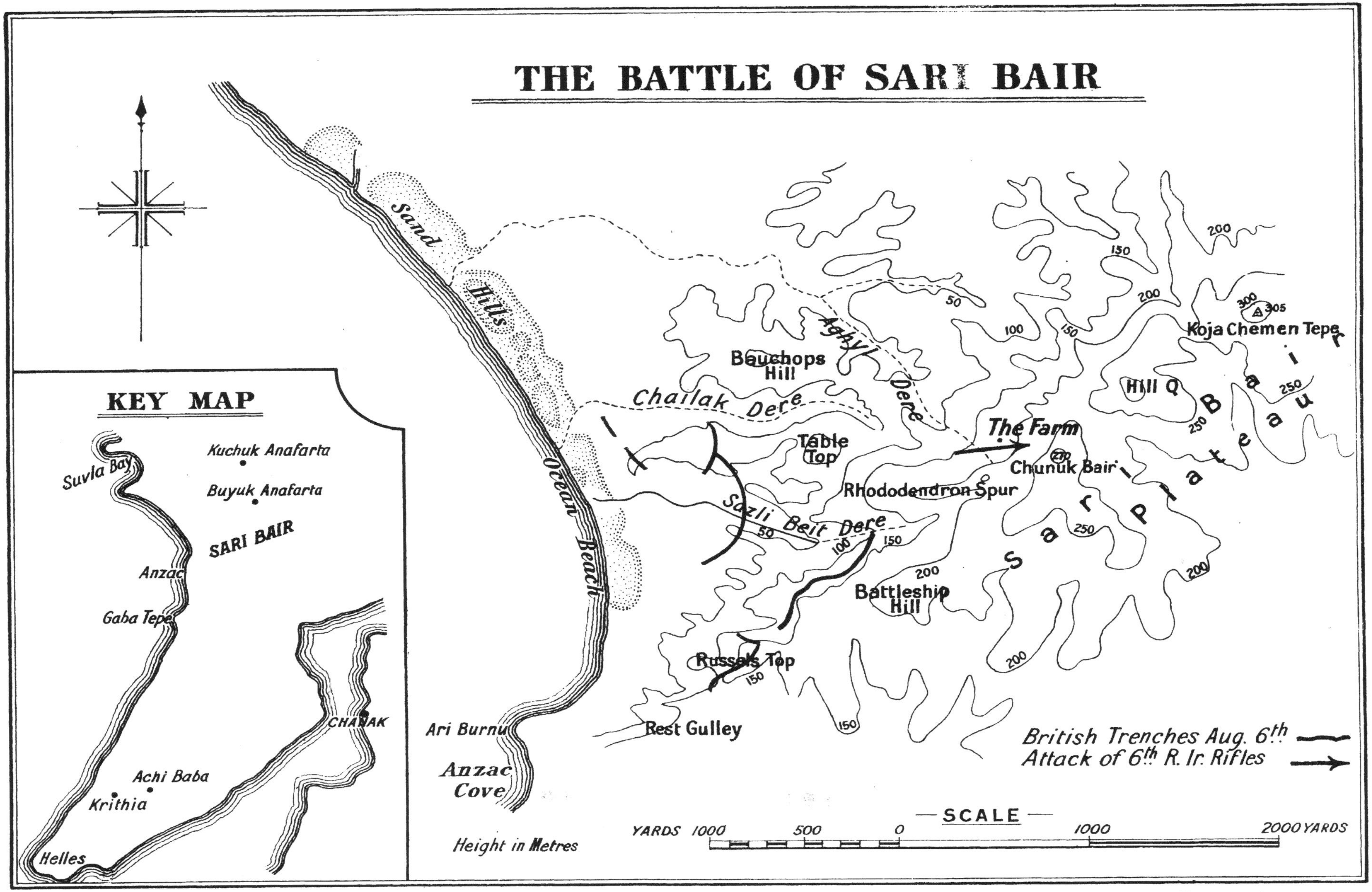

Facing page 52

The Royal Ulster Rifles.

was in command. Moreover, and still more important, Bulgaria, seeing an opportunity to avenge the defeats of the second Balkan War, had suddenly entered the ring. It was clearly impossible that the Serbians could at the same time hold their northern frontier against the Austro-Germans and the long eastern frontier against the Bulgars, outnumbered by two to one or more, without help from France and England. Each did send help, but it was utterly inadequate to save Serbia from her fate. It consisted in the first instance of a French Division from Cape Helles, and the 10th (Irish) Division from Suvla and Anzac.

III.—THE MOVE TO SALONIKA.

On September 29th the embarkation of the 29th Brigade began at Walker's Pier. It was complete at 2 p.m. next day. Some confusion was caused by the fact that the baggage of the whole force had to be put aboard one ship, the *Prince Abbas*. Units were much broken up. The 6th Royal Irish Rifles was about equally divided between the *Prince Abbas* and the *Ermine*. The Battalion disembarked at Mudros Harbour and moved into a camp. It had four days for rest and reorganization, both badly needed. Here Captain R. O. Mansergh arrived and took over command from Captain Rose. On the evening of the 4th it re-embarked on H.M.S. *Albion*, with Brigade Headquarters and the 6th Leinster (strength, 15 officers and 714 other ranks), sailing for " an unknown destination."

The unknown destination was well known to be Salonika, where the Battalion landed on the 5th, marching to a camp on the Seres road outside the town. For some reason unexplained, the French division at once moved north, while the British remained at Salonika. What kept these latter idle may have been the lack of first-line transport, with which they were entirely unequipped, but it seems probable the French were in the same predicament. A few transport mules had indeed been issued, but without nosebags, pegs or ropes ; and those who know that excellent but peculiar animal intimately will realize that they were, in the circumstances, difficult to handle. Moreover, Greece was mobilizing, which made it almost impossible to hire transport. Meanwhile reorganization proceeded, but with many hindrances. The worst of these were the Greek refugees from the north, who sold the men vile liquor and offered them money for boots and blankets. There were two courts-martial a day in the Brigade for drunkenness or stealing kit. There was heavy and persistent rain from the middle of the month onwards. Frequently 10 per cent. of any given unit's strength reported sick in the morning. Altogether, if the troops were not in action, it cannot be said that their " repose " was particularly valuable.

By the end of the month most of the transport had arrived from Basingstoke, and soon a move forward was made, the 29th Brigade being the last of its division to go up-country. On November 13th the Battalion entrained at Salonika, and was detrained at Doiran at night, having taken ten or eleven hours to cover some fifty miles upon this single-track railway. On the 17th, leaving one company behind, it moved to Hasanli, and two days later took over an outpost position at Causli.

A few words are necessary to define the general situation. Early in October, Mackensen had launched his great offensive upon the Serbians' northern frontier, driving them from the Danube and Save and capturing their capital. Bulgaria had waited calmly within her frontier till they were in retreat, then attacked them in flank. Nish had fallen by November 5th, and the enemy had come near to encircling the Serbian remnant and destroying it. Fighting desperately and well handled, they had extricated themselves, and after one of the most terrible retreats in history their remnant had passed through Montenegro to the sea at Durazzo. The French, advancing from Salonika, had made an effort to join hands with them, but without avail; and when Serbian troops appeared on that front, it was in Italian ships which landed them at Salonika. The French had moved up to a point not far south of Veles in their attempt to gain touch with the retreating Serbians; then, finding themselves in imminent danger of being cut off and annihilated by the advancing Bulgars, had fallen back across the Tcherna, though they kept posts along the left (northern) bank of the Vardar from its junction with the other river. They were thus holding a triangle pointing northwards. Echeloned back on their right rear were the two other brigades of the 10th (Irish) Division—the 30th with headquarters at Robrova and the 31st with headquarters at Causli.

On November 19th troops of these brigades began relieving the French at Kosturino, due north of Lake Doiran, and the 6th Royal Irish Rifles and 6th Leinster took over the line of the former from Causli to the lake. From the 20th onward came into operation the sensible plan that the British should operate east and the French west of the Doiran—Strumnitza road. On the 28th of the month, Captain C. M. L. Becher—who was to have, with his regiment, an extraordinarily varied service—arrived and took command of the 6th Royal Irish Rifles.

The next few days were quiet, and were taken up with trench-digging, there being minor reliefs between detachments of the Rifles and Leinsters at various posts and blockhouses. The 10th Hampshire was moved up into front line on the Kosturino Ridge, on the left of the 31st Brigade. The French, in a very ugly position, had already evacuated the Tcherna line, and were now level with the British.

IV.—THE ACTIONS OF KOSTURINO AND RETREAT ON SALONIKA.

On December 4th the Bulgars began their attack upon the Kosturino Ridge. The men of the Battalion could see the shells bursting upon the heights in front of them, but they had no news of what was happening. On the 6th came orders for a withdrawal, during which the 29th Brigade was to act under the orders of General Leblois, commanding the 57th French Division. Most of the Bulgar attacks that day were beaten off. But early next morning came an incident which in that difficult country, with its poor communications, might well have brought about disaster. The Bulgars captured Rocky Peak, south-west of Ormanli, taking the 10th Hampshire and 5th Connaught Rangers in enfilade. At 2 p.m. they launched an attack all along the line, which gave way at this menaced point. The Hampshire broke first, but was first rallied. The Connaught Rangers retreated headlong into Dedeli. Fierce fighting continued that evening and all next day, when the troops of the 10th Division fell back to a line through Dedeli and Causli, just north of the Doiran—Strumnitza road. Both the Hampshire and Connaught Rangers had had very heavy casualties. On the 9th the Causli line was reorganized, the 6th Royal Irish Rifles being moved up in support to the 6th Leinster Regiment. There were no fresh attacks that day in any force, and, with the right resting upon Lake Doiran, the position was temporarily secure. But the French were being heavily pressed on the left, and a further withdrawal was necessary.

On the 11th the Allies crossed the Greco-Serbian frontier, their right still upon Lake Doiran. Second-Lieutenant McKenzie and a platoon of the Battalion had been left in the village of Pozarli, with orders to remain, if possible, till noon; but the advance of the

Bulgars forced him to retire at 9.30 a.m., when he marched to Doiran Station. The night was a critical time. The roads were choked with French and British guns, and the troops moving into position had to march across country by compass. But march discipline was excellent, and before dawn the troops were in their new position, along the frontier from the lake on the right, the 6th Royal Irish Rifles in support to the 5th Connaught Rangers on the left of the 29th Brigade's lines. Subsequently, at a time given differently in the Brigade and Battalion diaries, the Rifles relieved the Connaught Rangers in front line. On the left of the Brigade were the French of the 57th Division, while east of the lake French cavalry was patrolling to prevent the line being turned. The orders were to send no patrols across into Serbia, but to wait and see if the Bulgars would violate the Greek territory.

After a quiet day on the 13th came one of those little incidents which breed trouble between allied troops unless they are handled in the right spirit, as this was by Brigadier-General Vandeleur, commanding the 29th Brigade. The Brigade was, as has been stated, under the orders of General Leblois. Early in the morning there was received a cipher message to the effect that General Sarrail, now in supreme command of the Allies at Salonika, had ordered General Leblois to withdraw the 29th Brigade. As a fact, no such order had yet reached the French General, who was naturally somewhat upset, seeing that he was holding a difficult rearguard position, when shown the message. General Vandeleur simply told General Leblois that, having been put under the latter's orders, he was not going to withdraw without his permission. Later in the day General Leblois issued orders for a withdrawal on the morrow, the British to move first. The 29th Brigade was to assemble at Kilinder, on the Salonika railway.

The orders, a model of their kind, were well carried out. It must be remembered that care was necessary, for it was a "toss-up" whether or not the Bulgars would enter Greek territory. As a fact, doubtless counselled by the Germans, they refrained from so doing for a long time to come. Kilinder was reached at 7.30 a.m. Here the 5th Connaught Rangers and 10th Hampshire entrained, the rest of the Brigade moving on, with a rearguard of French Chasseurs, to Uruslu. After a terrible night march, terrible because it was conducted in heavy rain upon a road already cut to pieces by traffic, by men already much fatigued, Kurus was reached. The following day the two remaining battalions, 6th Leinster and 6th Royal Irish Rifles, entrained at Sarigeul for Salonika.

V.—The Move to the Rendina Gorge.

The Allies had come to Salonika—they now had eight divisions there—and it had been decided, although their enterprise had failed and the primary reason for their presence, that of aiding the Serbians, no longer existed, that they were to remain. Greece, which had now in power a Cabinet favourable to Germany, suggested that the troops which retreated across her frontier should be interned, but the argument can hardly have been expected to be taken seriously, since the former Greek Government, that of M. Venizelos, had facilitated the landing on her soil. It was decided that the town should be denied as a submarine base to Germany and her Bulgar allies. For this purpose it was necessary to occupy a line well in advance of it and hold the whole peninsula between the Gulfs of Salonika and Orphani. The new defensive line was to run from the mouth of the Vardar, where it runs into the former gulf, in a curve round the city of Salonika; then, using as a natural barrier the two great lakes, Langaza and Besliek, to the Gulf of Orphani at the Rendina Gorge. The position was naturally strong, and could easily be improved so as to make it practically impregnable. But it had curious complications. The Greek mobilization was now complete, and though the Salonika zone had been evacuated by Greek forces, there were actually Greek soldiers so close as Seres, on the Salonika—Adrianople railway. Their presence there was for the moment not unwelcome, since they may have helped to induce the Bulgars not to cross the frontier while the Salonika defences were being completed. But they were on the whole embarrassing. In the first place, their attitude was not clear. On the whole, it was found that the soldiers were friendly. Their officers, and especially the senior ones, who took their tone from the King, were, however, strongly pro-German, even if not pro-Bulgar. In the second place, they were potential spies, whose movements, if they had a reasonable explanation, could not very well be stopped.

It having been decided to hold Salonika, there was a rush to complete its defences, even though the Bulgar armies still hesitated on the frontier. On Christmas Day orders were issued to the 29th Brigade that it was to occupy the extreme right of the line, and, the distance to the shores of the Gulf of Orphani being fifty miles, over bad roads, that it was to move by sea.

East of the lake, the deep cleft which contains its waters is continued in a steep, rocky valley known as the Rendina Gorge,* some seven miles in length. Through it runs a country track, considerably used by the peasants, who cannot otherwise move from north to south save by boat on the sea or the lake. At the gorge's end on the coast is the poor little village of Skala Stavros.

The Battalion, after ten days' rest from its labours in camp outside Salonika, marched down to English Quay and embarked on December 28th upon a ship which was an old acquaintance, the *Prince Abbas*, which bore it down the bay, round the south of the Chalcidicean Peninsula, and disembarked it next afternoon at Stavros, where it bivouacked on the beach. In the village itself there was little accommodation. Brigade Headquarters were installed in the solitary inn which it boasted. On the last day of the year 1915 the Battalion left its bivouac and marched up the Rendina Gorge to its centre, where it again bivouacked, prepared to push forward outposts on to the hills to north of it.

The 10th Division had had an unlucky start, and had been illtreated in being split up into detachments for its first great action. The 6th Royal Irish Rifles had had about as cruel an initiation to warfare as can well be imagined. It had been landed and thrown at once into an attack, and immediately afterwards subjected to a very severe counter-attack. Within a few hours half its strength had disappeared. Of the officers who left England in the *Transylvania*, three subsequently went sick, one of whom died. Every one of the rest was killed or wounded. But henceforth, though it was to see fighting of a highly diversified nature, it never had casualties on the scale of the Western Front or Gallipoli. It was to be a very long time, upwards of two years, on the Salonika Front, which must have had its periods of dreariness, but throughout that time its casualties were in battle probably less than those in the first ten minutes of the fighting on Sari Bair. The Army of Salonika had to deal almost entirely with the Bulgar, and in minor warfare at that. And it was kept in the position that its forces were just too weak for a grandiose offensive and far too strong for the mere task of defending the city. But if the troops had not to endure the fire and mud of the Western Front, they had few of the Western Front's compensations: reasonably frequent leave, occasional

* The name is also sometimes given to the Gulf of Orphani.

rests in inhabited country, comfortable billets at most times behind the line, beer, quick posts from home. And while in winter thay had cold almost as great as that of France, in summer they had excessive heat, flies and dysentery. Yet it would be hard to persuade anyone whose service was in the infantry on the Western Front that they had not the better of it. They had at least a reasonable chance of life, and, as Guido cries in " The Ring and the Book," " Life is all !" for all men, or almost all, even though they are ready to give that life for the cause which has engaged them.

BOOK III. 1916

CHAPTER I

I.—January–June, 1916 : The 1st Battalion.

It has been recorded that the 1st Battalion Royal Irish Rifles returned in early January to the line in the neighbourhood of Fleurbaix from its long rest. The trenches were found in a deplorable condition, wet and ruinous. And, as in such circumstances was always the case, the German snipers were active and troublesome. One, who did great damage, was for long unlocated, and seemed to be able to hit men even when behind a parapet. The secret was revealed when at last some movement was detected in a tree behind the German lines. A rattle from a machine gun, and a body pitched out to the ground. The Brigadier at once set about the reorganization of our snipers, who improved with practice in the use of their telescopic sights, till at last it was their pride that no German periscope could remain ten minutes with its glass whole.

On January 19th the Brigade Machine Gun Company was formed, by withdrawing the machine gun section from each of its four battalions. For a time there was close connection between the section of the company and the battalion from which it had been taken. Soon, however, the old personnel passed away as battle casualties or sick, and was replaced by the Machine Gun Corps, which did not do its recruiting or training upon a territorial basis. The companies began to have less and less connection with the infantry, and to look upon themselves as brigade troops, which for tactical purposes they were, till a later period of the war, when they became divisional troops. The Vickers machine-guns were replaced by four Lewis guns per battalion, these being gradually increased, as they became available in greater numbers from the workshops at home, till a Lewis gun section formed part of each of a battalion's sixteen platoons. The new gun was a less accurate weapon than the old, but more mobile and more suitable for infantry in trench fighting or open war. Other belligerents were finding the truth of this. The Brigade Diary for February records that there was a " fast-firing " machine gun shooting on our lines. The old German machine gun was rather slow-firing, and its " stammering " noise was only too well known. There is little doubt that the new gun heard was their light machine gun, just then coming into use.

In mid-February the 25th Brigade was relieved by the 102nd, and had a week's rest in divisional reserve near Sailly. At the end of March it quitted the area it had known so long, without any regrets. On the 28th the Battalion entrained at Merville, detraining that evening at Longueau, marching through the night to Montonvillers, north of Amiens, some twelve miles away. It was a dark, wet night, and the guide, not the only one of his kind in France, lost his way. But the Adjutant, Captain Browne, brought the Battalion at last to its destination and its billets.

On April 4th the Battalion moved towards the line, billeting that night at St. Gratien, and the next at Millencourt. On the evening of the 6th it entered the trenches, with the 2nd Royal Berkshire on its left. The new line was on the ridge above Albert, facing the village of La Boisselle in the German lines, which had been converted by the enemy into one of the strongest fortresses upon the Western Front. The country was chalky and the trenches fairly good, certainly much drier than those the Battalion had just quitted. But they were also very much more disturbed.

In those days reliefs were frequently talked about on the telephone, a most dangerous proceeding, as was subsequently proved when the German apparatus for tapping telephone conversations was better understood. There is no doubt that in this case the enemy was aware that there was a change in the troops opposite him. On the 10th he began to bombard the Battalion's front line with heavy trench mortars, doing a great deal of damage. At evening quiet fell, which continued all next day till about 7 p.m. Then there burst out a terrific bombardment, lasting an hour and a half, with shells of all calibres, lachrymatory and gas. The front-line trenches were blown to pieces, and, as in those days they were very strongly held, the casualties were heavy. Then the Germans entered our trenches in three parties. It is impossible to obtain an account of what followed, as all the men in that front-line trench were killed, wounded, or missing. But the casualties were, for a raid, enormous : 1 officer, Lieutenant P. M. H. Maxwell, and 9 other ranks killed, 39 other ranks wounded, 28 missing, of whom the majority were undoubtedly prisoners.

The Battalion was very severely criticized for its behaviour, but this was a case where criticism is easier than example. The bombardment had been of a violence such as no man in it had seen, and the survivors must have been completely dazed when the raiders attacked them. Even then they fought well, as was subsequently proved in a curious manner. Their vindication came from the enemy, in the form of a pamphlet issued for instruction in the art of raiding by the German command, a copy of which was captured by us during the Battle of the Somme. The German report states that the Battalion created a most favourable impression by its physique and its manner of repelling an assault, and goes on to declare that the latter would not have been successful but for the gas. This was indeed the deciding factor. The survivors of the bombardment were wearing the old and bad bag-shaped gas-masks, and fighting in these at night against the picked men of a raiding party is not likely to be crowned with success. The Battalion was not relieved till two days later. On the 14th, Major G. H. Sawyer, 2nd Royal Berkshire, came and took over command.

When next it entered the line it was ordered to make a raid in retaliation. This was one of those hastily prepared affairs which were sometimes forced upon units, and were rarely successful in the days when German *moral* was high. It was carried out by Lieutenant J. S. Muir with twenty men upon a point in the German trenches opposite Bécourt Wood. The Germans put down a heavy barrage on " No Man's Land " in reply to our bombardment. Lieutenant Muir, who did not know his men, nor they him, had as objective a machine-gun post in the enemy's line, 120 yards from our wire. He himself entered the gap in the enemy's wire, and one German was apparently killed, but his men did not support him owing to machine-gun fire, and no identifications were made. We had one man killed and several wounded. There had been no time to practise the raiding-party on " dummy " trenches, and, though they had viewed the spot from an observation post, they did not know it on the ground. On the whole, it was an example of how not to conduct a raid. On the 25th the Brigade was relieved and went into divisional reserve till the end of the month, at Millencourt.

On May 3rd the Battalion, less " B " Company and two platoons of " C," moved to Henencourt Wood, for work under the orders of the 23rd Brigade. The detachment was sent to Dernancourt, where it was put to work upon a new railway. Preparations for the great Somme battle were now in full swing, and, with the situation at Verdun still highly precarious, were being pushed forward as swiftly as possible. Most of all was hard work on the roads necessary if they were to support such traffic as a great offensive would entail. On the 11th the detachment at Dernancourt rejoined, being replaced by one consisting of " D " Company and the remaining platoons of " C." Then, on the 19th, the Battalion moved to Albert, and four days later re-entered the line. The new position was between the villages of La Boisselle and Ovillers-La Boisselle, and was for the time being very quiet.

Everyone knew that a great attack was to take place, though few had any idea how soon it was to come. The officers of the Battalion had some intimation that it would not be long delayed when, on being relieved from the trenches, they were shown a piece of ground at Bazieux, marked out with flags to represent the German front which their Brigade was subsequently to assault. Over this ground a tactical scheme was carried out on June 1st. On the 12th the Battalion returned to Albert. On the 18th a new Commanding Officer, Major C. C. Macnamara, arrived, Lieut.-Colonel Sawyer returning to his own regiment.

The final preparations for the Battle of the Somme must be left till the next chapter, while we return to the Regiment's 2nd and 7th Battalions.

II.—2nd Battalion's Raid at Le Touquet.

The 2nd Battalion was, it will be remembered, in line opposite Le Touquet, with billets at Le Bizet, not far from Armentières. This large town had a curious reputation until it was taken by the enemy in 1918. Though so close to the line, with actually field-gun batteries among its houses, it was comparatively little shelled, and constituted a distinct " amenity " for the front-line troops of the neighbourhood. Its breweries worked right up to the opening of the Lys battle, and it had surprisingly good shops and eating-houses. It helped to make popular with the troops a front which had already the merit of being quiet, if wet.

This quietude the Battalion itself rudely disturbed for a time by a raid on a very big scale. The German front-line trench at Le Touquet ran just west of the main street of the village, some of the ruined cottages of which were within the British position. There was at the moment uncertainty as to the constitution of the German troops opposite. But a comparatively small-scale raid would have resulted in identifications. This was intended, in addition, to kill as many Germans as possible, to destroy machine-gun emplacements and, as mining was suspected, any mine-shafts that might be found. The total strength of the raiding-party was to be no less than 9 officers and 220 other ranks, including 2 officers and 8 other ranks of the Royal Engineers, for demolitions. The northern party was to have two separate points of entry, some forty yards apart ; the southern party, one, on its right. The former party was, if possible, to penetrate to a big building known as Crown Prince Farm, which lay about a hundred yards east of the village street and was in the German third line. This fact alone shows how ambitious was the undertaking. The raid was to be preceded by a discharge of gas on the left of the front to be attacked, to divert attention from the latter. At the same time smoke was to be discharged on the other flank of the attack to screen the raiders from observation while they crossed " No Man's Land." The artillery preparation was to be a deliberate wire-cutting " shoot " lasting over four hours. The Battalion was not holding the line during the attack, the 13th Cheshire being in the trenches. The men who were to make it moved up in small parties during the morning of January 19th.

At 4.30 p.m. the gas discharge on the left took place. Within a minute all machine-gun and rifle fire upon that front had ceased, and it is highly probable that the 373 cylinders which were emptied caused considerable loss. Five minutes later came the discharge of smoke on the right. This drew a heavy bombardment from the enemy upon the trenches opposite, but allowed the large bodies of Riflemen to cross unobserved.

Entry was made at each of the three points without difficulty. The German trenches were unrecognizable from the fire of our trench mortars. The first prisoners were in our lines within five minutes of the launch of the attack. The southern party fought its way into an important stronghold, known as Red Tile House, in the second line, where it bombed and destroyed the dug-outs, killing many of the enemy. Opposite Crown Prince Farm the Germans were driven back to their third line with heavy loss, but the farm itself was too strongly defended to be captured. The Germans tried a counter-attack from its locality, but a party of picked bombers, one officer and four men, held them back while the work of destruction was completed. No mine-shaft was found, but every dug-out and emplacement that had survived the bombardment was blown up.

At 5.15 p.m. bugles were sounded in our front line, as a signal for retirement. Amid the din they were not heard, but watches had been carefully synchronized, and all the parties returned at the same time, carrying back their wounded. The total casualties were: 2nd-Lieutenants C. H. Wale and S. J. Lennox killed; 4 wounded, Captain E. Workman, 2nd-Lieutenants H. Phillips, W. O'Reilly, A. A. Broomfield (one, Captain Workman, died subsequently in hospital from a blow on the head with a rifle-butt, and one was so slightly hurt that he remained at duty); 11 other ranks killed, and 37 wounded.

These casualties were not light, but reports agree that a considerable number of Germans were killed. In addition, 11 prisoners were taken, who identified the troops opposite, and much useful documentary information brought in. The whole affair had been carried out with great coolness and courage, and admirably organized. It won for the Irish battalion high praise and much popularity in its new division. The Corps Commander, Sir Charles Fergusson, came in person to congratulate it. Three Military Crosses and three Distinguished Conduct Medals and a Clasp were awarded to officers and other ranks who had taken a leading part in the raid.

III.—2ND BATTALION IN MINE WARFARE NEAR ARRAS.

The Battalion now had over a month's rest from the trenches, the 74th Brigade being in corps reserve. It was not, however, far from the line, being all the time at a village called La Crèche, between Bailleul and Armentières, where on February 9th it was inspected by Sir Herbert Plumer, commanding the Second Army. Here there was plenty of football. Early in March the Division was sent to join the Third Army, and marched down from Flanders to Artois. On the 6th the 74th Brigade marched to the area of Neuf Berquin, the Battalion billeting at Vieux Berquin. On the 10th it moved south to the neighbourhood of St. Hilaire, the Battalion marching sixteen miles in falling snow to Ham-en-Artois. Then, on the 12th, the Brigade continued its march to Bailleul-aux-Cornailles, just north of the main Montreuil—Arras road. Here the Battalion billeted, with two of its companies in the neighbouring village of Monchy-Breton. It was now in country only just handed over by French troops of the Tenth

Army, being gradually relieved to join in the defence of Verdun, and it is recorded that for some of the inhabitants of these villages it represented the first English seen.

On the 14th the Battalion moved to the little village of Acq, on the Scarpe, near the famous hill and ruined abbey of Mont St. Eloy. It was attached to the 139th Brigade, of the 46th Division, for work, chiefly carrying stores and spoil to aid the mining operations of British and French, very active in this part of the line. It afterwards moved to the hamlet of La Targette, on the Arras—Béthune road, where the men lived in the support and reserve trenches, to be close to their work. On the 27th it moved back to Chelers, and comfort, and later on to Ternas, nearer St. Pol, where vigorous training was carried out in comparatively open country. Its casualties in the line had been Lieutenant E. Price killed, 2nd-Lieutenant Getty and 4 other ranks wounded.

From April 20th onward the 25th Division began relieving the 46th in the line opposite the Vimy Ridge. On the 22nd the Battalion moved up by bus and took over the trenches. This was a very disturbed area, and one of constant mining. Each side was trying to burrow under and blow up prominent points in its opponent's front line, but each was also continually blowing craters in the narrow " No Man's Land," for which there generally followed sanguinary hand-to-hand battles.

The day after taking over the new line, the Battalion was very heavily shelled, having 4 men killed and 23 wounded. Next day a mine was exploded by us on the right of the Battalion's sector, and occupied and consolidated by its neighbours. The affair did not concern the Riflemen, but they came in for a share of the German bombardment which followed, and had half a dozen casualties, including 2nd-Lieutenant H. E. White wounded. But next day was a more serious affair. This time the mine was a German one, and it was blown just at the junction of the Battalion's front with that of the 11th Lancashire Fusiliers, on its left. The explosion was accompanied by very heavy artillery fire, under cover of which the enemy entered the crater and from it attempted a raid upon one trench. The bombers of the 11th Lancashire Fusiliers counter-attacked, and the Germans ran, pursued by our men to the crater, which, however, could not be held, as it was commanded by another on higher ground. The men of the Royal Irish Rifles were drawn into the struggle and acquitted themselves well. They had thirty-four casualties, including 2nd-Lieutenant H. Stone killed, Lieutenant J. Jenkinson, T. J. Thompson (both Royal Irish Fusiliers), and 2nd-Lieutenant J. H. Grey wounded.

But this was no more than one incident in a constant mine warfare, and by no means the worst. The shaking of the ground following an explosion became so common that it was hardly noticed. Nevertheless, the constant tours in the line, any portion of which might " go up " at any moment and destroy a whole platoon in a single flash, constituted a very serious strain upon the endurance of the men, which they bore admirably. Some men have declared, and the thing sounds plausible, that it is worse as an experience to spend six days in trenches where mines are always expected than to advance in an attack through a heavy barrage, against machine-gun fire.

The most serious affair of all during this period took place on the evening of May 13th, when the Battalion was out of the line, but there had been minor battles on three separate occasions earlier in the month. On the 2nd, when the Battalion was in rest at Camblain l'Abbé, the 13th Cheshire had been raided after a mine explosion, and had repelled the enemy. On the night of the 5th, after the Battalion had returned to the line, the Germans made no less than three attempts to reach and destroy our mine-shafts at the point where its line joined that of the 11th Lancashire Fusiliers. Fierce fighting with the bomb ended in their eviction on each occasion. The Battalion again lost heavily, having 5 killed and 12 wounded. On the night of the 9th, when the Battalion was awaiting the 13th Cheshire to relieve it, two large mines were sprung on the front of the 9th Loyal North Lancashire, on its left. A desperate struggle followed in the darkness, as a result of which the Lancashire men, aided by bombers of the Royal Irish Rifles, established themselves on the near lips of the German craters and took one prisoner.

On the 13th the mine went up at 7.12 p.m., a very usual hour with the enemy. The British front line at this point was obliterated and the second rendered untenable by the bombardment. At 8.35 p.m. the Cheshires carried out a prepared counter-attack, capturing the crater and killing many Germans in it. They had themselves upwards of eighty casualties. Two platoons of the Royal Irish Rifles were rushed up to their aid, and likewise suffered severely, the Battalion's casualties for the day being twenty; 2nd-Lieutenant A. G. Mitchell being killed and 2nd-Lieutenants H. E. White and J. H. Starkey wounded. On the 15th was further liveliness, when we exploded a series of mines and occupied them, beating off a heavy counter-attack with loss. This time the Battalion was not engaged, but it had fifteen casualties from shell-fire in its support position at Zouave Valley.

The following night the Battalion relieved the Cheshires, and came in for fresh trouble. At 11 a.m. the enemy opened a heavy bombardment on "Q 88 Crater" and its approaches, soon afterwards launching an attack. Second-Lieutenant Thompson and his platoon held the place till 1.25 p.m., beating off attack after attack. Supports could not be got to him owing to the barrage. At the end of this time his party had dwindled from a platoon to two unwounded men, and he was forced to withdraw a little, to the communication trench which led to the crater. At 9 p.m. a small counter-attack was carried out, but became disorganized for lack of preparation and failed to retake the crater, which was eventually abandoned by the British. At all events, the Battalion was not called upon to attack it again. Relieved two nights later, it did not again return to those trenches. Its losses in this last affair were over one hundred. It was at Averdoignt till the end of the month, and for the next fortnight at Bailleul-aux-Cornailles.

The month's experience had been a trying one. The constant explosions were shattering to the nerves of the strongest men. The hard fighting which almost invariably followed them, when troops, still dazed and shaken from noise and shock, were called upon to clamber in counter-attack across mounds of broken chalk, exposed to machine-gun fire from the enemy's trenches, and at the end to meet the Germans in a bomb-fight—a form of war in which "Jerry" was always at his dour best—was no less wearying. And in this sort of trench fighting not only were losses very heavy, but they were largely composed of the best and most enterprising men. The Battalion had sore need of a rest when it came out of this sector.

For the first fortnight in June, in weather generally fine, brigade and battalion training, running, bayonet fighting, and especially tactical exercises against trenches, in preparation for the coming Battle of the Somme, were carried out. Under the influence of good sleep by night, open air and exercise by day, the men were fit and well again when they began to march down to the Somme. These marches were generally carried out at night, to cheat enemy aviators. On the 14th the Battalion marched to Ecoivres, on the 15th to Maizicourt, near Auxi-le-Château. These two marches totalled about twenty-five miles, and not a man fell out during either, sure proof of the Battalion's health. On the 17th it continued on its way to Fransu ; next day to St. Léger. Here there was a week's halt, in pleasant country untouched by war, during which the 2nd Royal Irish Rifles carried off the Brigade's cross-country race.

Then they turned their heads toward the line, marching first to Canaples, then Bonneville ; then, on the night of the 28th, to Mirvaux, twelve miles due west of Albert. On the 30th they moved up to Bouzincourt, close to the trenches, ready to " go through " should the German defences be captured on the following day, as General Headquarters, in its optimism, expected.

IV.—THE 7TH BATTALION AND THE APRIL GAS ATTACKS.

The 7th Battalion, as has been stated, was already in France at the beginning of 1916, but its active service does not really start till then. Its first casualty, in fact, occurred on New Year's Day, when its transport officer, Lieutenant J. P. Farrelly, was wounded near Hulluch. Throughout January it carried out steady training. On the 20th it lined the road in honour of a visit from General Joffre. On the 28th, when it was at Hesdingeuil, near Béthune, Major S. G. Francis, D.S.O., West Yorkshire Regiment, took command in succession to Lieut.-Colonel Hartley. He remained with the Battalion throughout its career, till it was disbanded two years later, when his fine service was rewarded with the command of a brigade.

On February 18th the Battalion moved to Sailly Labourse, being now attached to the 12th Division, and next day its companies began entering the trenches, each being attached to a battalion of the 36th Brigade. On the 25th it took over for the first time a sector of its own, not far from the Hohenzollern Redoubt, and that night got its two first prisoners, a couple of Bavarians who surrendered to a patrol. After this first taste of the trenches it moved back to billets at Ham-en-Artois, returning to the line after a month's further training, especially in bombing, in front of Hulluch. The very night, March 26th, on which it entered the trenches, the enemy blew two mines, accompanied by a heavy bombardment. Our Lewis-gun fire prevented him from occupying the craters, the near lips of which were eventually occupied and consolidated by our bombers. The Battalion came very lightly out of this affair, with no more than four casualties.

The Battalion was not in the trenches when there occurred one of the most serious gas attacks made by the enemy since the Second Battle of Ypres. The gas was released upon a wide frontage, on the front of the 8th Dublins and the right of the 49th Brigade, at 4.30 a.m. on April 27th. The " sack " gas helmets of those days were very inferior to the type evolved later, and casualties were numerous. It was, however, the tremendous bombardment, which knocked to pieces our front trench upon a front of upwards of half a mile, that caused most loss. An hour after the release of the gas the Germans entered the line at several points, but were ejected after heavy fighting, in which the 7th Royal Inniskilling Fusiliers, of the 49th Brigade, particularly distinguished itself. The 7th Royal Irish Rifles sent up one company to the 8th Dublins in front line, and another to the 9th Dublins in support, with fifty bombers. The losses in the 48th Brigade were about two hundred, but heavier in the 49th.

Two days later the performance was repeated. This time there was no infantry attack upon the Brigade's front, and those upon that of the 49th Brigade never reached our trenches. The losses in the 48th Brigade were huge for an affair of trench warfare— 100 killed and 180 wounded or gassed. It is doubtful, however, if the Germans got any profit out of this later venture. In the first place, some of the gas blew back over their lines, and their ambulances were afterwards seen to be hard at work. In the second, large bodies were caught by machine-gun fire and the barrage of the artillery covering the 49th Brigade and dispersed with loss. Second-Lieutenant Whitford was killed on this occasion.

There is little to record of the next two months, which were passed in the same area, except that the difficulty of obtaining recruits for battalions of the 16th Division began to make itself felt within six months of its arrival in France. At the end of May the 9th Munster Fusiliers was disbanded to provide drafts for other battalions, and replaced by the 1st Battalion. There were very few casualties, the only loss in officers being 2nd-Lieutenants P. Holden and F. S M'Carthy wounded. The Division remained in this region after the opening of the Somme battle, in the early stages of which it was not engaged.

In the following chapter we shall see that all three battalions, 1st, 2nd, and 7th, were in action in that battle within the first ten weeks.

CHAPTER II

I.—The Battle of Albert: 1st Battalion.

The Battle of the Somme was in the main the battle of England's New Armies, now at last considered ready to take the field in a great offensive. The French participation in the early stages was powerful and successful, but there were not engaged half the divisions of Joffre's original plan. Verdun had made too many demands for the original figure to be adhered to. On this occasion a second deduction from former battles had been made by General Joffre. The first, as we have said, reached before Loos and Champagne, was that any breach must be upon a wide front. The argument of the second, though perhaps none of the commanders realized it at the time, was to the effect that a " breach " in the old sense was very improbable. The new theory was that of the " limited objective," with fresh troops to exploit the success. Limited as they were, the objectives were seldom reached by our troops in the first day's fighting, and the casualties were enormous. In fact, the whole attack from Gommecourt to La Boisselle, eight miles as the crow flies, was a total failure. As a fact, though the concentration of artillery seemed very great to the troops that witnessed it, the British had even yet by no means sufficient weight of metal for such an enterprise. Above all, they were short of field artillery, and as a consequence the German wire at several points was inadequately cut. The effect of heavy artillery upon the German dug-outs, frequently thirty feet down in the chalk, had been extraordinarily overestimated. These causes, and perhaps even more the inexperience of the young soldiers engaged, were chiefly responsible for the defeat which met the northern section of the attack. On the right there was success, and it was subsequently exploited.

The 8th Division was attacking with all three brigades in line, the 25th in the centre. The right flank of this brigade was to be on the north of the ruined village of Ovillers. The final objective was to run through the eastern portion of Pozières. Beyond Ovillers the ground dropped away to a slight valley, rising again to Pozières. The attack was to be carried out by the 2nd Royal Berkshire on the right and 2nd Lincolnshire on the left, each with one section of the Brigade Machine Gun Company. The first phase was to consist of the capture by these battalions of the first four German lines, the last of which was over a thousand yards from the British front line. The 1st Royal Irish Rifles was to advance at " zero " to the British front line and follow the leading battalions at a distance of five hundred yards. It was to have attached to it the Brigade Grenade Company (less two platoons with leading waves) and one section of the Brigade Machine Gun Company. Its attack on the intermediate line was to be supported by two companies from each of the leading battalions, which were to garrison and consolidate the position when taken. The 1st Royal Irish Rifles was then to reorganize, and allow the 2nd Rifle Brigade to come in on its left. The two together were then to assault the final objective, or Pozières line. The criticism that at once arises in the mind is that, had all the first part of the attack gone well, the plan for the capture of the final objective was highly complicated. The 1st Royal Irish Rifles was to attack with three companies in line—from right to left, " B " (Captain A. J. Ross), " C " (2nd-Lieutenant H. M. Glastonbury), " D " (2nd-Lieutenant S. D. Smith)—with " A " (Captain G. Gartlan) in support.

The original plan had been to have six days' preliminary bombardment, gas to be liberated from cylinders on two days. Owing to bad weather, however, the attack was postponed two days, being launched on July 1st instead of June 29th. The postponement had some advantages, as further attention could be given to the cutting of wire. On the 23rd the Battalion had heavy casualties—1 killed and 19 wounded on the 28th, 19 wounded on the 29th, 5 killed and 23 wounded on the 30th. A big raid was carried out on the 25th by the 2nd Rifle Brigade, many Germans being killed and one prisoner taken.

The great attack was launched at 7.30 a.m., after a final hurricane bombardment. The leading battalions were at once met by a storm of fire that in a minute sealed the fate of the assault. Very few of the Royal Berkshire ever reached the German front line, and the small party that did was eventually driven out. The 2nd Lincolnshire did rather better at first. Two hundred yards of front-line trench were taken, but both flanks were in air. The few officers that remained led an attack on the second line, but were beaten off. A frontal counter-attack by the enemy was repulsed, but at 9 a.m. attacks from either flank captured half the ground won. This also was lost to a third counter-attack.

If the front companies had met heavy fire, those of the 1st Royal Irish Rifles met heavier still. So severe were the losses in moving up that two companies never got beyond our front line. " C," the centre company, just reached the German front line as a scanty remnant, but could not maintain its position. " D," on the left, entered the German front line and penetrated to the second, inflicting considerable loss on the enemy, but was obliged to withdraw in conformity with the troops on right and left. Colonel Macnamara was terribly wounded, losing an eye and being also hit in the leg, but would not let the stretcher-bearers take him back till he had handed over command to Major Fitzmaurice. It was all over by about 10 a.m.

That night the remains of the Battalion was withdrawn to Long Valley. It had lost its Commanding Officer, Lieut.-Colonel Macnamara, who died some days later of his wounds, and its Adjutant, Captain D. A. Browne. Second-Lieutenant Glastonbury was wounded and missing, 2nd-Lieutenants S. D. Smith and W. H. Gregg missing. Wounded were—Captains Ross, Gartlan; Lieutenants G. Lawlor, E. Blake-Murphy; 2nd-Lieutenants E. A. Mahoney, J. Marshall, M. A. Palethorpe, W. S. Maitland, H. J. McConnell, W. N. Tyrell, A. McDorrell, P. B. Hill. Of other ranks there were 17 killed, 348* wounded, 27 missing, and 8 classed as wounded and missing.

The men had done all they could. They had gone into action with the highest hopes. They expected victory, and fought as though they expected it. But their task was an impossible one.

But for Thiepval, a little farther north, Ovillers was probably the strongest fortress upon the whole front of the British attack. Its cellars had not been destroyed by the bombardments, and they made admirable shelters for the machine gunners, who were the great stumbling-block to success from end to end of the line. The counter-battery work here, as upon many sections of the front, had been quite insufficient. As a consequence, the German artillery, while the machine guns dealt with the first waves, to a large extent destroyed the supporting companies, and the impetus of the attack was at once lost. It is absurd to suggest, as is sometimes done to-day, that the attack went according to plan, or that the limited success achieved on the right represented anything approaching what had been hoped. We had learnt new lessons, but at a terrible price. We are not aware that the casualties for that first day have ever been

* It will, of course, be understood that the figures of "wounded" apply to the numbers passing through Dressing Stations, a considerable proportion of whom die later.

published, but those of the British were almost certainly over 40,000. As for the Battalion with which we are concerned, it well merited the phrase in the letter of Major-General Hudson, the Divisional Commander: " It [the Battalion's conduct] was, from all account, magnificent—no hesitation, and every man doing his level best. It is a day of which the Royal Irish Rifles will rightly be proud."

The 8th Division was in no case for further attacks. The day after the opening of the battle the Battalion entrained at Dernancourt, arriving on the 3rd at Ailly-sur-Somme. On the 6th it entrained at Longueau, detraining at Pernes next day and marching to Allouagne. Here there was a week of rest, training and reorganization, during which drafts amounting to 1 officer and 130 other ranks arrived. On the 14th the whole of the 25th Brigade marched to Béthune, the favourite town of the British front, with good billets and well-stocked shops. The Battalion remained here another week, during which Lieut.-Colonel E. C. Lloyd, Royal Irish Regiment, arrived to take over command. On the 21st it moved into brigade support, in front of Vermelles, and on the 26th once more entered the line, in what was known as the Hohenzollern Right Subsector.

II.—The Battle of Albert: 2nd Battalion.

It is convenient to leave for a moment its fortunes and turn again to the Somme, since the 2nd Battalion was to come into action at practically the same point. As a result of the first day's fighting, though neither Ovillers nor the neighbouring fortress of La Boisselle had been taken, a dint in the enemy's line had been made between them. On July 2nd the 19th Division captured half of La Boisselle, and the 12th some of the trenches in front of Ovillers. South of the former village the advance had been more considerable, and our line was facing more nearly north than east, as at the start. On the 5th the whole of La Boisselle was in our hands. To open wider the breach, the 74th Brigade, at the disposal of the 12th Division, was to be employed. It was to attack almost due northwards, from La Boisselle toward the eastern side of Ovillers.

The new attack was to be carried out by the 9th Loyal North Lancashire on the right and the 13th Cheshire on the left, with the 2nd Royal Irish Rifles in support. It was launched at 8 a.m. on the 7th, at which hour the Battalion moved up into the assembly trenches vacated by those which had advanced. The leading battalions went forward with great dash. Soon after 9 a.m. the whole of the first objective, a line some thousand yards south of Ovillers, had been won, with the exception of a gap of four hundred yards in the Cheshires' line. At 9.50 a.m. the 2nd Royal Irish Rifles and one and a half companies of the 11th Lancashire Fusiliers were sent forward to consolidate this line, while the attack moved on to the next objective. This was partially attained, and the line was now not more than seven hundred yards from Ovillers. Units were as far as possible sorted out and reorganized at dusk. The casualties of the Royal Irish Rifles were about 160. The men were amazed by the German dug-outs in the chalk, palatial dwellings with separate quarters for officers, kitchens, telephone exchanges, bunks for the men. None in the British Army had ever seen the like.

Further bomb-fighting in the night rounded off the gains, and the following day fresh attacks were made, the 75th Brigade, on the left, drawing level with the 74th before dawn. Three local counter-attacks upon the Loyal North Lancashire and Cheshire were beaten off. Bombing parties of the Royal Irish Rifles made further progress, but it was decided to postpone the advance to the final objective till night, when, there being signs of disorganization in the enemy's ranks, it was hoped a sudden and silent

THE BATTLE OF THE SOMME

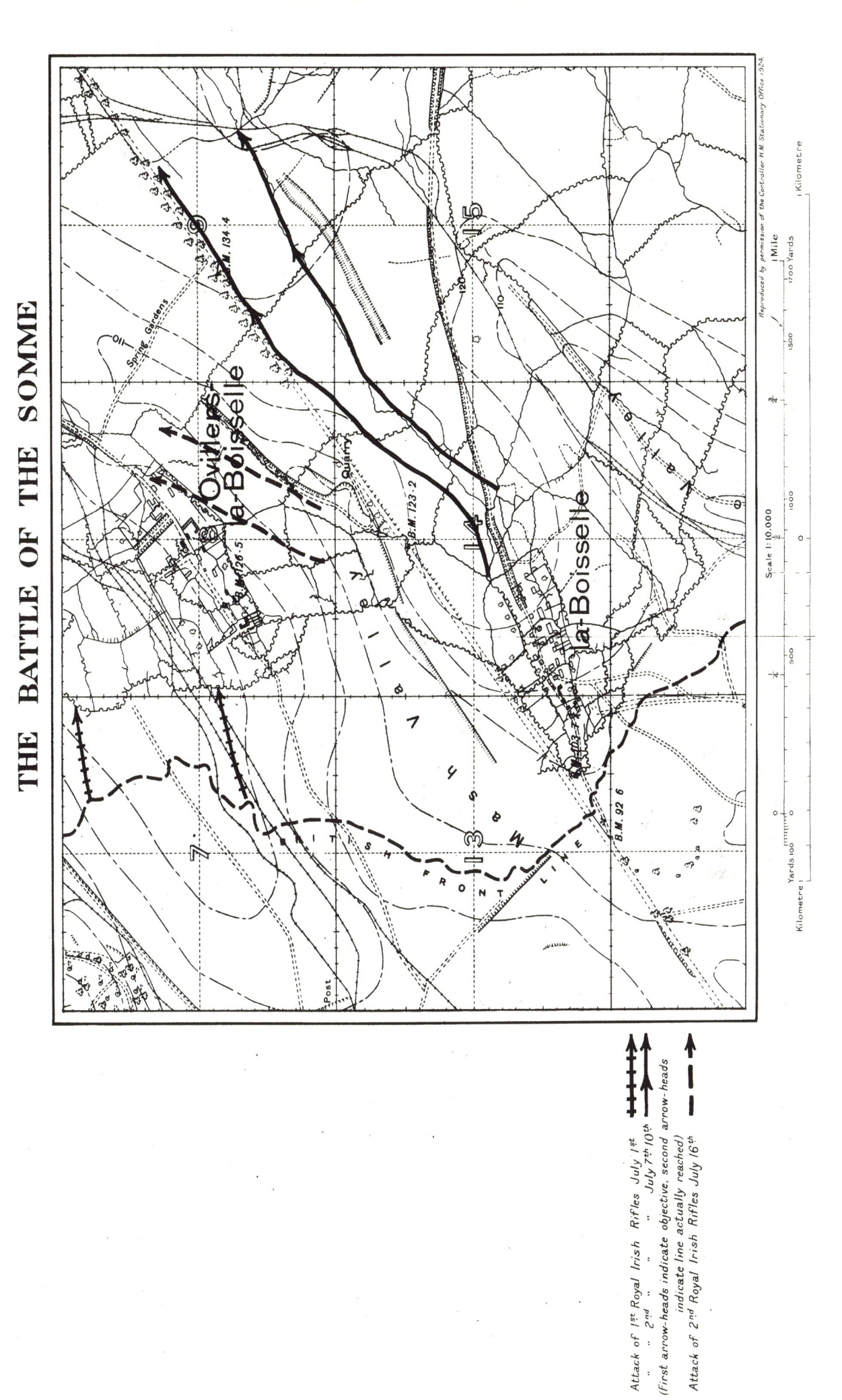

Attack of 1st Royal Irish Rifles July 1st
    "   " 2nd   "   "   July 7th,10th
(First arrow-heads indicate objective, second arrow-heads
indicate line actually reached)
Attack of 2nd Royal Irish Rifles July 16th

movement might yield profitable results. It had rained during the day, and the trenches were filling with what looked like whitewash, the fine chalk crumbled to powder by the heavy bombardments mingled with water. The men were smeared with it from head to foot. Many of the trenches were battered out of all recognition by the fire of our own and the enemy's guns, and maps gave little or no idea of the position.

It was this fact that brought about a hitch in the scheme of operations. The Battalion, with two companies of the 11th Lancashire Fusiliers, mistook its objective—one battered trench line amidst the general desolation—and went nearly six hundred yards beyond it. Fourteen prisoners were here taken by the Lancashire men. They went to ground in the trench they had decided to hold, but suffered before morning light some casualties from our own barrage fire. At dawn they found themselves "in the blue," without British troops on either side. At 10 a.m. a German counter-attack was launched from the neighbourhood of Contalmaison. By Lewis gun and rifle fire it was beaten off with heavy loss. But fresh attacks followed, and German bombers attempted to pinch in the flanks. It was evident that unless it retired the little force would be completely cut off. The retirement was carried out in orderly fashion, rearguards holding in check the German bombers. Finally, at 4 p.m., the Battalion had withdrawn to the trench which had been its true objective, but had been overpassed in the darkness. It was now in touch with troops on right and left, the latter flank being on the Albert—Bapaume road at a point about a thousand yards due east of the southernmost houses of Ovillers. Its casualties for the day, for this highly successful operation, had been over one hundred.

Relief came to men who had been fighting practically thirty-six hours, under continuous bombardment, moiled with chalk which was now drying from the consistency of whitewash to that of putty, in the early morning of July 10th. The Battalion marched back to Senlis, remained that day in bivouac, and went into billets in the houses at night. The 74th Brigade had done brilliant work in opening wider the gate through which the troops were now pressing northwards and eastwards, making their way upward on to the great plateau of Bapaume. Fighting had never ceased. Men had snatched a few hours' sleep when they could in the mud, and then gone forward to attack again. The wounded had to be dressed lying on their stretchers in the trench-bottom, and sometimes had to lie there for hours beneath a waterproof sheet till the stretcher-bearers could carry them farther back. Supports moving up, bomb carriers renewing the supply in the fighting-line, had to stumble over them as best they could. Farther forward British and German dead lay, pushed aside so that they should not obstruct the passage, khaki and field-grey so whitened with chalk and water that it was hard to tell one from the other. Amid all this strain and horror, the men had never lost their will to victory. When they came out they were bone-weary but in good spirits. They had done what they had been sent to do in face of all the known difficulties and many unforeseen. It was a great achievement. The cost was heavy, but not higher than was inevitable in such circumstances. The casualties in the Brigade were 1,277, of which the 2nd Royal Irish Rifles had suffered more than a quarter.*

* Total 334, thus divided: July 7th, 2nd-Lieutenants W. Workman (Connaught Rangers) and J. Watson killed; Captain H. Ireland (Leinster Regiment), Lieutenant W. P. Moss, 2nd-Lieutenants J. MacLaughlin, C. Weir, C. E. Wilson, wounded; other ranks, 28 killed, 116 wounded, 17 missing. July 8th, Lieutenant W. McConnell killed; 2nd-Lieutenants P. MacMahon, D. O. Turpin, wounded; other ranks, 7 killed, 22 wounded, 11 missing. July 9th, Captain W. A. Smiles killed; 2nd-Lieutenants P. E. Murray (Connaught Rangers), P. Windle, J. M. Clarke, wounded; other ranks, 12 killed, 62 wounded, 45 missing.

III.—THE BATTLE OF BAZENTIN RIDGE.

They were not out of it yet. They remained two days in Senlis, resting and scraping themselves clean. But they were still tired when, on the 14th, they marched through Albert and entered our old line in reserve. The following afternoon they moved up and took over the line, this time east of Ovillers, but not more than three hundred yards from its ruins. The village was, in fact, actually now to be attacked almost from the east, it having been partially cut off by the British advance, but being still strongly garrisoned and defended with bravery and tenacity deserving the highest tributes. An attempt was to be made to finish it off before dawn. It was a most ambitious venture to be attempted in the darkness, since three brigades were to be employed, the 143rd, the 74th and the 75th, though none of them had a frontage of more than three hundred yards, and the 74th, in the centre, attacking Ovillers itself, hardly two hundred.

The attack was not a complete success. The attack of the 74th Brigade was carried out by the Royal Irish Rifles and two companies of the 13th Cheshire. The Battalion attacked with three companies, from right to left " D," " A " and " C," in six waves. But, despite the darkness, the advance was raked by machine-gun fire from the right flank, where there were still Germans in the continuation of the trench which formed the " jumping-off " line. As a consequence of the subsequent loss and disorganization, the Battalion was forced to withdraw. On their left, however, the 143rd Brigade had made progress, and its right battalion, the 5th Warwickshire, once gone to ground in its objective, was completely cut off, owing to the trenches behind it having been bashed out of existence by the German fire and rendered useless for communication. To join up with them, the only method which now appeared practicable was for the 2nd Royal Irish Rifles to bomb its way up a trench which led to their right flank.

From 9 a.m. that morning till noon the bombers of the Battalion fought desperately to make ground up the trench, without avail. Their total gain at the end of the period was ten yards. As a barrier was destroyed and captured, the enemy put up a new one behind it. In the afternoon bombing squads of the 11th Lancashire Fusiliers came up to help the attack on. With this new impetus, and a supply of rifle grenades, the attack began to make slow progress. A Stokes mortar was hauled forward, with a score of bombs, and after great trouble got into action. It was a strange affair. The men were absolutely " dead beat." Those not fighting flung themselves down in the trench and slept, while twenty yards away bombs were flying and bursting with their disquieting noise. It seemed as if the attack might die away with the dusk from sheer fatigue.

And then suddenly came the dramatic end. A white flag was hoisted upon a pole. Orders were passed to our men to stand upon their guard. It might be a trick. But no ! From all corners heads appeared, arms were raised, more flags waved, shouts of " Kamerad !" heard. The whole party had surrendered.

They were at once passed down the trench. Their officers, a captain and a lieutenant, had to be fetched from a dug-out, so apparently the surrender had not been made by their orders. The other ranks numbered 126. Their defence had been a splendid one, but now they seemed delighted to be prisoners and out of it all, insisted upon shaking hands with their captors. As for the Riflemen, new life was put into them by their triumph, fatigue forgotten. Within a few minutes they had linked up with their comrades of the Warwickshire, who had passed an uncomfortable and difficult day. Then they pressed down towards the village, clearing a whole block of trenches, adding to their prisoners

THE ULSTER DIVISION MEMORIAL AT THIEPVAL, FRANCE
Erected in Memory of the Attack by the Ulster Division, July 1st, 1916.

two heavy and one light machine guns and a great quantity of booty of all kinds. The remaining Germans fled into the cellars of the village, where they continued to resist till "mopped up" the following day. Later that night another battalion of the 143rd Brigade, the 6th Royal Warwickshire, relieved the Royal Irish Rifles, which marched slowly back to Bouzincourt. The men were so weary that they could scarcely set one foot before another, but delighted with their triumph. One in two of them wore German helmets, these being still the days of the peace-time *pickelhaube*, a very pretty trophy.

The operation had been one of the most brilliant of the minor attacks on the Somme, cleverly planned, and carried out, by men who might have been expected to be too weary for the work, with a dogged persistence that would take no denial. Losses had been, considering the volume of the artillery fire, extraordinarily light. Not thirty men were killed in the 74th Brigade, the total casualties of which were less than two hundred. The casualties of the 2nd Royal Irish Rifles were, for the two days, fifty-seven[*]. It must of course, be remembered that the Battalion had gone into action on this second occasion very weak in numbers, and it was now at about half strength. During the next few days, however, when back in rest at Beauval, it received drafts of more than two hundred other ranks.

IV.—Trench Warfare on the Somme.

Beauval, just south of Doullens, is one of the best small towns of the Somme area, and the Battalion would have been happy to have had more time to make its acquaintance. But so many fresh divisions were being called upon, week by week, for the Somme battle, that small opportunity was given for rest to those that came out of it. The best for which they could hope was a comparatively quiet line. After six days the 74th Brigade marched back to Mailly-Maillet Wood, and on the night of the 24th relieved another Ulster battalion, the 1st Royal Inniskilling Fusiliers, of the 29th Division, opposite Beaumont Hamel, the right flank being upon the famous salient known as the Mary Redan. This was part of that front north of the Ancre where the first day's attack had been a total failure, and "No Man's Land" was still full of the 29th Division's dead. No new operations had been attempted after the first rebuff, and the line was quiet, full of excellent deep dug-outs constructed for shelter during the bombardments preceding the offensive. It was exchanged in August for another sector, just farther north, in front of the ruined village of Auchonvillers. Then, on the 10th, came a week's rest and training, at Bus-les-Artois. On the 18th began another tour in the line, this time opposite Thiepval Wood, and on the 28th one in newly conquered territory just south of it. The British were still creeping from the southward toward the Ancre valley, and the line here still faced northward. Battalion Headquarters were actually located in the very "nest" of dug-outs in which the Riflemen had taken their big haul of prisoners in July, while the right flank was a thousand yards due south of Mouquet Farm, subsequently so notorious. Father Gill describes the Albert—Bapaume road, which had been practically unrecognizable where it passed through La Boisselle, as now steam-rolled, so that cars could run upon it at full pace. The British advance was still progressing, and their admirable rear services were aiding them wonderfully. The superiority of "Q" to "G" in the British Armies had become almost a commonplace. On August 30th there were serious casualties, 2nd-Lieutenant J. J. Daly and 16 other ranks being wounded, and 5 killed.

[*] Second-Lieutenant J. Lecky killed; Captain D. H. Kelly, 2nd-Lieutenants T. H. Gallwey and R. A. Bennett (Cheshire Regiment) wounded; 2nd-Lieutenant T. E. Barton missing. Other ranks, 4 killed, 42 wounded, 6 missing.

The Battalion spent the first week of September in this area, the middle fortnight in the much pleasanter situation of Domqueur, not far from Abbeville, where it carried out vigorous training, and the last week in the same part of the line. It was in the trenches when the 18th Division captured the Schwaben Redoubt, at Thiepval, a formidable work taken on July 1st by the 36th Division, which had to be abandoned because no advance had been made at Thiepval on the right flank. It was not engaged actively here, though the 11th Lancashire Fusiliers of its brigade saw some hard fighting and took over thirty prisoners; but it came in for its share of the German bombardment, and had several casualties, 2nd-Lieutenant J. Stein being killed and 2nd-Lieutenant K. Elphick wounded. Meanwhile the 7th Battalion had also been in action on the Somme during September, and we will now turn to consider how it fared.

V.—The Battle of Ginchy.

The 7th Battalion was in the Hulluch area throughout the months of July and August. The line, after the great gas attacks, was generally quiet, and casualties comparatively few. On the night of July 31st there was a curious incident. A raid was attempted by the Battalion, without success. The enemy's wire was found to be insufficiently cut. After an effort to penetrate it by means of its wire-cutters, the raiding party returned to our trenches. A few minutes later the enemy raided in his turn. If, as seems probable, this raid was made in retaliation and organized on the spur of the moment, it was creditable to the German battalion or company concerned. A raid carried out immediately after the failure of one by the other side has advantages so obvious that the uninitiated may wonder why it was not more often attempted. As a fact, the most successful raids were generally those prepared for weeks in advance, over "dummy" trenches, reproduced from aeroplane photographs of the trenches to be attacked, worked to a strict time-table, with every man trained to carry out exactly and without hesitation his particular part of the programme. Raids hurriedly improvised often ended in hopeless confusion, the men losing their way in the dark, and being comparatively helpless when once out of the control of their officers and non-commissioned officers. Among Colonial troops, who had a highly developed personal initiative, such raids were commoner and frequently successful. The Australians, the country-dwellers among whom had an extraordinary sense of direction and power of memorizing the features of ground seen in daylight, practised them frequently, though for the most part at a period later than this; asking no more of their artillery than that it should not shoot upon such-and-such trenches over such-and-such a period.

In this case the Royal Irish Rifles were nearly caught napping. Somewhat imprudently, the majority of the officers in the front line had gone back to report to the Commanding Officer at Battalion Headquarters upon their attempted raid. The men themselves, showing, for young troops, very creditable presence of mind, saved the situation. When the sentries in the saps fell back to the front line trench to give warning of what was coming, bombing squads, formed under non-commissioned officers, rushed into position to cover these saps. Showers of bombs kept the enemy from pushing down them into the main trench. By the time supports had moved up from the second line he was gone. Our losses were 4 killed and 6 wounded, and the enemy took no prisoners. One officer was wounded during August: 2nd-Lieutenant Macnamara.

On August 24th the 48th Brigade was relieved by a brigade of the 32nd Division, which had had heavy losses on the Somme. After a few days' rest it entrained for the battle area, detraining at Longueau on the 30th and marching to Corbie, on the Somme River. Thence it moved slowly forward to the ruined village of Guillemont, where the 7th Royal Irish Rifles relieved two battalions of the 47th Brigade, in the support line. The village had been taken but four days earlier, as part of the series of attacks which had advanced our line at this latitude to a point nearly six miles from the original front. To the north-east was the village of Ginchy, already taken but lost to a German counter-attack. It was now to be attacked by the 16th Division, in conjunction with other attacks upon the southern portion of the British battle-front.

For three days the Battalion remained in the village, consolidating it with the aid of the Engineers. There was no shelter but a few dug-outs, in which in the darkness men sometimes happened upon strange and grisly house-mates, and the shelling was very heavy. Casualties were numerous. On the night of the 6th the Battalion, though holding the support line, sent forward three strong patrols to locate the enemy's position at Ginchy. They were fired upon, and Lieutenants Morgan and Williams were killed. Next evening the Battalion took over the front, which was about half-way between the two villages. What the war diaries, ever optimistic, knew as the " accommodation," consisted in this case of shell-holes, sometimes linked together by little trenches. The night of the 8th was spent in digging assembly trenches. At this point Germans and British were widely separated, and the diggers, moving forward quietly in the darkness, were enabled to tape out and dig their front line nearly two hundred yards in front of the position held, thus giving themselves so much shorter distance to go in the attack. They dug before morning light four successive lines, forty yards apart, each capable of holding four platoons, west of the sunken road between Guillemont and Ginchy, while the men of the 1st Munsters were employed on the same task east of the road. They then took up their assembly positions, four companies in line, from right to left " B," " A," " C," and " D," each in four waves on a frontage of a single platoon. Though the attack was not to take place till late in the afternoon of the following day, it was obvious that no movement would be possible after dawn.

The 16th Division was attacking with the 47th Brigade on the right and the 48th on the left, the latter having the village of Ginchy as its objective, the boundary between the two being at the " jumping-off line," the Hardecourt—Ginchy road. The boundary between the 48th Brigade's two first-line battalions was, as has been stated, the Guillemont—Ginchy road. The experience of early defeats in this battle had taught the advisability of short objectives, and in this case, though the final line beyond Ginchy was not more than a thousand yards from the assembly trenches, the attack was to be made by four battalions, two " leap-frogging " the two in the lead upon the first objective, the road running from Delville Wood to the middle of the village. The second two battalions were to pass through the leaders at " zero " plus forty minutes. The attack was to be made by the 1st Munsters and 7th Royal Irish Rifles in front line, the 8th and 9th Dublins in second, named from right to left in each case.

" Zero " was fixed for 4.45 p.m. The intention was presumably to vary the usual dawn attack which was expected by the enemy. Another advantage was that, with a short objective, there would be just time for some consolidation before dusk, and very little for an organized German counter-attack. Such were the advantages of the scheme, and in other parts of the front they may not have been balanced by serious hazards. In the case of the 48th Brigade, and above all of the 7th Royal Irish Rifles, the plan caused very heavy loss of life, and might easily have led to a disastrous failure of the attack. The assembly trenches were only too visible to the German observation officers, and they had a good nine hours of daylight to pound them with their guns. It is easy to imagine that losses were high. But there was loss from a reason less creditable to the authorities in rear. At 7.55 a.m. the Brigade received a report from the Royal Irish Rifles, and soon afterwards one of a like tenor from the Munsters, that our artillery was bursting shells in their front line and causing heavy casualties. Apparently the account of these battalions having gone forward two hundred yards to dig their assembly trenches had not reached all the batteries of the numerous artillery brigades supporting the attack, or had not been understood. According to the Brigade's report, it was batteries of the Guards' Divisional Artillery and the 61st Brigade R.F.A. that caused the trouble. However this may be, what with the bombardments of the enemy and our own side, Colonel Francis reported to his brigadier, at 2 p.m., that his battalion, which had gone into action somewhat weak, had not much more than a hundred and fifty bayonets for the assault. As there was grave doubt whether this force would suffice to take the first objective, the 48th Brigade asked for further troops, and was given the 7th Royal Irish Fusiliers, of the 49th Brigade. To bring this battalion up into line there was none too much time, while from the moment it left the cover of Guillemont it was exposed to heavy fire. Largely through the skill and energy of its commanding officer, it was in its place in time, behind the Royal Irish Rifles. There were thus five battalions under the command of the General Officer Commanding 48th Brigade to carry out the assault.

At "zero" the waves went forward, energy and dash unabated by the dreadful pounding of the day and the toil of the preceding night. The Riflemen, backed up by the Royal Irish Fusiliers on the left, the Munsters on the right, reached the German front line, on the outskirts of the village, and took it in a moment, killing or taking prisoner most of the Germans in it, though a handful managed to escape and run back to the second line. The "going" being fairly sound, Stokes mortars of the 48th Light Trench Mortar Battery arrived with the men of the Royal Irish Rifles, and very useful they proved. Just behind the German front line a stout-hearted officer had rallied a party of forty men, possessed of one or two light machine guns, which prepared to dispute the second advance. The mortars were withdrawn a little, set up in shell-holes, from which their rapid fire of small shells was opened over the heads of the infantry. In a few minutes the whole German party surrendered to the latter. The range of the Stokes was then lengthened to aid the troops about to pass through to the second objective.

Punctually at 5.25 p.m. the 9th Dublins came through. But, as happened not seldom in such cases, when men's blood was up and they were excited by a preliminary success, a number of the Riflemen could not be held by the few officers remaining, and went forward with the Dublins, through the village, to the second objective, which was also taken. They even went beyond the objective. This was risky, as the attack had not gone too well elsewhere, and the advance had been checked east of Delville Wood, A subaltern officer of the 7th Royal Irish Rifles, whose name is not recorded, brought back his own men and the Dublins to the proper line. The former were then led back to the first objective, and the work of consolidation set in hand. Colonel Francis had been knocked down by a shell-burst and severely shaken. Lieut.-Colonel E. Bellingham, the officer commanding the 8th Dublin Fusiliers, the supporting battalion on the right, accomplished very fine work in the organization of the whole line. By midnight the village was in a sound state of defence. Half an hour later what remained of the Battalion

Facing page 74

was relieved, staggered back to Carnoy, was shipped into motor-buses and taken to the Happy Valley, near Albert, where the men lay down and slept, and marched next day to the comfort of Corbie.

The losses in this affair were enormous. Those of the 48th Brigade amounted to fourteen hundred, about half its infantry strength in going into action. The Battalion had killed, Major Cairnes and 2nd-Lieutenant Capper; missing, believed killed, 2nd-Lieutenant Keown; wounded, Major Lash, Captain Taggart, 2nd-Lieutenants Bayham (who died soon afterwards), Devereux and Boyle. Of other ranks, 39 were killed and 260 wounded and missing. A large proportion of this loss was, of course, due to the terrible bombardment from dawn to the hour of the assault. The Battalion had fought with hereditary Irish dash. The success of the 16th Division on this occasion was the more creditable in that upon the rest of the front the attack failed. To complete the work begun by it was needed one of the greatest attacks of the whole Somme battle, when tanks were employed for the first time.

A few days of rest followed, but hardly had men emerged from that strange and merciful trance which seems to follow such experiences, when they were moved back by bus to Longpré and entrained for the north. They reached Godewaersvelde on the afternoon of September 21st, and marched to billets at La Clytte, a mile and a half north of Kemmel Hill. On the evening of the 23rd they relieved Canadian troops in the neighbourhood of Vierstraat, at the southern corner of the Ypres Salient.

VI.—The 1st Battalion at Loos.

The 1st Battalion, it has been recorded, had gone into line in the Loos Salient at the end of July. This area, like that held ealier in the year by the 2nd Battalion a little farther south, was one of constant mining activity and warfare among the craters. German artillery was far less violent than of old, most of the heavy pieces having been moved down to the Somme, but the enemy was strong in trench mortars, and used them with vigour. The dug-outs were good and deep, but swarmed with rats and mice, and the whole region had the indescribable dirtiness and sordidness of an old battle-ground, lying like a pall upon a country-side singularly unattractive at the best of times. There were frequent bombing fights, in one of which the Battalion suffered severely, losing eight prisoners, in the early morning of August 21st. Later in the month there was a raid even heavier upon the 2nd Rifle Brigade, after a terrific bombardment with 200-pound trench mortars. Outside the front line, with its mortars and constant threats of mine explosions, which shook men's nerves, there was nothing of which to complain, there being little or no long range artillery fire. September passed very quietly. On October 9th a small raid was attempted by 2nd-Lieutenant Palmer with twelve men. The Germans were on the alert, and he could not get in. He shot two of the enemy, however, with his revolver, while his party threw bombs into the trench. The casualties were comparatively light in this period, the losses of officers in two months and a half being 2nd-Lieutenants J. L. Millar and W. K. Adrian killed, and 2nd-Lieutenants C. N. Champney and J. C. Cooke wounded. On October 14th the Battalion entrained at Lillers for its second venture on the Somme.

CHAPTER III

I.—THE BATTLE OF THE ANCRE HEIGHTS.

THE autumn fighting of the Somme battle, the bulk of which took place in the neighbourhood of the Ancre Valley, made less impression upon the public mind than the earlier part of the campaign, except so far as it bred a certain impatience with the methods pursued, called in question the merits of the limited objective, and undermined the position of the director of operations, General Joffre. Yet it has from the military point of view high interest and importance. It was warfare carried out under the most difficult conditions, often in the worst of weather. It imposed upon the troops concerned a strain even more heavy than that endured from July to September. It marked, on the other hand, a distinct improvement in tactical methods, as well in the employment of artillery, now considerably increased in volume, the disposition of troops, as in the local leadership of subordinate commanders. In the fighting of October the 74th Brigade, which had done so well in July in the neighbourhood of Ovillers, carried out one of the most brilliant actions of the campaign. This must here, however, be treated without entering into detail, as the men of the 2nd Royal Irish Rifles, who had had the lion's share at Ovillers, played in it a comparatively minor part. At least, their part was not the striking one of capturing trenches, but of taking them over when won, and carrying up munitions to aid the attack farther forward.

On October 5th the Battalion took over positions in reserve to the newly won line. On the 8th it had a company in the notorious Mouquet Farm, which had proved a nut so hard to the British teeth, one in a trench south of it, one west of Courcelette, and one near Pozières Cemetery—this last a position with reminders of the fate of all flesh rather too grim to be pleasant in war. Here, it need scarcely be said, it was kept fully occupied with "fatigues." On the 9th the 7th Brigade captured Stuff Redoubt, on the 74th Brigade's flank, holding it against counter-attacks next day.* On the 13th the Battalion took over a portion of the front line. The moment was unpleasant for the change, since our guns had begun to cut wire for the next advance to the Ancre Valley, and the German retaliation was considerable. The Battalion had, however, no more than eleven men wounded in the first twenty-four hours, and held itself lucky.

In the early hours of the 21st it was relieved by the three other battalions of the Brigade, which were to carry out the new advance. The trench which the Battalion evacuated and was to take over again as soon as the assault was launched was called Hessian Trench, and ran from the Courcelette—Grandcourt road, a thousand yards northwest of Courcelette, to the neighbourhood of the Thiepval—Grandcourt road, due east and west. The objective was Regina Trench, which ran parallel to it, four to five hundred yards farther north. The attack was carried out by the 18th Division on the right and the 25th on the left. The 74th Brigade was in touch with the 18th Division, and had the 75th Brigade on its left. Immediately the attacking battalions had left Hessian Trench, two platoons of "A" and two platoons of "B" Companies of the Royal Irish Rifles filed into it to garrison it. The assault was successful, and the remainder of the Battalion at once began its work of carrying forward bombs and ammunition to Regina Trench. This work was of the greatest difficulty. The ground was literally ploughed

---
* Second-Lieutenant C. R. Cooney (Leinster Regiment) was killed on this date, and 2nd-Lieutenant F. R. Fowler of the same regiment a few days later.

up—there had been heavy rain of late—and it was no light task for a man to cross it with only his own rifle and equipment. To carry forward buckets or bags of bombs and boxes of small-arm ammunition, to say nothing of petrol-tins of water, in the face of heavy artillery fire, was a job for which many of the men would have not unwillingly exchanged that of advancing to the attack. Fortunately, the great German bombardment did far less damage than might have been expected. The casualties of the Riflemen were light.* Those of the whole Brigade were less than a thousand, of which over 650 were wounded, while the Brigade had taken 4 officers and 474 other ranks. It had been one of those actions, not too frequent in the Somme fighting, of which we can say with certainty that the losses of the defenders must have been considerably in excess of those of the attackers. The 25th Division had added new fame to the high reputation already won in this campaign.

The Brigade was relieved next day, and on the 24th marched from Harponville to the coveted quarters of Beauval. Here it was inspected by the Fifth Army Commander, General Sir Hubert Gough, who complimented all the battalions upon their great work in the Somme fighting. This marked the end of the Battalion's sojourn in this part of the line, which, as the fates willed, it was not to revisit. On the 30th it marched to Candas and took train to Caestre, in Flanders, on the main road between Cassel and Bailleul.

II.—The 1st Battalion in Attack on Misty Trench.

The 1st Battalion Royal Irish Rifles was in an attack on the Somme on October 23rd, only two days after the advance near Grandcourt in which the 2nd had been engaged. This was, however, nearly eight miles from the scene of the former action, and at the other flank of the British front of attack. Here the Allies had bitten deeply into the German positions, the British right being ten miles from the old front line in the same latitude. All the three main German lines of defence which had existed in July had been penetrated, but, the advance having taken upwards of four months, the Germans had had time to dig and wire as they fell back, and now had equally strong defences in front. The object of the attack in question was to get within striking distance of the village of Le Transloy, on the Bapaume—Peronne road, from the present position between Morval and Lesboeufs. The 8th Division was to attack with all three brigades in line, the 23rd on the right, the 25th in the centre, and the 24th on the left. The 25th Brigade had two successive objectives, the first partly represented by a trench known as Zenith Trench, and partly represented by an imaginary line prolonging this trench to the left (and north-west) to another trench known as Misty Trench. The second objective was three hundred yards beyond the first. The advance to these objectives was to be carried out by the 2nd Lincolnshire on the right and the 2nd Rifle Brigade on the left. Somewhat unfortunately, " zero," originally fixed at 9.30 a.m., was postponed five hours, till 2.30 p.m.

At the time appointed two companies of each of the leading battalions sprang forward so closely upon the heels of the barrage, which they had been instructed to hug, that a few men were hit by our shrapnel in the advance. On the Lincolnshires' front there occurred a curious incident, as a result of which, through the supreme gallantry of a single German officer, the Battalion's attack failed to win its section of Zenith Trench. Those who know anything of the war need not to be told that the psychological moment in an infantry attack following a creeping barrage is that when the barrage lifts off the trench

---

* One officer, 2nd-Lieutenant S. A. Bell, and 8 other ranks wounded.

to be captured. However closely the leading wave has kept to the moving wall of the barrage, it is impossible to avoid giving the enemy opportunity to man his parapet to some extent before the attacking bayonets are on him—if he be resolute enough to take that opportunity. But men who have crouched in the shelter of a dug-out or have lain shuddering in the bottom of a trench upon which shells are crashing down often take longer to recover themselves than it takes for determined and well-led troops to cross the intervening ground. If they do, they are commonly lost. The moral and physical impetus of attacking, supposing the troops on either side to be of equally good quality, is worth a reinforcement of one hundred per cent. At Ypres, in the following year, not only was the defence fluid, but the soil was also. Over and over again the most gallant men in the British Army lost the barrage at the last moment from sheer inability to drag their feet from the glue-like mud. On the Somme at its worst the mud was bad, but never so bad as this, and it was above all the close and resolute following up of the barrage that was bringing us our successes.

In this case, as we have shown, the troops had closed up as much as they dared, having even had some men hit by our shrapnel. Just as the barrage moved off Zenith Trench, a German officer was seen to spring up and run along the parapet, signalling to his men to line it. Almost immediately there burst out such an intense fire from light machine guns and rifles that the attack was stopped dead. If ever one man held up an assault by his own exertions, this German officer did so.

The incident has been described in detail partly because of its interest and partly because of its important after-effects. On the left the 2nd Rifle Brigade went forward with its accustomed dash. The platoon directed upon the junction of Zenith and Eclipse Trenches (the latter a communication trench running into the former at right angles) was beaten off by machine-gun and rifle fire; several of the Germans, doubtless inspired by the high example they had been given, had been observed to kneel upon their parapet. On the left of this point, however, the objective was attained—that is, the line between Zenith Trench and Misty Trench was reached.

Now the 1st Royal Irish Rifles advanced by platoons, at fifty paces interval, in single file to take over Rainbow and Spider Trenches, from which the leading battalions had gone forward. The Battalion had to pass through a heavy barrage, and had serious loss, but went through with remarkable steadiness. It was in position at 3.15 p.m.; but it was found impossible to organize the speedy attack upon Zenith Trench which would have had the best chance of success. Not till 8 p.m. did orders arrive for the new attack, to be carried out by two companies of the 2nd Royal Berks on the right, and two of the 1st Royal Irish Rifles on the left, at 3.50 a.m. next morning.

This assault was likewise a failure. The two companies of the Royal Irish Rifles, " A " in the lead, " B " following it at twenty-five paces distance, went forward well enough, but the assault was simply swept away, losing fifty per cent. of its strength in a few seconds. The line was thus left in a curious position, in which it was to remain for several days. On the right the 23rd Brigade held a considerable length of Zenith Trench; then came a gap of over two hundred and fifty yards held by the enemy; then a line of shell-holes, linked together in a few cases by now, held by the 2nd Rifle Brigade. The attack, it will be seen, had achieved a very limited measure of success.

The Royal Irish Rifles remained three more days in line, under heavy and continuous bombardment, and then, on the 26th, relief took them to no better place than Trones Wood, where the bivouacs were full of water. On the 28th they were back again in close

WINTER CONDITIONS ON THE SOMME

support in Spider Trench. A new attack to secure the still uncaptured portion of Zenith Trench had been planned for next day; the 2nd Devons, of the 23rd Brigade, and 1st Sherwood Foresters, of the 24th, being lent to the 25th Brigade for the operation. It had, however, rained incessantly, and the ground was becoming wellnigh impassable. According to the report, the attack was for this reason postponed. Actually it would appear that the commanding officers in front line decided it would be madness and wanton throwing away of lives to attempt it under these conditions, and announced their respectful refusal to do so. It was necessary to leave the half-done job to be finished off by someone else. On October 30th the Battalion returned to the doubtful comfort of Trones Wood. It had suffered very heavily in numbers and in health and strength. Its losses were—1 officer killed, 8 wounded*; 20 other ranks killed, 143 wounded, and 43 missing, of whom the great majority must have been killed also. As for the other side of the case, the exposure, the cold, the wet of winter warfare practically without cover, beggar description. No man can long withstand them, and none can endure the period these had endured without an almost intolerable strain, which had frequently serious after-effects upon the constitution of individuals.

Citadel Camp, where the Battalion passed the night of the 31st, was no Elysium. It was a camp of tents, never very comfortable in winter, even when those tents have floor-boards, as in this case they had not. Here, about midnight, there arrived suddenly, quite unheralded—in accordance with that sense of humour for which the transport services were famous—and as it were " out of the blue," an enormous draft of 6 officers and 425 other ranks. Like everyone else, they were wet through; but, unlike everyone else, they had had neither tea nor supper. Those who have known its like will be able to call up for both ear and eye what followed among those clammy tents in the darkness, as food and accommodation were found for that forlorn and rain-sodden draft, half a battalion in strength.

It was to be some weeks before the newcomers were to have an opportunity of settling down, for there was no rest yet for the Battalion, but for a few days at Méaulte. On the 11th it re-entered the line in front of Le Transloy, to be relieved after two days of tremendous shelling, in which gas was largely used, and to endure a bombardment even more severe while in brigade support. The casualties for November were 66 other ranks. But for the last week of November and all but the last three days of December there was to be rest, broken, it need hardly be said, by training, but rest nevertheless. The Battalion took train at the new station of which the name stood for the winter fighting as that of Longueau had stood for the summer—Edgehill, outside Dernancourt—to Airaines. Thence it marched to the village of Laleu, which was small, but none the worse for that, since it was impossible for another unit to share it. And there it remained till December 28th, while the veterans recovered from the effects of the Somme, and the new men learnt to know their companions and their officers. On that date it returned to the battle area, to a camp near Bray-sur-Somme, and two days later was again in line, between Combles and Sailly-Saillisel.

III.—THE 2ND BATTALION AT PLOEGSTEERT.

The 2nd Battalion, which had reached Caestre on October 30th, was at Shaexhen, near Meteren, on November 1st, in a camp on the Bailleul—Armentières road next day,

---

* Second-Lieutenant S. Gault killed; 2nd-Lieutenants A. H. Nicholson, T. Benson, G. F. Wolfe, G. C. Holt, E. W. Lennard, A. J. E. Gibson, V. Noonan, G. S. Sinclair wounded.

and on the 3rd marched to Ploegsteert Wood, in the support line. " Plug-street " had few rivals in popularity on the British front. It was always one of the quietest places along our whole line. The shelter of its trees made communication easy, and a light railway brought rations within a short distance of the front line. In summer, life in it was really pleasant, and its garrison was enabled to forget all the worst horrors of war. At this time of year there remained one, the wet in the trenches, but by the period we have reached rubber thigh-boots were plentiful. With their aid, with a supply of whale-oil for rubbing the feet, and dry socks sent up each night with the rations, the troops were able to make light of the wet. Casualties were always light. The Diary reports that on November 10th, when gas was discharged along the whole front of the 25th Division and there was a fair amount of retaliatory fire, the Battalion, then in front line, had not a single casualty. On November 25th Major H. R. Goodman arrived and took over command.

In December some wire-cutting operations were carried out by our artillery, but retaliation must have been light, for the whole brigade had only 82 casualties for the month, while the Royal Irish Rifles had 4 men killed and 5 wounded. Christmas was celebrated out of the line, at Nieppe, with sports and a good dinner, visited by the new brigadier, General Bethel. The last Christmas had been passed at Le Bizet, but a few miles away. During the month a draft of 124 other ranks arrived, of whom half were Londoners of the 1st/4th London Regiment. The shortage of Irish recruits was becoming serious for Irish battalions which wished to preserve their traditions.

IV.—THE 7TH BATTALION IN FLANDERS.

Of the 7th Battalion there is little to record during the period of October to December, 1916. It occupied different parts of the divisional front facing the Messines—Wytschaete Ridge. In brigade reserve it was usually at Kemmel, and in divisional reserve at Locre. There was comparatively little artillery fire on this part of the front during all the fighting on the Somme, where both sides had sent the majority of their heavy guns, and for which both sides husbanded their shells. Of this area it was well said by a soldier of the 36th Division, then on the 16th Division's right, that it was the pleasantest front in the world, if only one were far enough away from it. The statement had less of the " bull " in it than may appear, for it was only necessary to be far enough away to avoid the German trench-mortars. Five hundred yards from our front line, for practical purposes, sufficed. On the Somme, Battalion Headquarters had little advantage over the outposts. Here, in that historic villa known as " Doctor's House," they lived in comfort. But the front line was undoubtedly unpleasant at times. One glance at the mortar-craters, lip to lip in some parts, was enough to tell the initiated that on the quietest of days. There were constant bombardments by British and German mortars, which the British Staff and trench-mortar personnel—and probably the German also—called " trench-mortar duels." The infantry, perhaps, considered the term misapplied, as the duel consisted in each side firing as hard as it could at the opposing infantry.

The 36th (Ulster) Division, it has been said, was on the 16th Division's right, while in November the 25th Division came in next farther south. There was thus a very remarkable assemblage of battalions of the Royal Irish Rifles. Between Nieppe and Kemmel, six miles apart, there were the 2nd, 7th, 8th, 9th, 10th, 11th, 12th, 13th, 14th 15th and 16th Battalions. Eleven battalions of one regiment within six miles probably constituted a record.

CHAPTER IV

I.—THE 6TH BATTALION'S LIFE IN MACEDONIA.*

THE history of the 6th Battalion in the East during the first seven months of the year 1916 is marked by more movements than important events. It is in miniature the history of the whole Allied Army of Salonika, admirably christened by M. Mermeix, the French historian, " l'armée qui s'ennuyait." It has been stated that the Allies had determined to hold the town, and had prepared lines of defence for the purpose. For this their forces were amply strong, and when reinforcements began to arrive, including the reconstituted Serbian Army and detachments of Italian and Russian troops, they were far too strong. But they were not strong enough for a major offensive. The Bulgars they might have beaten, but there was always Mackensen in the background, who could, even during the Somme fighting, even during the Russian offensive, have spared divisions enough to hold them. From January to August, 1916, the Salonika Army was inactive, and even in the latter part of the year its offensives were of a minor nature. In these circumstances it was a task of some difficulty to keep the troops, not merely occupied, but interested in their occupations. That task would appear to have been better carried out, on the whole, by the British than by the French commanders. This is not a political history of the war, but only a history of certain battalions of the Royal Irish Rifles. But it is not out of place to remark that the French Army at Salonika was first a bored army, and in 1917 a disaffected army, which it took all the vigour of General Guillaumat, the successor of General Sarrail, to restore to the highest efficiency. If the British suffered far less from these effects, even though boredom was to some extent inevitable and military crime not unknown, it was due to the energy of the British commanders and their ingenuity in keeping their men " at concert pitch " by means of work and play. The 29th Brigade was especially fortunate in having a brigadier who spared neither himself nor his staff Its War Diary at the slackest times makes most interesting reading. Whether engaged in manœuvres behind the line or holding a wide and scattered front, General Vandeleur appears to have been constantly in the saddle, and nothing escaped his eye. He must have ridden thousands of miles in 1916 and 1917. These rides are chronicled at length in a diary that was always admirably kept. They will not here be referred to in detail; but if the history of the 10th Division is ever written, it will be the task of its historian to analyse them and draw the appropriate moral. It was a situation in which British commanders, with the lessons of military life in India before them, have often shone, and their achievements at Salonika, too often forgotten in the general impatience with which the campaign—rightly, in all probability—came to be regarded, are memorable in this respect.

The holding of the Rendina Gorge was a task light enough. The Bulgars had not yet crossed the frontier, and, as has been stated, there were Greek garrisons in front which would probably at this date have disputed their passage, though no one could be certain of that. Traffic through the gorge was stopped, and there were boat patrols on

*In this and subsequent chapters dealing with the 6th Battalion, some of the names are spelt differently in the text and on the maps.

Lake Beshik to watch for suspicious persons who might try to cross the water. Greek officers and soldiers, however, were allowed passage on explaining in a satisfactory manner the nature of their mission. The work of entrenchment at once began, and wire entanglements were put up to bar approach at points favourable to attacking troops. The Brigadier reported that, in the event of an attack, at least three more battalions would be necessary to hold the line, and in February the 80th Brigade took over the right half of it, the 29th Brigade having now no coast to watch. There would be ample naval support if wanted, and the *Endymion*, from the Gulf of Orphani, carried out registration in front of the position. There was a succession of naval visitors to study the situation. Two other visitors were the well-known war correspondents, Messrs. Nevinson and Price, who walked from Salonika, a distance of over forty miles. The troops were not uncomfortable, and their rations were greatly improved when an arrangement was made to purchase fish from a company which fished the Beshik Lake under a licence from the Greek Government.

In February, after much good work upon the new defences, the 29th Brigade was relieved. The 6th Royal Irish Rifles marched back by stages to Ajvasil, half-way to Salonika, on the shore of Lake Langaza, and was occupied in training and work upon rear defences and upon roads. The weather at this time was intensely cold, and there were several heavy blizzards. Otherwise there is little to record for the next two months. St. Patrick's Day was duly celebrated by a holiday and battalion sports in camp. In April important manœuvres were carried out by the "29th Mobile Column," as a test and training for speed in a war of movement upon broken ground with few roads worthy of the name. All transport was pack, save for ten G.S. limbered wagons with small-arms ammunition and a few with the train. A battery of artillery and three light ambulance wagons were the only other "wheels" with the column. After a postponement, caused by a snow-storm, the manœuvres began on the 19th. The next four days were fine, and long marches were carried out. An attack was practised on the 21st. On the 23rd the manœuvres came to an end, the whole Brigade marching to camp at Hortakoz. The day was intensely hot, and the troops felt the effects of the sudden change of weather. Yet two men only of the Battalion fell out, and these were the only two to fall out during the manœuvres, out of seventy-six in the Brigade. The percentages of men falling out to total numbers are carefully recorded in the Brigade Diary. They were: 10th Hampshire, 5·1 per cent.; 5th Connaught Rangers, 4 per cent.; 6th Leinster, 2·17 per cent.; 6th Royal Irish Rifles, 0·25 per cent. It was considered that in the difficult and trying conditions all the percentages were satisfactory, so the achievement of the Royal Irish Rifles must be reckoned as splendid. Moreover, out of nine mules in the Brigade found with galled backs, one only belonged to the Battalion, showing that its animals were as fit as its men, and that its saddlery was properly adjusted.

In May the Battalion lost its Machine Gun Section, withdrawn, with those of the other battalions, to form the 29th Machine Gun Company, thereafter attached to the Brigade. Early in June the Battalion, with the rest of the Brigade, moved to Likóvan, half-way between Salonika and Seres, for work upon the main road connecting those towns. Each company had to find one hundred men a day for the work, in two shifts, two companies working in the morning and two in the afternoon. That did not last long, for a few days later arrived orders to take over from French troops a considerable portion of the Struma line held by them. The move began on June 9th.

The great river, after crossing the Serb-Bulgarian frontier, runs south-east into the

Gulf of Orphani, through a broad valley between the heights of the Rhodope Mountains and the range known as the Kruzabalkan. Before it reaches the sea it forms a large sheet of water, in the deepest part of its valley, known as Lake Tahinos. This is some fifteen miles long, and there is only another seven or eight miles of river between it and the gulf. At the western end of the lake is the village of Gudeli, where there is a ferry which, like many institutions in that country, probably dates from a thousand years back. It was from this ferry westward that the new line of the 29th Brigade was to run. The Royal Irish Rifles did not enter the front line during its first occupation by the Brigade, but had two companies at a hamlet called Marian, near the lake-shore, in control of wells and watering arrangements. In the middle of July the Brigade was relieved and moved to Dremiglavia, north of Salonika, west of the Seres road. Here, and not before it was time, sun-helmets were issued, and a few days later " shorts." Here also a new system of transport was organized, entirely on the pack basis. There were now no less than 127 pack mules, while the transport personnel amounted to 100, and the transport officer was given an assistant. With all this mighty aid, there was a very small battalion to transport anywhere. Men were going down right and left with fever as the heat increased. Soon there were over a thousand sick in the Brigade, the ration strength of which fell to less than 1,800. It seemed useless to preserve the old formation, and General Vandeleur suggested that a composite battalion should be formed temporarily, till the heat was over and the sick had returned to their units.

Permission was given after some hesitation, but the reorganization had to be carried out in the midst of a move. For before it could be done orders were received for the Brigade to return to the Struma line from Gudeli Ferry to the bridge at Komarjan. The headquarters and one company of the new battalion were provided by the 10th Hampshire, and one company from each of the three other battalions. All the details marched back to Dremiglavia. On the night of August 27th the line was taken over, and as a few Bulgar shells fell next day near Komarjan Bridge, the Battalion may be said to have been in action that day for the first time since the previous year. It was rumoured that the Bulgars meant to do more than fire a few shells, and work in strengthening the position at once began. But whatever the intentions of the enemy may have been, they were not carried out owing to the ill-fated but seemingly promising entry of Rumania into the war.

Komarjan, north of the river, on the composite battalion's left flank, was known to be occupied by the Bulgars, and it was decided to carry out a reconnaissance in force to ascertain their disposition and inflict upon them as much loss as possible. Attacks were to be carried out simultaneously at either flank, that on the left, upon Komarjan, by the company formed from the 6th Royal Irish Rifles.

The company crossed by rafts after a ten minutes' bombardment by the 67th Brigade, R.F.A. and "A" Battery of the 54th Brigade, R.F.A., deployed on the left bank, and advanced in open order upon the village. From Komarjan there came fairly heavy rifle fire during the advance, but it was high, and caused little or no loss. Where the Riflemen reached close quarters the Bulgars for the most part did not stand. Such as did were taken prisoner. The attack passed through the village and a line beyond it was taken up. The position was risky, for there was always the chance that the company might at any moment be attacked by a force of three or four times its own strength. At 6.15 p.m. orders were issued for the withdrawal, and by 8.30 all the men were back on the right bank. The losses were 1 man killed, 1 wounded, and 1 missing, while 24 prisoners had been taken. The operation was essentially a minor one, and very different to what were known as minor operations on the Western Front. But it had been carried out with courage, speed, and high efficiency, which earned the praises of the powers that were. It had been established that the enemy held Komarjan as a piquet.

On the 23rd the Rifle Company, under Major Graham, again crossed the Struma, this time at the opposite end of the Brigade's front, at Gudeli Ferry, to cover the left flank of the 7th Mounted Brigade, which carried out a more distant reconnaissance. This operation also was carried out smartly, and apparently without loss. There being one raft only here available the troops were not back on the right bank till 3 a.m. on September 24th.

From this date onward the 6th Royal Irish Rifles was reorganized at a strength of three companies, but, according to the 29th Brigade's diary, the composite battalion did not cease to exist till October 11th.

II.—Operations in the Struma Valley and Capture of Jenikoj.

The reconnaissances which have been described were the prelude to an advance of some importance. Five miles north of the western end of Lake Tahinos is the town of Seres, through which runs the railway from Doiran to Adrianople and Constantinople. For some distance this railway runs parallel with the Struma. The Salonika—Seres road crosses both river and railway, the former near Orljak. On this road, about half-way between the two, is the important village of Jenikoj. It was determined to capture this place as a preliminary to cutting the railway, which must obviously have been of great assistance to the enemy. The beginning of the operation was to be the capture of the villages of Karadzakoj, Bola, and Zir by the 81st Brigade of the 27th Division, the left flank of which was to be covered by the 6th Royal Irish Rifles, two companies of the 6th Leinster, and six machine-guns; the whole force under the command of Lieut.-Colonel C. M. L. Becher, 6th Royal Irish Rifles. The attack was fixed for September 30th, the crossing to begin at 3 a.m.

The attack was a complete success, the Bulgar outposts being driven in before their troops in reserve realized what was happening. By 8.45 the force was digging in upon its position. But the enemy quickly recovered. A first counter-attack was beaten off by machine-gun fire at 11 a.m. An hour later another, from Jenikoj, directed upon Zir, was checked, but not without some difficulty, by the troops of the 81st Brigade. At 12.23 p.m. Colonel Becher reported that in view of the aggressive spirit shown by the enemy, his force was none too strong. Later in the afternoon the Cyclist Company was moved across to his right flank, and he also brought up his reserve platoon to close a small gap between his force and the 81st Brigade. His casualties had been not inconsiderable for fighting of this nature, one officer, Lieutenant Miller, having been killed, and 2 officers, Lieutenant A. T. M. Poore and 2nd-Lieutenant H. O'Halloran, and 16 other ranks wounded. The Bulgars had apparently lost heavily in their counter-attacks.

The dispositions of Colonel Becher's force on the morning of October 1st were then as follow:—One platoon 6th Royal Irish Rifles, the 10th Cyclist Company, the 6th Royal Irish Rifles (less one platoon), two companies 6th Leinster Regiment, from right to left. There was no infantry attack upon his force, though there were counter-attacks elsewhere. The line was, however, subjected to some shelling by the enemy's artillery. Patrols of the Royal Irish Rifles reached a point a thousand yards from Jenikoj. The following day the situation remained the same on the front of the force commanded by Colonel Becher. On its right there were repeated counter-attacks in the early hours of the morning. Twice the Bulgars entered Zir, but were each time ejected, many being bayoneted. Colonel Becher was now under the orders of the 30th Brigade, which was to continue the advance on the morrow, October 3rd.

The troops of the 30th Brigade duly passed through to the attack upon Jenikoj. They went forward in good style, and were in possession of the place by 7.20 a.m. But the Bulgars, well aware of the British object in making the advance, were not going to give in without stern resistance. A really heavy counter-attack was launched upon the village, and the next news Colonel Becher had, at 4.10 p.m., was that the 6th and 7th Dublins had been driven out in some confusion and that he was to go forward to their support. As it proved he had to do more than this. The two Dublin battalions were considerably disorganized. Colonel Becher, who had gone forward with his own battalion alone, therefore collected such bodies of them as he could, and sent back for the Leinster companies to move up also. By 5.15, when he had reached the southern end of the village, in face of considerable fire, these companies closed up with the Riflemen. The Bulgars did not await the new attack, and soon afterwards Jenikoj was again in our hands. The losses of the Battalion were one killed and 23 wounded.

There followed an absurd muddle. At 8.15 p.m. Colonel Becher received orders from the 30th Brigade to retire to his original position. An hour later, immediately after his return, a message arrived to the effect that the retirement was "cancelled." The order had been due to an error, but it was impossible to rectify it that night. Next morning the attack was carried out by the two Dublin battalions, now reorganized, the Royal Irish Rifles on the left, and the Composite Battalion on the right advancing in support. The village was taken for the third time, on this occasion without opposition. Work upon the consolidation of the new position, in both front line and support, was at once begun.

On the 9th the Battalion relieved the 6th Dublin Fusiliers in front line. Large numbers were now rejoining from hospital, and the sick-list was falling rapidly as the troops became to some extent acclimatized, and—still more important—as the temperature fell. On the 11th, as has been stated, the 29th Brigade was restored to its basis of four battalions. Next day the Crown Prince of Serbia visited Jenikoj and the trenches in its vicinity and congratulated the troops upon their advance. On the 24th the 6th Royal Irish Rifles took over the duties of outpost battalion at Kalendra, being relieved after two days.

III.—The Affair of Barakli-Jama'a.

We were not yet fully established upon the railway, and there was a further advance to be made from Jenikoj, astride the Seres road. This was carried out on the morning of October 31st by the 5th Connaught Rangers on the right and the 6th Royal Irish Rifles on the left. There was a "preliminary bombardment" at 7 a.m., which consisted in fact of a few ranging shots only. At 9 a.m. the troops went forward. Some of the spirit seemed to have gone out of the Bulgar infantry after their recent defeat. There was considerable shelling and musketry fire, but the fact that there were no casualties is conclusive proof that the latter was not at short range and that the enemy did not wait till our troops came to close quarters. The Connaught Rangers occupied the railway embankment south of Seres, and the Royal Irish Rifles, which had advanced as far as the Prosenyk Stream, the other side of the railway, was later withdrawn to the same line on the left. The advance had been conducted with good leadership, and the fact that it had been made with slight loss was due to its steadiness and even progression. The Bulgar may not be a first-class fighting man, like the Turk at his best, as the latter was seen on the Gallipoli Peninsula, but he is a sturdy enough peasant soldier, quick to act upon signs of hesitation in his opponent. Had he been in this campaign fighting with his heart in the business he would doubtless have been far more formidable and more like what he had been in the First Balkan War. The Battalion had 2 officers killed, 4 wounded, 4 other ranks killed and 24 wounded, the names of the officer casualties not being given.

On November 3rd the Battalion was relieved, the front being taken over by the 31st Brigade. At this time the 29th Brigade lost the 10th Hampshire, which had had a high record from the first, which was exchanged for the 1st Leinster Regiment with the 27th Division. Work on rear positions with some training continued throughout the month, till the 23rd, when the 29th Brigade re-entered the front line. The 6th Royal Irish Rifles was now at Nevoljen, with " D " Company some miles farther north at Topalova, on outpost duty. There it remained till December 28th, when it was relieved, and the whole Battalion withdrew to Orljak. The year ended with hard work on the Struma defences and the construction of a camp for divisional headquarters.

CHAPTER V

I.—THE 3RD, 4TH, AND 5TH BATTALIONS.

THIS is a suitable point in the history to give a short account of the work at home of the three battalions with which we are concerned that did not quit the British Isles, the 3rd, 4th, and 5th. The greater part of their record is not one that can be dealt with at length. It is for the most part a long list of recruits joining, of drafts sent to France, with occasional moves. Very hard and very important work was accomplished by their commanding officers and staffs in the training of the necessary reinforcements. But their existence was for the most part eventless. They lived, it may be said, only half their life at home. The other half was bound up with the battalions on active service abroad, which they fed with reinforcements, from which, in return, they received the sick and wounded when sufficiently recovered to leave hospital. They had, therefore, always in their ranks, particularly after the war had been going on for some time, a considerable number of officers and men not fully fit, but possessed, on the other hand, of priceless knowledge of the conditions of modern war.

The 3rd Battalion had but a short stay at Portobello Barracks in August, 1914, moving next to Wellington Barracks. On the 26th it sent out its first draft, under the command of 2nd-Lieutenant R. Magennis, consisting of 42 rank and file of the Army Reserve, and 2 sergeants and 49 rank and file of the Special Reserve. This draft joined the 2nd Battalion in France as its second reinforcement. Thereafter, for some time to come, drafts were sent to the 2nd Battalion, and a little later to the 1st, at the rate of two or three a month. The four-company formation came in at the end of August in this as in the other reserve battalions. A notable recruit was " Billy " the famous dog of the 2nd Battalion, who was brought over from Tidworth. He was now fifteen years old, and was said to have been taken from General Botha's farm in South Africa, being brought home by the 2nd Battalion on its return to England. The Battalion remained through the winter of 1914-1915 in Dublin, sending its recruits to Kilbride for their musketry. At the end of a year of war it had sent out forty-six reinforcements. On August 23rd, 1915, it despatched its first draft to the 6th Battalion, with the Mediterranean Expeditionary Force. It had now sent out since the beginning of the war 3,000 men. At a review of the Battalion on July 30th Major-General Friend, commanding the troops in Ireland, spoke in the highest terms of the work of Colonel McCammond and his staff.

The 4th Battalion moved to Carrickfergus from Hollywood in April, 1915. There Colonel McFerran took over command in succession to Colonel F. Findlay. Detachments were found for Kilroot Battery, Larne Harbour, and the very important cable station at Whitehead. Bombing instruction was given to the men during the spring. It is believed that the Battalion was the first in Ireland to give men this very useful training before they went out to France.

The 5th Battalion remained in Victoria Barracks till May, 1915, when it moved to Palace Barracks, Hollywood. Numerous drafts were sent out from it to France. In December, 1915, Lieut.-Colonel T. V. P. McCammon temporarily vacated the command in order to raise a new battalion (the 20th), which he did in a very short time. During his absence Major Swettenham was in command, and he a few months later succeeded him as Commanding Officer. Colonel McCammon, after many applications, was sent to France, and fell mortally wounded at Monchy in April, 1916, a very short time after his arrival in the country.

II.—The Rebellion of Easter Week in Ireland.

In that month there broke out the disastrous revolt known as the " Easter Week Rebellion." There were risings all over the country, but the only place in which it can be said to have been a serious menace to England, then in the midst of her preparations for the Battle of the Somme, was in the capital. The civil authorities had shown an almost criminal remissness in refusing to see the danger signals. Fortunately, the military, under Sir John Maxwell's leadership, acted promptly and efficiently. It was necessary not only to strike hard but to strike very quickly. Otherwise the whole country might have risen and England been involved in a guerilla warfare like that which came after peace had been signed with Germany, which would have distracted her energies and robbed her of the reinforcements for her great offensive campaign in France. Moreover, a long campaign would have brought far more suffering and misery, with destruction of life and property, to the country.

The 3rd Battalion was in Portobello Barracks, Dublin. It was much depleted in strength owing to the large number of drafts sent out. A great proportion of the rank and file was composed of recruits in training, but all, when called upon, behaved most gallantly, acted with forbearance, and worthily upheld the traditions of the Regiment.

On Easter Monday morning the troops were off parade, prepared to enjoy themselves, and a holiday mood pervaded the barracks. The alarm was brought by 2nd-Lieutenant C. R. W. McCammond, of the 19th Battalion, who was on leave from his own battalion on a visit to his father, Lieut.-Colonel W. E. C. McCammond. The latter, unfortunately, was in bed with an attack of pleurisy, and the Battalion was deprived of his leadership during the days that followed. The command had devolved upon Major J. Rosborough in his absence.

Lieutenant McCammond had been in Dublin, and about noon, when returning on horseback to barracks, was set upon by rebels at Portobello Bridge. These had established themselves in Davy's public-house, which overlooked the bridge and commanded the Rathmines Road and Richmond Street. A number came out of the house to attack him, while others fired at him from the windows. Fortunately they were incredibly bad marksmen. Lieutenant McCammond got clear, only slightly wounded, and rode on to barracks to give the alarm.

Orders were received at 12.40 p.m. from the Garrison Adjutant to have all available men paraded with 50 rounds of ammunition. Some minutes later the Officer Commanding the troops in Dublin, Colonel Kennaird, rode into barracks. Small columns were then organized. The first party to leave Portobello consisted of 2 officers and 50 other ranks under Major W. S. B. Leatham. It had orders to move to Dublin Castle. On approaching Portobello Bridge the rebels in Davy's public-house opened fire from the barricade and loop-holed windows, and as the building was in a commanding position it was decided to capture it from the Sinn Feiners. During the attack Major Leatham was severely wounded, and Lieutenant Battersby was shot through the hand. A second column under Major W. G. T. Rigg, which left barracks at 1.10 p.m., for the Castle, reinforced Major Leatham's party, and the assault upon the rebel stronghold was successfully carried out.

Information being received that the Telephone Exchange was in danger of falling into the hands of the insurgents, 2nd-Lieutenant J. Kearns left with 25 men at 1.45 p.m. to forestall them and take possession of the building. After an adventurous journey through the streets the party just managed to get there first, being fiercely attacked soon after its arrival. The rebels were beaten off, and the Exchange remained throughout the period in the hands of our men. It was a remarkable and fortunate circumstance that the leaders of the revolt, at the time when they " captured " the much less important General Post Office and other public buildings, neglected to possess and garrison the Telephone Exchange. The telephone afforded the principal means of military communication, and proved invaluable.

At 1.50 p.m. 100 men under Captain Rodwell left with orders to push through to the Castle by way of Camden Street. The column was fired on from houses on both sides of the street and eventually held up at the junction of Cuffe Street and Camden Street. Here 2nd-Lieutenant J. H. Calvert was killed by a bullet, which passed through his head, fired from a window just above him. After some fighting the party reached the Castle by way of South Circular Road. The Bank of Ireland guard was furnished by the Battalion, and the small party did splendid work in resisting the attempts of the rebels to obtain possession of the Bank. Sergeant W. Morris was in command during the whole period. The defence of the barracks was left to employed and unfit men and to non-commissioned officers and Royal Irish Constabulary attending the Portobello School of Instruction. During the day many officers and men of various units, in the city on business or on leave, took refuge there, making a welcome addition to the garrison.

On Tuesday, April 25th, reinforcements arrived from the Curragh, Belfast, and England, and a military cordon was drawn round the city. Martial Law was proclaimed. But no attempt was made on this day to oust the rebels from the central fortresses, and there is nothing of importance to record for this period of twenty-four hours.

On Wednesday officers were told off to deal with the notification and collection of reports, search parties, examination of rebel prisoners and documents. Small parties were sent out to search houses reported to be occupied by Sinn Feiners. Many of these were fired on, and some sustained casualties.

On Thursday, the 27th, a party of 150 under Major Sir Francis Fane, attacked the South Dublin Union Workhouse, held in force by the rebels. It was found impossible to obtain complete possession of it without artillery, but the principal object was achieved, as a supply column from the Curragh, which had been held up here, was enabled to proceed to its destination. Armoured cars now appeared on the streets for the first time. They had been ingeniously planned by Colonel H. T. W. Allatt, who had, as draft conducting officer, taken many men of the Battalion across the sea, and were made up under his direction at the Inchicore Railway Works. Each was formed of an engine-boiler mounted on a large motor-lorry. The lorries were placed at the disposal of the military by Messrs. Guinness. They were extremely useful. The Battalion, save for its garrisons on detachment, was now outside the main zone of operations, in the centre of the city, but heard all day long the rattle of machine-gun fire and the boom of artillery. The glare of burning houses lent an awful grandeur to the nights. About 6 p.m. on Saturday news arrived of the unconditional surrender of the rebels in Sackville Street, and at the Royal College of Surgeons, Stephen's Green. On Sunday the remaining 600 rebels in Jacob's

Biscuit Factory, which had been bombarded from the Liffey, also surrendered. There was no more of the rebellion beyond a little desultory sniping, which continued for the next two days.

The Battalion had had casualties comparatively severe. Second-Lieutenant J. H. Calvert was killed, Majors Rigg and Leatham, 2nd-Lieutenants Battersby and McCammond wounded. Of other ranks there were 5 killed, including C.Q.M.S. J. Coyle, and 20 wounded.

On May 4th the Battalion was inspected by the Commander-in-Chief, Sir John Maxwell, who at the conclusion of his inspection spoke in very high terms of its conduct during the recent disturbances. These men had been called upon to perform a duty always distasteful to soldiers, and may have had to fire upon friends or even relatives. They had done their duty without question. On the other hand, they had acted with forbearance. Sir John added that His Majesty the King had learned with great pleasure of the loyalty of his Irish regiments in these trying circumstances. Colonel McCammond received also from the Commander and Secretary, Royal Hospital, Kilmainham, the Chief Ordnance Officer, Island Bridge, and the Governors and Directors of the Bank of Ireland, letters of warm praise for the conduct of the garrisons supplied by the Battalion during the outbreak. The Bank of Ireland, with the consent of Colonel McCammond, presented £5 to Sergeant Morris, £3 to Lance-Corporal Lehane, and £2 each to the six Riflemen of the Guard. It is interesting to find among these No. 14430 Rifleman J. Emerson. It was he who, having been given a commission in the Royal Inniskilling Fusiliers, won a Victoria Cross by an action of outstanding valour on Welsh Ridge, in December, 1917. With a hole in his steel helmet and blood running down his face from a bomb-splinter in his skull, he held off German attacks with a handful of men for several hours, finally counter-attacking over the open and driving the enemy back. His wounds were mortal.

On May 6th the 3rd Battalion left Portobello Barracks, Dublin, for Victoria Barracks, Belfast, where it remained for the rest of the year.

The 4th Battalion likewise was concerned in the Easter Week Rebellion. It sent one company under Captain W. E. S. Howard, which formed part of a composite rifle battalion despatched from the north. The Company's casualties were two Riflemen killed and several wounded.

In August, 1916, all men under 18 years 8 months were transferred to the 5th Battalion. In November the 4th Battalion moved to Newry, where, though an active anti-enlistment campaign was being carried out by the Sinn Fein element, it had a good reception from people of all creeds, and had always cordial relations with the people of the town.

The 5th Battalion remained at Hollywood till April, 1918, when it moved for the summer to Clandeboye Camp, which had been built for the training of the 108th Brigade of the 36th (Ulster) Division.

BOOK IV: 1917.

CHAPTER I.

I.—THE GERMAN RETREAT TO THE HINDENBURG LINE.

THE year 1917 opened with high hopes and ended in deep disappointment. The offensive plans worked out by Sir Douglas Haig and General Joffre were modified by the latter's supersession by General Nivelle, and by the German retirement to the Hindenburg Line. We had fine successes at Vimy Ridge and Messines, but the latter was to be but a prelude to a very ambitious scheme for the clearance of the Flanders coast, and it was only the prelude that was successful. " Third Ypres " was the most terrible of the battles fought by British soldiers, and it had to be continued under impossible conditions owing to the failure of Nivelle's great offensive and its crippling effect upon the French Army. None of the battalions of the Royal Irish Rifles were to take part in the Arras fighting, but all three were to be heavily engaged in the battles of Flanders.

The 1st Battalion we left in line in the Sailly-Saillisel area. The front here was now comparatively quiet, but it was very exposed and the outposts could not be visited by day. There were no continuous trenches. If the posts could not be visited by day, they were not very pleasant to visit by night, for officers inspecting, or reliefs, or ration-carriers, for then the visitors stumbled blindly about amid shell-holes and tangled wire, with about equal chance of being shot by their friends or walking into the lines of their enemies. After relief on January 3rd, the Battalion, somewhat to its surprise, was sent back by train to its former very pleasant abode at Laleu, and there remained training till the 23rd, when it returned to the front line at Rancourt, slightly south of the former position. Snow had now begun to fall and there was setting in one of the bitterest six weeks that Northern Europe has experienced for many years. The fiercest cold of all was between February 1st and 18th. On one occasion 32 degrees of frost were recorded. The men bore the cold well. Indeed, acute as were the sufferings which it caused, the intensest cold had far less effect upon the health of the troops than the wet. The frost had also certain advantages with regard to the work necessary to improve the position. Digging was impossible; so was wiring. Neither spade, pick, nor iron picket could be driven into the ground. But the engineers' stores, so hard to bring up over swampy ground, could now be easily dumped near the front line.

A thaw came just before the 25th Brigade, after some more training near Bray-sur-Somme, returned to the line at the end of February. The roads and trenches were now in a frightful state. The men of the 11th Brigade, whom they relieved, before Bouchavesnes, were in pitiable condition. Some had to be dug out before they could go. One died of exhaustion. Those who have experienced these horrible nights in mud and water above the waist, with men whimpering in the darkness from sheer fatigue and calling to their comrades to aid them with shovels or to hold out to them the butts of rifles, will realize why our troops on the Somme did not fear the frost.

During this period the 25th Brigade came under a new commander, Brigadier-General C. Coffin, D.S.O. By a curious coincidence it was to be under his leadership, as divisional commander, in another division, that the 1st Battalion Royal Irish Rifles was to march to final victory, the following year. But victory was a long way off still, and much was to happen in the intervening eighteen months.

It was under the terrible conditions which have been described that the 8th Division carried out a new attack on March 4th. It was quite a small operation, which had for object the capture of ground from which the enemy had close observation of the Bouchavesnes Valley and the valley north-west of it to Rancourt. On the right of the 24th Brigade the 25th was to attack upon a narrow frontage, with one battalion, the 2nd Royal Berkshire. From the British trench to the final objective the distance was under 500 yards. This was a trench known as " Fritz Trench." The German front line, a couple of hundred yards west of Fritz Trench, and parallel to it, was known as " Pallas Trench." On the 25th Brigade front no other infantry than the Royal Berkshire, except six platoons of the 2nd Lincolnshire, acting as " moppers up," were to take part but the Royal Irish Rifles knew they would probably be called upon to bring up S.A.A. and bombs at a later period.

The attack of the Royal Berkshire was a complete success. It was launched at 5.15 a.m. At 5.40 a.m. it was reported that Pallas Trench was in our hands, by 5.55 the first prisoner was in the Battalion headquarters, and at 6.10 it was learnt that the three companies were in Fritz Trench. Some of the troops overshot this battered trench and went on to the next, Bremen Trench, but were driven back by our barrage. At noon came the first call upon the Royal Irish Rifles. One company was ordered to carry up ammunition to the Royal Berkshire, and two Lewis-gun teams were put at the disposal of the latter Battalion. Then, at 6 p.m., came orders to relieve the 2nd Lincolnshire in the old British front line. This was accomplished with some difficulty, amidst heavy shelling. About 7.30 p.m. the Germans counter-attacked heavily, and regained about a hundred yards of Fritz Trench, but within two hours had been driven out. The Lewis gunners of the Royal Irish Rifles were engaged in this affair, three being killed. The total casualties in the Battalion were thirty, those of the Royal Berkshire very heavy.

Next evening the Battalion took over the new line, with " D " Company in Fritz Trench, and " C " Company in Pallas Trench. Shelling was heavy, and the inevitable consolidation, amid dead friends and foes whom there was no time to bury, an unpleasant task. As proof of the weight of the enemy's fire it may be noted that the Battalion had 5 killed and 19 wounded during the twenty-four hours of March 7th. The following evening it was relieved by the 2nd Rifle Brigade and withdrew to Bouchavesnes, where Captain G. W. Calverley was gassed, 2nd-Lieutenants L. Bayly and P. Quinn (Munster Fusiliers) wounded, 5 other ranks killed and 18 wounded. By the time it returned to the front line the latter had grown much quieter.

It had for some time been apparent to the British command that the enemy was about to carry out an important retirement. In February he had evacuated his positions west of the line Le Transloy—Loupart Wood and north of the Albert—Bapaume road. Hurried by successful attacks, of which that recorded by the 8th Division had been one among many, he was now preparing to move back to the famous Hindenburg Line, which ran from south-east of Arras, across the Bapaume—Cambrai road about half-way between the two towns, east of St. Quentin, through La Fère. The retirement was, it has been said, expected, and the troops had been warned to be prepared for it and to keep in touch, but in the present weather conditions, with the destruction which the enemy was known to be carrying out, there was small hope of being able to inflict serious injury upon him.

The 1st Royal Irish Rifles was in front line on March 17th. About 2 p.m. its patrols found Bremen Trench unoccupied, and by evening they were approaching Moislains. This village was entered about 4.30 a.m. next morning, and later in the day posts were established on the Canal du Nord. On the 19th other troops took up the pursuit, the Battalion withdrawing to rest at Bouchavesnes. With the best will in the world the British could do little. Every possible device to hinder them had been employed. At every cross-roads huge craters had been blown, while trees had been cut down and thrown across the roads. On the Bapaume—Cambrai road there must have been thousands of the big poplars that so often flank national roads in France dealt with in this manner. The villages outside the shelled area had been systematically destroyed. The destruction of the fruit trees is too well-known to be discussed here, but it was one of those petty acts of vileness peculiarly significant of a barbaric nation, which filled the whole civilized world with disgust.

On March 26th, when the Battalion marched up again to the front line, the latter was beyond Riverside Wood, near Manancourt. The enemy was still holding Fins and Sorel, as was proved by patrols which pushed down the valley towards these villages at night. Some progress was made on the 27th, but not a great deal. The enemy was not prepared to step into the Hindenburg Line at this point—probably his demolitions were not finished—and he was resisting strongly at Fins and Sorel. The Battalion was back again at Riverside Wood when these villages were finally occupied, the first by the 2nd Royal Berkshire, the second by the Rifle Brigade. On the afternoon of the 30th the Battalion marched to Equancourt, just as the Rifle Brigade was about to attack Dessart Wood, east of Fins and north of the road from that village to Gouzeaucourt. This operation the Battalion was ordered to cover on the right, and one platoon was detailed to move forward south of the Fins—Gouzeaucourt road to support the attack.

Heavy machine-gun fire met the attacking battalion as the men rose from the cover of a sunken road, and for a moment it seemed that the attack would fail. Then Colonel Brand, the commanding officer of the 2nd Rifle Brigade, seeing what was happening, got out of the road and led his men forward. Meanwhile No. 5 Platoon " B " Company 1st Royal Irish Rifles, attempting to fulfil its task on the right flank, also came under fire, apparently from two German machine guns. Lieutenant Brown, in command of the platoon, then worked his way forward with his Lewis-gun team to engage them. The southern of the two German guns, on the main road, was quickly silenced, but the detachment, thinking discretion the better part of valour, fell back in safety. The second German team held on longer, which was its undoing. Lieutenant Brown's gun killed half the team, the others were captured, and his Corporal, Massey, captured the gun. Without doubt this brilliant little action was of great service to the Rifle Brigade, which soon afterwards took Dessart Wood with several prisoners.*

In the evening two companies of the Battalion, " B " and " C," were pushed forward to Revelon Farm, while Battalion headquarters moved into Sorel-le-Grand. " Booby-traps " had been left everywhere by the disagreeable Boche, and nothing seemed safe to touch. Headquarters found a good dug-out, but decided to move out of it as soon as a hut could be put up, since they suspected an acid time-fuse bomb, a very favoured device of the enemy, and one which caused us heavy loss at the Town Hall in Bapaume.

* For this action Lieutenant Brown received a Bar to his M.C.

The British were working their way forward to the Hindenburg Line, driving back the last German rearguards which remained between them and it. The Battalion did not come in for any of the fighting in which its brigade was engaged during this phase. On the 4th it was in reserve to an attack on Gouzeaucourt Wood, as a result of which the front was advanced very close to the Hindenburg Line. Gonnelieu, however, still held out, and the 2nd Lincolnshire did not take it till the 21st, as the result of a fine action, in which the Germans fought most stoutly but lost over a hundred prisoners. On the 24th the 40th Division took Villers-Plouich and Beaucamp, and the two sides were now in the positions they were to occupy till the Battle of Cambrai at the end of the year.

Hard work began as soon as a regular line was formed. It was very necessary, for the present position was that the enemy was behind almost impregnable fortifications, and our troops were in the open, in great danger in case of a surprise attack. No one minded work here, however. The men were in good spirits after the advance, and above all after leaving behind them the horrible muddy waste of the battlefield. Here the country was somewhat dreary, because the villages had been destroyed, but it was pleasant country in more or less its natural state, not ploughed up by shell-fire. It was a new sensation to hold trenches in the midst of such. In mid-May the Brigade moved back to Nurlu, in corps reserve. Here there was plenty of sport intermingled with the training for battle. The Royal Irish Rifles particularly distinguished themselves. In football they won the Brigade Championship very easily, scoring fourteen goals to one in three matches, while in the boxing championships they won both light and feather-weight events. The end of May, the period covered by this chapter, found the Battalion once more on the move, on its way north to Flanders.

II.—THE 2ND BATTALION IN EARLY 1917.

The 2nd Battalion in Ploegsteert Wood began the New Year with a liveliness rather unwonted in that sector. The Battalion was in the support trenches of the wood, on the afternoon of January 22nd, when an intense bombardment broke out all along the front. By 4.30 p.m. it had become very heavy indeed, so heavy that for a time it seemed likely that an important attack was coming. S.O.S. rockets went up at various parts of the front, and the order came to reinforce all the forts in Ploegsteert Wood. What the Germans were actually about to attempt was a whole series of raids, after having, as they hoped, almost destroyed the front-line garrison by their fire. One party entered our line at a wet gap between the 74th and 75th Brigades. This was beaten back by our cross-fire, and subsequently a wounded German officer and dead soldier were brought in by our men. A second party had no better fortune, and, as it was retiring a shell from one of the great German *minnenwerfers* was seen to drop in its midst and completely destroy it. One party only, out of four, entered our trenches opposite St. Yves, and it was driven back by a counter-attack. When the entry of this party was reported, at 5.30 p.m., "A" Company of the 2nd Royal Irish Rifles was moved up to support the 11th South Lancashire, but the enemy was gone when it arrived. The 11th South Lancashire had had very heavy casualties, there being 16 other ranks killed, and 3 officers and 23 other ranks wounded, but the enemy must have had serious losses also, and his venture had been a complete failure. The Battalion had 2nd-Lieutenants W. J. McDonnell and W. J. S. Kydd wounded. Its other losses in officers during this period were Lieutenant Leach and 2nd-Lieutenant Jackson killed.

THE NORTHERN BATTLEFIELD OF THE SOMME

British Line July 1st 1916 marked in blue
Hindenburg Line marked in red.

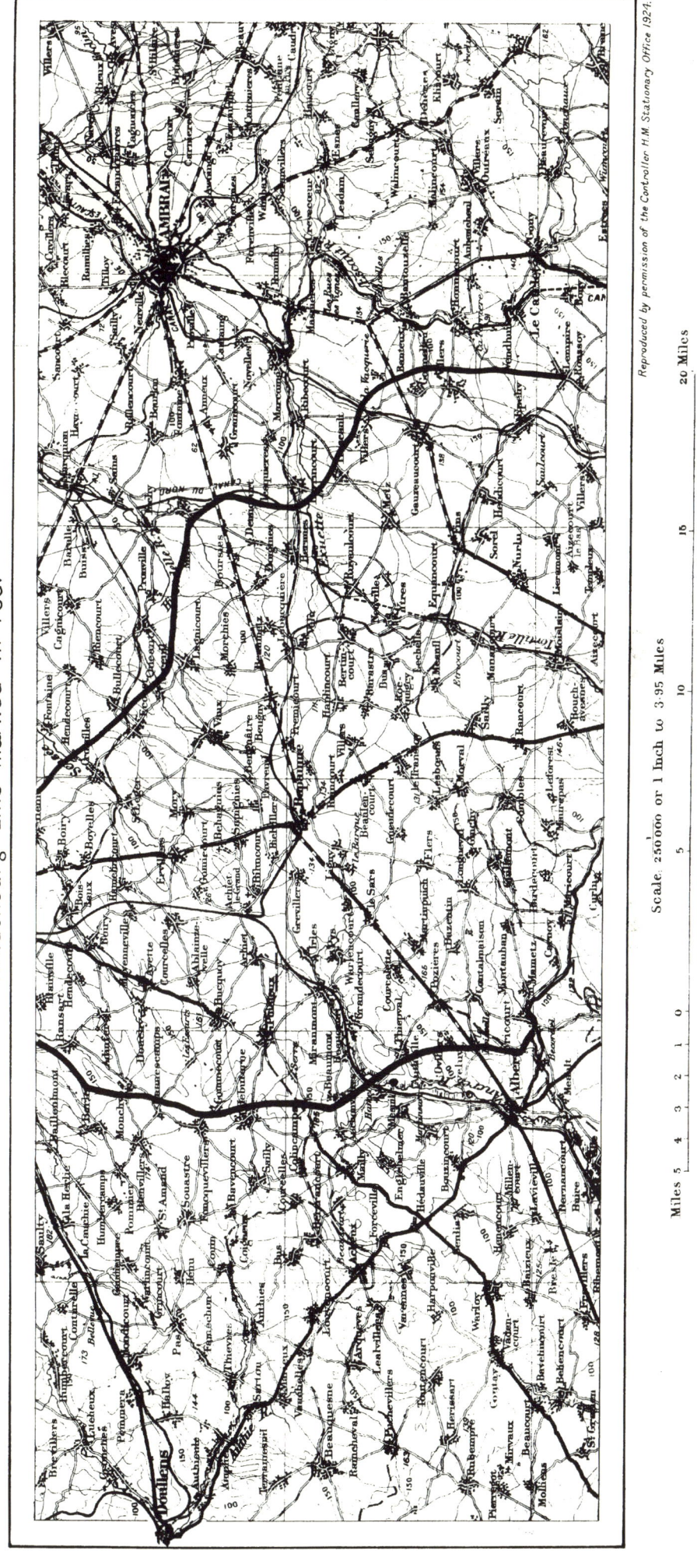

The cold here was even more intense than upon the Somme. One used at that time in Flanders to come upon rows of dead thrushes by the roadside, and it is said that certain rarer types of song-birds have not been seen in that country since then. But the conditions under which the troops lived were very different from those of the Somme. They had adequate shelter, and generally adequate fuel. When the latter was lacking, the " duck-boards " of trenches and other timber disappeared mysteriously, and it became necessary to take severe disciplinary measures—even to the cancelling of a battalion's leave allotment for a certain period in some cases.

Early in February the Brigade went into divisional reserve, at Le Romarin, and began training in the attack. Fuller and more thorough training followed from the 22nd onward, when the 74th Brigade moved back to the Caestre area, the Royal Irish Rifles being located at Tattinghem. Here the billets were excellent for everyone, and a battalion mess was established. Some battalions always made a point of establishing a single officers' mess whenever they were far enough from the line to make it possible, but in general there were none except on the comparatively rare occasions when troops found themselves in back areas and engaged in training. Practice attacks were the chief features of the new training, with some musketry on the range, and the troops began to think they were " in for " an immediate operation. Perhaps such was the intention, but, if so, it was altered by the German withdrawal to the Hindenburg Line.

At the end of March the Battalion returned to its old area. It was for some time engaged in working parties, then, in the middle of the month of April, re-entered the line, this time north of Ploegsteert Wood, with headquarters at a rather famous ruined house known as St. Quentin Cabaret. The great Messines offensive, the most thoroughly prepared of any of our attacks in the course of the war, was drawing near, and there was hard work at this period, battalions out of the trenches having to find large parties for carrying. The Battalion attempted several silent raids, but none were successful. The great increase in our artillery and infantry activity upon this front had caused the enemy to evacuate his front line—permanently, as it appeared—and his second whenever there was the merest hint of aggression on our part.

The Battalion was singularly lucky in the amount of training it was given for the coming battle. On May 25th it was entrained from Bailleul to Watten, and marched to Tournehem, where the British Army had rented a large tract of land, which it used as a training area. Here on three days attacks were carried out against " dummy " trenches marked out to represent those on the Messines—Wytschaete Ridge which the Battalion was to attack. Then the Battalion returned to La Crèche and was engaged in final battle-practice up to the very eve of the attack.

III.—THE 7TH BATTALION IN EARLY 1917.

The 7th Battalion, in line opposite Wytschaete, began the year 1917 with a raid on the Petit Bois Salient in the enemy's lines. This was carried out under the command of Captain D. Scallard, by three parties, under the leadership of 2nd-Lieutenant H. Boyle, 2nd-Lieutenant M. Hartery, and Captain Barnett, at 3 a.m. on January 4th. It was a surprise, and all three parties entered the enemy's trenches, inflicting considerable loss on him. But the Germans rallied, and a hard bombing fight ensued. Unfortunately it was impossible to take any prisoners. Our casualties were very light, two men only wounded.

There is little to record for the next two months. This part of the line was fairly quiet and casualties as a rule were light. There was a curious scare on the Second Army front at this time, the fierce frost having turned the inundations which protected the Belgian front to solid ice and made them no longer an obstacle. The Battalion was called upon to do a lot of wiring when it was out of the trenches—difficult work, when the ground was like iron. On one occasion the Battalion missed its baths at Locre owing to the frost.

On March 8th the Germans carried out against the Battalion one of those monster raids, the memory of which causes in the private soldier's breast mirth or anger, according to his temperament, when historians gravely inform him that the enemy was markedly inferior to us in the organization of such enterprises. From morning till 2.30 p.m., there was intermittently heavy fire, which damaged our wire defences. Then, at 3.30 p.m., a terrific bombardment, with all calibres of artillery, and huge trench mortars, followed an hour's pause. Portions of our trenches were so battered as to be completely obliterated and large numbers killed and wounded. After seventy minutes of this terrible punishment, while the survivors in the first two lines were crouching in what remained of their trenches, dazed and stunned by its violence, the German artillery put down a regular creeping barrage, behind which three parties, each almost fifty strong, advanced to the attack. The right party was beaten off with loss by a plucky Lewis-gun team. The centre and left entered our trenches and penetrated to the second line, driving back the remnants of the garrison. A counter-attack by the reserve company, organized and led with great gallantry by Major Rigg, drove out the enemy within a quarter of an hour of his entry into our trenches. He left 4 wounded prisoners and 3 dead in the hands of the Riflemen. The latter's losses were, for a raid, very heavy indeed. Lieutenant Henley was killed, Captain Barnett, 2nd-Lieutenants Thompson, Corrigan, Owens, Young, and Hartery wounded. There were 7 other ranks killed, 31 wounded, and 25 missing. The affair must count as an important success to the Germans, though probably not nearly all the missing were prisoners of war. Most of the Battalion's casualties were caused by the preliminary bombardment, in which some men were doubtless blown to pieces. The enemy, on the other hand, suffered also somewhat severely, for besides those left in the Battalion's hands, dead and wounded were also observed in " No Man's Land."

In April the 7th Battalion visited the area in which the 2nd carried out its training a little later, Tournehem. It remained here twelve days, four being devoted to company training, four to battalion, and four to brigade. Then it returned to its old Vierstraat sector. Almost at once there was an unfortunate occurrence, Captain Scallard, M.C., who had carried out the raid already recorded, being waylaid by a German party in " No Man's Land " and captured with two men. May was occupied with work, digging miles of new trenches, laying miles of tram-way, dumping hundreds of thousand shells and thousands of trench-mortar bombs for the Battle of Messines.

CHAPTER II

I.—The Battle of Messines, 1917: The 2nd Battalion.

The Flanders front had been selected for a great offensive in the summer of 1917 for good reasons. The German submarine menace was becoming more and more serious, and Zeebrugge and Ostend were its most dangerous bases. From our present line to the Dutch frontier the distance was comparatively short, not thirty miles, but it would require a very much shorter advance to cause the enemy to evacuate the coast. To have brought the Bruges—Ghent—Brussels railway under the effective fire of our howitzers would have been at any rate the beginning of the end, so far as the enemy's hold upon the coast was concerned. Plans were prepared for a coastal landing with the aid of naval forces and an attack by tanks which were to scale the sea-wall at Ostend, but these operations were only to be carried out if and when the main assault of the Fifth Army, attacking from the Salient, had progressed sufficiently far for them to have a chance of success. That moment, as all the world knows, never arrived. The Battles of Ypres, 1917, were a strategical failure. The weather was against us, and wet weather in Flanders soil constitutes a very exceptional handicap. Some writers have spoken as if this had been the sole cause of our failure. But one of equal importance was the skill of the German commanders, above all Sixt von Armin, in instituting a new system of group-defence in depth to meet our attacks, and the tenacity of the German troops who carried it out, fighting as well in little isolated bodies under junior officers or non-commissioned officers as they had fought in continuous trench lines, where they were under the control of battalion and regimental commanders. On our side the devotion was as great or greater, and the success that was achieved was due to a bull-dog courage in the British soldier which in all his long hard fighting history even he has probably never equalled.

The first step in the Flanders operations was to be the capture of the important Messines—Wytschaete Ridge, which would cut away the southern flank of the Ypres Salient and deny to the Germans high ground which would have been of priceless value in combating the major attack. In this preliminary battle the 2nd Battalion Royal Irish Rifles took part, while the 7th was in divisional reserve on the same day.

The 74th Brigade was to attack the ridge just north of the Wulverghem—Messines road, with its right upon Swayne's Farm on the Messines—Wytschaete road, and its left a hundred yards south of Four Huns Farm. The frontage of the Brigade was about 1,100 yards at the starting line, and narrowed down to about 700 yards on the Messines—Wytschaete road. This narrowing of the frontage was universal, as the British were attacking a marked salient, the capture of which would reduce the length of their line upon the front of attack by at least a third. The attack was to be carried out by the 2nd Royal Irish Rifles on the right, and the 13th Cheshire on the left in front line, followed by the 9th Loyal North Lancashire on the right and the 11th Lancashire Fusiliers on the left. The objective of the two first battalions was the line of the Steenbeke Brook, which runs across the slope of the ridge in a marshy valley, and was here almost exactly parallel to the British front line, at a distance of 800 yards from it. Upon this line the other two battalions were to pass through the leaders, for the attack on the Messines—

Wytschaete road, their exact objective being a trench known as " October Support," just beyond it. Upon the line of October Support the 75th Brigade was to pass through the 74th (and the 7th, upon its left) to attack the enemy's third main line of defence, running through Fanny's Farm. The final objective of the British attack, the Oostaverne Line, was to be captured by the troops of the 4th Australian Division.

" C " and " D " Companies were to advance in three waves, the objective of the leading wave being the German support line, Ugly Support, one platoon being allotted the " mopping up " of any dug-outs that might exist between it and the front line. Meanwhile, on the right, " B " Company was to advance in line of platoons, with sections in file, twenty yards interval between sections and thirty yards distance between platoons, and the two leading platoons to capture the very important " pill-box " stronghold of Ontario Farm. The third platoon, when the barrage lifted, was to go forward with " A " Company, which passed through " C " and " D " to the attack upon a strongly fortified work known as Ozone Strong Point, just west of the Steenbeke, known to be full of dug-outs, where heavy fighting might be expected. After capturing its objective it was to advance to the stream and, so far as was possible, clear the wire from its bed. After the 9th Loyal North Lancashire had passed through, " B " and " C " Companies with the Lewis-gun sections of " A " and " D" were to form up in artillery formation east of the Steenbeke and advance behind that battalion, to take over from it the intermediate line, half-way between the stream and the Messines—Wytschaete road. The task of the other companies would then be the consolidation of the ground captured by them.

The artillery scheme for this battle, which cannot be dealt with in detail in a regimental history, was as perfect as had ever been worked out upon the Western Front. The barrage was highly complicated, as the advance varied in pace owing to the varying distances to be covered, but the whole thing had been worked out so carefully that there was no hitch.

At 1 p.m. on June 6th two platoons of " B " Company entered the trenches and took over the Battalion's frontage from the 75th Brigade. At night the remainder of the Battalion, 21 officers, 616 other ranks, marched up through Wulverghem to its position of assembly. This was the fifth day of the preliminary bombardment of the ridge, and the enemy was fully alive to what was coming. He was shelling heavily the neighbourhood of Wulverghem, which caused a few casualties. Otherwise, the assembly was very successful and there were few casualties between the time of its completion, 11 p.m., and " Zero," at 3.10 next morning.

At " Zero " came the deafening roar and flash and dust-cloud of the great semi-circle of mines which have made the battle famous and will never allow it to be forgotten. The mine on the front of the Battalion did rather more than had been expected of it. The platoons detailed to attack Ontario Farm found their occupation gone. The strong-point was completely destroyed. Where it had been was a vast crater.

Closely following the barrage, the waves went forward. In the German front line resistance there was little or none. The moral effect of the mine had without doubt been enormous. Dazed and terrified, the survivors surrendered at once. Our barrage was perfect ; the enemy shelling negligible. Behind the German front line there was a certain amount of resistance, but it was isolated and was speedily overcome. At 3.30 a.m. all ground west of the Steenbeke was in our hands. The 9th Loyal North Lancashire passed through successfully.

At " Zero+90," that is at 4.40 a.m., " A " and " B " Companies went forward across the stream to fulfil their task of consolidation farther forward. It was then perceived that there was trouble in front. The 9th Loyal North Lancashire was meeting with stubborn opposition upon the crest, at Middle Farm, on the Messines—Wytschaete road. " B " Company, under Captain T. J. Thompson, then pushed forward to work round the farm from the right. Largely owing to the skill and gallantry of this officer the manœuvre was completely successful, and the resistance of the enemy brought to an end. Consolidation, that inevitable task, which made demands so high on the soldier's energy, when the excitement and strain of attack had brought reaction, was then everywhere begun, to be continued throughout the day and the following night. The farther advance to the Oostaverne Line was carried out in the afternoon with complete success.

Messines was a triumph of organization in every form. The pack transport, which brought up food, ammunition, and wire, worked without a hitch. Within a few hours of the advance hot tea was brought up to the men in large containers. The men were so delighted with their success that they had to be restrained from walking about in the open under the fire of German artillery, now bombarding the ridge from behind the rampart of the Ypres—Comines Canal. Losses had been heavy, but there was, most happily, an exceptionally small number of killed, and captures had been so large that they can hardly have been exceeded in many cases by any one battalion in the whole course of the war. Two officers had been killed, Lieutenant S. J. O'Brien and 2nd-Lieutenant W. Dobbie ; while Captain Thompson and 2nd-Lieutenants R. S. Noble, H. C. Mallett, H. Marshall, and E. J. Williams had been wounded. Of other ranks, 14 were killed and 216 wounded. The captures were 200 prisoners, 5 machine guns, 2 trench mortars, and a great quantity of ammunition and stores. The Battalion remained two days longer on the slopes of the ridge, frequently under very heavy fire, before being withdrawn to bivouac in the old British front-line trench. After a tour of duty in the support trenches, during which it was visited by the corps commander, Sir A. Godley, it moved up on the 17th to relieve the 8th South Lancashire of the 75th Brigade in the new front line near Warneton. This was a very unpleasant position, as it was on a forward slope and exposed to the enemy's artillery. The Battalion had, however, but three days in front line followed by two in the support trenches southeast of Messines. On the 23rd the whole Brigade was relieved. The Battalion was taken back by bus to Caudescure, and then had a three days' march to Fruges, where it began a fortnight's training for the further fighting which awaited it in the Flanders battle.

II.—THE BATTLE OF MESSINES, 1917 : THE 7TH BATTALION.

The 36th Division attacked on the left of the 25th in the Battle of Messines, with the 16th Division on its left, the latter having its right flank upon the centre of Wytschaete, the northern half of which village was captured by the troops of the division. The 48th Brigade, in which was the 7th Royal Irish Rifles, was in reserve for the battle. On the front of the 16th Division all went likewise according to plan. The Battalion took up its position an hour before " Zero " in the Vierstraat Switch, a reserve line. At 8 a.m. it received verbal orders to move up and occupy our old front line, with the 2nd Royal Dublin Fusiliers. It was in position by 9.30, and remained there all day, sending up some carrying parties to the troops of the 47th and 49th Brigades upon their objectives.

At 4 a.m. on June 8th the Battalion moved forward to relieve the troops of the 47th Brigade on the " Black " and " Blue " lines which were positions, the former about 500 yards east of Wytschaete, and the latter about 400 yards west of it, through

Wytschaete Wood. They were, of course, support and reserve positions, since the Oostaverne Line had been captured, but they were of high importance, in the event of a strong counter-attack, since the Oostaverne Line was not yet very strongly defended. Headquarters moved to cellars in the ruined village. Lieutenant Drought was killed here. At 11 a.m. it was reported that the enemy was massing in front, but, if a counter-attack was projected, it did not develop in face of the terrific barrage put down by our guns. The Brigade was relieved next day by the 34th Brigade of the 11th Division, and after some marching and counter-marching in the ensuing days, due to a change of intention as to which troops were to hold the line here, moved back to the Rubrouck training area.

III.—THE BATTLE OF PILCKEM RIDGE.

During the latter part of the month of June, all three battalions—1st, 2nd, and 7th—were, therefore, training for the great attack at Ypres. The 1st Battalion, which had been in the Strazeele area from the 4th, had ten days' more training, from the 19th, at Steenvoorde. Almost all the training consisted of practice for attack on trenches, and it was obvious that the Battalion was to be highly tested within the next few weeks. There were changes in command during June. Lieut.-Colonel E. C. Lloyd was succeeded by Lieut.-Colonel R. Daunt, but the latter returned to England at the end of the month, and was succeeded by Lieut.-Colonel A. D. Reid, Royal Inniskilling Fusiliers. On June 29th the Battalion moved to Dominion Camp, west of Ypres. The Salient, which had been comparatively quiet during the height of the Somme battle, had now flared up again, and its back areas were certainly more dangerous and unpleasant than at any time since the beginning of the war. The cause of this was the great increase in long-range shelling, with high-velocity guns, and in the number and size of bombs dropped by aeroplanes. There was, therefore, little rest in the camps, which were generally bombed at night and shelled during the daytime. It is scarcely necessary to add that as one moved east of Ypres the shelling increased in at least arithmetical progression, though in the actual front line it was lighter than upon its approaches. And yet the supreme memory left by the Salient during the summer months of 1917 is one rather of disgust than fear. Rather even than the shelling and the bombing one recalls the all-pervading stench of dead horses, mingled with whiffs of gas, that lay upon it like a pall in those days.

The Battalion did not have a long spell in the line under these conditions. On the night of July 6th it relieved the 1st Sherwood Foresters of the 24th Brigade in the trenches about the Ypres—Roulers railway. It was a wild night, and the shelling of the Ramparts by big howitzers as the Battalion moved up was a sight of mingled terror and magnificence. By luck and good judgment companies* were got through between the storms, and the relief accomplished almost without loss. Headquarters, in a good dug-out in Railway Wood, had a narrow escape of being completely destroyed within a few hours of its arrival. At 5 a.m. next morning there was suddenly a fearful flash and explosion, and the electric lights went out. On candles being lit, two dead bodies were found at the foot of the stairs, the wood ceiling had been rent in pieces, even the papers on the table were torn and scattered all over the place. Apparently a large trench-mortar bomb had burst in the very mouth of the dug-out and blown it in. The dead bodies were those of two orderlies who had been sitting on the stairs, probably asleep. In the circumstances

* Three companies only entered the line for this tour, "C" returning to Dominion Camp.

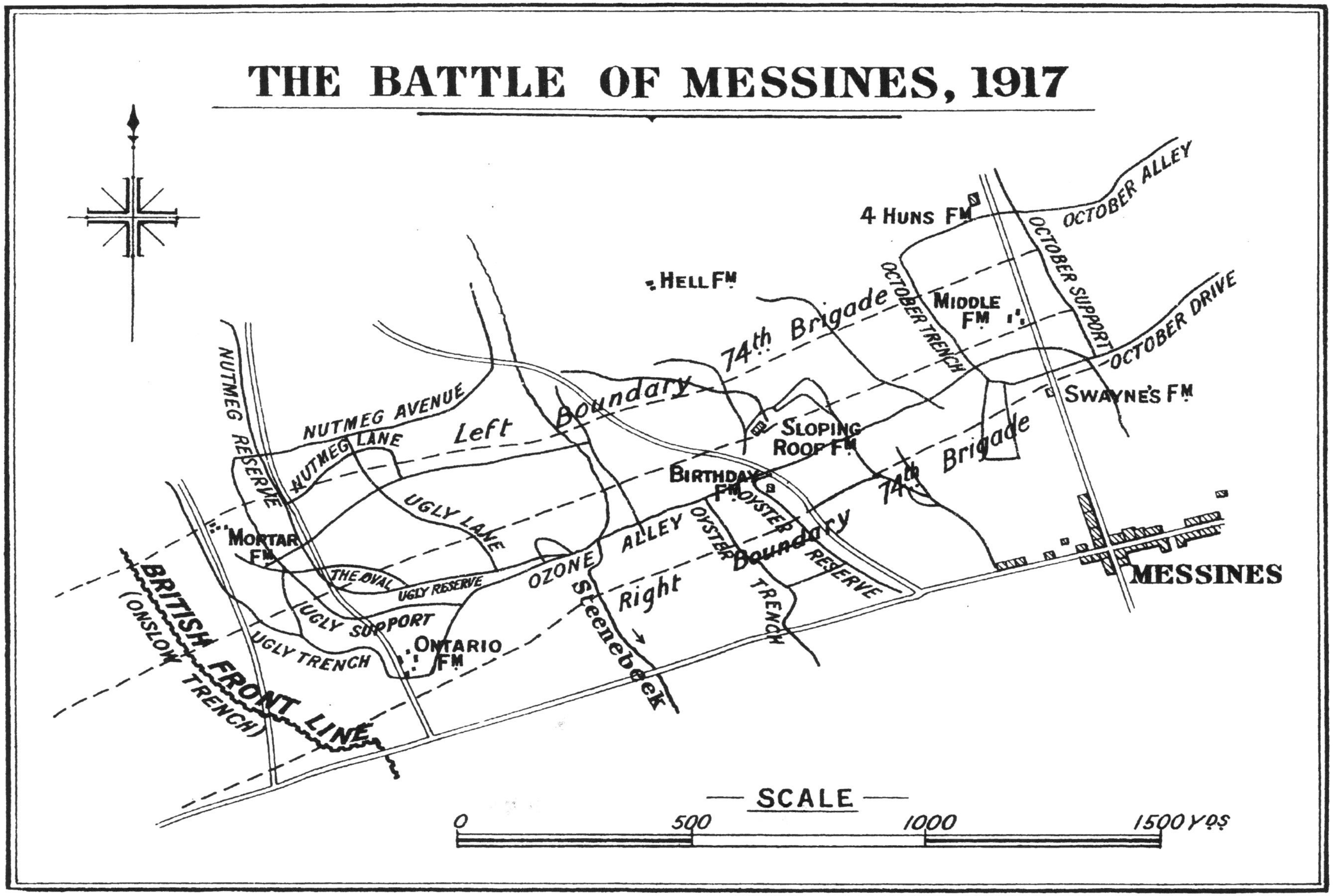

Facing page 100

The Royal Ulster Rifles.

the escape of the rest of the headquarters was little short of marvellous. The orderly-room sergeant is described as having been "blown through the table," and yet was not seriously hurt.

On July 9th the Battalion was relieved by the 10th Cheshire, and moved to Dominion Camp. Two days later it was entrained at Ouderdom to the Tournehem training area. The officers knew that the attack would be made from the trenches they had been holding, and had studied the ground carefully from observation posts and the front line. Then Colonel Reid set himself to train his men to the utmost. Everything was worked out in smallest detail. Lectures were given daily to the men and photographs circulated giving views of the enemy's position taken from aeroplanes. Mingled with hard training, as much amusement as possible was provided for the men in the training area, and after a fortnight spent in the open air in fine weather, the Battalion was thoroughly fit and in good spirits. On the 24th it entrained at Audricq for Hopoutre, expressively known to the troops as "Hop-out," since it was the chief detraining station for the Salient for troops returning from their training. On the 30th came the approach march for the great battle. The description of the movement may be given in the vivid words of Captain G. Whitfeld, the Adjutant :—

"All companies having reported present, we proceeded on our way, going by a cross-country route. Our route led us right through the heavy batteries just north of the Kruisstraathoek—Ypres road. We reached this place at twelve midnight, and were floundering along in the dark in single file, the Commanding Officer and myself leading, while there were blinding flashes all around us. The great counter-battery bombardment had opened.

"The 'going' was frightfully slow owing to the weights the men were carrying and the fact that we had the whole of the 2nd Lincolns in single file in front of us. However, we pushed on and crossed the canal at 12.30, having taken three and a half hours to do four miles—we still had four to go. Soon after crossing the canal a message came back to say that the Germans were shelling Shrapnel Corner. I knew this corner of old. It was one of the most terrible places in the Ypres Salient. It was on the main route and situated about a quarter of a mile from Lille Gate on the Ypres—Messines road. On arrival at this dreaded spot we were fortunate, for, owing to a lull, the whole Battalion got past with only one casualty. Then commenced one of the most terrible marches I ever experienced. Try to imagine for yourself a dark night, a shell-swept track, the stench of dead horses (for no man dared wait in that region), and the sickly smell of asphyxiating gas; then, perhaps you can realize more or less what that night was like. It is a horrible sensation to be floundering along in the dark with a gas helmet over one's head, and falling into shell-holes. I got so 'fed up' that I removed the helmet from my eyes, keeping, however, the tube in my mouth. At last we reached our destination, Halfway House, where it had previously been arranged that all men should be under cover. This, however, was not the case, and the men just flopped down and fell asleep, regardless of gas and high explosive shells that came over at frequent intervals. The Colonel, Browne, and myself then went down into the dug-out, which was half under water, and full of troops, and got into a small recess which had been reserved for us. All three sat on a bed and in five minutes were asleep, but only for one hour—I never remembered an hour passing quicker."

In these Ypres battles it often appears as though the extraordinary difficulties of assembly and the fact that after accomplishing it troops had, through fatigue, frequently lost three-fourths of their fighting value, were not fully realized by the higher command. Let it be remembered that in this case the Battalion was not even moving to the trenches. It was to take part in the second phase of the attack, and its destination, Halfway House, was at least a mile from the British front line.

The 25th Brigade was to pass through the 23rd and 24th Brigades on the Westhoek Ridge, along which ran the Frezenberg—Westhoek road. Its own objective was the "Green" Line, an imaginary line running west of Zonnebeke village and through the western edge of Polygon Wood. This second phase of the attack was to be carried out by three battalions in line—the 2nd Lincolnshire on the right, 1st Royal Irish Rifles in the centre, and 2nd Rifle Brigade on the left.

At 6.50 a.m. it was reported that the attack of the 23rd and 24th Brigades had been a complete success, and the Battalion was ordered to move forward to the Westhoek Ridge in artillery formation. There was a certain amount of shell-fire, but by careful "dodging" the old German front line was safely reached. Here wire and shell-holes slowed down the advance. But on approaching the ridge it was soon discovered that the position was not exactly what had been anticipated. The leading brigades had, in fact, carried out a very fine attack, but were not, unfortunately in possession of the "Black" Line on the Westhoek Ridge as their commanders believed. General Coffin, who did not like the look of the situation, was informed that there were only a few snipers and one or two machine guns still holding out. It was accordingly decided to carry out the attack as originally planned. When the new barrage for the attack on the "Green" Line fell, at "Zero+6 hours 20 minutes," the Battalion went forward in perfect order. Unfortunately, General Coffin's apprehensions had been only too well-founded. The left company found itself pinned to the ground by the fire of machine guns *beyond* which our barrage had fallen. The company commander ordered section rushes, but casualties in the first minute were so heavy, and obviously so fruitless, that he was forced to desist, and withdraw to his original line to consolidate it. The right company was held up for similar reasons, and owing to the fact that the division on the right was held up. The centre company got to the Hannebeke Brook, a truly magnificent feat in the circumstances. But it was found impossible to maintain this isolated position, and the company had to be withdrawn likewise. Colonel Reid, who had been in command but a short time, but had already won the affection and confidence of all ranks, was killed shortly after the opening of the action.

Some local counter-attacks were beaten off. But at 3 p.m. there was one much more serious, delivered by fresh troops in marching order, who had, according to the subsequent reports of observers, been brought into Zonnebeke in lorries. Its full weight fell upon the Lincolnshire and Irish Rifles, and in places it reached our front line. Then the men who had fallen back were rallied by the few officers remaining, and led back to the attack. The Germans were driven out, leaving many dead. A machine gun which the attacking wave had brought forward was captured. The counter-attack was definitely broken, and the ground won by the 23rd and 24th Brigades, which represented a substantial success, held. The Battalion was relieved at 11 p.m. that night, and as the word is suggestive of an orderly exchange, the words of Captain Whitfeld, who now found himself in command of his battalion, may again be quoted :—

" It was impossible to send the message round to the company commanders, because there was no definite line, and the orderlies would in all probability walk into ' No Man's Land ' and be captured. How that relief was completed I do not know to this day.

The order was that on relief the Battalion was to take up its position in the old German front line. This I was unable to communicate to the non-commissioned officers, but I fancied I should find them at Halfway House next day, and I was right."

These are the words of an experienced campaigner. One with less knowledge of human nature would have pictured the remnants of the Battalion wandering about Flanders in the dark. But the soldier, after an attack, with no orders and almost too tired to think coherently, trudges with a dog-like instinct straight to the point where he slept or lay an hour or two for rest before he moved to his position of assembly.

The Battalion moved back to the Steenvoorde area on August 5th, where it received orders that all deficiencies were to be made up forthwith, and was set to carry out training and reorganization. Its losses had been heavy enough, but were on the whole less than might have been expected from the nature of the fighting. It had left considerable reinforcements out of action, going in at a strength of only 20 officers and 620 other ranks. Of the officers 6 were killed, including the colonel, and 7 wounded.* Of other ranks 30 were killed, 145 wounded, and 18 missing. The Battalion had gone into the battle at a very high pitch of efficiency, trained to the hour and full of goodwill. General Coffin, whose splendid courage and leadership in the reorganization of his troops won for him the supreme award of the Victoria Cross, spoke in highest terms of the work that had been done. Major-General Heneker, commanding the 8th Division, after speaking of the victory, won by the 23rd and 24th Brigades, added :—

" The 25th Infantry Brigade's attack went well until held up by cross-fire from the high ground. The Army Commander recognizes this."

IV.—THE CAPTURE OF WESTHOEK.

As a result of these operations, then, an advance had been made of 2,000 yards, but the Westhoek Ridge had not been taken on the front of the 8th Division. It is quite clear to any reader of the reports of this and the succeeding fighting that even less had been consolidated than was believed. After reading Captain Whitfeld's account of the conditions of the relief it will not be difficult to understand the cause. In that welter of mud, amid shell-holes lip to lip, the most advanced posts had not been taken over, and so ground once won had to be taken again. By a coincidence the 2nd Battalion was to attack over almost the same ground as the 1st.

After its victory of Messines the Battalion had, as has been stated, moved to Fruges for training. This was a very pleasant and pretty little place, not far from the battlefield of Crécy, which was visited by many of the officers. Father Gill, the Chaplain, was informed by the Curé that the numbering of the houses in the village dated from the English occupation one hundred years before, after Waterloo. On July 8th the Battalion exchanged Fruges for Radinghem, to finish its training. This was also an agreeable village, but the stay here was short. On the 12th the Battalion marched to Delette and Reckinghem, where brigade manœuvres were carried out, bivouacked for the night, and returned to Radinghem on the morrow. Here a draft of 102 other ranks joined—about half the casualty list of Messines.

The Battalion then moved to the inevitable goal, Pioneer Camp, west of Ypres. For the next ten days it found parties for work on roads varying from 250 to 400. There

* Killed : Lieut.-Colonel Reid, 2nd-Lieutenants L. C. Byrne, R. K. Pollen, T. Furness, H. Brown, P. Doherty. Wounded : Captain G. Mockett, 2nd-Lieutenants C. Reid (Leinsters), P. Breen, E. L. Burke-Murphy, R. A. Veitch, E. Daniel, M. H. Jeffares.

was heavy shell-fire on back areas and a considerable number of casualties, fifteen being recorded on the first day. On the 30th the Battalion moved to Swan Château, and on the 31st, "Zero" day of the attack, two companies were employed on the corduroy roads, which were such a feature of the battle and without which it could scarcely have been fought, and on laying pipes for water. On August 4th it moved into the dug-outs under the Ramparts of Ypres, and next day into line before Westhoek Ridge. Very unfortunately "A" Company was caught by a heavy barrage moving through Château Wood, and had numerous losses. The front line also was heavily bombarded, and the casualties for the first twenty-four hours, including the relief, were upwards of seventy.

The operation to be carried out was to complete the capture of the Westhoek Ridge and bring the line level at this point, so that a further major operation could be undertaken. The 74th Brigade was the only one of its division to be employed, while the 18th Division was attacking on its right. The brigade was to attack upon a front of 2,000 yards, south of the Ypres—Roulers railway line. The distance of its objective varied considerably along its front, being about 450 yards on the right, 650 in the centre, and 250 on the left. With a frontage so wide, the Brigade used all its four battalions, from right to left—the 13th Cheshire, the 2nd Royal Irish Rifles, the 9th Loyal North Lancashire, the 11th Lancashire Fusiliers. The 2nd Royal Irish Rifles had to go the extreme distance, and had, moreover, to take the village of Westhoek itself; and, if Westhoek were hard to find on the ground, at least the "pill-boxes" might be expected to be thicker on its site than elsewhere.

The Battalion's advance was to be made in four waves, "A" Company in rear forming the fourth. The other three companies were to form the three leading waves, advancing in lines of platoons in depth.* There was one slight aid to direction not always present in this shattered area, as "B," the left company, was to have its right, and "C," the centre company, its left, on the Westhoek—Zonnebeke road, which might be expected to be just recognizable. These three companies were to take and consolidate a line which corresponded exactly with the "Black" Line of the first attack, and "A" to pass through them to a position 150 yards farther on. Colonel Goodman was left out of this action, it being laid down that commanding officers and seconds-in-command should take turns in going into battle, to avoid the chance of both becoming casualties the same day, and Major R. de R. Rose was in command.

The attack had been fixed for August 9th. Very heavy rain having fallen on the evening of the 8th, filling the shell-holes to the brim with water, it was postponed twenty-four hours. In this period some small improvement may have taken place in the state of the surface, but a faint idea of the conditions may be gained when it is stated that it required eight men to carry down a wounded man on a stretcher to the advanced dressing station on the Menin road, and that there were reports of wounded men having been drowned in shell-holes.

"Zero" was at 4.25 a.m. on the 10th. The men went forward with extraordinary bravery. Met by heavy machine-gun fire, their feet clogged by the mud, they advanced heedless of casualties, and with such speed that the Germans in the opposing "pill-boxes" were largely taken by surprise. In many cases the enemy ran back from their concrete shelters before the barrage reached them, and ran only to their own destruction. For the barrage caught them up as they floundered knee-deep, and it was, in the expressive

* Companies were, doubtless, organized in three platoons. This was sometimes forbidden by the higher command, but a weak battalion had no other choice.

term of French gunners, so " well-nourished " that it was impossible for any man to pass through it in the open without being hit. Moreover, the Riflemen fired from the hip as they advanced, a method which had sometimes been scoffed at by our military opinion when employed by the Germans, and are said to have brought down several of those who were retreating. On the front of " B " Company, one " pill-box," which had not been seen amid the general welter, though not far from our original line, gave trouble, checking the assault till an officer rushed forward and fired his revolver through a slit in the wall, when the machine-gun team fled. The fight resolved itself chiefly into a " mopping up " of dug-outs which had been passed. From these considerable numbers of prisoners were taken. The objective was reached at 5.20 a.m., and a line of posts pushed out behind a protective barrage to cover the consolidation, which was at once begun. Connection was established with the Cheshires and Loyal North Lancashires, whose attacks had been equally successful.

From 10 a.m. onwards it was observed that the enemy was trickling men across the next ridge in front into the valley of the Hannebeke, where they were in dead ground. At 3.30 p.m. the enemy made what is described as a rather feeble counter-attack, which was beaten off by machine-gun and rifle fire before our artillery barrage fell. The enemy, however, continued to push men into the Hannebeke Valley, and at 5.50 p.m. S.O.S. signals were put up by the Royal Irish Rifles, as a new attack appeared likely to develop, and the numbers in position in the valley must by now have become considerable. The signal was not seen, but a runner got to advanced brigade headquarters at 6 p.m. with a message from Major Rose, while other battalions reported that the Germans were thick in Polygon Wood. Intense fire was concentrated on these areas at 6.45 p.m. and by 7.15 the enemy's fire, which had likewise grown heavy, slackened off. Our bombardment then stopped, and it seemed as if the counter-attack had been broken up.

It came after all, and only a quarter of an hour later, preceded by a heavy bombardment, with a smoke barrage to cover the assaulting troops. Again the S.O.S signal was not seen, while, as need hardly be said, no telephone wire could be kept going for five minutes in that inferno. But, most fortunately, one of our airmen did see the signal, or else saw that the enemy was attacking, and himself dropped the rocket which called for a barrage. The result was that our barrage completely smashed the attack in the space of a minute. It seemed as if the front wave was annihilated. Survivors of the others could be seen flying in all directions. The German losses must have been very heavy indeed.

But the enemy was persistent, and was not yet done with. At about 4.15 a.m. next morning strong patrols were pushed forward by him. All but two were checked by Lewis-gun fire and got nowhere near our line. Of these two one came on very pluckily and threw bombs, but was attacked with the bayonet and all the twelve men in it killed. The larger patrol retreated before our fire, and was seen to enter a " pill-box." A patrol sent out in turn by the Royal Irish Rifles took it in entirety—1 officer and 19 other ranks. It was a remarkable ending to one of the most splendid incidents in the history of the Battalion.

How splendid its self-sacrifice was can only be measured if we consider its losses. They were extraordinarily high, and it is quite clear to anyone examining them that no troops but those of the very highest quality could have achieved what the Battalion did in face of such fire as these losses imply. The Battalion went into action at a strength of 15 officers and 479 other ranks. Their losses were 8 officers and 342 other ranks ;

or 53 per cent. of officers, and the enormous proportion of 71 per cent. other ranks. But it had been largely a machine-gun battle, and most of the casualties were caused by machine-gun bullets. The proportion of wounded to killed was fortunately high—over 80 per cent. The officer casualties were: Killed, Lieutenants E. Brown, S. V. Morgan, 2nd-Lieutenants P. McKee. Wounded: Captain R. Jeffares, 2nd-Lieutenants R. S. Walsh (Munsters), B. J. Murphy (Munsters), P. D. Alexander, R. Carruthers. The Medical Officer, Lieutenant A. B. Ross, was also killed. On the other hand, the Battalion had captured 4 officers and 150 other ranks, as well as a trench gun and five machine guns, and had undoubtedly accounted for a great number of Germans in its attack and in beating off the numerous counter-attacks.

After the battle the Battalion moved back to the Steenvoorde area for training and reorganization. It had gone twice into action within little more than two months, and had been completely successful in each case.

V.—THE BATTLE OF LANGEMARCK: THE 1ST BATTALION.

The 1st Battalion's two actions were to be even closer together, but it did not have so good fortune in them. The attack in which its sister battalion had taken part was, as has been said, a local one. That of August 16th was the second main stroke of the battle, the first having been that of July 31st, in which the 1st Battalion had also been engaged. The first attack had been in all the circumstances a success. The second, made in conditions much more difficult, when the ground had been soaked in the rain which began with the opening of the action, and ploughed up by the constant bombardments of both sides, was generally a failure. On August 16th the 8th and 16th Divisions attacked side by side, and both the 1st and 7th Battalions of the Royal Irish Rifles were in the assault, the former south, the latter north of the Ypres—Roulers railway line. The 8th Division had as its objective a " Green " Line, which was, however, not quite that of July 31st, but slightly less distant.

The 8th Division was attacking with the 25th Brigade on the right and the 23rd on the left. On the 25th Brigade's front the 2nd Royal Berkshire was attacking on the right and the 1st Royal Irish Rifles on the left. The Battalion was to go into action under yet another in its long list of commanding officers, Lieut.-Colonel H. McCarthy-O'Leary, M.C., Royal Irish Fusiliers. It was moved up by bus on the afternoon of August 14th, and after a very difficult march, with a quantity of gas-shell about, reached Lille Gate, Ypres, at midnight, and slept in the dug-outs there. Next day was spent in distributing stores and reconnoitring the route to be followed that night.

At 9 p.m. the Battalion started, six hours having been allowed for the march, which was under five miles. It had been arranged to start from a sally-port in the ramparts to avoid the notorious Menin Gate. But even as it was a " five-nine " fell in the ranks before the Menin road was reached, and caused thirteen casualties. The best description of the march and of the assembly and opening of the attack is again to be found in Captain Whitfeld's diary:—

" The Germans, as luck would have it, were exceedingly quiet on our front, having, as I found out from the forward observation officer, received three hours' gas on their batteries. The ' going ' on the Menin road was good, and we made quite fair progress as far as Birr cross-roads, where we were to meet guides from the —— and start our journey across three miles of mud and shell crater. After waiting half an hour, finding the guides, we heard the cheerful news that only one out of sixteen knew the way. We started, and from 10 p.m. to 3.45 a.m. were trying to cover those three miles. If I did the journey once I did it five times, for the Commanding Officer and I would hear the messsage come up to say ' company has lost connection,' and so it went on till at last I saw the ridge in front and knew we were there at last.

"Now came the job of getting the companies into position. We had only three-quarters of an hour to do it in. At this moment someone reported to me that one of the companies was ' missing.' The rear of the preceding company had seen them, they said, about an hour before, but had lost sight of them. At anyrate, finally only half turned up and the other half went over with the 23rd Infantry Brigade. The Colonel assembled the men in a very able manner, whilst I went to Brigade headquarters and reported to the Brigadier. I then gave Battalion headquarters men some cover against the pending Boche barrage, and finally made my way to Rifle Brigade headquarters. In doing so I passed the companies lined up all ready. A few of the men were muttering to each other but most were too excited to speak. We probably all had that extraordinary feeling which only those who have ' been over ' have experienced. On arrival at the 2nd Rifle Brigade headquarters I found the Colonel waiting, and as the barrage was timed to commence in three minutes, I went outside to see the beginning. The first streaks of a summer dawn were already showing in the east when suddenly the whole sky lit up behind me with dull red flashes and the roar of guns commenced. In less than half a minute the German line was lit up with marvellous colours—green, red, blue, gold, and silver, intermingled with the red glare of our bursting shrapnel. The German barrage dropped within three minutes."

Each of these somewhat unfortunate attacks at Ypres by the Battalion had been a subject of misgiving to commanders under which they fought, in the first case to their Brigadier, in the second to Major-General Heneker, commanding the 8th Division. The former had mistrusted the reports on July 31st that the whole of the "Black" Line had been captured, and he had been right. In this General Heneker had represented very strongly to the Corps Commander the difficulties in which his troops were likely to be involved owing to the troops on the right not being in possession of the high ground about Glencorse Wood and not being level with his division. He also was correct in his appreciation of the position.

All the opposition and the bulk of the machine-gun fire came from the right flank. Despite it, the troops, which had formed up on tapes laid in front of their positions, went forward in excellent style, keeping close to the barrage. The important "pill-box" known as Anzac Farm gave some trouble, but was finally surrounded and captured with a number of prisoners, by Lieutenant C. D. Quilliam and his platoon, and held till the counter-attack. The final objective was reached about 6.20 a.m., and an effort made to consolidate it, but owing to the heavy losses in the advance and sniping from the rear, this was found to be impossible. At about 7.50 a.m. the enemy was seen to be working round the right flank, while the position of the left was also unsatisfactory. The line was accordingly withdrawn 200 yards.

When Colonel McCarthy-O'Leary heard that the "Green" Line had been reached, he went forward as arranged previously towards the Hannebeke Wood. The account of what follows, much more vivid than anything to be found in any of the diaries, must again be given in the words of the Adjutant, Captain Whitfeld :—

"Entering the Hannebeke Wood the forward observation officer and I moved forward, but were driven into a trench by a German airman, who swooped down upon us.

We again went forward and crossed the stream, which by now had been reduced to a series of small lakes. No officers could be found, and very few men, and it was reported to me that all the former had either been killed or wounded. I have never seen so many dead as there were in that Hannebeke Valley, both Boche and British, the majority of them the former.

"About half an hour later I met the Colonel coming back, and could see at once that he had been hit, for his right arm was hanging limp and blood was all over his coat. He decided that we must go back at once and report the situation to the Brigadier, which we did, having again been chased by bullets all the way. The Commanding Officer was by this time very weak, and the Medical Officer ordered him to go back at once to the rear dressing station. He therefore handed over command to me and I again proceeded forward. The shelling now became very heavy (far worse than on the 31st), and I took cover in a trench where some men were, which I soon found was 'marked' by the German gunners.

"From then on the shells came pouring in without cessation. Shrapnel and high-explosive—mostly the latter—kept bursting with a deafening roar. I might have guessed that this bombardment was nothing less than an attack by 'storm troops,' and this was the case. They came—six battalions in six lines—and owing to our heavy casualties we were nearly forced back to our original position.

"At 8 p.m. I sent up the S.O.S. signal, and this was replied to, as I heard afterwards, by about 980 guns. Dusk came at last, and except for a violent barrage by both sides at 8 p.m. comparative quiet set in. Just before dusk I had met the doctor for the first time that day, and he informed me that I was the sole survivor of all the officers, and, therefore, again in command of the Battalion.

"At 9 p.m. I received orders to take the remnants of the Battalion to Birr cross-roads. . . . After much tripping and stumbling in shell-holes I and my orderly arrived safely at 1 a.m., and went down into the deep dug-out, where I was given some food and drink, and then slept."

It is improbable that the most practised and skilful writer could describe better the simplicity of the mental machine after a day such as this than does Captain Whitfeld in these words. There is no room for sentiments of horror, hardly even for regret for lost friends or a fine battalion destroyed at such a moment. They may come on the morrow. For the moment one can only pray to be given some food and drink, and then allowed to sleep.

Only sixty men accompanied Captain Whitfeld to Birr cross-roads, but a number more, who had lost their ways, joined later. The losses were enormous, about two-thirds of those who had gone into action. Two officers were killed, 5 wounded and missing, 3 wounded (including the commanding officer)*, 27 other ranks were killed, 7 wounded and missing, 170 wounded, and 63 missing.

VI.—The Battle of Langemarck: The 7th Battalion.

The 7th Royal Irish Rifles, as has been said, also attacked on August 16th. The Battalion had been in the Tilques training area till July 25th, when it moved up to Toronto Camp. For the opening of the battle, on July 31st, it was for some reason not quite

---

* Killed: 2nd-Lieutenants E. A. Mahoney, J. E. G. Wilson. Wounded and missing: Captains A. J. Ross, A. F. Nicholson, J. F. Clery (Munsters), 2nd-Lieutenants W. Kingston (Munsters), R. Ennis. Wounded: Lieut.-Colonel H. W. D. MacCarthy-O'Leary (Irish Fusiliers), 2nd-Lieutenants J. K. Boyle, C. D. Quilliam.

7TH BATTALION IN BATTLE OF LANGEMARCK: AUGUST 16TH

clear put at the disposal of the 15th Division, which was attacking on that date. At 4.30 a.m. it moved to a position in our reserve line, and that evening, after the 15th Division had made a considerable advance, was moved forward to occupy the old British front line north of the Ypres—Roulers railway. It remained here, receiving various orders which were cancelled before they could be acted upon, till 2.15 a.m. on August 2nd, then moved back to Toronto Camp. The 16th Division had meantime relieved the 15th, in accordance with the disastrous policy carried out not only here but on other parts of the front, of not keeping in the divisions which had carried out the first attack, however tired or depleted, till the next was prepared, so as to have fresh troops to make it. This policy meant that divisions were thoroughly jaded and shaken, and had suffered in some cases upwards of two thousand casualties, before they were launched to the attack.

The Battalion entered the front line, its right on the Ypres—Roulers railway line, on the night of the 7th. The ground was now in a state that defies description. Men became literally caked with mud to the eyes. The shelling was, at its worst moments, as heavy as experienced at any moment of the war. The first day in Major H. S. Allison was killed by a shell, and 2nd-Lieutenant G. P. Roche wounded. The next, all the runners and observers of the headquarters were either killed or wounded by another. On the night of August 10th the Battalion dragged itself out to the Asylum and was entrained back to its old camp. Its casualties for this tour in the line were 12 killed, 75 wounded, and 4 missing.

There it rested till the 14th, moving up to its assembly positions, in the trenches it had lately held, that night, being in position by 2.30 a.m. on the 15th. The objective of the 16th Division was the " Dotted Green " Line, which ran through the point where the railway bridges the Hannebeke Brook. It was attacking with three companies in line, and one in support.

At " Zero " there burst out very heavy machine-gun fire. Some of the guns, safe in their " pill-boxes," actually continued to fire as the barrage passed over them. All officers were hit before the " Green " Line, half-way to the final objective, was reached, and the centre and left companies were stopped by their enormous losses. The right company, however, to some small extent protected from view, worked most gallantly up the railway, cleared a nest of dug-outs upon it at the " Green " Line, and sent back thirty prisoners. This was an advance of over 500 yards, but a few splendid and devoted survivors were seen to go forward behind the barrage, over the Hannebeke, and on towards the final objective. The rest of this company's attack was held up by the strong nest of concrete buildings known as Potsdam. Nor was an effort to work round these from the railway line successful. Lieutenant Kingston was killed here, most gallantly attempting to storm a " pill-box " by firing his revolver through a loop-hole. Finally a small body made an effort to consolidate its position at the captured dug-outs, where the " Green " Line crossed the railway.

Colonel Francis had none of his own officers left, and at 10.15 a.m. Captain Cowley, 8th Dublin Fusiliers, went forward with his company to ascertain the position on the " Green " Line, but was unable to reach it. There was touch with the battalion on the right of the 23rd Brigade 8th Division on the " Green " Line.

So the situation remained till late afternoon, when there was launched the great counter-attack described by Captain Whitfeld. The battalion of the 23rd Brigade fell back in disorder, and actually was driven beyond the " Black " Line. Colonel Francis sent all the men he could scrape together, five Stokes' gunners and a few details from his headquarters to form a defensive flank. The enemy, however, did not follow up his success, being checked by our artillery and machine-gun fire.

As for the body of men on the railway, it was now reduced to six. The troops on the right having been driven back, it was attacked likewise. The post fell back 200 yards, and took up a new position, keeping off the Germans by its fire. The men who had crossed the Hannebeke were cut off, and no more was heard of them. A few may have been captured, but the majority must have been blotted out by the successive bombardments of each side. The last men west of Potsdam, mostly Dublins, fell back to our line at dusk.

The Battalion was not relieved until the following night, when it was withdrawn to Vlamertinghe. Its losses were 4 officers killed, 7 wounded, 6 missing, 39 other ranks killed, 269 wounded or missing.* On the 21st it entrained at Esquelbecq for the Third Army area.

So ended the summer battles where the Regiment was concerned, though the 1st and 2nd Battalions were to see more of the Ypres area before the year was out. The casualties sustained by the three battalions in five actual attacks, two by the 1st at Ypres, one by the 2nd at Messines, and one at Ypres, one by the 7th at Ypres, amounted to just 1,400, of which Ypres accounted for over 1,150. These do not in most cases include losses while holding the line during or after those actions, which cannot now be accurately determined, but must have been very heavy. The 7th Battalion, we have seen, had 93 casualties in one spell in the line a week before it attacked. Nor does it include the losses in back areas or on working parties behind the line from shell-fire and aeroplane bombs. The total cannot have been far short of 2,000.

" Third Ypres " is indeed something of a nightmare to those who look back upon it. The difficulties were undoubtedly enormous. The tanks, which might in other circumstances or on other soil have been of vast assistance, were seldom here if any, owing to the weather. The terrific shelling in some ways defeated its own ends, often making obstacles only less difficult than barbed wire for attacking troops to negotiate. These difficulties were recognized by all. But when men were sent to a second attack and found themselves opposed by machine-gunners in the identical " pill-boxes," that had defeated the first, still absolutely intact, they did begin to feel, to put it mildly, that something was wrong. But, whatever we may think of the leadership—and on that point no full judgment can really be made till all the circumstances are known and the events analysed in the Official History—the battle will always remain one of the most extraordinary monuments to the courage and endurance of the British soldier. Those hard-used words are indeed inadequate to describe his virtues. If mortal men could have pulled down reinforced concrete with their naked hands, these men would have done it.

---

* Killed: Captain C. McMaster, Lieutenants A. N. Oakshot, W. Kingston, 2nd-Lieutenant Hatte. Wounded: Captains J. Craig, R. L. Henderson, Lieutenant W. J. B. Wilson, 2nd-Lieutenants Beatty, R. Greaves, R. L. Cramp, M. J. Hartery. Missing: 2nd-Lieutenants A. C. Hill, G. B. C. Elmott, R. Hannah, W. Owens, H. M. Hoops. 2nd-Lieutenant K. Pelton (Leinsters) was killed on August 2nd.

THE BATTLES OF YPRES, 1917

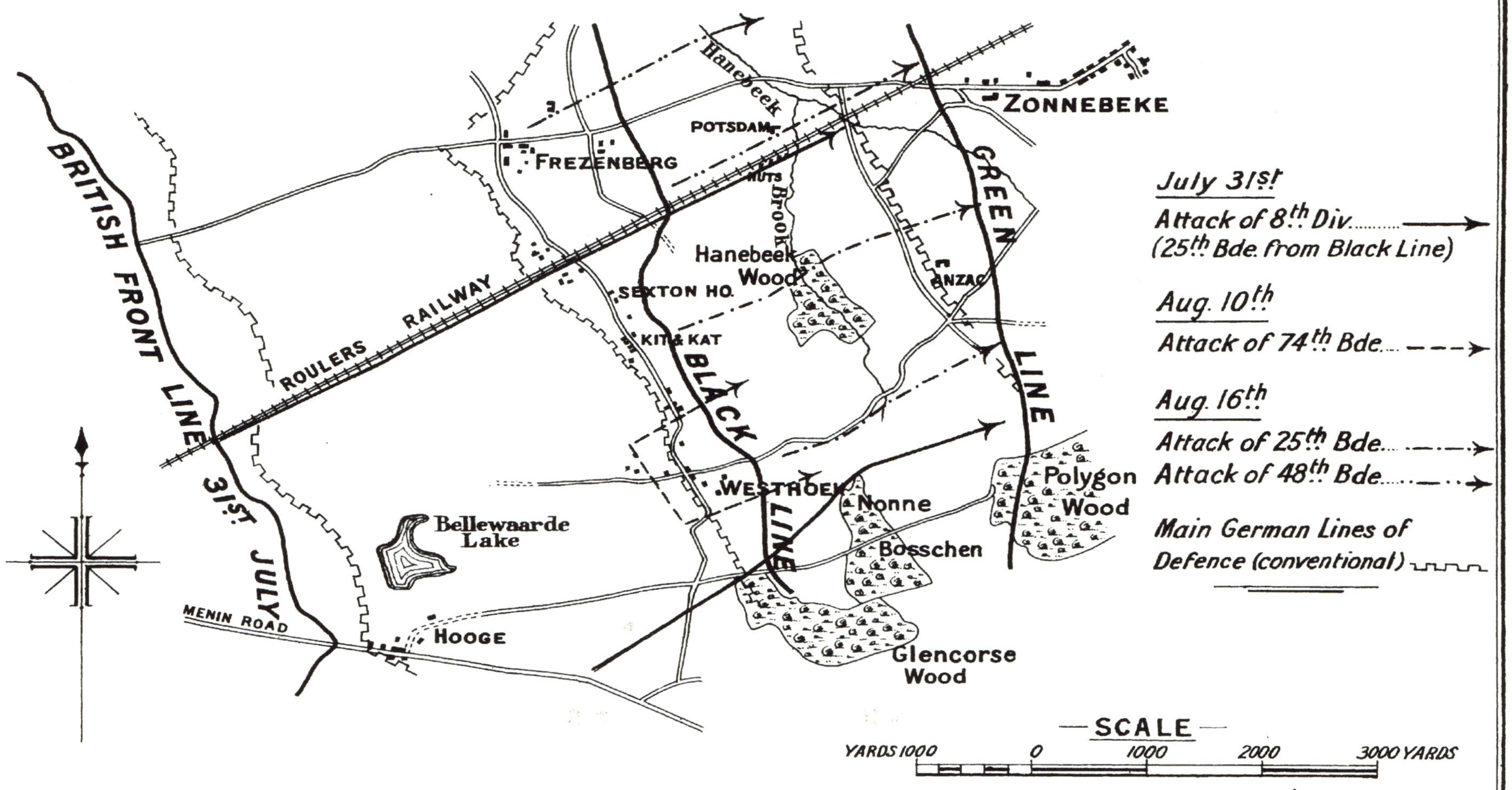

CHAPTER III

I.—AUTUMN, 1917: THE 1ST BATTALION.

AFTER its two terrible struggles at Ypres, the 1st Battalion Royal Irish Rifles was inspected at Halifax Camp by the Corps Commander, General Jacob, who spoke in very high terms of the manner in which it had fought. He was, alas! addressing not more than about a hundred of those who had come through the second action. On August 19th the Battalion was taken back in buses to the Hazebrouck area, where it was inspected by Sir Douglas Haig, who took this method of expressing his appreciation of the work of the 8th Division. On the 27th it moved to De Seule, a village east of Bailleul, where yet another commanding officer, Lieut.-Colonel J. H. M. Kirkwood, D.S.O., Household Battalion, arrived. The Battalion was fated to have bad luck with its best commanding officers, who seldom survived long. Colonel Kirkwood was neither killed nor wounded, like most of the others, but was evacuated sick to England a little more than a month later, being succeeded by Major T. H. Ivey.

The Battalion moved up to the well-known Bulford Camp, on September 3rd. On the 11th the 25th Brigade entered the line, and on the 19th the Irish Rifles relieved the Lincolns in the "Plug-street" area, with its left flank on the Douve. Here a dummy attack, with stuffed figures in khaki and trench helmets, and a liberal amount of smoke, was arranged to make the enemy believe that offensive operations were being renewed on this front. The Germans put down a heavy barrage, while their machine guns made accurate shooting against the dummies, knocking most of them over. There was a little later an unhappy incident when the enemy raided a post and took prisoner two men whose resistance was not in accordance with the Battalion's great traditions. Many battalions had trouble about this time with "combed out" men from safer avocations, who did not relish the change in their existence. To do them justice, all but a negligible proportion speedily acquired the proper spirit, particularly when they found themselves in a really good battalion. The total casualties for September were 29, including Lieutenant G. C. Robb wounded.

When relieved the following night the Battalion found a welcome draft of 1 officer and 100 other ranks awaiting it at Nieppe. On October 2nd another of 71 other ranks arrived. Then the Battalion relieved the 2nd Royal Berks in a sector farther north, at La Basseville, upon ground captured in the Battle of Messines. The trenches here were very muddy and unpleasant, but the Battalion did not have to hold them long. The rest and training which were certainly due after Ypres were coming. On the last day of the month the 25th Brigade, having been relieved by the 24th, moved to the area round Steenwerck.

Twelve days were spent here in rest and training, in the course of which news arrived that Passchendaele had fallen. But it was too late. What would have meant a great triumph two months earlier had no strategical significance to-day. Winter was upon us, and the Flanders campaign, with its casualty list already approaching a quarter of a million, must soon inevitably close. But the 8th Division was to have one more throw before that horror was at an end.

On November 12th the Brigade moved to the La Motte—Caudescure area, where it expected a fair period in pleasant surroundings. But plans were apparently changed, for on the 15th it moved to Caestre and entrained for the Salient. The movements are altogether difficult to understand, as the 25th Brigade relieved troops of the 3rd Canadian Division, remained in line for two days, and was then entrained from Wieltje to Ridge Camp near Vlamertinghe. Here word was given that the Brigade was due to make another attack. It was news that could arouse no enthusiasm in the boldest breast. No one by this time went into the Ypres battle expecting victory. However, training was carried out with the old vigour, attacks being practised daily for a week. The account of the action may be left till the next chapter.

II.—AUTUMN, 1917 : THE 2ND BATTALION.

The 2nd Battalion, after its action on the Westhoek Ridge, moved back to rest at Steenvoorde, near Cassel. Training was carried out, but the necessary drafts from home arrived in very small numbers. Recruiting in Ireland, at least outside the north-east corner, had to all intents and purposes stopped since the Rebellion, and, as we shall see, there was about to be a disappearance of Irish battalions all over the world. On September 1st the Battalion returned to the Salient, and next night entered the trenches on the Westhoek Ridge. It is recorded that its strength in the line was 10 officers and 242 other ranks. The enemy made a local attack on the Battalion's line under cover of a very heavy barrage on the night of the 6th. Our S.O.S. signal went up in good time, and under the weight of the resultant barrage the attack faded away without a man reaching our wire. The Battalion was relieved on the night of the 8th, and after a week in camp moved back by bus. It remained at Raimbert till the end of the month, having thus an opportunity to train some drafts which had at last arrived.

Father Gill, the Chaplain, relates one story of the Salient, which those who remember the war will recognize as typical. A dog named "Sticky" which had been long with the Battalion but had disappeared during the Somme battle a whole year ago, was seen by Father Gill's batman, and "rejoined." He remembered his old friends. But alas! "he had," says Father Gill, "contracted the bad habit of promiscuous friendships, and would at a moment's notice attach himself to any unit which happened to attract his attention. By care and watching over his erring feet we recaptured his affections, and kept him with us for a few months. But finally we lost him again, and I have never seen nor heard of him since." Such were too often the fashions of soldiers' dogs, who seemed to consider themselves as attached to the British Army rather than to any particular unit, still less to any particular man.

The 25th Divisional Horse Show was held on September 26th, and the Royal Irish Rifles lived up to their usual standard on this occasion by winning a prize for the mess-cart. A week later the welcome rest came to an end. The Battalion marched to Bethune, and on October 5th entered the line in the Cambrin sector in relief of troops of the 2nd Division. It had just had news that it was shortly to be transferred from the 25th Division to the 36th (Ulster) Division. Very keen regret was felt at leaving the 25th Division, in which it had been two years, having established an excellent reputation and become very popular.

The new line was very quiet and highly in favour with troops. The good old custom of newspaper boys bringing the Paris *Daily Mail* to the end of the communication trenches was preserved. People whispered rumours of espionage and said it was bad for discipline, but the Corps Commander was too wise to destroy a " feature " of his area which made men happy, more from the excitement of seeing the newspapers sold than because of their pleasure in getting news earlier than usual. How quiet the front was is shown by the fact that two men who were out on patrol, one having been slightly wounded, being caught by dawn and deciding to remain in a shell-hole till the next night, on repenting of this resolution were able to crawl in to our lines in broad daylight. One good draft of 3 officers and 62 men arrived here. The Battalion had Portuguese troops attached to it for instruction in trench warfare.

Another event of interest was the visit of Cardinal Bourne to the Battalion. He came to Beuvry when it was out of the trenches, and gave an address, followed by Benediction, to Catholic officers and men, afterwards having tea with the Brigadier in his command post, quite close to the trenches.

During the rest of the month nothing of importance occurred, but for the unfortunate loss of 2nd-Lieutenant A. Davison and 5 other ranks, ambushed and captured on patrol. The time was drawing near when the Battalion should leave the 25th Division. It entered the line under the old command for the last time on October 31st and came out on November 8th. Two days later it marched off to Bethune for the move. It was given a fine send-off, the bands of the other three battalions of the brigade playing it out. It was a sad moment for many. But, just as there had been deep regret on leaving the 3rd Division, after which the Battalion had settled down and done remarkably well in the 25th, so in a short time it was to take its place and win a new name in the 36th.

On November 12th there was a farewell inspection by General Sir H. Horne, commanding the First Army, outside Bethune. Next day it moved by bus to the Third Army area. It billeted that night in Arras, and went on next day *via* Bapaume and Rocquigny to Ytres, where it was billeted in Little Wood. Here it found the 7th Battalion, at a strength of 17 officers and 515 other ranks, waiting to be broken up and absorbed by it. It had four days only for reorganization and training, during which the staff of the 36th Division had small time to make its acquaintance or assist it. For it had arrived on the very eve of the Battle of Cambrai. On November 19th it moved to Lebucquière to bivouac in reserve for that action.

III.—AUTUMN 1917 : THE END OF THE 7TH BATTALION.

The 7th Battalion after its share in the Ypres battle, entrained at Esquelbecq on August 21st, arriving at Bapaume that evening and marching to Courcelles-le-Comte. The whole of the Somme battlefield area was now an abomination of desolation. Bapaume had been first damaged by British artillery fire and its destruction completed by German explosives before the retirement to the Hindenburg Line early that year. It was, indeed, a remarkable spectacle at this time, each house being laid flat in an orderly fashion by the German demolition parties, so that in some streets there were rows of houses with their roofs almost whole, but only a few feet above the ground upon the mass of bricks of the blown-in walls. At some villages, such as Courcelles, a certain amount of repair had been carried out by British troops, to make out of roofless barns a shelter for men and beasts of units passing in or out of the line, but these were, of course, outside the real zone of the battle, where nothing remained to repair and the sites of whole villages were almost impossible to discover.

Immediately after its arrival in this area, the Battalion left the 48th Brigade, in which all its combatant life had been passed, and was transferred to the 49th. There was already a break-up of Irish battalions. In this case the 7th and 8th Inniskilling Fusiliers of the 49th Brigade were amalgamated, and the 7th Irish Rifles brought in to make up, while a Regular battalion, the 1st Dublin Fusiliers, was transferred from the 29th Division and brought into the 48th Brigade. General Ramsay, commanding the 48th Brigade, made a farewell speech to the Irish Rifles, expressing his regret at losing them.

The 49th Brigade remained for some time in reserve, the Battalion being in the neighbourhood of Ervillers, another village of which the memory only remained, though some hutments had sprung up on its site. On September 4th it entered the trenches, near Croisilles, on the Sensée River, with its headquarters in the celebrated tunnel under the Hindenburg Line, which at this point only and on a narrow frontage had been captured by our pursuing troops after the great German retreat. The line was quiet in the extreme, and almost the only casualties were due to a German bombardment in retaliation for the release of gas by neighbouring British units.

In the middle of the month of September, when it was out of the line, very bad news came to the Battalion. It was in a short time to be broken up, to cease to exist. Everyone who had served in a temporary battalion, knew, of course, that its life would end with the end of the war, but there was nothing unreasonable in the hope that it would live to take a part in the final victorious battles, which only the most pessimistic feared would never come. In the case of Irish battalions, however, this hope was not for the most part realized. As has been stated, recruiting in Ireland had practically ceased since the Rebellion, and in consequence of the rising power of Sinn Fein and the Government's decision not to apply conscription to Ireland. For the last year of the war the Regular Irish battalions could only be maintained by eating up their temporary sisters, and even then received a certain proportion of English recruits. It is believed that not more than half a dozen Irish Service battalions on active service survived to the end, including two battalions of the Royal Irish Rifles, the 12th and 15th. The prospect was none the less bleak for officers and men. It was not as if for them the war was over. They would have to go on fighting till the end, or till they became casualties. But the traditions they had inherited and built up together were to be taken from them, and they were to finish the war in other associations.

The first days of October saw some minor fighting in the line over a concrete machine-gun emplacement occupied by the troops of the 49th Brigade. On October 4th the 7th Royal Irish Rifles was relieved by the 7/8th Royal Irish Fusiliers. That night marked the end of its fighting service as a battalion. It remained in the reserve area about Hamelincourt till the 14th, when orders came for it to be transferred to the 36th (Ulster) Division, then on the Cambrai front. It was there to be broken up, and its troops absorbed by the 2nd Royal Irish Rifles, as has been recorded when dealing with that battalion. It had the better part of a month to await this event, which took place at Ytres. Various officers and other ranks were transferred at their own request to the Royal Air Force or Tank Corps. Lieut.-Colonel Francis was promoted to the command of a brigade.

CHAPTER IV

I.—THE BATTLE OF CAMBRAI: THE TANK ATTACK.

THE 7th Battalion having been broken up, after only two years of active service in France, we have now to chronicle once more simply the records of the two Regular battalions in that theatre. This chapter deals mainly with the 2nd Battalion, which took part in November and December in one of the most interesting actions of the war, the Battle of Cambrai, while the 1st Battalion was in the Salient and concerned with the last dying flickers of " Third Ypres."

Cambrai was indeed an interesting battle. It proved that the tank, useful, indeed, on the Somme in its undeveloped stage, but very ineffective in the heavy, water-logged and shell-churned flats of Flanders, was capable, on good ground and if employed in sufficient numbers, of revolutionizing the theories of warfare which the trench fighting of the last three years had built up. The scheme of the surprise attack was brilliant, and the execution successful. Unfortunately the British Army was now upon a front so wide and had been so terribly ground in the mills of the Salient that Sir Douglas Haig found himself short of men at the critical moment. Nor was the training for open warfare adequate. Indeed, it is quite possible that had a greater success been achieved an even heavier rebuff from the enemy's counter-offensive might have resulted than that which actually occurred on the right flank. The plan was simple. The tanks were to roll out gaps in the enormously powerful wire defences of the Hindenburg system of trenches, through which the infantry was to press in columns. The infantry " drive " was to be east and north, and the troops of the Cavalry Corps were to pass through at the earliest opportunity, push towards the Canal de l'Escaut on the east, and the River Sensée on the north, thus turning the whole enemy line south of the Scarpe. The 36th (Ulster) Division, of which the 2nd Royal Irish Rifles now formed part, was to have on the first day one brigade only, the 109th, engaged, which was to clear the important system of hostile trenches west of the Canal du Nord, as far north as the Bapaume—Cambrai road. The 108th Brigade, in which the Battalion was now included, was to be in reserve. There was little likelihood of its being employed on the first day, as it was not to be called upon unless the dominating height of Bourlon Wood should be captured that afternoon by our troops, which appeared unlikely.

The attack upon the Hindenburg system depended on surprise, and the surprise was complete. The great assault, launched at 6.20 a.m. on the morning of November 20th, swept through the front and support Hindenburg Lines, the most formidable continuous defences in the world, as though by magic. The German officers found it impossible to organize resistance. Their men, terrified by the line of great engines bearing down upon them out of the mist, surrendered or ran away. At 8.35 a.m., at the same moment as the Hindenburg Support Line was attacked all along the front, the 109th Brigade began its bombing action—one of the most celebrated of the war—up the trenches west of the Canal du Nord. This was prefaced by a bombardment of the Spoil Heap upon the canal bank, which was chosen as the point of entry, with the demoralizing incendiary shell known as " thermit." By 3.30 p.m. the troops had crossed the Bapaume—Cambrai road, having captured over 500 prisoners. Everywhere else the infantry attack had gone well, except at Flesquières, a village on a hill-top, just inside the Hindenburg Support Line. This place was defended with great gallantry by a German officer, who shot down the tanks as they breasted the slope, with a field gun, at point-blank range. The failure of the 51st Division to capture it on this first day had an unfortunate effect upon the battle, since it prevented the cavalry in some cases from moving to its allotted positions. Moreover, though the 62nd Division on the right of the 109th Brigade, carried out its task brilliantly, capturing Graincourt and crossing the Bapaume—Cambrai road, Bourlon Wood was not taken, so there was no question of employing the 107th and 108th Brigades of the 36th Division, which could probably on this date have captured the village of Mœuvres without much difficulty.

The 2nd Battalion Royal Irish Rifles had, as stated in the last chapter, moved into bivouac with the 108th Brigade at Lebucquière on November 19th. At 8 a.m. on the 20th, after the opening of the battle, when there was still a prospect of the Brigade being used against Mœuvres, it moved forward till its head was at the village of Hermies. Then in the afternoon it moved farther east, three of its battalions taking up positions in our old trenches, while the 2nd Royal Irish Rifles moved to Yorkshire Bank, a large spoil heap at the point where the Canal du Nord turns abruptly west along the Grand Ravine. The 107th Brigade later crossed the canal and moved into Havrincourt, captured in the morning by the 62nd Division. The two brigades in reserve had an unpleasant afternoon, as rain fell heavily, and they had not much shelter. The Royal Irish Rifles remained all night upon and around Yorkshire Bank. The general position at the end of the day was that Flesquières, which had not been captured, formed the point of an extraordinary salient into the territory taken by the British. Our line now ran due east, just north of the Bapaume—Cambrai road, cutting at right angles across the Canal du Nord and the two Hindenburg lines. But at the Factory on the Bapaume—Cambrai road it ran due south, east of Graincourt, round Flesquières and then north-east, to north of Noyelles, in our hands.

The salient was very quickly cleared on the morrow, when Flesquières was found unoccupied and Anneux, Cantaing, and Fontaine captured by the 62nd and 51st Divisions. Unfortunately, however, the delay had been very serious. It had spoiled whatever chances the Cavalry Corps possessed, and these chances were at once reduced to zero when German resistance, after the first staggering shock, began to stiffen. Nor had the attack on the heights of Bourlon and Bourlon Wood been successful. Had this very valuable ground been taken, the intention had been to employ the 107th and 108th Brigades to move up east of the Canal du Nord and hold its line from Mœuvres to Sains-lez-Marquion. In the circumstances these brigades were not employed, while the attacks of the 109th, northward in the direction of Mœuvres, only succeeded in gaining about eight hundred yards. The only move made by the 108th Brigade on this day was to advance slightly northward, astride the Canal du Nord, the 2nd Royal Irish Rifles passing the night in old German trenches on the west bank.

Next morning, however, the 108th Brigade came into action, in relief of the 109th, which had had two days of hard fighting. At 7 a.m. on the 22nd the leading battalion of the Brigade, the 12th Royal Irish Rifles, took over the 109th Brigade's trenches south of Mœuvres, ready to attack that village at 10.30. Behind it the 9th Royal Irish Fusiliers was well closed up on the Bapaume—Cambrai road. Then came the 2nd Royal Irish Rifles, and in rear the 11/13th Battalion of that Regiment. East of the canal the 107th

Brigade was to roll up the remainder of the Hindenburg Support Line, which crossed the canal east of Mœuvres, at the same time as the 108th Brigade captured the village.

The attack of the 12th Irish Rifles on Mœuvres was well carried out and succeeded after considerable trouble in capturing the whole of this formidable *point d'appui*. But it was quite out of the question to capture the Hindenburg trenches flanking the village without either tanks or a serious artillery preparation. Consequently the attacking battalion was upon a narrow front and harassed on either flank. When the German counter-attack, apparently by two battalions, was launched, our men north and west of the village were pinched by its converging pincers, and forced to fall back to avoid capture. Unfortunately the supports of the 9th Irish Fusiliers did not arrive in time to give them such numbers as would have made a stand possible in this awkward situation. Three companies of the Irish Fusiliers made another attempt after dusk, but were held up by wire. It was decided that the 12th Irish Rifles should attack again next morning, and at 7.30 p.m. the 2nd Battalion moved up across the Bapaume—Cambrai road to be ready to support it. The Battalion had now passed three winter days in the open without coming into action.

II.—THE CAPTURE OF BOURLON WOOD: THE 2ND BATTALION AT MŒUVRES.

The attack of the 23rd on Mœuvres was a bigger one than that of the preceding day. On the right one company of the 9th Royal Irish Fusiliers was to make a feint attack upon the Hindenburg trenches east of the village, it being thought almost impossible to clear these without tanks. The remaining three companies of the Battalion were to enter the village at the south-east corner and take its eastern edge. The 12th Royal Irish Rifles was to capture and clear the rest of the village, the 2nd Battalion being in close support, to follow up any success achieved and clear the Hindenburg Line north-west of the village. An attack was being launched at the same time by the 107th Brigade east of the canal.

From 9 a.m. onwards heavy artillery shelled the village. Three-quarters of an hour later the enemy, who had from the higher ground evidently observed the assembly of our troops, began a counter-bombardment. At 10.30 the troops advanced to the attack through the trenches of the bottle-neck south of Mœuvres, behind a creeping barrage. On the right the company of the Royal Irish Fusiliers succeeded by means of the bluff of their feint attack and got a footing in the first line trench, which they then proceeded to clear up to the canal. They could make no impression on the second line, which was strongly held. The other three companies entered the south-east of the village and made a certain amount of progress. On the left the 12th Irish Rifles had made little. It was evident that the place was strongly held and that many more machine guns had been brought in.

At 2 p.m. "A," "B," and "C" Companies of the 2nd Irish Rifles moved into the village to the support of the 12th Battalion, while half an hour later "D" Company moved up the trench on the west flank of the village. Progress was much impeded by machine guns on either flank of the village, even after, as the result of a pigeon message, the approximate positions from which these were firing had been pounded by heavy artillery. The three companies of the 2nd Irish Rifles advanced slowly, making skilful use of cover, but "D" Company was unable to enter the Hindenburg Support Line on the west.

By 3.30 p.m. the 2nd Irish Rifles had captured three-fourths of the village, and reached a point not far from its northern edge. But the 9th Irish Fusiliers were stationary in the south-east portion, while German machine guns, sweeping the main street, prevented co-ordination of the attacks. Dusk, too, was now beginning to fall. It was decided that consolidation of the ground won, with the enemy pinching either side of the village, was impossible, and that there was serious risk of losing a considerable number of men, to no useful end, if they were left in this position overnight. At 4 p.m., accordingly, the troops were withdrawn, and a line established through the southernmost houses of the village. The Battalion was relieved in the early morning of November 24th by the 11th Inniskilling Fusiliers of the 109th Brigade, and moved back to the neighbourhood of Hermies, where it remained till the evening of the 26th. In this, its first action in the 36th Division, it had fully lived up to its reputation, proving itself skilful and bold in village fighting, and, though prisoners were few, taking four German machine guns. It is easy to be wise after the event, but it seems clear that Mœuvres ought to have been attacked on the first day of the action, even if Bourlon Wood were not taken, that it would have been fairly easily captured then, and that, on the other hand, there was never much prospect after the first day of capturing *and holding* it, without the aid of tanks to roll up the trenches of the Hindenburg Support Line. No tanks were employed west of the Canal du Nord from the beginning of the battle to the end. The Battalion had had heavy losses ; 2nd-Lieutenant Rainey and 16 other ranks killed, Captains McArivey and Smith, 2nd-Lieutenants Stuart and McAlindon, and 99 other ranks wounded, 7 other ranks missing.

Bourlon and Fontaine had been captured on the 23rd, both subsequently to be lost to counter-attacks, but Bourlon Wood remained in the hands of the British. No new attempt to advance west of the Canal was made on the 24th or 25th, but there was considerable shelling, and it was evident that the enemy had brought up much fresh artillery to compensate for his heavy losses in guns on the first day. On the evening of November 26th the whole of the 36th Division was relieved, and at 7 p.m. the 2nd Royal Irish Rifles marched from Hermies to Beaumetz. The relief was a very unpleasant experience. It was blowing and snowing hard, and the ruined village which was to shelter the troops after their week in the open was full of the details of other divisions. Next day the Battalion moved to Rocquigny, and on the 29th entrained at Ytres for the Fosseux area, west of Arras.

III.—The German Counter-Attacks.

The 36th Division was being transferred from the battle-front to the XVII Corps in this area. The infantry moved north by train, the transport by road, staying a night by the way. But the very day after the move occurred the great German counter-offensive, admirably planned to apply pincers north and south to the salient caused by the successful attack of the British. On the left or northern front, where the artillery of the 36th Division, which had been left in line, played a remarkable rôle in the fighting, the Germans suffered a complete and bloody defeat. On the right or southern front they broke through in most sensational fashion, retaking La Vacquerie, capturing Villers-Guislain and Gonnelieu, which had been in our hands before the attack, and actually holding Gouzeaucourt till thrown out of it by a counter-attack made by the Guards' Division just after midday. The 36th Division received instant orders to retrace its steps and re-enter the battle. But there was now no time to find trains. The troops had to march back. As for the transport, which had moved north by road, in many cases it was turned about without the unfortunate beasts being unhitched.

The Battle of Cambrai,
1917.

The 2nd Irish Rifles detrained at Beaumetz les Loges, Rivière Station, five miles south-west of Arras, at 1.30 a.m. on November 30th, and marched to the neighbouring village of Simencourt. Soon after its arrival came the orders for the return. It marched that day to Gomiecourt, off the Arras—Bapaume road, arriving at 9 p.m. The distance was about thirteen miles, which does not sound excessive; but it had already had a two-mile march that morning, and came from a week's fighting and a night in cattle-trucks. Next day, December 1st, it left Gomiecourt at 12.30 p.m. and marched to Rocquigny, about eleven miles. On the 2nd it left Rocquigny at 10 a.m. and marched to fields outside Metz-en-Couture, going into billets in the village as soon as a corner could be cleared for it, about 5 p.m.

On December 3rd the 36th Division got orders to enter the line on Welsh Ridge, the most vital part of the threatened front, and on the 5th, 6th, and 7th the 109th Brigade was engaged in desperate bomb-fighting, with constant attacks and counter-attacks along the Hindenburg trenches where they crossed the ridge. The 108th Brigade, however, had a rather quieter and less important front on the left of the 109th, for the most part in the wooded Couillet Valley. After two days in reserve trenches, the 2nd Irish Rifles entered the line here, leaving the neighbourhood of Beaucamp at 8 p.m. on the 4th, and not reaching the front line till 3 a.m. next morning.

From the Battalion's position one could look along the valley into the large village of Marcoing, which had been captured by us on November 20th, and recaptured by the enemy on the 30th, but did not appear to be seriously damaged. From the village small patrols of the enemy were constantly coming up the sunken roads in the dusk of morning and evening. Two men were captured by the Battalion on the 6th, one on the evening of the 8th, and a fourth on the night of the 10th: 2nd-Lieutenant Phillips was wounded on the 6th. It was important to strengthen the position, and hard work was done on a new trench begun by the Battalion's predecessors. On the 12th the Battalion was relieved by the 9th Irish Fusiliers, and moved back to the reserve line, west of Couillet Wood, where it bivouacked. During this period Lieut.-Colonel Goodman, the Commanding Officer, was forced to "go down" owing to a breakdown in health due to overwork and strain. He had given all his energy to the welfare of the Battalion which he had led so ably, and had now no more to give.

It was now over three weeks since the launching of the attack at Cambrai, and there was hardly a man of the infantry but was suffering from fatigue and exposure. The weather had been, perhaps, no worse than that of any normal November and December, but it was not the climate in which one would naturally choose to live three weeks in muddy ditches, with frequent intervals of heavy fighting and heavy marching. The men were at a very low ebb, and the sick wastage became enormous. Promise of relief came at last, but it was not possible to relieve the left brigade frontage till after the right. Now, as has been stated, the left was the quieter front, but the 108th Brigade had held it continuously, while the 107th and 109th Brigades had taken turns on the right. Two battalions of the 107th Brigade, the 1st Irish Fusiliers and 10th Royal Irish Rifles, were therefore exchanged with two of the 108th, the 2nd and 11/13th Battalions, and remained in line with the latter Brigade. On the night of the 14th the 2nd Battalion was relieved by troops of the 63rd (Royal Naval) Division, and moved to Metz under the orders of the 107th Brigade. On the 15th the Battalion moved to Etricourt, and on the 17th entrained to Mondicourt, billeting in the neighbouring village of Warlincourt, on the Doullens—

Arras road. Here it was joined next day by the 108th Brigade, relieved at last, and returned to its command.

The men, after all their work in the open, were bone-weary. Unfortunately, they did not reap the full benefit of a rest in very pleasant country and good billets owing to a remarkable series of snow-storms occurring at this time, which necessitated the employment of working parties to keep the roads clear. Even in the course of the two miles' march from Mondicourt to Warlincourt, the Battalion on its arrival had lost its way in the snow, some of the smaller roads being unrecognizable. However, it was possible to obtain, at a price, plenty of good cheer, and the Battalion's last war Christmas was happily spent.

The rest was not a long one. The Fifth British Army was about to relieve the French over a considerable portion of front, and the 36th Division was to move down south as part of it. On the 28th the Battalion again marched to Mondicourt and entrained, *via* Doullens and Amiens, to Boves, on the Avre, south-east of the latter city. Once again there was trouble through snow on the march to billets in Gentelles, and the lorries carrying stores from the station stuck in drifts by the roadside. The transport, travelling by omnibus train, was snowed up at Flesselles, and did not arrive till the 30th. Apparently affairs were not yet quite ready for the relief of the French, for the whole Division halted for some days in this area. The Battalion saw out the year 1917 in Gentelles, doing some training to pass the time, and did not continue its passage south till January 7th.

IV.—THE SECOND BATTLE OF PASSCHENDAELE.

We left the 1st Battalion about to take part once more in fighting in the Salient. On the night of November 30th it marched up from Haslar Camp, St. Jean, to the neighbourhood of Passchendaele. Unfortunately, it came in for a serious bombardment of the duck-board track, and had no less than thirty casualties during the move. And when the duck-board was cut by shell fire, the mud made progress terribly slow. However, the relief was at last accomplished, though the right post, Teale Cottage, which the Battalion had been ordered to take over, was found to be in the hands of the enemy. " C " and " D " Companies were in front line, the other two in support.

The assault was to be carried out by the other three battalions of the Brigade, 2nd Lincolnshire, 2nd Berkshire, and 2nd Rifle Brigade. These battalions moved up on the afternoon of December 1st to the positions from which they were to attack. The Irish Rifles covered their assembly, then withdrew into brigade support in trenches and shell-holes behind. In the darkness and confusion, however, the orders to withdraw did not reach " D " Company, which remained in line during the fighting that followed, and had more casualties from shell-fire than would otherwise have been the case.

The object of the attack was to gain possession of two important redoubts, one three-quarters of a mile due north of Passchendaele, the other a thousand yards north-east. The moon being but just past the full, it had been decided to carry out a night attack. The Germans were used to attacks at dawn, and always prepared for them. It was to be supposed that they would be less on the alert several hours earlier. These night attacks, however, added new elements of risk, because men so frequently lost their way in them. On this occasion there was a particularly bright moon, so that individual figures could be distinguished at a hundred yards' distance. The ground, as the Brigade Diary expressively remarks, was " Ypres," and it may be added that the month was December. On the whole, however, the surface was unexpectedly dry.

The attack was launched at 1.55 a.m. behind a very heavy barrage. At once the inevitable blast of German machine-gun fire burst out. Despite it, however, the three battalions fought their way forward, and almost everywhere reached their objectives. But on both left and right defensive flanks had to be formed running back to the assembly position owing to the inability of other troops to advance. There was also a German salient in the middle of the attack, where progress was held up along the road leading north-east of Passchendaele. On the rest of the front the objectives were taken. The Germans allowed more than twelve hours to pass before they attempted a counter-attack. This, when it came, was beaten off by the weight of the British barrage and by machine-gun fire. The Brigade was relieved at night by troops of the 14th Division and moved back to St. Jean. The Royal Irish Rifles had taken no part in the action beyond covering the assembly and performing some carriers' duties. All the more significant, then, is it of the ferocity of the German artillery fire that in the two days in the line their casualty list reached the enormous total of a hundred—enormous for a battalion not directly engaged in an attack.*

A good rest followed the battle. The Battalion entrained at St. Jean and went direct to Wizernes, near St. Omer, marching thence to Noir Carme and Zudausques. Here mornings only were devoted to training of all natures. In the afternoons there were sports—boxing, football, and cross-country running. The weather during early December was fairly good, and the troops recovered their fitness in the open air. Christmas celebrations were held on December 20th, as an early move was in prospect. This took place on Boxing Day, when the Battalion marched to Wizernes, entraining at 6.0 a.m. for the eternal Salient. Once again the men got out at St. Jean, marched *via* Wieltje, which had been in our front line of July, and went into dug-outs in the California trenches, which marked the " Black " Line of the summer attacks, a little north of the point where the Battalion had been twice engaged. While in this area, Lieut.-Colonel McCarthy-O'Leary, who had been wounded here in command of the Battalion on August 1st, returned and again took over command. On December 30th the Battalion entered the line in the unpleasant Goudberg sector, north of Passchendaele.

---

* The great majority of the losses occurred during the relief or in reconnaissance of Teale Cottage. The officer casualties were : 2nd-Lieutenant A. B. Wilkie, killed ; Captains W. R. L. Patterson, G. C. Robb, 2nd-Lieutenants P. Windle and E. W. Lennard, wounded.

CHAPTER V

I.—THE STRUMA VALLEY.

THE 6th Royal Irish Rifles began the year 1917 in billets in the village of Orljak, south of the River Struma. Three companies were employed in various fatigues, strengthening the river defences and constructing new divisional headquarters for the 10th Division. The fourth carried out training. The Commanding Officer, Lieut.-Colonel C. M. L. Becher, went on leave to England on January 8th, Major F. R. W. Graham taking command. The strange vicissitudes of South-Balkan weather were very trying to troops. In summer the climate was sub-tropical, with swarms of flies and the typical disease of malaria. Now, in January, there were such heavy falls of snow that the whole aspect of the country was changed and its features hidden. All work had to cease for some days. The Struma was in flood, causing considerable trouble. At the end of the month the Belica Stream also flooded, flowed round the dam which had been built, and swamped the outposts, which had to be withdrawn to the right bank. The comfort of the troops had now, however, greatly improved. The Battalion had an excellent canteen in Mekes, where tinned foods of all kinds were on sale and good teas could be served. Given time, the British Army could always be trusted to work out administrative arrangements in any part of the world superior to those of any other nation among the combatants on both sides, though, as those who remember the war scarcely need to be told, at considerably greater cost.

On February 4th the Battalion relieved the 5th Connaught Rangers in line at Jenikoj, with outposts in Kalendra. Bulgar patrols occasionally approached the outposts, always to be driven out by our musketry fire. Kalendra received about six shells a day, and our casualties were very rare. We also took a good few deserters. The Struma and Belica were now both falling, and the positions became more comfortable. On the 26th of the month the 29th Brigade was relieved by the 31st, and the Battalion moved back to Orljak. The first part of March was spent in training and work on the roads, the Brigade returning to the line on the 15th. The Battalion was now at Elisan, in support to the right section of the Brigade frontage on the left of its previous position at Kalendra. The outposts were at Kumli and Barakli on the Belica Stream. The enemy evidently saw the relief and welcomed the incoming troops with a good deal of shelling. On March the 31st the Royal Irish Rifles were ordered to reconnoitre the ground in advance of their present outposts at Kumli, with a view to forming a new line from Barakli to Prosenik, to serve as a bridge-head over the Belica. This was done by the 24th, and the enemy permitted the troops to establish themselves without opposition in the new positions. Six small front-line works were established, and a number of supporting keeps. The scouts of the Battalion worked well forward and identified the positions of Bulgar posts round the village of Kjupri. A raid on the trenches in front of the village was planned for April 25th, but postponed owing to rain.

On April 28th an outpost on the left bank of the Belica was raided by the enemy. The Bulgars, about forty strong, crawled up through the long grass and threw a shower of bombs. The post withdrew in good order on to the main piquet line. Two men were, however, missing, both believed to have been killed. Next day the raid took place, with the object of feeling the strength of the Bulgars in and around Kjupri. The force consisted of two parties, each of one officer and twenty men, supported by two Vickers machine guns and a section of A/54 Battery R.F.A. The scouts of the left party walked right on top of a listening post of three men, who resisted pluckily. One was killed and one taken prisoner, the third escaping. We had two wounded, one by a bayonet. But the alarm had been given, the Bulgars in the trench behind fled into Kjupri, and the party could do no more good. The enemy fired a volley on the right party, which caused no loss, and then likewise bolted. It was estimated that the garrison of the village consisted of not more than about sixty or seventy men.

The way was now cleared for a more important operation. The 29th Brigade, on the left of the 30th, was to make an attack and hold the ground won. The most important task was assigned to the 6th Royal Irish Rifles, which was to capture the village of Kjupri. The 6th Leinster were to attack on their left. The artillery support would sound meagre on the Western Front, but was quite powerful for fighting of this nature. It consisted of the 54th Field Artillery Brigade, one section of D/68 (Howitzer) Battery, and one section A/64 Battery, with the 153rd Field Artillery Brigade for counter-battery work. The attack was to be carried out at 7 p.m. on May 5th. Colonel Becher had meanwhile returned from England, and was in command of the Battalion.

Of the assault itself there is little enough to record. The men went forward with that speed and confidence which was generally the undoing of the discontented Bulgarian soldier. The Irish Rifles had not to encounter a serious resistance from the enemy, though there was fairly heavy artillery fire. All objectives were attained, and there was touch with the battalions on either flank. Then the work of consolidation began. Four posts were taken up by " C " Company in a semi-circle beyond the village. In the darkness No. 4 post was sited rather far forward, out of line with the rest. Colonel Becher made a last tour of them at 3.15 a.m. on the 6th, when the work accomplished was excellent.

The enemy's artillery kept up its fire all night, the intensity of the barrage increasing at 3.30 a.m. At 5 a.m., when he had light enough, the enemy attacked. The exposed No. 4 work was his evident objective, and a body of about 150 men was seen attempting to outflank it on the left. Checked by the Lewis gun in the post, the Bulgars fell back to reform. At 6 a.m. there was another attack, slightly farther to the left. It was rather half-hearted, and was dominated from the first by Lewis-gun and musketry fire.

But at 6.45 came the real effort. A strong force attacked the front between works Nos. 3 and 4 and 100 yards each side of them, after a bombardment which caused considerable loss in Work 4. Runners all became casualties, and for a time the two posts were completely cut off. Our barrage was late owing to bad communications. Each platoon of the enemy crept forward till fired on, then got up to charge with the traditional cheer. Our fire took considerable toll of the attack, and then our artillery opened to complete the check. The lateness of the barrage proved a blessing in disguise, for it fell right along the whole Bulgar line when the latter was within 150 yards of Work 4 and about to make an attempt to rush it. The enemy now fell back, having evidently suffered heavily. Voices of the officers were heard urging their men forward once more, received, observes the war diary, " by frenzied cries of discord by the rank and file." The rank and file's opinion evidently prevailed, for there was no further attack. Our barrage lengthened in pursuit of the enemy.

The losses in the works were—in No. 3, 2 other ranks killed, 6 wounded; in No. 4, 5 other ranks killed, 1 officer and 11 other ranks wounded. The defence had been very resolute, particularly in No. 4, of which the garrison was reduced to a handful. The Battalion received the following message with reference to the affair from Brigade Headquarters:

"The Divisional Commander congratulates you on gaining the required objective and repulsing all enemy counter-attacks. He is confident that the 6th Royal Irish Rifles will treat all subsequent attacks in the same way. The Brigadier adds congratulations also."

There was hard work digging and putting up wire obstacles till May 19th, when the Battalion was relieved by the 5th Connaught Rangers. A fine patrol action was fought by the 6th Leinster at this time, resulting in the capture of about a dozen Bulgars and, what was more important, a German non-commissioned officer. The amiable Teuton had in his possession a number of clips of ammunition with the bullets reversed. Such bullets make a hole into which a man might put his fist. It is to be trusted that his captivity was not passed under the most pleasant conditions.

II.—The Evacuation of the Struma Valley.

The recent advance was to have no value beyond keeping up the fighting instinct of the troops and causing loss and depression to the enemy. At the end of May it was decided that the unhealthy valley of the Struma should be evacuated for the hot months, in order to avoid the risk of another serious malarial epidemic. June 1st and 2nd were spent by the Battalion demolishing observation posts and dug-outs. It was not in line for the actual retirement, having been relieved on the 4th by the Connaught Rangers. The withdrawal was by stages, covered by detachments of the Connaught Rangers and 1st Leinster. By the night of the 5th the Struma Valley was practically clear, the last outposts moving up the slopes in the early morning of the 7th.

On June 10th the Battalion settled down at Pekovo on its new position. This was on the high range south and south-west of the Struma, and over two thousand feet up. The line now held ran from Camel Hill, south of Bestavuk, through Kairahman, to the junction of three roads north-north-west of Calimah. The front was held by two companies, with four Vickers guns and two trench mortars. Two companies were in support. The front was enormous, upwards of eight miles long, so that posts were many hundreds of yards apart. But the position was strong, and the excellent observation from it would allow it to be reinforced while an advancing enemy was still miles away.

Mobile columns were organized to dislodge the enemy from villages in front of the Brigade, with Yeomanry co-operation. The Connaught Rangers carried out an expedition to Ormanli, now six miles from our front line, but the enemy fled on the advance of our column. It began to appear as though the Bulgars also, though more used to this sort of climate than our men, had evacuated the valley of the Struma, or at all events had no more than a screen of troops in it.

Everything possible was done to keep the troops fit. Special sun-shelters were constructed. In July men in front line and close support had ten grains of quinine every second day. There were, nevertheless, a fair number of men who suffered from a mild form of malaria. On the 28th of the month the Battalion exchanged frontages with the 6th Leinster, who had been on its left. Mosquito netting made its appearance about this time, and was at least as valuable as the quinine in the fight against malaria.

In August the Battalion moved to Mirova, which was no less than 2,600 feet above sea-level. Here intensive training began. The new platoon formation of a section of grenadiers, a rifle-grenade section, a Lewis-gun section, and a section of riflemen was introduced. General Vandeleur laid stress on the importance of training the men of the first two as riflemen also, as on this front they were more likely to be required in that capacity. He was certainly right, and the " specialist " craze was found on the Western Front to have some evil results, as it made men forget the use of their rifles. The trouble with regard to these schemes in the British Army was that the authorities behind drained the battalions so remorselessly that there were never men enough to keep sections or platoons up to strength. It was useless to talk magnificently of a " section of grenadiers " when that numbered only three or four men.

Suddenly there came orders which completely altered the last months of the Battalion's existence. The 10th Division was to move to Palestine.

III.—THE MOVE TO PALESTINE.

The warning for the move was short. On September 4th the Battalion marched to Lakana, on the main Seres—Salonika road, and on the 9th was taken down to the Base in motor lorries. Here re-equipment was hastily carried out, the wheeled transport being issued instead of the pack which had been used on this front. On the 14th the Battalion, at a strength of 27 officers and 870 other ranks, embarked at Salonika, but remained two days in harbour waiting for its escort of two destroyers. Then came the voyage through the blue waters of the Ægean, with a halt at Skiros, where the troops bathed. Alexandria was reached on the 19th, and next day the Battalion entrained for Moascar, and went into camp.

The position in Southern Palestine may be shortly summarized before we embark upon the Battalion's participation in the great campaign, in which it arrived at the very moment that victory was about to turn its face towards our armies. The original British policy in Egypt had been defensive. No attempt had been made at the outbreak of war with Turkey to hold the Turco-Egyptian frontier, which ran through the waste of the Sinai Desert, over a hundred miles east of the Suez Canal. All we desired was to assure the Canal itself, which was strongly garrisoned with Indian troops; while Territorials and Anzacs were training in Egypt and available as reinforcements. In February, 1915, a Turkish force of some 20,000 men, led with extraordinary skill across the desert by the German Kress von Kressenstein, had attacked the Canal, and actually got three boatloads of men across it, but had suffered heavy defeat. Later the policy had changed. We began the great coast railway from Kantara, on the Canal, out into the desert, through Bir el Abd and El Arish, and a pipe-line for water, both marvellous feats of engineering. In January, 1917, we captured Rafa, on the old frontier line, and this point was reached by the railway in March. We had now left behind the desert, but Southern Palestine was by no means the land flowing with milk and honey which Biblical students may have expected to find. It was stony, hilly, almost waterless in summer. In March we attacked Gaza, and suffered what can only be described as an important defeat. In April we attacked again, Sir Archibald Murray being apparently urged on from home by statesmen who did not realize the strength of the enemy's position, and desired a success against Turkey to march with the offensive in Europe. The result was a failure still more marked. Then quiet fell for the rest of the summer, during which General Sir Edmund Allenby succeeded General Sir Archibald Murray. The British front lay from Gamli to the sea west of Gaza. The Turkish position lay mainly along the Gaza—Beersheba road, which was defended by a series of very strong works. Gaza itself was particularly strongly fortified. The Turk, at least without German guidance, was backward in some of the arts of war, but in that of fortification he was, as always in his distinguished military history, thoroughly up to date. Sir Edmund Allenby determined to capture Beersheba first of all, as the works here were the least formidable in the line, and also because its capture would give him an open flank against which to act, and allow him to make full use of his superiority in mounted troops. In order, however, to keep the enemy in doubt as to his object, it was necessary to attack at Gaza simultaneously with the main assault on Beersheba. The attack was fixed for October 31st.

After a short stay in Egypt, during which there was a big boxing tournament held by the 29th Brigade at Ismailia, the journey to the front began. On October 4th the 6th Royal Irish Rifles entrained at Kantara, reaching Rafa next day. Here training began, and the fact that this training was largely in deploying from a column of route and advancing to the attack was evidence of the British commander's confidence that the Turkish line would be broken. Mobility was the essential. To aid in the acquirement of this, eight small arms ammunition pack mules were equipped as machine-gun mules. Practice was also carried out in the quick striking of camp and in the loading of camels, which now formed the principal part of infantry transport. The men, it was noticed, were very fatigued even after short marches. They had not wholly recovered from the malaria in the Struma Valley. On the 28th the Battalion marched to Kemp Station, arriving at 11 p.m. The route was across loose sand, and it was found necessary for the Camel Column to move parallel to that of the infantry, as under such conditions the beasts outpaced the men. The following night the march was continued to Shellal, close to the front line and near the British right flank. The 29th Brigade camped in broken ground, where it was completely hidden from enemy observation save from the air, which the Turk was to be given small chance of employing. The men were somewhat fatigued, and had not yet grown used to their meagre daily water ration of a gill per man.

IV.—THE THIRD BATTLE OF GAZA.

On October 31st, the day of the attack, officers of the Royal Irish Rifles were ordered to reconnoitre the line of the 30th Brigade in front, but before this could be carried out the sudden order came to move to Goz el Bazal. This was reached at 9.30 p.m. Half an hour later there arrived in camp the splendid news that Beersheba had fallen.

It had been taken as the result of a brilliant action almost entirely carried out by Australians and New Zealanders. The main road, through Hebron, to Bethlehem and Jerusalem, had been cut early in the day by a great encircling movement, and the town captured from the east by the 4th Australian Light Horse Brigade. Over two thousand prisoners had been taken, but the Turks had robbed us of the good water-supply which was one of the chief reasons why Beersheba had been attacked as a prelude to the general action, by blowing up most of the wells.

Next day the Royal Irish Rifles moved to Karm, on the road from Khan-Yunus to Beersheba. The railway, which stretched out as if by magic, was already beyond this place. On November 2nd the officers reconnoitred the line of the 30th Brigade in front. On the 3rd the Battalion moved a few miles nearer Beersheba, to Beit Abu Taha. On November 1st a holding attack on the Gaza defences, to prevent the enemy reinforcing

THE SALO
Attacks by 6
indicated

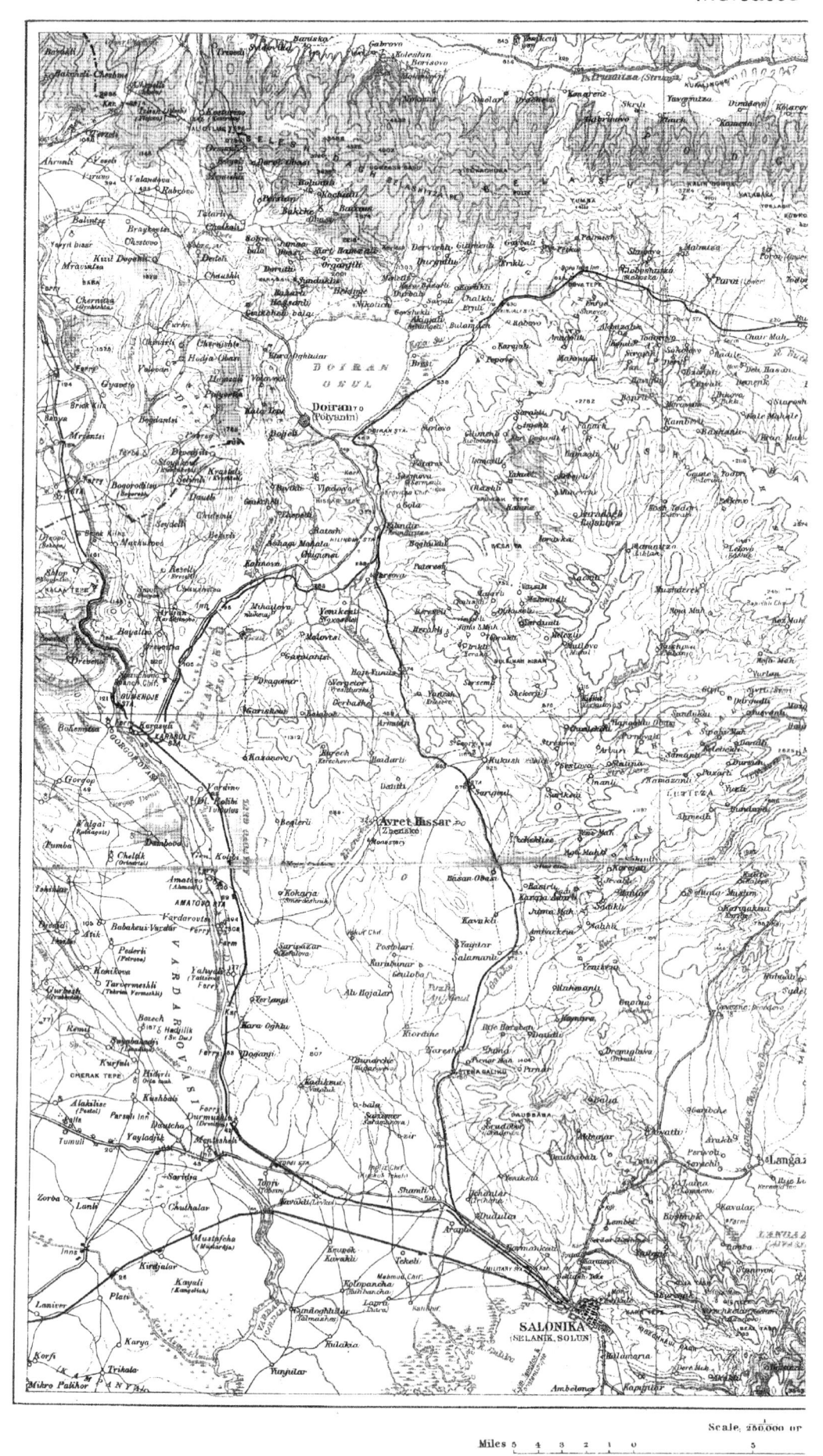

NIKA THEATRE

th Royal Irish Rifles
by red arrows.

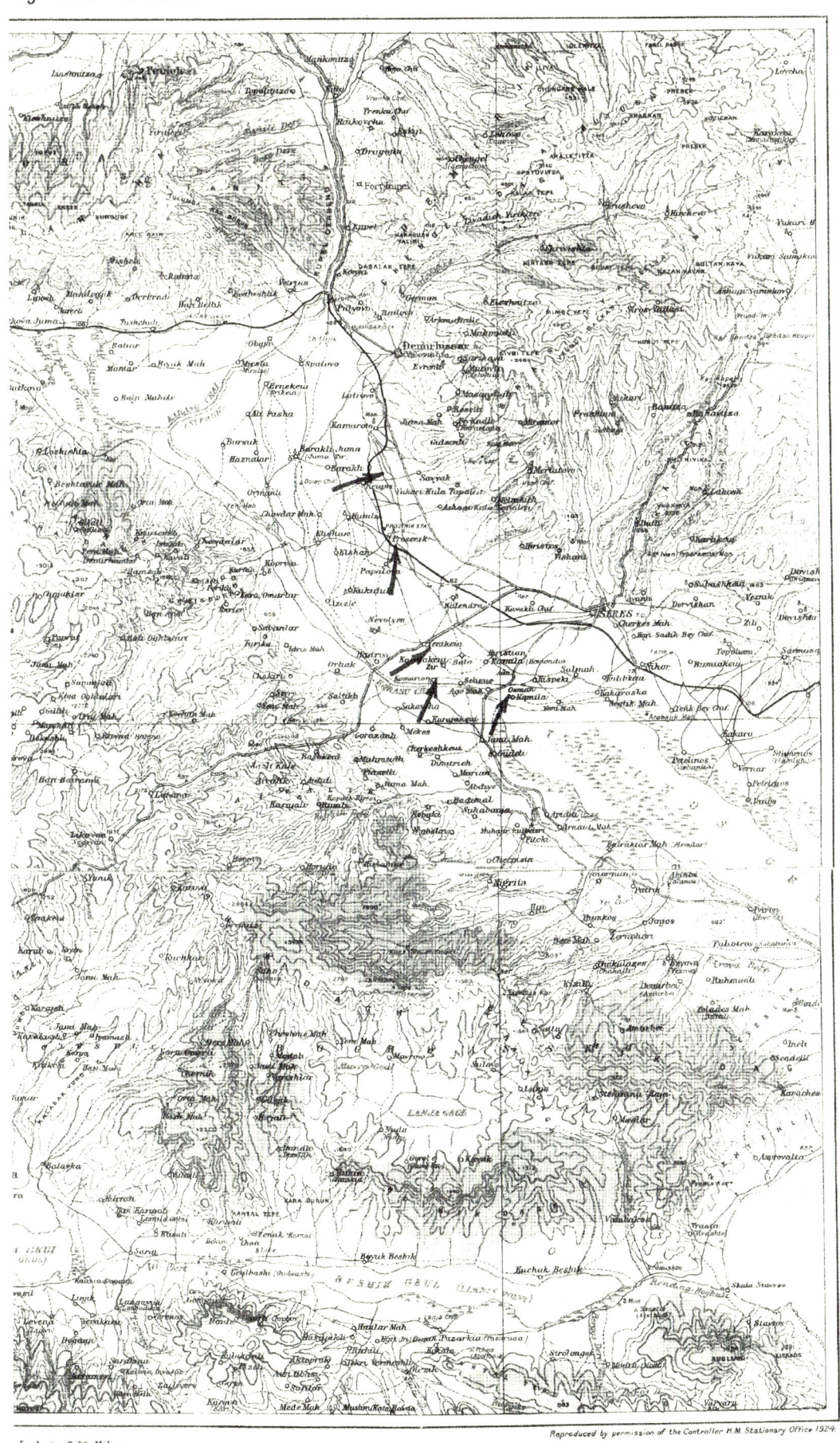

Inch to 3.95 Miles

Reproduced by permission of the Controller H.M. Stationary Office 1924.

his line elsewhere, had succeeded in reaching most of its objectives. The way was now prepared for Sir Edmund Allenby's main attack.

On November 5th the Battalion was ordered to relieve the 6th Munsters in the outpost line, west of the Wadi Imlieh, south of the Beersheba—Gaza road. It was a very difficult march, and though the crossings of the wadi had been reconnoitred carefully, it took a long time to find them again in the dark. The Battalion was not concerned with the still greater difficulties which were encountered by the wagons of the train in its rear, but the latter were floundering about all night. Lieutenant C. F. Everson and one other rank were wounded on this date.

The 6th was an important day, when the enemy's line was definitely breached. Sharia Station, six miles north of the Beersheba—Gaza road, was taken The 31st Brigade was the only one of the 10th Division that was in action, and it got its objectives. On the 7th the advance continued, the 29th Brigade being still in divisional reserve. To the Royal Irish Rifles was given the task of clearing the battle field in its area, and the Battalion buried 34 Turkish dead.

Gaza had been evacuated in the course of this day by the enemy, and next morning the Battalion was ordered to march up west of the Beersheba—Gaza road till touch was obtained with the troops working down from Gaza. The meeting of the two columns took place at 11.30 a.m. A number of trench mortars were found, and the men had an opportunity of studying the excellent Turkish defences. Those at Hareira, on the main road, were in particular wonderful. The trenches were ten feet deep, and the whole work was a maze of trenches and wire, probably one of the finest fortresses in the world, built on the lines which had been taught by the experience of this war.

From this date onwards the enemy was in flight. With the mass of cavalry at his disposal, Sir Edmund Allenby must have hoped to be able to destroy the army opposed to him. Unfortunately, however, he had found very much less water than he had hoped for. And without water it was impossible to move his cavalry at the necessary speed. Moreover, the infantry had not in all cases been able to take over the work from the cavalry, which had "opened the ball" for it, swiftly enough. As a consequence, the cavalry, retained in action when it should have been resting, was too weary for the gigantic marches necessary to rout the retreating columns and press on into Jerusalem. A great victory had been won, but the Turks were to be able to take up a new line of defence, and one, in the opinion of the very able German, Baron Kress von Kressenstein, who had commanded them in the action, better suited for resistance to a stronger force. The Turk is always a magnificent marcher, at least equal to the Frenchman in any climate, and far superior to any European in a climate and country such as Palestine. When his troops broke off the action at night, they were able in the darkness to do a fifteen mile tramp, while our cavalrymen were searching for water for their tortured beasts, and, if caught up the following afternoon, to repeat the performance. Nevertheless, the cavalry pressed on magnificently. Tortured by flies, by thirst, by sand-storms, in clothes they had not changed for ten days, till the stuff was caked as hard as a board with sweat and sand, often on half rations, they pushed the enemy back. On the 14th the vital point of Junction Station, twenty miles west of Jerusalem, was taken. The Turkish Army was cut in two, one half retiring eastward, the other northward.

The Battalion had no part in this attack. On November 10th it marched to the Wadi Hareira, and on the 18th to Sheikh Nebhan, due south of Gaza. It had a few days of training, particularly in scouting, of vast importance in the work that was to come.

A Brigade Lewis-Gun Competition held on the 24th was won by the Royal Irish Rifles. It was growing colder now. Drill jackets were exchanged for the ordinary service dress, and great-coats drawn. The greater coolness by day was welcome, but there was now only too much cold at night for men who had no shelter from it. On the 27th the march forward was resumed, the Battalion reaching the famous Junction Station on the 30th. The men were given all the following day to themselves, to bathe and wash clothes in the Wadi Katrah.

On December 2nd the Battalion, less "D" Company, detailed for water duties by the XX Corps, marched to Beit Nuba, north of the Jerusalem—Ramleh road, and on the 4th to Beit Anan. The 29th Brigade was now in front line, but the Royal Irish Rifles were in support. The 6th and 7th were mainly employed in conducting southwards parties of refugees. Rain had now begun, and a wet season was setting in. In Beit Anan five Turkish deserters were captured. At midday on the 9th came the great news that Jerusalem had fallen. It had been said by native prophets that when the Nile flowed into Jerusalem, a great king from the west would drive out the Turk. As a fact, though the Nile did not precede Sir Edmund Allenby, it followed him very shortly, for the marvellous pipe-line, upon which the whole expedition so largely depended, reached the Holy City or its neighbourhood.

Next day, December 10th, the Battalion marched north to Beit Sira, having been joined by "D" Company. On the 12th it relieved the 2nd Royal Irish Fusiliers at Suffa. It was over two months since it had crossed the frontier, but now for the first time it found itself in front line. "C" Company on the right had two platoons in line, "D" on the left all four. That the front was quiet and sparsely held by the enemy is proved by the fact that work on the rough country tracks was carried out by the support companies. The Army Commander was eager to continue the advance, but operations were continually put off by the rain. It had been decided that an attack was hopeless unless preceded by thirty-six hours of fine weather to allow the tracks to dry, and to await this there was postponement after postponement. There was a scare that the Turks, for political and religious reasons, would attempt a minor counter-offensive on Christmas Day. The line of the Royal Irish Rifles was reinforced, but the Turks remained quiet.

As the crow flies, the men were less than twenty miles from Bethlehem, that poor village where the history of the world had been changed nineteen centuries before; but, in squalor and wet, on scanty rations, their outposts without shelter on the bare hills, they had little to remind them of the celebrations commonly dedicated to the anniversary. And yet, to those of them that had imagination, there must have been a peculiar interest and solemnity in the associations, which the insignificance of the country must have served only to heighten. In these bleak and stony hills, in the green valleys with their primitive cultivation, the modern world was born. Away on their right flank was Jerusalem and the Mount of Olives, with one of the few splendours due to man, the fine mosque on the site of the Temple. Beyond was Jericho and the Hill of Temptation; farther still the Jordan and the desert. Ahead of them were Nazareth and Capernaum and the Sea of Galilee, not changed in any of its surroundings since the miraculous draught of fishes broke the net. Farther still was the range of Lebanon, with that one scanty grove of cedars, surely the most sacred trees that exist, since, through many of the long generations that mark the lives of trees, they are descended from the forests that built Solomon's Temple. And great forests then there must have been, when

Hiram, King of Tyre, let Solomon have what he would of them, even if we take it that the latter was something of a boaster. For we are told that he organized an army for the work under Adoniram, and gave them more leave than Allenby's army ever got, sending them to Lebanon " ten thousand a month by courses ; a month they were in Lebanon and two months at home." And he had " three score and ten thousand that bare burdens, and four score thousand hewers in the mountains," besides three thousand three hundred officers. If we could believe him, which is difficult, we should feel convinced that those officers had their hands as full as Sir Edmund Allenby's Administrative Staff.

The attack took place at last on December 27th. From right to left the 29th Brigade had in line the 1st Leinster, 5th Connaught Rangers, 6th Royal Irish Rifles. Patrols went forward at 5.45 a.m., the general advance beginning a quarter of an hour later. The first ridge was reached without difficulty at 6.45, when the Riflemen were in touch with the Light Horse on their left. Attempts to advance from it were, however, met with hot machine-gun fire. On the right the Turks attempted to counter-attack the Leinsters, but were beaten off. But the line was now temporarily hung up. Communication was difficult, and the 9th Mountain Battery, supporting the Irish Rifles, could not be got to bring fire on the hostile machine guns. The Brigade Headquarters ordered the 263rd F.A. Brigade to shell the ridge Sheikh Abdallah to Kefr Namah. At 10.15 a determined effort was made to advance, and within a few minutes all objectives were taken, including the hamlet of Deir Ibzia, captured by the Leinsters. Six Turkish officers and 51 other ranks were captured by the 29th Brigade, which had only 46 casualties. Of these the Royal Irish Rifles had 1 officer (2nd-Lieutenant J. W. Wilson) and 1 man killed, and 1 officer (2nd-Lieutenant R. Warnock) and 8 other ranks wounded.

The Royal Irish Rifles were not called upon next day, when the line was further advanced and Abu el Anein captured. This attack was almost a "walk-over." We had no more than 2 men wounded, while we captured about fifty of the demoralized enemy, and counted 32 dead Turks upon the field. On the 29th patrols covered the right flank of the Australian Light Horse, which was pushing forward, and another occupied Ras Kerker without opposition. On the 30th the Battalion took over the line from the Australians between Ras Kerker and Jurdeh.

So ended the year 1917. At this moment, as we have seen, prospects on the Western Front were bleak enough, and the war was, as it were, to be fought over again. Here, however, victory was in sight. The moral and discipline of the Turkish Army at this time can be judged by the following captured order, by the officer commanding the 2nd Battalion, 81st Regiment, dated December 1st, 1917 :—

" To-morrow the G.Os.C. the Army Corps and our Division will certainly come here and go down to Bethlehem. Care should be taken to have the ground clean and the men properly dressed. The officers should not stroll about in their slippers and nightcaps.

" It was noticed by the G.O.C. that an officer on patrol duty was in communication with a filthy woman in a cave. The Battalion will not hesitate to punish that officer for the disgrace he has brought upon us. . . .

" I see soldiers sleeping in and wearing their overcoats during the day. This lowers the moral of the soldier, therefore I ask the officers to give tactical lessons to their men in shooting and how to take advantage of ground during their free hours.

K

"I expect the O.C. Transport to grease the camels regularly, to clean their sores, and to send them to the veterinary officers if necessary.

"A list of armed and unarmed soldiers, with the amount of ammunition, number of rifles, entrenching tools and animals, should be sent to the Battalion Headquarters before 6.30 p.m."

BOOK V.

CHAPTER I

I.—JANUARY—MARCH, 1918.

THE 6th Battalion Royal Irish Rifles was not fated to see out the year 1918, or even the war. We may therefore deal first with its final campaign, and then turn to the 1st and 2nd Battalions, which can be followed straight through to the Armistice.

The Battalion was, it will be remembered, in line at Ras Kerker, about fourteen miles east of Ramleh and half that distance west of the Jerusalem—Nablus road. How quiet was the position may be judged from the fact that the natives, during January, began to plough, not only behind the line, but in front of it! A patrol carried out as far as the village of Jemmala, some three miles away, encountered no enemy. The line of posts, by which the Brigade's front had been hitherto defended, was abandoned in favour of strongly held defended localities, one in each battalion front, wired all round.

The chief occupation of the troops was, however, work on the tracks, which was of greater importance than improvement of the defences. The position was not over comfortable, nor was it improved by the heavy rains of that period. However, some of the minor amenities of warfare, which always appeared at every pause in active operations, made life more bearable. More comforts could now be brought forward, a wash-house was opened in Ras Kerker, and a certain amount of leave to Jerusalem—not exactly a paradise of pleasure—was granted. The wisest men were those who took all the chances that offered themselves without prejudice to hopes of better things.

The Battalion also received a few drafts, which tended to raise its spirits, for there is nothing more depressing to a unit than to be seriously under strength. " A " Company, which had been disbanded for a short time owing to the Battalion's weakness, was re-formed on January 20th.

In early February the weather continued wet. Practically all the Battalion's available strength, 9 officers and 450 other ranks, was now engaged daily upon the roads, a few sentries sufficing to assure the line. Due north of the present position was some high ground, crowned by a hamlet called Beit Ello. It was decided to occupy this as a preliminary to a further advance. Some of the procedure of this warfare against an enemy weak in numbers and seriously weakened in moral would have appeared to the soldier on the Western Front madder than the campaigns of the knights in " Through the Looking-Glass." Such would certainly have been his opinion had he been informed that sometimes, when there was question of occupying ground in the hands of the enemy, distinguished generals, screened and escorted by a handful of troops, galloped all over the area in question to ascertain whether this would be worth while. Yet so it was, and on February 11th the 6th Royal Irish Rifles covered such a reconnaissance of the Beit Ello plateau by the Brigade Commander. " A " and " B " Companies, with the Battalion scouts, furnished the necessary covering parties, throwing out Lewis-gun sections upon all the heights after the enemy had retired before their advance. One platoon cleared the village of Beit Ello and made good the high ground to a distance of 600 yards to north-west of it. A second platoon, from the left of the first-named, made good the highest ground, known as the Beit Ello plateau. Then patrols pushed out towards Deir en Nidham, a village two miles north of Beit Ello. Most elaborate communication was carried out, two miles of cable being reeled out to Beit Ello. The reconnaissance was successfully carried out without loss, though the Turks did a certain amount of sniping. When, however, a similar reconnaissance was carried out on the 26th, covered by parties of the 6th Leinster, the enemy was alert and stubborn, and a hard fight followed before he was driven off with a loss of 18, the Leinsters having 1 killed and 6 wounded.

The occupation of the plateau, by three companies in line, with one in support, and three Vickers guns, took place in the evening of March 2nd. The Battalion's right flank was now in air, but this, in the circumstances, did not constitute a great danger, particularly as the advance was about to be resumed.

The new advance was preceded on March 5th by a reconnaissance somewhat similar to the last, of the village of Deir en Nidham and the tracks leading up to it, which was likewise carried out by the Royal Irish Rifles. A party of three platoons, under Captain Pollock, approached the village, which was found to be held. After a short exchange of fire, however, the Turks withdrew. Our men then pressed into the village, where they captured a Turkish officer and 2 men, one of them wounded. The officer had a telephone, with three lines running in northerly and north-westerly directions. While the reconnaissance was being carried out about a hundred Turks concentrated in front of the village, and later another two hundred appeared on the ridge north of it, but our men were able to carry out their retirement at the proper time and practically unmolested. The Battalion had 2 men wounded.

II.—The Actions of Tell 'Asur.

On March 7th patrols of the 1st Leinster made good the Deir en Nidham ridge, the Irish Rifles being in support of that battalion. On the 9th there was a general advance which continued all day. The Irish Rifles were not engaged, but they followed up, marching through Deir en Nidham, half-way to Arura, where they took up a covered position in a small wadi, and remained in brigade reserve.

The Battalion was, however, to take part in a further attack on the morrow, in conjunction with the 30th Brigade, upon the high ground west of Abwein, of which the really important part, which commanded a good stretch of country, was known as Hill 30. The plan was for three firing line companies, "B," "C" and "D," to advance, the first at 5.30 a.m., as advanced guard, the second at 5.45 on Sheikh Redwan and Arura, and the third at 6.15 on Hill 30.

Not much opposition was met with at first, but it soon became evident that the Turk meant to make a stand on this line, and resistance grew fierce. Heavy machine-gun fire broke out along the front, and " D " Company was brought to a halt almost at once. Two platoons attempted to attack the hill from the north, but were held up by enfilade machine-gun fire from a watch-tower. " B " advanced by short rushes over difficult ground, but was likewise checked. " C " did best, and within an hour of the start its leading platoon was on Sheikh Redwan, where it came in for considerable shell-fire. The company was reorganized and began an attack on Arura, but was soon stopped by machine guns. It then withdrew slightly to a good position commanding Arura, so that at least the Osmanli should not be able to use the village.

Led by officers who constantly exposed themselves, " B " Company attempted to creep forward, and by 7.30 was within 600 yards of its objective, but out of touch on either flank. By 8.30 all was at a standstill. Runners were hit if they attempted to move with a message, and it was impossible to get the artillery to knock out the machine guns. The worst trouble was due to enfilade machine-gun fire, as the 30th Brigade on the right flank had not succeeded in advancing. Away to the left large bodies of the enemy were seen moving south on Nabi Saleh, where the 5th Connaught Rangers were fiercely counter-attacked at noon, the Osmanli getting to within a hundred yards of their position.

It was decided to attempt a new advance in the afternoon after further artillery preparation. This took place at 3 p.m. But a few field guns firing on several square miles of broken country had not much effect upon the machine guns, which were as bad as ever. " D " Company succeeded in advancing about another hundred yards, " B " rather less. It was therefore resolved to re-form the right flank of the Battalion, which was seriously in air, and consolidate the ground already gained for the night, and this was carried out without great difficulty. At 9 p.m. another attack on the Connaught Rangers was repulsed. Orders were issued to renew the attack in the morning, in conjunction with the advance of the 30th Brigade on Abwein.

In this affair the 6th Irish Rifles had 4 other ranks killed, and 8 officers and 51 other ranks wounded. The officer casualties are very high in proportion, and prove that the officers exposed themselves freely in their attempts to advance.* The losses are high in themselves for this sort of open fighting upon a very wide front. The Turk on this occasion had had orders to stand, and he was always a difficult man to shift when he made up his mind to stay where he was.

The attack had, however, loosened the masonry of his defence if it had not quite dislodged it. There was no need of another. At 9 a.m. next morning the advancing screen of scouts found no obstacle to their progress, and the Battalion moved to the top of Hill 30. It also took over Arura, and by 10.30 a.m. was in possession of all its objectives of the previous day. The left flank of the Brigade was in a doubtful position till the 12th, when the advance of the 75th Division assured it. On this date the Battalion's position on Hill 30 was subjected to considerable shelling by the Turks.

The enemy in front evidently held no definite position, but moved about in small bodies. This was proved by the fact that on the night of the 13th a patrol of the Irish Rifles was able to advance from Arura to the village of Mezra, a mile north-west, without encountering any enemy, while the following night there was a determined attack by the Turks upon an advanced post outside Arura. The enemy was beaten off, but the Battalion had 1 man killed and 2 wounded.

From now to the 20th of the month the Battalion remained in front line, in heavy rain and very inclement weather. On the morning of the 20th it was relieved, and moved into wadis in rear of the position. While it was here the Duke of Connaught visited the 10th Division. On the 20th he presented decorations for recent acts of gallantry. On the 22nd, with Sir Edmund Allenby and Brigadier-General Vandeleur, temporarily commanding the Division, he rode to Deir en Nidham, from which points of interest in the recent fighting could be pointed out to him.

The moment was a fateful one. Here, indeed, victory was in sight. On the Western Front, however, the Germans had just launched their tremendous attacks upon the British Third and Fifth Armies, and, incidentally, the 1st and 2nd Battalions of the Irish Rifles. The ensuing days were among the most critical of the war. And, far away as

* The names are not available, but one officer, Captain Danks, died of his wounds a fortnight later.

was the scene, it had a marked effect upon the campaign in Palestine, certainly hastening, if it did not bring about, the end of the 6th Battalion's career.

III.—The End of the 6th Battalion.

The Battalion remained in divisional reserve during the next few days of the halt and the early part of the new advance. On April 9th the 1st Leinster made an attack and reached the outskirts of Karawa Ibri Zeid, but were unable to capture it. On the 11th the place was found unoccupied and taken over by the Leinsters. The Royal Irish Rifles was at this time employed upon road-making in the neighbourhood of Deir en Nidham. On the 21st the Battalion moved into position in Deir es Sudan, in relief of the 1st Leinsters, and that evening captured two Turks. On the 27th a detachment from the Battalion rushed some enemy posts near Furkha, capturing three men and killing some others. The only British casualty in this affair was one officer (2nd-Lieutenant Ruddell) wounded.

On April 29th the 30th Brigade attacked and captured Mezra, while the 6th Royal Irish Rifles were ordered to assist it by the capture of a hill known as Sausage Hill. There was considerable musketry and machine-gun fire at first, but the Turkish spirit was broken and there was no defence once our men began to push to close quarters. The high ground was eventually occupied with a loss of 2 men killed and 2 wounded. Apparently owing to an error, it was withdrawn on May 1st. On the 2nd it received orders to reoccupy the position, and was able to do so without loss. This was its last action. It remained in line, under very unpleasant conditions, with constant rain, till May 13th, when it was relieved by a Sikh battalion and withdrew to the Wadi Reiya, near Deir en Nidham, for disbandment. For word had come that it was to meet the same fate as the majority of other Irish Service battalions. This fate it might possibly have escaped in the East had all gone well on the Western Front. But Sir Edmund Allenby was being called upon for large reinforcements of white troops for France, and his army was undergoing reorganization.

May 15th was the last date in the Battalion's annals. It was addressed by Major-General Longley, commanding the Division, and Brigadier-General Vandeleur, commanding the 29th Brigade, who spoke of its good record, and expressed the hope that officers and men would take with them the spirit that had hitherto accompanied them to the units to which they were being transferred. These were to be, in the case of seven officers and all the non-commissioned officers and men, excepting the transport, other battalions of the 10th Division, particularly the 1st Leinster. The remainder of the officers went to the Base, to await employment as they were called upon. Colonel Becher returned to England, and ended the war in command of a battalion of the Royal Irish Rifles in France, where the first part of his service had been performed. The transport marched to Ludd, where all stores were handed in to Ordnance and animals to the Remount Depot. The personnel of the transport was then distributed among companies of the 10th Division Machine-Gun Battalion.

The Battalion had been upwards of four years on active service, during which its life had resembled rather that of those Roman legions which were often left for long periods on the outskirts of the empire than that of most British units in the late war. Except for its first few days of fighting, when it had been cut to pieces, it had never been in one of those bloody actions such as battalions in France with its length of service had entered on half a score of occasions. But it had seen much diverse fighting, tackled

JUDEA

Advance after Third Battle of Gaza and Attacks of 6th Royal Irish Rifles indicated by red arrows

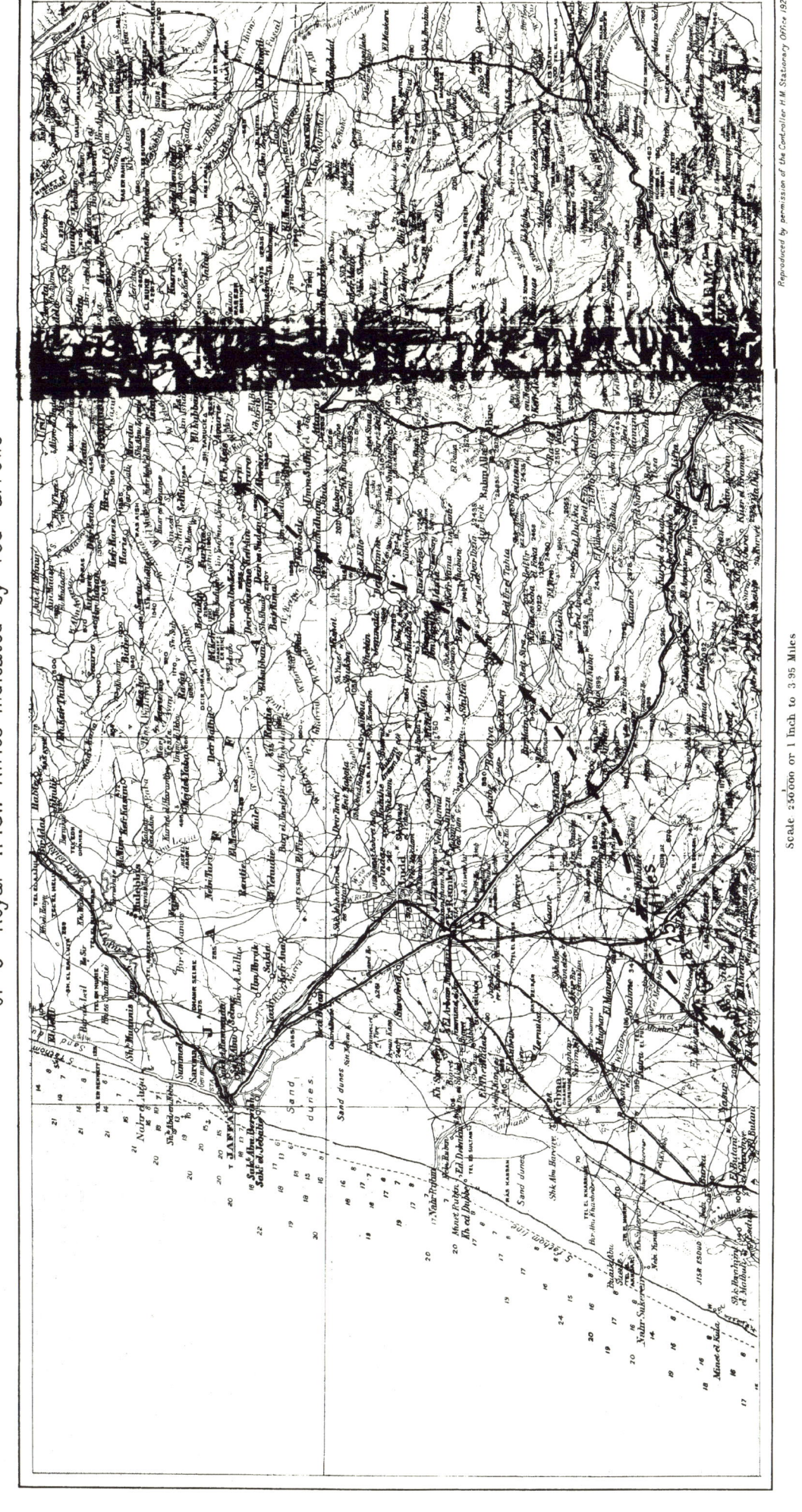

the Turk on the Gallipoli Peninsula, the Bulgar in Macedonia, the Turk again in Palestine. In all that time, with the exception of a few days at Salonika and a few in Egypt, it had been remote from civilization, had hardly seen a town. Dirty hamlets of the Struma Valley, sometimes washed away between one dry season and the next, wretched villages of the Palestine uplands, had formed its best billets. But for the most part it had lived in the open, in the most astonishing varieties of weather, from almost tropical heat, when flies disputed their food with the troops and mosquitoes heralded fever on their shrill trumpets, to times when the snow lay ten feet deep in the sunken hill-tracks. There had been very little leave home, and a very small proportion of men could hope to see England till they got a bullet somewhere in their anatomy, and not by any means always then. Leave had generally meant the dubious attractions of Salonika or the inevitable disillusionment prepared for visitors to Jerusalem—not home and family. Its separate sea voyages had been remarkable in number—Liverpool to Alexandria and Mudros in the *Transylvania*, Mudros to Anzac in the *Partridge*, Anzac to Mudros in the *Prince Abbas*, Mudros to Salonika in the *Albion*, Salonika to the Gulf of Orfani in the *Prince Abbas*, Salonika to Alexandria in the *Huntsgreen*. The men had been wanderers, and the survivors must have brought home many strange impressions upon which to ponder in after life. This at least they surely brought back—the knowledge that they had served their country well and carried out boldly and cleanly every task that was put into their hands.

CHAPTER II

I.—EARLY 1918.

FROM now onwards—from February 6th, to be precise—both Regular battalions of the Royal Irish Rifles were not only in the same division, the 36th, but in the same brigade, the 107th. Their record for 1918, through defeat and subsequent victory, and up to the day of demobilization when their cadres returned to England, can therefore be given in a single continuous narrative. First of all, however, there remain a few words to be said about their existence during the month of January, before their reunion.

The 1st Battalion began the last year of the war in lively fashion at Goudberg, gallantly beating off two German raiding parties on the evening of January 1st. The first attempt was on a post of " A " Company, on the right of the line. One German was killed and several wounded, the necessary identification of the unit and formation being obtained. The second, a little later, was on posts of " C " Company. The whole credit for its defeat rests with a Lewis-gun section, commanded by Corporal Hanna, which swept away the attacking party. Five dead were left on the ground when it retired.

On the night of the 3rd the Battalion was relieved, the Headquarters' " pill-box " being bombarded for over two hours while the change was in progress, and two of the relieving battalion killed. After a week at St. Jean, it returned to the front line, now worse than ever owing to a thaw and melting snow. It was left in twenty-four hours only, during which time the " C " Company took a prisoner, but at the end of that period, when it moved into the reserve position at Bellevue 1,000 yards back, many of the men were suffering from almost complete exhaustion. A number were buried in mud and shell-holes, and had to be dug out. On the 18th the Battalion was relieved at Bellevue, entrained at Wieltje, and reached the comparative decency of Abeele at 2 a.m. on the morning of the 19th.

After a short period of rest, when clothes had been cleaned, numbed minds and bodies brought back to life and duty by the disagreeable but efficacious tonic of steady close-order drill, and drafts amounting to about a hundred absorbed, there came the order to transfer to the 36th (Ulster) Division. It had for some time been anticipated and deeply regretted. For over three years, since the day it landed in France, the Battalion had served with the 8th Division. That division had not been, as those who have followed the Battalion's story up till now will admit, lucky. Compared with the 25th, for example, in which the 2nd Battalion had been serving, it had few successes. But it had been—above all, under its present energetic commander, Major-General Heneker—a very good formation, with an excellent spirit, always ready to do its best under the most impossible conditions. The officers and men were genuinely attached to it. Perhaps the hardest parting of all was with that fine battalion the 2nd Rifle Brigade, which had frequently been their " sister battalion " for purposes of relief when holding a line of trenches. Close friendships had been formed between the two units of Riflemen in all ranks.

The Battalion entrained at Hopoutre on February 3rd and detrained at Ham next day, marching to Cugny, five miles east of that town. Here it received 8 officers and

200 other ranks from the 8/9th Royal Irish Rifles, of the 36th Division, which was being disbanded, and relieved that battalion in brigade support to the 107th Brigade. From this moment onwards it was part of the 107th Brigade.

The 2nd Battalion had meanwhile moved slowly east with the 36th Division towards the St. Quentin front, where the latter was to relieve French troops. It left Gentelles on January 7th, and had a disagreeable march, owing to a sudden thaw, to Guillaucourt, a village which had been fairly close to the front line. More snow began to fall soon after its arrival. Here a new commanding officer, Lieut.-Colonel P. A. Cox, D.S.O., arrived. He was, however, in command for a few days only, leaving afterwards to command temporarily a brigade while senior officers were on leave, and not returning till after the great German attack. On the 11th the Battalion marched across the old trenches of 1916, and was billeted in ruined villages, Herly and Billancourt, near Nesle. Nesle itself, a large town, had not been destroyed. The Germans, when retiring to the Hindenburg Line, had spared it, and not only left in it all the women and children and men above military age of its population, but herded into it a large number from neighbouring villages which they had destroyed. At Ham, farther east, they had done the same thing.

On the 13th the move was continued, through Nesle and Ham, to a village called Pithon, on the banks of the Somme, a march of twelve miles. French artillery officers, who knew the area well, befriended the Battalion, and, as the French heavy guns remained for some weeks after the relief, were able to help it in many matters. On the 15th the Battalion moved on to the completely destroyed village of Fluquières, on the Ham—St. Quentin road, where it billeted in little huts constructed by the French from the ruins of the houses. There were with the Battalion a few men who remembered this neighbourhood from the days of the Retreat from Mons. The Battalion spent a few days training, and on the 25th began work on the " Battle Zone," as the reserve system of defence was called. The other two brigades of the Division had meanwhile relieved the 6th French Division astride the Somme, and on the 29th of the month the 108th Brigade relieved the 109th in the right sector, the 2nd Irish Rifles being in brigade reserve at Essigny Station, in dug-outs along the railway cutting.

The moment was coming when the 36th Division, with all the others in France, was to be cut down from twelve to nine infantry battalions, owing to the shortage of man-power. Three new regular battalions, the 1st and 2nd Royal Inniskilling Fusiliers and 1st Royal Irish Rifles, in addition to the 2nd Royal Irish Rifles, which, as we have seen, had been some months with the Division, and the 1st Royal Irish Fusiliers, which had been present still longer, were joining; and six of the Division's old battalions were being broken up or formed into " Entrenching Battalions." The immediate duty of these was work on defences, but they were eventually to be used as drafts for the Division. Few guessed how soon they would be wanted, or how far short of filling the gaps their reinforcements would be.

The 2nd Battalion was transferred from the 108th to the 107th Brigade on the evening of February 8th. This Brigade now consisted entirely of Royal Irish Rifles—the 1st, 2nd and 15th Battalions. The same evening as the transfer took place the Battalion entered the line.

On February 22nd another division relieved the troops of the 36th north of the Somme in the front line, and at the same time the system of defence was reorganized. All three brigades now entered the line, with one battalion in the Forward Zone, one in the Battle Zone, and one in reserve. The 107th Brigade had the centre sector. One of the three battalions held the front line trenches, with headquarters and one company in a fortress known as Racecourse Redoubt, a mile behind them; the second, that which garrisoned the Battle Zone, was in deep quarries near Grand Séraucourt; and the reserve battalion in that village, which huts and little cottages built amid the ruins had made fairly comfortable.

There was now nothing to be done but work and wait. A great German offensive was accepted as a certainty. The point at which it would be launched was at first doubtful, though as time went on it became quite clear that it would certainly include the Fifth Army front. And the Fifth Army was holding an enormous front—from Barisis, away down on the Oise, to Gouzeaucourt, thirty-five miles as the crow flies, and forty-five taking into account the curves of the line, with eleven divisions in front line and a mere handful of reserves! Important work had to be carried out in the Forward Zone—above all, upon Racecourse Redoubt, which had been made very strong by the time the attack was launched. Chief attention, however, was given to the Battle Zone, which on the 107th Brigade's front included the village of Contescourt, close to the marshy valley of the Somme, and was sited on the forward and reverse slopes of a ridge across which ran the Essigny—Contescourt road. It was a well-planned line of defence, but unfortunately there was not nearly enough labour to perfect it in the allotted time; while an accountable and highly blameworthy shortage of wire held up work in February and the early part of March. The troops were ordered to dig quite shallow trenches, which were—in theory—to be deepened out when the moment came to occupy them for defence. In the rear defence line of the Battle Zone were three large wired-in forts, to contain a company and battalion headquarters. That on the front of the 107th Brigade was just east of the quarries where the Battle Zone battalion was stationed, and was known as Quarry Redoubt. The rest of the position was divided into a series of smaller, semi-isolated keeps.

The three battalions of the Brigade had spells of five days in the Forward Zone, five in the Battle Zone, five in reserve. In the two latter periods they worked as a rule on the Battle Zone defences, but a little sorely needed training was done in March. The period of waiting was very trying to the nerves, especially as the XVIII Corps, in order to be certain that all units knew their positions and could reach them quickly when the order "man battle stations" was sent out, practised the troops by trial messages. A humorous situation arose when an orderly at Divisional Headquarters, roused to take the message at an early hour, went to sleep before handing it to the officer on duty. The officers of the Corps Staff, who hastened out from Ham without their breakfasts in a chill and foggy dawn to see the assembly, had to wait an hour before the troops arrived. They seemed to be of opinion that this was clear proof that the Division was unready. A mild suggestion by an officer of the Divisional Staff that, had the Germans really begun their bombardment, nobody within ten miles of the front could have slept if he wanted to, was considered trivial, as it doubtless was; and the unfortunate orderly duly appeared before a court-martial.

The only important event before the all-important one was a very big raid on the 107th Brigade's front, the 1st Royal Irish Rifles being then in front line. After a heavy bombardment of twenty minutes, the sentries in the outpost line, which was very thinly held, saw a large body of the enemy attempting to crawl through or cut the wire. Lewis-gun and rifle fire was opened, and for ten minutes the defenders, a platoon in strength, kept off the enemy. Then there suddenly appeared a body of about eighty Germans *behind* the trench, having doubtless crept through at an unoccupied point under cover of the other attack. The Lewis gun was broken in two by a direct hit with a bomb, and the men could not fire over the parados owing to its height. Having thrown fifty bombs, and having their platoon officer, Lieutenant H. D. Sinclair, wounded, they fell back right and left along the trench. The Germans then advanced and threw bombs into empty dug-outs, retiring before a counter-attack could be organized. The lance-corporal holding the Lewis gun was killed, and the Germans doubtless got an identification from his body, which they carried away. But it was dearly won, for their losses were very considerable, while the Battalion, besides the officer and the lance-corporal, had only 1 man killed and 7 wounded.

On St. Patrick's Day, March 17th, the 1st Battalion was holding the Battle Zone, and the 2nd in reserve at Séraucourt. The Roman Catholics of the two battalions united for Mass on this day for the first time since the year 1854, a fitting prelude to the terrible moments that were coming.

On Wednesday, March 20th, the officers of both battalions learnt that the attack was, according to deserters' reports, to be expected the following day. There had been previous reports of this nature, and no one could be certain whether or not these were reliable. It made little difference. All that would be required in the way of preparation next morning would be to collect the blankets in which the men had slept, and to move to the battle stations. Heavy bombardments on likely positions of assembly were carried out by our artillery during the night.

II.—THE BATTLE OF ST. QUENTIN.

At 4.30 a.m. next morning upon the whole front sleepers most hardened to shell fire were awakened by the sudden opening of the most terrific bombardment any man there had ever heard. Its greatest weight was upon the Forward Zone and the artillery positions, but Grand Séraucourt, which had not had a shell since the Division arrived, was soon a smother of high explosive fumes and brick-dust.

Ten minutes later the signal " man battle stations " was received by the 1st Battalion. The morning fog, so celebrated in accounts of the battle, was of a density that prevented men from seeing ten yards ahead. But they knew the ground. Within a few minutes column after column had moved quietly and in good order out of the quarries: " A " Company (Captain Reed, M.C.) to the Battle Zone trenches on the right; " B " (Captain Brown, M.C.) to those on the left, in the Contescourt section; " C " (Lieutenant Kerr) to the counter-attack position, between and in rear of the other two; " D " (Captain Bayley) to Quarry Redoubt, in the second line. Unfortunately, the platoon of " B " destined to occupy Contescourt ran into a large shell on the way up and was almost destroyed. This was not learnt till afterwards, and it was at Contescourt that the enemy made the only serious hole in the Division's Battle Zone. The counter-attack company made later in the morning an attempt to regain the village, but was held up by very heavy machine-gun fire.

At 9 a.m. intensive shelling of the Battle Zone began. The enemy had by this time broken through the Forward Zone, though the Headquarters of the 15th Irish Rifles was resisting heroically and continued to fight on till 5.30 p.m. By about noon the enemy was attacking the Battle Zone all along the front, and, as the fog was just beginning to clear, his men in the open became visible to our machine gunners and suffered heavy loss.

Attack after attack was launched, the Germans bringing up ladders to cross the barbed wire. But they were kept out. Even at Contescourt they made no farther progress, the Battalion clinging to the cross-roads south-east of the village.

The 2nd Battalion, meanwhile, had moved out at 6.30 a.m. to the Quarries vacated by the 1st, to await events. At 10 a.m. 2nd-Lieutenant McFerran, M.C., the intelligence officer, who had gone forward to reconnoitre, was killed near Grugies, in the Forward Zone. Lieutenant C. R. W. McCammond was wounded about the same time. About 2 p.m. orders were received to take up a position on the Essigny—Grand Séraucourt road. But the move was unnecessary. The 1st Battalion was holding its difficult post faithfully and well, and repulsing every effort of the enemy to advance. At 4 p.m. the 2nd Battalion, which was suffering from the heavy shell-fire, was ordered back to the shelter of the Quarries.

At 7 p.m. there came orders for a company to attack Contescourt and recapture it. " D " Company was selected. Advancing with the greatest gallantry, it reached the village. The enemy, however, at the same moment poured considerably superior numbers into Contescourt, evidently for a new attack on the 1st Battalion's position. Great losses were inflicted on him, but the odds were too heavy. Both officers with the company, Lieutenant G. E. Lynch and 2nd-Lieutenant W. L. P. Dobbin, M.C., were killed, and there were not more than forty survivors left to fall back.

The division on the right had been meanwhile completely broken. The enemy had burst through its Battle Zone about noon, and made steady progress thereafter, completely turning the 36th Division's flank at Essigny. Finally the situation grew so serious that the Fifth Army decided to withdraw the III Corps behind the Crozat Canal. And in conformity with this withdrawal, the 36th Division, which had hardly lost a foot of ground in its Battle Zone, had to go also. It was a bitter moment. The 1st Battalion was ordered to retire across the Somme to a position at Hamel, the 2nd to Happencourt, after which the bridges would be blown. The move began at 11 p.m. the 2nd Battalion covering the withdrawal of the 1st, and not completing its own move till 11 a.m. next morning. The Battalion's losses, with the exception of unlucky " D " Company, had been light hitherto, though it had fierce fighting before it could be disengaged that night. The 1st Battalion, on the other hand, had lost nearly half its fighting strength. Captain J. Brown was wounded and missing ; Lieutenants S. Kerr, P. O'Kane, B. T. Hodgson, 2nd-Lieutenants J. Kennedy and J. C. Thompson, killed ; 2nd-Lieutenants H. Oliver, T. A. Valentine and J. Aiken wounded.

March 22nd dawned in mist almost as thick as that of the preceding day, but became clear rather earlier. The Division's right flank, represented by the 61st Brigade, of the 20th Division, which had been put at General Nugent's disposal, was behind the barrier of the Crozat Canal, and was held all day. The other flank, however, was now in trouble. The 1st Battalion was heavily engaged all day, but, with its flank on the marshes of the Somme, and with the 1st Inniskillings, of the 109th Brigade, most gallantly holding out in Ricardo Redoubt to the north, it was beyond the enemy's power to dislodge it, Across the river valley large bodies of enemy troops could be seen moving southwards from St. Quentin.

About 2 p.m. Ricardo Redoubt was surrounded, and the 1st Battalion ordered to fall back to Happencourt, where it maintained itself till dusk. That afternoon, however, the Higher Command decided on a further withdrawal, behind the line of the Somme, from St. Simon to Ham, in consequence of which all positions north of the river had to be

Map V.

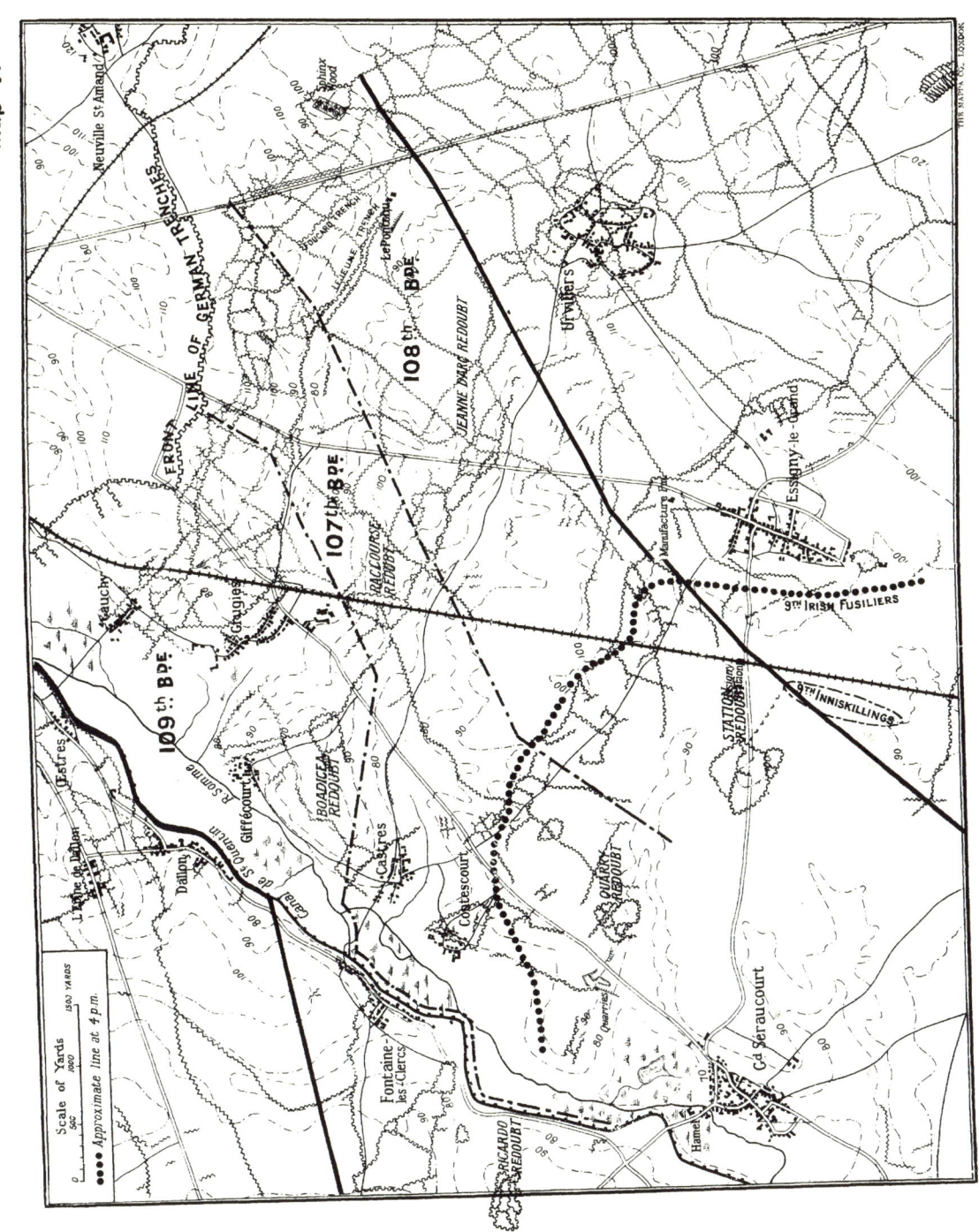

The Position before the German Attack, March 21st, 1918.

abandoned. The retirement began as soon as there was darkness enough to cover it. The 2nd Battalion marched along the river road, through Tugny, to Pithon, where it had billeted nine weeks earlier, and there crossed the river, marching into Cugny. Here, as the 107th Brigade was for the moment in reserve, the 61st and 108th holding the lines of the Crozat Canal and the Somme, the Battalion went into billets, posting piquets round the village, and had a much needed rest. Its commanding officer, Major Rose, had been wounded about the time the retirement began, and Captain T. Thompson, D.S.O., assumed command. The 1st Battalion followed across the bridge at Pithon, and reached Eaucourt at 3 a.m. after a march of eight miles. It likewise had a few hours' rest.

The great break-through had begun, and was to be completed the moment the Germans forced the line of the Somme and the Crozat Canal, as they did very early on the 23rd. Returned civilians were fleeing for the second time from their homes. From Ham many of the lightly wounded in the hospital had had to begin their movement to the rear on foot, the nurses walking beside them, as there were not enough ambulance cars for all. It goes without saying that vast quantities of food and munitions had been and were to be abandoned. A great proportion of the shell dumps were found intact when the French had advanced over this area in October.

Owing to an error on the part of a brigade on the left of the 36th Division and of some engineers, not only was the main bridge at Ham not properly demolished, but the crossing of the river at this point was not guarded. The enemy speedily crossed here, and was also across the Crozat Canal at several points at 11.30 a.m. The two battalions of the Royal Irish Rifles were summoned from their rest at 10 a.m., and each moved out of its village, the 1st digging in north and north-west of Eaucourt, the 2nd north-east of Cugny. In the latter case the remains of " D " Company, strengthened by a draft of sixty-seven other ranks from courses and leave which had arrived that morning, was put in reserve, just outside the village. At noon word came that the enemy was in Flavy-le-Martel, two miles east down the road and well west of the Crozat Canal. The Brigadier, General Withycombe, told Captain Thompson that Cugny was to be held at all costs. In early afternoon there were a couple of minor attacks, mere " feelers " by patrols, which were dealt with suitably. Then comparative quiet fell.

At 11.30 a.m. the 1st Battalion also received orders to move towards this threatened point on the main road, and took up a position on the right of its sister battalion, but with its right considerably refused. On its right were dismounted French dragoons. Second-Lieutenant W. N. McNeill was wounded here.

At 6 p.m. a general attack astride the road was launched by the enemy. The 2nd Battalion did not yield a foot, though a few men temporarily fell back into the village. The troops on the right of the 1st Battalion retired. The enemy got round its flank and tried to rush the Headquarters, Lieut.-Colonel McCarthy-O'Leary being wounded, but remaining at his post. It eventually fell back upon Beaumont-en-Beine, where it consolidated its position. And now the enemy had penetrated between the 2nd Battalion and Cugny, and the position was desperate. As darkness drew on, " A " Company was ordered to cover the withdrawal of the rest to a point west of the village. The enemy infantry pressed forward to the attack with the great dash and boldness shown by the Germans throughout this offensive, but " A " Company, and particularly its Lewis gunners, did magnificent work, raking the advancing waves and killing men in clumps. It then withdrew, skirting Cugny, now in enemy hands, and losing several prisoners by the way. A party of "C" Company trying to approach the village was challenged by a body of the enemy. Lieutenant R. B. Marriott-Watson, M.C., called out a reassuring answer in German, and quietly approached. There was a short and bloody scuffle in the darkness, and the Germans were bayoneted. Throughout the night the position just west of Cugny was consolidated by men who, though worn out and hungry, were strung up by good leadership to a point at which they were almost literally unconquerable. During the night the 1st Battalion got orders to take up a line in support of the 2nd. It dug in 700 yards behind the latter astride the Villeselve—Cugny road, with battalion headquarters in a sunken road near Montalimont Farm. Had it been known that the troops on the 2nd Battalion's right had retired in the darkness before enemy pressure, the 1st Battalion would doubtless have been moved farther forward to cover that flank. As it was, the 2nd Battalion was isolated.

III.—THE ACTIONS AT THE SOMME CROSSINGS.

About 10 a.m. on the 24th a new attack developed on the 2nd Battalion, the enemy making desperate efforts to debouch from Cugny, and also sweeping in on the flanks. Once again the attack was beaten off. By this time, however, there was a shortage of ammunition, and orders were given to fire at good targets—that is, at considerable groups of Germans—only. In view of the isolation of the position, orders were likewise issued for the companies on the flanks to be slightly refused. In executing this movement, "D" Company had heavy losses, Lieutenant Marriott-Watson being among the killed. Soon afterwards Captain Thompson met a like fate, courting death in his efforts to inspire his men. The bravery and good leadership of this fine officer on the Messines Ridge has been recorded in an earlier chapter.

Captain J. C. Bryans now assumed command, and took advantage of a short lull to reorganize the line. This had hardly been completed when a new attack began. Colonel McCarthy-O'Leary sent forward messengers with orders for the 2nd Battalion to withdraw through the 1st. No answer was received, runners being all killed or wounded. In any case, Captain Bryans had orders to fight to the last, and had, moreover, come to the conclusion that an attempt to retire over open ground, with machine guns on either flank, would mean annihilation. If his little force was to be destroyed it should die to better purpose.

The attack, accompanied by a flight of low-flying aeroplanes, swept in in overwhelming strength from the left, and a desperate hand-to-hand fight ensued. Sergeant-Major Ferris, commanding "B" Company, stood out as one of the most heroic of an heroic band. When the Germans finally closed, many men had not a round left to fire. They sprang from their entrenchments and met the enemy with their bayonets. In a few minutes all was over. The defenders were simply engulfed by superior numbers. It is impossible to give exact figures, but Captain Bryans estimates that there were some hundred and fifty men in the final fight, and that over a hundred were killed or wounded in the last hand-to-hand struggle, among the former being the Acting-Adjutant, Lieutenant M. E. J. Moore, M.C.; Lieutenant J. K. Boyle, M.C., and 2nd-Lieutenant E. C. Strohm were wounded and taken prisoner with Captain Bryans.

There cannot be many instances, even in the late war, of a battalion being blotted out so completely as this. Only the transport, a handful of employed with it, a few officers kept back, and those on leave were left. And if the incident was exceptional in this respect, it also stands out as an example of supreme heroism that should live for ever in the Regiment's memory. While the war lasted its details could only be guessed at, and it never received the public recognition it deserved.*

By 3.30 p.m. the 1st Battalion also was almost surrounded, and was compelled to fall back on Villeselve, where it took up a covering position north and west of the village. Here it held the enemy in check by its fire till 6.30 p.m., when it received orders to fall back, through Guiscard and Bussy to Sermaize, near Noyon, arriving about 3 a.m. The 36th Division had been relieved by the French 62nd Division. It was not, however, to enjoy a long respite.

The French were fighting a delaying action, and it was quite clear the bone-weary men would have to move quickly. And, in fact, at 9 a.m. on the 25th the 1st Battalion marched along the main Amiens Road, to Avricourt, which was reached at noon. Here there was a halt of six hours, during which men slept like logs as they had fallen out. Accompanying the Battalion was a force of fifty officers and men, who were all that could be collected of the 2nd Battalion. At 6 p.m. the retreat was continued to Guerbigny, on the bank of the Avre, a march of over twelve miles.

This last move was a nightmare. The men had reached a condition of fatigue when they seemed lost to all sense of what was happening about them. In some cases their boots were giving out. The roads were choked with pitiful columns of refugees, carrying their goods piled high on country carts, the poorest actually pushing wheel-barrows. It is certain that a proportion of the men simply could not have completed the march had it not been that a few lorries were placed at General Withycombe's disposition, which took the most footsore to their destination and then returned to meet the slowly advancing column and pick up a second load. Even with this aid it took seven and a half hours to complete the move.

IV.—The Battle of Rosières.

There followed now the most desperate moment for the Allies of the whole war. The British were retiring due west, the French south-west, being preoccupied by their lines of communication and the safety of Paris. The inevitable gap appeared at Roye on the morning of the 26th, and the enemy pushed into it with extraordinary speed. To close it there were no available troops but the tired and depleted 30th and 36th Divisions. The 36th was ordered to turn out instantly and take up a line, represented over much of its length by old French trenches of 1916, from the River Avre, at l'Echelle St. Aurin, to the Amiens—Roye road north of Andechy. The task of holding this line was allotted to the 109th Brigade on the right and the 108th on the left. The 107th remained for the time being in reserve.

Fast as the troops moved, they were only just in time. In fact, the enemy groups with light machine guns prevented their occupying Andechy, and their line was bent back on the Amiens—Roye road, because machine guns were already in position at the point where their left should have been. In these circumstances the 107th Brigade was ordered out also, and at 10 a.m. was standing by in readiness to intervene when called upon. General Withycombe had now a great many units under his command, since a Field Company, the Pioneer Battalion, and an Entrenching Battalion had been put at his disposal. He therefore formed his force into two groups, one consisting of the units named above, the other of the 1st Irish Rifles and the remnants of the 2nd and 15th Battalions. The latter group was under the command of Lieut.-Colonel McCarthy-O'Leary.

* The story was, it is believed, first given to the public in the present writer's " History of the 36th (Ulster) Division."

The line of the 108th and 109th Brigades, protected by a certain amount of the old barbed wire, held splendidly all day. Towards evening, however, it became apparent that the enemy was preparing a heavy attack on Erches, in its centre. He had brought up guns and mortars, and was bombarding it heavily. Colonel McCarthy O'Leary's group was, therefore, formed up along the road from west of Erches to Bouchoir, which was partly sunken and well adapted for defence; the 2nd Battalion on the right, the 1st in the centre, the 15th on the left.

About eight o'clock the enemy forced his way into Erches, making use, according to reports from several quarters, of French uniforms, and certainly crying repeatedly in English, "Do not fire! We are French!" The line of the 108th Brigade was broken, and its headquarters attacked and dispersed. A little later it was discovered that the enemy patrols had entered Guerbigny, on the right. The 2nd Battalion was thereupon moved slightly to the left, to cover the right flank of the 1st.

At 5.30 a.m. on March 27th a ration party, bringing up food for the men of the 2nd Battalion, and ignorant of the situation, actually entered Erches and was charged by a German cavalry patrol. It succeeded, however, in getting clear, and—better still, for the men were well-nigh starving—in delivering its rations.

At 9 a.m. the enemy, who had been pounding the position with guns and mortars, attacked again. Colonel McCarthy-O'Leary, ordering a counter-attack to ease the position, was wounded a second time, and had to be evacuated; and Captain P. Murphy, commanding the remnant of the 2nd Battalion, was also wounded. The men of the 1st and 2nd Battalions then fell back to the neighbourhood of Arvillers, where Captain Patton, of the 1st Battalion, reorganized them, and they began to dig in again. Captain Miller, commanding the remnant of the 15th Battalion, held his ground till noon, when his trenches were being blown in. He then managed with difficulty to fall back upon Captain Patton. Finally General Withycombe ordered the little force to fall back upon Hangest-en-Santerre, as large bodies of the enemy could be seen advancing on Davenscourt and disappearing in the woods behind it. This withdrawal was complete at 5 p.m. That evening a French division moved up and relieved the party, which then marched to rejoin the division at Sourdon, *via* Plessier-Rozainvillers. There was, however, another party of 3 officers and 68 other ranks of the 1st Battalion, which did not receive General Withycombe's message. This little body of men put another fine achievement in the retreat to the credit of the Regiment. Having dug in north-west of Arvillers, facing due east, it was in action throughout the night of the 27th. On the following morning also it kept the enemy in check by its fire, with no other troops in its vicinity. It was not relieved by the French till 11 a.m. on the 28th. By this time the enemy was between it and the rest of the division. It marched to Sourdon to rejoin, *via* Mezières, Villers-aux-Erables, and across the Avre at Moreuil, a distance of fifteen miles, arriving at 7 p.m. This march was in itself no mean feat after what the men had previously endured. In addition to the Commanding Officer, the 1st Battalion lost Lieutenant E. V. Manico, and 2nd-Lieutenants T. Enright, R. Moore and F. W. Hoyle, all wounded on the 26th.

V.—THE END OF THE RETREAT.

There was one more call to answer for the remnants of the two battalions, less the detachment just mentioned. Early in the morning of the 28th an enemy column had found a gap in the French ranks at Montdidier and had crossed the Avre. General Nugent, commanding the 36th Division, received an order signed by General Débeney,

Map VI.

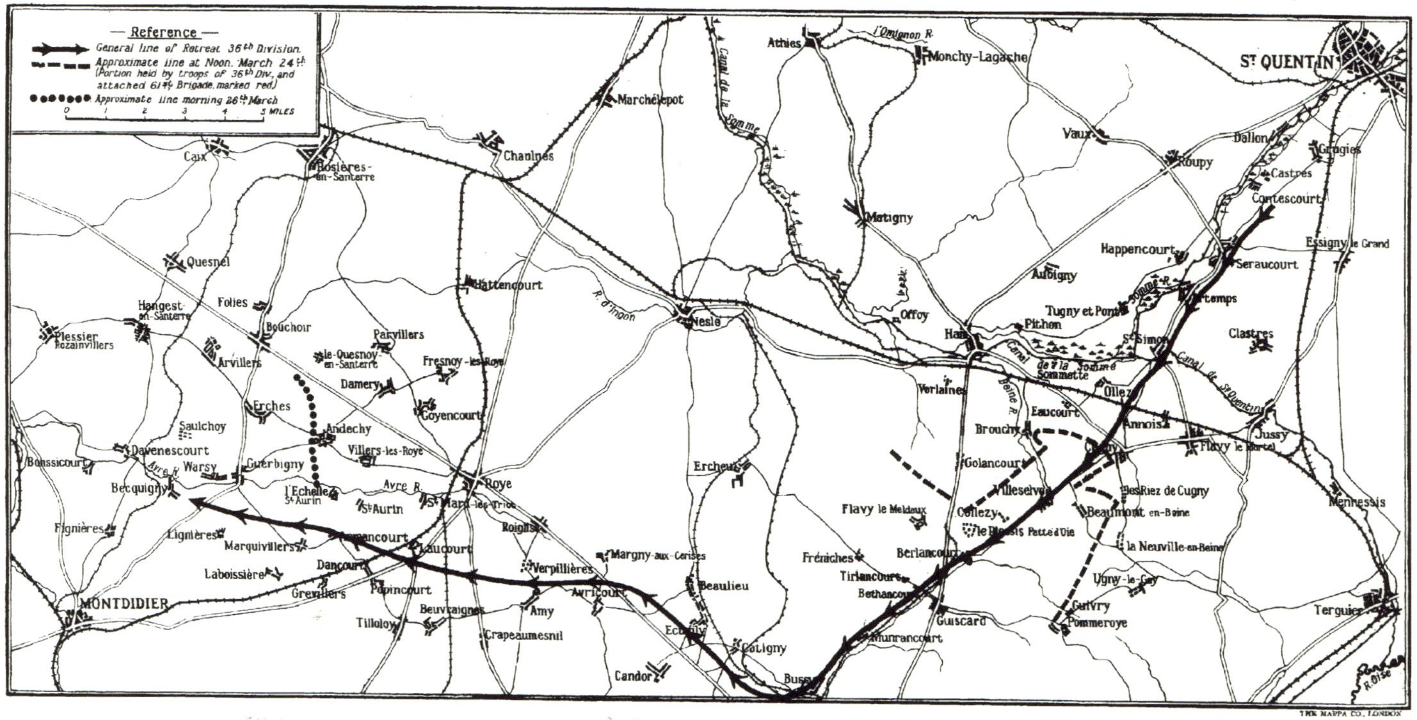

The Retreat of March, 1918.

commanding the First French Army, to cover the artillery he was massing at Coullemelle to command the main Bréteuil—Montdidier road. All troops that could be collected of the 107th and 109th Brigades were, therefore, turned out and marched to this village, putting out posts south and east of the village. Later on a message from the French was received requesting that troops should be moved forward to Villers-Tournelle. This order did not reach General Withycombe till nearly 4 a.m. on the 29th. It was very wet and cold, many of his men were at their last gasp, and, wonderful to relate, the messages from in front were more reassuring than those from the rear. Before he moved his weary men on what might well be a wild-goose chase, General Withycombe therefore ordered a strong patrol to move to Villers-Tournelle and ascertain the situation. Twenty of the fittest men under Captain Taylor were chosen for the task. Villers-Tournelle was found unoccupied. The patrol trudged on to Cantigny, the next village. It was an uncanny moment for the scouts in front as they entered it in the murk of that wet sun-rise. For aught they knew their friends the enemy, who made had bigger advances than this in previous periods of twenty-four hours might be in possession. But no, the French were there. Their officers told Captain Taylor that the line out in front was holding firmly, and that there was no cause for anxiety. Though no one knew it, the German advance was, for all practical purposes, now held up. The patrol accordingly withdrew to Sourdon.

Orders had now been issued for the 36th Division to be withdrawn for reorganization. At 2 p.m. on the 29th the 107th Brigade, picking up the small party that had held the line at Arvillers, moved across the Noye to Chaussoy-Épagny, arriving at 5 p.m. After a halt of two hours, it set out upon what in all the circumstances must be reckoned a terrible night march, through Berny, Jumel, and Oresmaux, across the next of the great series of rivers which meet at Amiens, the Celle, at Wailly, to Velennes. It took about nine hours to cover the fifteen miles. Then it had twelve hours' rest, before carrying out another twelve miles' tramp, through Taisnil, to Saleux. This village had suddenly become of great importance, as it was at the junction of two lines to the south, to Beauvais and Rouen, while Amiens, now bombed and shelled, could be skirted from it to reach all the British communications to northward. Arrived at 11 p.m. the troops bivouacked at the roadside to await a train.

The retreat was at an end, and the cost could be counted. The 1st Battalion had lost in officers and men, 31 killed, 248 wounded, 9 wounded and missing, 155 missing, many of the latter being in fact killed or wounded ; a total of 439. The 2nd Battalion had been, as we have seen, wiped out, and its losses were far heavier. They are not given according to the above categories, but the total amounts to 10 officers and 616 other ranks—the fighting strength of a battalion. At least they had not been incurred in vain. Both battalions had played from first to last a remarkable part. Cases of weakness, due to the overwhelming burden of fatigue, had occurred here and there, but the general record is magnificent. The finest part of it all is perhaps the fashion in which the men answered call after call made upon them. The defence on the Avre, unsupported by artillery, was worthy of fresh troops of good quality, and it was made by men hungry, dispirited by continual defeat and retreat extending over a week. And, be it remembered, had the Battle Zone all along the front held as did the Battle Zone of the 36th Division, it is highly probable that the Germans could have been stopped on the Somme and the retreat would not have occurred.

CHAPTER III

I.—THE MOVE TO FLANDERS.

NEVER was reorganization carried out in pleasanter surroundings, and never, unfortunately for the troops, in greater haste, than was the case with the 36th Division. The whole Division, except the artillery, was entrained from Saleux to the green valley through which the Brèsle runs down to the sea between Mers-les-Bains and Le Tréport. There were some hopes that a week's rest might be given in this pleasant country, in villages which were unspoiled by the continuous billeting of troops. But such good fortune was too great for the black moment. The British divisions which had been cut to pieces had two fates only open to them. Either they were reduced to cadre, as happened to a number, and disappeared temporarily from the British "Order of Battle," or they were hastily filled up with drafts and put into the line to relieve a division that was fit. Many of them thus sent to reputedly quiet fronts were to meet the full force of the German offensives on the Lys and on the Aisne.

Both Battalions of the Royal Irish Rifles detrained at Gamaches and marched to billets, the 1st to several small villages, with headquarters at Monchelet, the 2nd to Maisnières. The 1st Battalion arrived early in the morning of April 1st, the 2nd on the afternoon of March 31st. Each received drafts from the Entrenching Battalions, which had moved north with the Division, that of the 1st Battalion amounting to 4 officers and 160 men from the old 10th and 14th Battalions of the Regiment.

The men had hardly time to look round and realize how comfortable they were before orders arrived for the 36th Division to move at once to the Ypres area, so well known by both battalions, and take over the line. Both battalions entrained on April 3rd for Proven, the 1st arriving that same evening, the 2nd next morning. Both marched to Siege Camp, near Brielen. On the 6th both entered the line, in relief of troops of the 1st Division, in the neighbourhood of Poelcappelle. Within the next few days drafts amounting to 1 officer and 234 other ranks from the Reserve battalions joined the 1st Battalion. A very large draft of 306 other ranks also arrived for the 2nd Battalion. This was, however, mainly composed of boys of nineteen, whose training was far from complete, while they needed also the toughening of close order drill and route-marching; and was accordingly kept at the Detail Camp for further instruction, and gradually sent on to the Battalion.

Ypres and the Salient was at this moment a picture of desolation, but, wonderful to relate, of placid desolation. It had never been so quiet. The line now included Passchendaele and Poelcappelle. Observers at home fondly believed that, however unsatisfactory in other respects "Third Ypres" had been, at least it had won us all the best of the ground. At Passchendaele this was, indeed, more or less true, but from Poelcappelle we stared up at the high ridge of Westroosebeke—and the Germans stared down upon our positions. Poelcappelle itself was a remarkable sight. There were half a dozen good "pill-boxes" built on top of former cellars. But for them it would have been impossible to have guessed that a village had ever been there. There was not a brick, not a stone, not a tree, not the outline of a garden. And, let it be remembered, these Flanders villages, on rich land, were not like those of the Somme, where half the houses and all the barns were of lathes and clay. They were substantial, with houses well built of brick and sometimes even stone, with strong churches big enough to contain the whole of a pious population. All this had gone before the blast of shell-fire like thistledown before a breeze.

Behind, typical British organization and industry—for wherever we failed, we never failed *there*—had been at work. There was a maze of railway sidings at Wieltje, in the original front line, and light railways ran all over the battlefields of August. There were camps as far forward as the old "Black Line," where so many men of the two battalions had given up their lives. "Duck-board" tracks, by which alone progress for infantry in the desolation was possible, led in all directions. There was actually an officers' club in Ypres.

This was, it must have seemed to veterans of the Salient, despite its discomforts, too good to be true. And, indeed, it did not long endure. On April 9th the troops in line heard a tremendous bombardment to the south, over their right shoulders. The second great German offensive, of the Lys, had been launched. It met with astonishing initial success. Within forty-eight hours of the assault, the German front at a point fifteen miles south of Passchendaele was fifteen miles west of it. The 108th Brigade, of the 36th Division, was hurriedly carried by bus and lorry to Kemmel, and was in action in the early hours of April 11th. In the Salient there was no fighting, but a withdrawal was absolutely necessary, and was delayed only long enough to evacuate artillery and as much ammunition as possible, tear up the light railways, blow up concrete dug-outs, and blow huge craters at every important cross-roads.

II.—WITHDRAWAL IN THE SALIENT.

Both battalions had been relieved when the withdrawal took place, and the 2nd was holding the line of the Steenebeke. The new front line was to be the present "Battle Zone," at this point practically the British front line of July, 1917; but an outpost line was to be maintained, for the present at least, on the Steenebeke. From the night of the 11th the withdrawal began of the artillery, a few single field guns remaining till the last moment to fire at night and prevent the enemy guessing what was happening. Then, on the night of the 15th, the two battalions of the 109th Brigade, which had had an anxious time of it, withdrew quietly across the stream. The 2nd Battalion now formed the outposts. But the enemy was superlatively cautious. He shelled Poelcappelle, now a mile and a half from our front, very heavily before he ventured to occupy it, and then advanced very slowly.

The Belgians on the left were now giving a helping hand by extending their front. On the 17th they relieved the 2nd Battalion, which returned to Siege Camp. Its casualties had been Lieutenant J. Cordner, M.C., killed, and 11 other ranks wounded. The two battalions for the next ten days had short periods in the new outpost line, in support, and in reserve. On the 23rd an officer and two men were taken by a patrol of the 2nd. Meanwhile Kemmel Hill had fallen, the Battle of the Lys was extending northward, and a further withdrawal was necessary. The new line of resistance was actually the Ypres Canal, but an outpost line 3,000 yards in front of it was to be maintained. As a matter of fact, on the 36th Division's front the British Army never retired behind its front line of 1917, for, as the Battle of the Lys died down, the lines east of the canal were strengthened, more troops were pushed beyond it, and it ceased to be regarded as the line of resistance. On the left the Belgians were far in advance of the line of 1917; on the right we were somewhat behind it, at the notorious Hell Fire Corner. It was a bleak and depressing moment for the troops—above all, for the survivors of " Third Ypres." Almost all the ground then won and so freely watered by the blood of their companions had now to be surrendered. The only consolation was that the gains of that battle, such as they were, could not be measured by the ground won, but by the effect on German moral.

This time it was the 1st Battalion which remained in line, the 2nd retiring through it. The month that followed was uneventful, save for a few skirmishes in " No Man's Land," of which the Riflemen had the better, each Battalion taking a few prisoners. The 1st Battalion had two officers, 2nd-Lieutenants H. C. Green (Munsters) and F. H. Levis, killed, and 2nd-Lieutenant E. B. Colles wounded on April 29th; the 2nd, Captain L. A. H. Hackett, M.C., and 2nd-Lieutenant V. E. Gransden killed a few days earlier, and 2nd-Lieutenant E. A. Cochrane wounded in May. All time out of the line was devoted to wiring. An attack here was always possible, but by the end of May the Second Army was well prepared to meet it. Between the canal and Poperinghe alone were four good, well-defended lines of entrenchments, with many more west of that town. During this period the Division and the 107th Brigade changed commanders, Major-General C. Coffin succeeding Major-General O. S. Nugent in command of the former, and Brigadier-General E. J. Thorpe succeeding Brigadier-General W. M. Withycombe in command of the Brigade. From one result of the policy of holding the ground east of the canal as an outpost position, the battalions in line suffered through May. The infantry was now thick upon the ground, but the guns were behind the canal. The German guns could reach the canal, and thus harass even infantry in support. Our 18-pounders could only just reach the line of the Steenebeke.

At the end of May came good news. The Belgians were taking over still more line, and the 36th Division was to be relieved for a rest. To say the truth, the bulk of its infantry were not the men who had undergone the retreat. They had passed to death or captivity. But the young drafts sorely needed further training. And a rest was as sorely needed by the staffs of battalions and brigades. The relief was doubly valuable, coming as it did in the best month of the year.

There was one unfortunate incident before it took place. Major Musgrave, the G.S.O. 2 Intelligence Duties of the II Corps, with the laudable desire to obtain information at first hand, went out on the night of June 2nd with a small patrol of the 2nd Battalion. The object of the patrol was to examine the road, parallel with our outpost position, which ran from the Zonnebeke road at Verlorenhoek to the Poelcappelle road some distance east of Wieltje, and particularly a suspected German post upon it at Jasper Farm. North of this point the patrol was suddenly bombed, and Major Musgrave killed instantly. Second-Lieutenant N. B. Munn, the Battalion intelligence officer, began to carry in his body to our lines, a distance of some five hundred yards, but was hit by machine-gun fire and forced to abandon it. Eventually it was brought in by others. Between machine-gun bullets and bomb splinters, Lieutenant Munn was wounded in twelve places, and three men of his patrol of five were wounded.

The relief took place on the night of June 5th, and both battalions moved by rail to Road Camp, three miles west of Poperinghe, on the Proven road. Here training began, intermixed with work on the " Blue " Line, just east of Poperinghe. But the defences were now excellent, and only a brigade at a time was required to work. After a week of work, from the 13th to the 19th, the 107th Brigade began training in earnest, with most of the afternoons devoted to games, cross-country running, football, and even cricket where a tolerable pitch could be obtained. The Belgian troops, its neighbours, were notably good players of Association football, and there were many excellent international matches. For the evenings there was the cinema, the concert party, and boxing competitions. The month of June made a wonderful difference to the young soldiers of the two battalions. By the end of it they were thoroughly fit and prepared for the new and difficult work before them. The end of the period was marked by the 36th Division's Horse Show at Proven, a very splendid function. At this the 1st Battalion covered itself with fame, winning more prizes than any of the other eight infantry battalions in the Division. For a team of two limbers, with four light-draught horses, it took first prize; for officers' chargers, second prize (won by Lieutenant Tate, the transport officer, one of the "oldest hands" with the Battalion); and for a travelling kitchen and a water-cart, third prize in each case.

III.—IN LINE AT BAILLEUL.

On July 3rd both battalions moved back to the region of Cassel, the 1st to Ste. Marie Cappel, and the 2nd to Hondeghem. The French troops which had been moved up to the support of the British in Flanders were now about to be relieved round the great salient made by the German offensive on the Lys. The 36th Division was to relieve the 41st French Division in the neighbourhood of St. Jans Cappel, which had been its headquarters a year ago. The 2nd Battalion moved up first, on the night of July 6th, to take over a portion of the support line. The following night the 1st Battalion took over in front line. The colonel commanding the French regiment relieved, before he marched away, presented to Lieut.-Colonel J. P. Hunt, D.S.O. (who had succeeded Lieut.-Colonel McCarthy-O'Leary in the command), a cow which his troops had found wandering without an owner and had appropriated. There was, indeed, a large amount of stray live-stock in this area, owing to the speed with which the unfortunate civilians had been compelled to evacuate it. There were also plenty of vegetables growing in the gardens right up to the front line, and new potatoes and green peas made a very pleasant addition to rations. For the troops, indeed, it was a delightful line after the Salient. The Division's position was on the outskirts of Bailleul, which was crumbling away under our artillery fire. The enemy's advanced posts were along the Haagedoorne sidings, the wonderful Second Army railhead which had been constructed before the Battle of Messines, and north of the well-known big asylum.

The British were now strong enough to embark upon some local offensives to improve their position. On July 19th the 9th Division, on the right of the 36th, recaptured Meteren. Two platoons of the 1st Battalion attempted to enter the enemy's trenches as a diversion. In this they were unsuccessful, but a patrol later captured a German in broad daylight. On the 23rd the 2nd relieved its sister battalion, and on the 29th carried out a brilliant little patrol action. Two officers, Lieutenant D. B. Wallington and 2nd-Lieutenant J. M. G. Stewart, with four men, crept out at 5.30 p.m. and made their way to a farm-house inside the enemy's wire, where they heard talking. A quick rush completely surprised the enemy post, numbering about ten. Four prisoners were taken, and the rest killed or wounded. Two of the prisoners broke away in "No Man's Land" on the return journey, and were shot. The patrol had no casualties, though heavy machine-gun fire was directed on it as it made its way back to our lines. Casualties were light, but the 1st Battalion had 2nd-Lieutenant W. E. Parke and the 2nd Battalion Lieutenants C. R. W. McCammond and E. Morrow wounded during July.

The ordinary tours in line and support continued into August, but the British had not given up their policy of eating into the enemy's defences and denying him any good ground that existed in his uncomfortable salient. At the end of July the 1st Australian Division, to the south, had retaken Merris. On August 18th the 9th Division resumed its offensive, and captured the Hoogenacker Ridge, south-east of Meteren. All men's hopes were rising now. It was a month since Marshal Foch's first great counter-blow had been struck, and the Germans driven out of the Château-Thierry salient, so menacing to Paris, with great loss in prisoners. Another great offensive on August 8th had cleared Amiens and carried the line forward to Roye, where the German break-through had occurred at the end of March. It was now the turn of the 36th Division to improve its position.

The task did not fall to either of the battalions with which we are concerned, though both suffered from the increased liveliness of the front. On the 14th of the month the 2nd Battalion came in for a bad bombardment with gas shell, about sixty men being more or less affected.* Two days later the 1st Battalion had its commanding officer, Colonel Hunt, wounded, Major J. A. Mulholland, M.C., taking over command. On August 18th the third battalion of the 107th Brigade, the 15th Royal Irish Rifles, carried out an attack, advancing the line on a front of half a mile a distance of 400 yards, and taking 22 prisoners and 2 machine guns. Two days later the 9th Royal Irish Fusiliers, of the 108th Brigade, carried out an even finer attack, under a barrage of smoke and shrapnel, advancing to make it through the 1st Royal Irish Rifles. The enemy was taken completely by surprise. The line was advanced to the Haagedoorne—Dranoutre road; 60 prisoners were taken, with 11 machine guns, and a great number of Germans killed.

IV.—THE GERMAN RETIREMENT.

The British were now only 1,000 yards from Bailleul, and had pierced its main defences. An attack upon the salient would now have resulted in a victory like that on the Marne. The enemy, however, did not await it. On the morning of August 31st, when the 107th Brigade had gone back again to the Cassel area for a rest, it was suddenly discovered that he had slipped away from in front of our positions. By 2 p.m. patrols had entered the asylum and were upon the Neuve Eglise road. By midnight they were within a mile of the summit of the Ravelsberg Hill. The 107th Brigade was accordingly moved up to the area of Mont Noir and Mont des Cats, to be in readiness to follow up the pursuit. The 2nd Battalion had now a new commanding officer, Lieut.-Colonel J. H. Bridcutt, D.S.O. Major H. C. Glendinning had been temporarily in command during the last month, Colonel Cox having gone to the Senior Officers' School at Aldershot. One event may be recorded, as of interest to the history of the Regiment, and also as typical of British imperturbability. The II Corps Horse Show had been fixed for August 31st, and the Germans were not allowed to spoil it by their untimely retirement. And again the transport of the 1st Battalion achieved a triumph. It was selected by General Coffin to represent the infantry transport team—one travelling kitchen, one

---

* On this date the following officers were gassed : 2nd Battalion—Captain C. E. Barton, 2nd-Lieutenants C. H. Lane, R. A. Gough, F. T. Pool ; 1st Battalion—2nd-Lieutenant F. R. H. Macauley, Rev. W. H. Hutchison. Of these the two officers first named died subsequently. Two further officers of the 2nd Battalion were wounded on August 24th 2nd-Lieutenants R. I. Johnston and W. H. Calwell.

water-cart, two limbers, two pack mules—of which one was entered from each division in the Corps. It carried off first prize. The transport sergeant, Sergeant Clarke, received a silver cup, and each driver a silver medal. Meanwhile the rest of the Battalion was marching forward. It was the case of Drake and his game of bowls over again.

On August 31st the 109th Brigade captured the Ravelsberg with some difficulty, then hustled the enemy rearguards down the further slope. The following day saw much severer fighting, which brought our troops to the outskirts of Neuve Eglise. On September 2nd that village and the old G.H.Q. line were captured by the 108th Brigade. By the evening of the 3rd the line ran from l'Alouette, a mile east of Neuve Eglise, to La Plus Douve Farm, south-east of Wulverghem. Another attack next day brought it from a point on the flank of the famous Hill 63, captured by the 29th Division, to Gooseberry Farm. The latter, however, was lost to a violent counter-attack, supported by three times the weight of artillery the British had been able to drag up across the bad roads, and the line on the left driven back some five hundred yards. Nor did further attacks on September 5th meet with better fortune. It was evident that fresh troops were wanted, as the 108th Brigade had been fighting constantly for four days.

That night the 2nd Battalion, with " D " Company of the 1st, was ordered to relieve the 9th Royal Irish Fusiliers, and to carry out a new attack on the 6th. But the relief was, if truth be told, something of a muddle. The orders gave little time for the necessary movements to be carried out. And in their course the enemy poured down upon the area one of the heaviest gas bombardments that any man there remembered to have experienced. Messengers, with their masks on, lost their way in the darkness, or were overcome with vomiting. It was the night of the new moon, and the officers and men in the Battalion who knew the country really well were but a handful. As a result, several platoons were late, and were not in position when dawn broke. And the road from Neuve Eglise to Wulverghem ran down a forward slope, completely exposed to the enemy's numerous and well-placed artillery, so that no movement of formed bodies of troops was possible in daylight. For the troops not in their positions of assembly there was nothing for it but to take cover by the roadside and wait.

Then came orders for the new attack to be launched at 4 p.m., with the objective of the old British front line of the days before the Battle of Messines, from Gabion Farm on the Douve on the right to the Wulverghem—Messines road at Boyle's Farm on the left. The 36th Divisional Artillery had now its batteries up, and was prepared to put down an effective barrage, advancing at the rate of 100 yards in three minutes, and then forming a protective curtain beyond the objective. " A," " B " and " C " Companies were disposed in front line, with " D " and " D " of the 1st Battalion in support.

Lieut.-Colonel Bridcutt had a difficult task, and organized it cleverly. At " zero " the platoons not already in position began to advance in columns of sections, taking what cover they could and picking their way through wire, largely uncut. Rain was falling heavily. It was impossible to complete the advance till dusk began to screen the troops from the German machine gunners. Germans appearing on the left flank, the men began to fancy they were surrounded, though the hard-pressed Germans were really in no mood to counter-attack at that moment. To reassure them, Colonel Bridcutt brought up his " D " Company to form a defensive line between the front and support lines. All objectives were taken eventually except Gabion and Boyle's Farms. These were later reached about dawn on the 7th, but the company commander on the spot decided not to hold the latter owing to its exposed position and the fact that it was a mark for the enemy's gunners. He established his line from thirty to forty yards west of it. In this his judgment was confirmed by his commanding officer. Nineteen prisoners and eight machine guns, as well as a trench-mortar, had been captured. So secure did the position appear that Colonel Bridcutt sent back the company of the 1st Irish Rifles, to save them from the bombardment. His own battalion had suffered severely, having 170 casualties, whereof 150 had been wounded, or gassed during the relief on the night of the 5th. It is sometimes said that there was by this time a falling-off in the dash and bravery of the British Army from the days of, let us say, Ypres, 1917. This may have been so in cases where the youths who filled the ranks of so many battalions after the defeats of the spring had not been fully trained and hardened. But it is obvious that there was not much wrong with a battalion that could go forward across open wire-strewn ground, in face of heavy artillery fire and machine guns so numerous that eight could be captured on its own front, could suffer loss such as this, and win its objectives.

On the morning of the 8th the enemy attempted a counter-attack, two groups moving forward, after a very heavy bombardment, upon posts in our front line. They were annihilated by Lewis-gun fire, and a wounded survivor of each captured. That night the front was widened, down to Hyde Park Corner, in " Plug Street " Wood, and taken over by the 1st Battalion on the right and the 15th on the left, while the 2nd Battalion was withdrawn for a well-earned rest at Neuve Eglise. While it was in line, Lieut.-Colonel Hunt returned to the command of the 1st Battalion from hospital.

Nothing happened but minor " bickering " till the 15th, when the 107th Brigade was relieved by the 109th, and withdrew first to the Berthen training area and later to that of Cassel. The 2nd Battalion had had heavy officer casualties, 2nd-Lieutenant Eaton having been killed, and Lieutenants V. C. Young, H. D. Mitchell, H. Cumming, and W. F. Hunter, wounded. Considerable drafts were received by each battalion, 90 other ranks by the 1st and 139 by the 2nd. Once again the old familiar process—scraping, cleaning, reorganizing of companies, drill, tactical exercises—was undergone. But the last experience had been by no means so gruelling as others that could be recalled, and both battalions were fit and in good heart. Victory was in the air. On the 12th Havrincourt had been captured, and the Hindenburg Line breached. On the 15th the attack in Macedonia, which was to put Bulgaria out of the war within a few days, was launched; on the 19th the last great offensive by Sir Edmund Allenby in Palestine. All men's spirits were aflame with hope. It began to seem that this year, so black for its first half, would see the victorious conclusion of the war.

For the last great offensive in Flanders the 36th Division was required, and it was to attack from ground very familiar to it, and still more familiar to the two battalions of the Royal Irish Rifles—the Ypres Salient. The concentration was carried out with great secrecy, all movements taking place after dark. On the night of the 26th the 1st and 2nd Battalions, then in the neighbourhood of Wormhoudt, moved to Tunnelers' Camp, near Proven. Next day the 2nd Battalion moved slightly forward, to " P " Camp, a mile and a half north-east of Poperinghe. All the final preparations, including the very impressive and gruesome one of sharpening bayonets on grind-stones, were made. Surplus kit was dumped. They were to travel light for the next month.

CHAPTER IV

I.—THE BATTLE OF YPRES, 1918.

THE great attack in Flanders was being carried out under the supreme command of the King of the Belgians, with the French General Degoutte as Chief of the Staff. The attack was to be made upon a front of seventeen miles between Voormezeele and Dixmude. The II Corps, to which the 36th Division was attached, was attacking on the right of the Belgians, and had its left flank on the Ypres—Zonnebeke road. The II Corps was employing the 29th Division on the right, and the 9th Division on the left. The 36th Division was not to be employed on the first day.

At 5.30 a.m. on September 28th the attack was launched, in heavy rain. The result was one of the most remarkable victories of the war. The Allies swept forward, and in one bound put behind them the waste of the old battlefields. By night the 29th Division was a mile east of Gheluvelt, and the 9th had Becelaere, distance some three and a half miles from the starting-point. The Belgians were well east of Zonnebeke. At 11 a.m., seeing how affairs were going, the II Corps ordered the 36th Division to move forward, with its infantry brigades in echelon. The 109th Brigade moved first by train to Potijze. The 107th Brigade was in rear. It entrained in the afternoon with orders to move as far as Vlamertinghe. When it arrived there, however, orders were received to the effect that, the advance having been so rapid, the men were to keep their places in the trucks and move east of Ypres. At Hell Fire Corner, for the first time since it had won its name far from the front line, they detrained. The men had little or no shelter for the night, which was wet and cold.

On September 29th the 109th Brigade entered the line between the 9th and 29th Divisions. Again a very remarkable advance was made, all the more remarkable because there was no artillery to support it, it being impossible to get guns up over the unspeakable roads. The 9th Division captured Dadizeele, and the 109th Brigade Vijfwegen, a village a mile south of it. Unfortunately, however, the 29th Division had not made much progress, and there was a very long open flank from Vijfwegen to a point south of Becelaere. On this date the 107th Brigade did not make a big move, merely forward to the Westhoek Ridge, of terrible memory, where both the 1st and 2nd Battalions had seen fighting so fierce the previous year.

At dawn on September 30th the 108th Brigade passed through the 109th to renew the attack, with the great embanked Menin—Roulers road as its objective. After heavy fighting the road was reached at two points north and south of a mound known as Hill 41, but the two flanks were unable to join hands. Hill 41 was a most important position, crowned with two or three farms and their outbuildings, which had been strengthened with concrete. A second attack made by the 12th Irish Rifles at 4 p.m. was pushed to within a short distance of the crest, but a heavy German counter-attack drove the somewhat thinned line off it.

Meanwhile the 107th Brigade had begun to move forward at 4.50 a.m., the 2nd Irish Rifles leading, to the neighbourhood of Becelaere. At 1.55 p.m. the Battalion received orders to move up on the right of the 108th Brigade and attempt to seize Klythoek, on the main road. It was, however, found impossible to advance owing to the machine-gun fire, which we had no artillery to neutralize, and the attack was not persisted in. The men lay on the ground, getting such cover as they could from their waterproof sheets, to await the dawn and make another attempt.

This had no better fortune. The day dawned in a dense wet mist. The leading companies, swept by machine-gun fire, lost direction. Lieut.-Colonel Bridcutt, attempting to reorganize them, was killed, and the attack died away, as attacks do in such circumstances. On Hill 41 the 108th Brigade had captured Twigg Farm, just short of the crest, with over twenty prisoners, but had been unable to gain complete possession of the hill. That night the 1st Battalion relieved the 2nd, suffering severe casualties from artillery and machine-gun fire on the way up.

On October 2nd another attempt was made to advance, which was again unsuccessful. On the left good progress was made at first, but the intense fire kept the right stationary. That the men had not spared themselves in their efforts to win ground was shown by the casualty list, 5 officers and 100 other ranks, happily for the most part wounded. Second-Lieutenant J. C. Haigh (Dublins) was killed, Lieutenant R. Murphy died of wounds, 2nd-Lieutenant A. A. McManus was missing, Captain H. Taylor and 2nd-Lieutenant W. C. Gardiner wounded. As a fact, further advance under present conditions had become all but out of the question. The very speed with which the Anglo-Belgian Armies had advanced, over the worst ground upon the whole of the Western Front, was now proving a handicap. They had outrun their services of supply. Across the Ypres Salient there were three roads only, the Menin, the Zonnebeke, and the Poelcappelle, of the slightest value for heavy transport, and these three were blocked with the mass of wheeled vehicles of all kinds struggling forward. There should have been a rigorous limitation of what should be moved east of Ypres, in which case twice as much would have reached the front line as was actually the case. Some wagons of the 107th Brigade took at this period, it is recorded, thirty-six hours to move from Potijze Château to Terhand. Sometimes for hours together there was not a move of an inch in the columns of traffic, and the drivers huddled themselves at night on top of their wagons or on the clammy and sodden ground at the roadside, and slept as best they might.

The Germans, on the other hand, had been driven back into civilization. They had roads and railways both excellent and numerous behind them. They had unlimited artillery. Without it the resistance of their infantry, by no means the infantry of the previous year, would not have been anything like so determined. The 107th Brigade, it must be admitted, had not had the best of the luck in this, the last Battle of Ypres. It had been brought up into action just as we had really shot our first bolt, as the German resistance was stiffening; too late to win the honour gained by the 109th in a remarkable advance, in time only to take hard knocks.

There was nothing for it now but to wait till some sort of order could be made in the traffic, and more guns and ammunition brought up. In these circumstances there was a double advantage in moving back as far as possible all troops not required to hold the line during the quiet period. They could be rested, reorganized, in some cases even given baths, and their rations would not be on the forward roads. The 109th Brigade had the best fortune. It was moved by train to the neighbourhood of Vlamertinghe, and had not only its baths, but training on unbroken ground. Some troops had to remain in reserve, against the unlikely chance of a counter-offensive. This lot fell to the 107th

Brigade. On the night of the 4th the 1st Royal Irish Rifles was relieved in the line and moved to the area of Terhand, where the 2nd was already. Next night both battalions moved back to Reutel, where they were accommodated in tents and bivouacs. During this period of rest, Lieut.-Colonel C. M. L. Becher, D.S.O., took command of the 2nd Battalion. As readers of the previous chapters will recall, he had had a very varied career with different battalions of the Regiment in France, Macedonia, and Palestine. Now he was back again to complete it by leading the 2nd Battalion to final victory.

II.—THE BATTLE OF COURTRAI.

The rest lasted till October 13th, on the evening of which the two battalions marched up to positions of assembly for the new attack. Artillery was now up in force ; the whole of the 36th Divisional Artillery, an Army Artillery Brigade, three batteries of a French Cavalry Division, and medium trench-mortars. The first objective of the II Corps was the important Tourcoing—Courtrai—Inglemunster railway line, upon which the 36th Division was to be directed from the Lys on the right at Courtrai to the northern outskirts of the town of Heule. There were two other towns, Moorseele and Gulleghem, on the front of the attack, lying in almost a straight line from west to east, at equal distances. Moorseele was about two and a half miles from the line now held, Gulleghem a mile and three-quarters farther on, Heule a mile and a half beyond that. The attack was to be made by two brigades, the 107th on the right, the 109th on the left. Each was to attack with one battalion, on a front at the starting-line of 500 yards, which was somewhat longer upon the final objective. The 107th Brigade's attack was to be carried out by the 15th Irish Rifles. After Moorseele had been captured, a line east of it was to be consolidated, and the 1st Irish Rifles was to pass through the leading battalion and advance with the road from Gulleghem to Wevelghem and the southern houses of the former town as objective. The plan thereafter was fluid, and the details for the final advance to the Lys would depend upon how quickly the resistance of the enemy was overcome. The attack was to be supported by a barrage almost equal in density to those of previous years, but moving much faster—at the rate of 100 yards in two minutes, with a pause of fifteen minutes every 1,500 yards. Batteries were to move forward during the pause beyond Moorseele to support the new advance. They would at this point be firing at extreme range.

At 5.32 a.m. on October 14th, in fine but foggy weather, the great assault was launched. The 15th Irish Rifles lost the barrage owing to the mist, but they went forward unchecked. By 8 a.m. they had reached the western houses of Moorseele, and within another hour had chased the German rearguards through its streets and were upon the line of their objective. Meanwhile the 1st Battalion had been following up in artillery formation. At 10.35 it passed through the leaders. All went well at first, and, in company with the 2nd Inniskilling Fusiliers on its left, the Battalion gained a mile of ground. Then, 1,000 yards west of Gulleghem, came a serious check. The town was defended by three lines of barbed wire, behind which snugly ensconced machine gunners sat. The Battalion had outrun the small amount of artillery support it had had since Moorseele. An attempt was made to outflank the town, and a little more ground was won. But it was madness to go forward unless the fire of the machine guns could be kept down, and the commanding officer ordered the attack to be broken off. The Battalion's losses had again been very heavy—23 killed, 92 wounded, and 8 missing. It had accomplished one feat very rare in the war's history, bringing down by rifle fire a German aeroplane, of which the occupants, an officer and a sergeant-major, were captured. It received 22 reinforcements that night, who must have felt some bewilderment at being conducted in the darkness into a line of figures muffled in waterproof sheets, sheltering in ditches and below hedges, and being told they were to carry out an attack the following morning. More than 250 prisoners had been taken by the Division, 15 field guns, a number of horses, and uncounted light machine guns.

All that was now wanted to enable troops to storm any position the Germans were likely to hold was a moderate amount of supporting field artillery. The German machine gunners frequently left their positions under a fourth of the volume of fire that their predecessors of last year would have withstood. Indeed, the Flanders offensive, had it stood by itself, could have been conducted with less cost by making movement more leisurely, and insuring that artillery was in position to cover each successive advance. It did not stand by itself. It was part of a general and carefully planned offensive along the whole front, and speed was essential.

The value of artillery support was proved the following morning, October 15th, when, at 9 a.m., the attack on Gulleghem was renewed under a barrage. The 1st Battalion then broke through the wire defences, passed through the town, and consolidated a line 1,000 yards east of it. And though, as will subsequently be shown, it was to come into action again before evening, its losses for the day amounted only to 8 killed and 24 wounded. Its officer casualties in the two days were, however, very heavy. Lieutenant E. J. Williams was killed, the Adjutant, Captain J. C. Leeper, Captain W. F. Hogg, M.C., Lieutenants A. H. Nicholson and J. G. Branford, 2nd-Lieutenants H. M. Jeffares, J. A. Maxwell, wounded.

It was now the turn of the 2nd Battalion. This battalion had on the 14th moved off at "zero" behind the 1st, and passed through the 15th. By evening it had taken up a line some five hundred yards behind the 1st Battalion, west of Gulleghem. On the morning of October 15th it had followed its leader through the town. The plan was for the Battalion to pass through the 1st at 1 p.m. and attack the southern part of Heule, while the 9th Inniskilling Fusiliers took the greater portion of the town, pushed on north of the Heulebeke, to the railway. Unfortunately, the Battalion was not up in time, lost the barrage, and was held up in front of Heule by machine-gun fire. The 9th Inniskilling meanwhile had reached its objective, and it was necessary to move up the 1st Irish Rifles to cover its right flank.

There was nothing for it but to arrange a new barrage for the 2nd Battalion. This was done at 3.50 p.m., when the Battalion reached its objective without serious difficulty. A patrol under 2nd-Lieutenant Rule entered Courtrai, and found the whole city on the left bank of the Lys clear of Germans, but all the bridges over the river destroyed. The 1st Battalion was now withdrawn, and marched to Rolleghemcappelle.

The Germans were holding the further bank of the Lys in some strength, and it was decided to make an attempt to cross at the quays. For this task fresh troops were needed, the 107th Brigade having had two hard days. At 5.30 a.m. on the 16th the 108th Brigade passed through the 2nd Battalion and occupied that part of Courtrai west of the Lys. There were scenes of extraordinary enthusiasm in the city, which had waited over four years for this deliverance. But the Germans held over half of it still, and any troops approaching the Lys were greeted with heavy machine-gun fire. In the course of the afternoon the 108th Brigade, with its attached Field Company, effected a remarkable crossing, two boatloads of men getting across under cover of a smoke-screen. The bridge of pontoons subsequently put across was, however, demolished by artillery fire.

Orders received that day altered the plans. It was not the object of the Allies to fight their way through the great industrial towns, a difficult operation, and highly destructive to civilian life and property. They were going to launch a new attack across the Lys farther north, which would complete the task very much more easily and effectively. For this the 36th Division, which had won a high reputation in the late fighting—" one of the best fighting divisions in the Army," as the Corps Commander put it a little later—was required. It was, indeed, to lead the attack, and carry out one of the most difficult and intricate operations possible to conceive in warfare.

On October 17th the 1st Battalion Royal Irish Rifles marched to Lendelede, the 2nd following the next day. It was a welcome change to find good billets, even if only for a day or two, and equally welcome were some excellent baths, in which 300 men an hour could bathe, left behind by the Germans. That night, much disturbed by enemy bombing, the 109th Brigade was relieving Belgian troops along the left bank of the Lys, with its left on the junction of the river and the Canal de Roulers. It had the task of forcing a crossing about five hours before the troops of the 9th Division on its right, and twenty-four hours before a French division, now hurrying into line, on its left.

The actual details of the crossing may be said not to be the concern of the historian of battalions of a brigade which was in reserve. But the details are so interesting, the manœuvre so difficult, and the importance of the first bridge-head over the Lys so great, that it is probable he will not be blamed for giving a brief account of the action before the 107th Brigade intervened in it.

The crossing was to be made at a sharp bend of the river due south of and three-quarters of a mile from the village of Oyghem. The troops, on reaching the farther bank, would be midway between two villages, each about half a mile from the river, Desselghem and Beveren. The plan was to ferry across in pontoons one battalion, the 9th Inniskilling Fusiliers, at dusk on the 19th. This battalion was to push forward to the main Courtrai—Ghent road and hold that position. Directly it was across, the Engineers were to throw across a " half-pontoon " bridge, to be complete at 10 p.m. On this a second battalion, the 1st Inniskilling Fusiliers, was to cross, and form flank from the Oyghem—Desselghem road to the left of the 9th. Then, the bridge-head being established, the 107th Brigade was to begin its crossing as early on the morning of the 20th as possible, to carry out the further advance in a south-easterly direction. It was a very difficult operation. In the first place, the enemy was holding the farther bank of the river in some strength. In the second place, the attack of the 1st Inniskilling was to be at right angles to that of the 9th, and it had after crossing to change front in the darkness. The scheme would have been impossible but for the moon, almost full.

The 9th Inniskilling crossed successfully, with a single casualty only, and began its advance. It met with considerable resistance, and did not quite reach its objective, being brought to a halt 400 yards short of it. The bridge meanwhile was thrown across, despite the heavy fire which the German artillery directed upon the river. At 10 p.m. the 1st Inniskilling began crossing. Then the Battalion swung left, and one company attacked each of the four villages, which lie in a nest, Spriete, Desselghem, Dries and Straete. The Battalion had sterner work than its predecessor, since the Germans were now fully on the alert. In fierce fighting, resort being frequently had to the bayonet, Spriete and Desselghem were cleared of the enemy. Then the supporting companies went through. Straete was captured, but the right company could do no more than reach the outskirts of Dries. However, that was not of great importance. The plan had succeeded in essentials. Eighty prisoners had been taken and numerous machine guns.

The Engineers had desperately hard work to keep the bridge, hit more than once by German shells, in repair. But they accomplished their task, and the 15th Irish Rifles, of the 107th Brigade, was able to begin its crossing at 2 a.m. It then moved forward to relieve the 9th Inniskilling Fusiliers. The 1st Irish Rifles then crossed. On the right troops of the 9th Division had begun crossing at midnight. For some time it was hard to find touch with them, and when this was accomplished the line at the point of junction was rather too close to the Lys for safety, the village of Beveren being still in the enemy's hands.

The new attack was launched at 6 a.m., Beveren being at once taken by a combined operation of the two Divisions. The 15th Irish Rifles had considerable casualties from machine-gun fire, and lost their Commanding Officer at an early stage. But the advance was very rapid. By 9 a.m. we were across the road from Deerlyck to Waereghem, or two miles beyond the Lys. A mill, in which were several machine guns, gave great trouble at this point, and a platoon of the 1st Irish Rifles was brought up to capture it, and succeeded in its task. By this time, however, our field guns across the Lys were firing at extreme range. It was decided to call a halt, to allow the French to cross that evening, while the 108th Brigade came into line on the left of the 107th. The 1st Irish Rifles relieved the 15th. The 2nd Battalion had crossed that morning, and moved forward in reserve. About two hundred prisoners had been captured by the Division.

The attack of October 21st, carried out by the 1st Irish Rifles on the 107th Brigade's front and the 1st Irish Fusiliers on that of the 108th Brigade, was of peculiar difficulty. There was no artillery support. The country was admirably suited to long-range machine-gun fire. And on the left the French, who had to fight their way from the bank of the Lys, were always considerably in rear. Nevertheless, the 1st Royal Irish Rifles carried out a very fine attack, the line at dusk being from the village of Knock to the Gaverbeek. Casualties in the circumstances had been light—1 officer and 4 other ranks killed, 2 officers and 14 other ranks wounded.*

That night the four batteries of the 153rd Brigade R.F.A. crossed the Lys, to fire a barrage the following morning in support of the advance of the 107th Brigade. It was thought that this comparatively small amount of artillery would yet make a very great difference. It was highly necessary. From the Gaverbeek the ground rises to a general ridge, crowned by a series of little heights, then drops down over two miles to the great river which runs parallel to the Lys at this point, the Escaut or Scheldt. The various little crests afforded admirable positions to the enemy on which to fight a delaying action before falling back on the Scheldt.

The artillery support was indeed most valuable on the morrow, October 22nd. At 9 a.m. the 2nd Royal Irish Rifles, supported by a company of the 15th Battalion, attacked the Klijtberg Hill, the first of the crests described above, and captured it almost without loss. The little hill was an easily recognized objective, since there was a windmill upon it. But it was to be an objective to the enemy also. A really vigorous attack,

* Lieutenant E. Daniels killed, Captain L. M. Bayly, M.C., wounded (died of wounds), 2nd-Lieutenant J. T. Gardiner wounded. On the previous day 2nd-Lieutenant W. J. Linton and the Rev. W. H. Hutchison were wounded.

by a Prussian Assault Battalion, drove in the left flank, which was considerably in advance of the 108th Brigade, and pushed the Battalion off the hill and back for a distance of 800 yards. Colonel Becher at once organized a new attack with two companies, which went forward very gallantly and again took possession of the knoll, driving the enemy off it. And that, though no man in the ranks can have guessed it, constituted the last action of the Battalion in the Great War.*

The 1st Battalion was to have one more turn. There were signs that the enemy's resistance was weakening, and it seemed possible that he might be about to retire to the Scheldt. Two companies of the Battalion, with a squadron of the 28th French Dragoons, were ordered to form an advanced guard and move toward the river. They passed through the 2nd Battalion on the Klitjberg Ridge. Vossenhoek was taken, but Kleineberg, a mile farther down the main road, was strongly held by machine guns. It was found impossible to make any further advance till these had been adequately dealt with by artillery. The Battalion had seven men wounded during the day. It, like the 2nd and 15th Battalions, was weary, and very low in strength. General Coffin therefore decided to relieve the 107th Brigade at once by the 109th. The relief was carried out without difficulty, the enemy being strictly on the defensive. The 1st Battalion marched back to Desselghem, which provided good billets; the 2nd to Bavichove. Both battalions then moved south-west by easy stages to Mouscron, practically a suburb of Tournai, but on the Belgian side of the frontier, arriving on November 3rd. It may be added that the other brigades of the Division only remained in line till the 27th, the 109th having the satisfaction of capturing the important Kleineberg Ridge, and were then relieved by troops of another division.

The men of the 36th Division were indeed suffering severely from fatigue. We had slipped into winter almost without realizing it. Two factors had contributed to strengthen the men and enable them to endure more than under normal circumstances of warfare. The first was that they had been fighting in inhabited and undamaged country, an experience new to most of them. That meant that battalions not actually in the firing-line had the shelter of houses at night. Such shelter was of enormous benefit in putting back the moment when fatigue and exposure made the troops unfit for further offensive action. But it was one factor only, and perhaps not even the most important. The other was the flow of victory on this and other fronts, and the sure hope that a few more resolute blows would bring the war to an end. That was a stimulus to all, to the young recruits as well as to the veterans of many battles. It nerved them to make a great final effort. The two battalions with which we are concerned, and, indeed, the whole Division, had written a splendid last page to their career in the war. Apart from the gallantry shown, there had been given proof, in dealing with the German machine guns which were the backbone of the enemy's resistance,† of a very high order of tactical skill. This was all the more creditable because there was in the ranks a small proportion of the non-commissioned officers and men who had experience of battle. The young successors of the men of Mons and Le Cateau, of Neuve Chapelle and the Somme, of Ypres and Cambrai, had lived up to their traditions worthily from every point of view.

* The 2nd Battalion's officer casualties for October, besides Lieut.-Colonel Bridcutt, were Lieutenant A. E. Buttle killed, Lieutenants A. E. Kemp, D.C.M., and F. K. McKeeman wounded.

† The German units were very depleted and weak at this time. But they missed numbers on the defensive comparatively little, because they had their full complement of light machine guns, on which the infantry now wholly relied. It was, in fact, an army of machine gunners, than which, in the defensive, nothing could be more formidable.

CONCLUSION

The 36th (Ulster) Division was not to form part of the British Army of the Rhine. It was to end its existence in the area about Mouscron, to which it had retired to rest after its last battle. Reinforcements from the Base arrived here, and all preparations were made to enter the line again. But that was not required. On November 11th came the Armistice, and warfare ceased after four years and three months. That was precisely the period of active service of the 2nd Battalion Royal Irish Rifles, while the 1st had served in France and Flanders exactly four years.

There is little to record for these final months. Almost at once the great British Army, formed for the war, began to melt away. The only difference between the treatment of regular and temporary battalions was that, while each were to be reduced gradually to cadre, the cadres of the latter were to be disbanded on reaching home, while those of the former were to form the nucleus about which regiments were to be built up anew. The events worth mentioning are few. On November 17th there was a great Thanksgiving Service in the central square of Roubaix, after which the troops marched past Lieut.-General Sir C. Jacob, in command at the moment of the Second Army. Training continued until the end of the month.

In December demobilization commenced, though men did not begin to return in great numbers till the New Year. The scheme of demobilization was theoretically perfect, but its operation caused considerable grumbling. Men were divided into classes, according to the importance of the trades which they represented, and the need for them in the resumption of national life in England. So the " key-men," on whom other trades depended, were to go first. The trouble was that it was these very men, just because they were " key-men," who had been called up most recently ! The comments of a boot-black who had volunteered in 1915, and had by extraordinary fortune kept his skin whole through ten battles, when he saw a printer who had waited for conscription sent back to his work and family before him, can be more fitly left to the imagination than described in cold print. To some extent the system was modified later, men with long service being demobilized early, whatever their classification.

Education was another feature of the period. The bulk of the infantry consisted of young men who had had little or no technical instruction to fit them for taking up a trade when they returned to civil life. It was, as is well known, this fact that made the employment of ex-service men a problem so difficult, even in the first two prosperous years after the war, before the general bad times set in. Classes were now set up throughout the Army to educate the troops, both in such subjects as mathematics and languages and in technical trades, such as carpentering and engineering. Attendance at these classes was voluntary, and they were very popular. They were worked out and organized with skill and enthusiasm, and the prospectuses, if carried out, would in many cases have produced valuable results. Unfortunately, they hardly ever were carried out in the case of most men. So soon as a man began to make progress, the order for his demobilization inevitably arrived. It is to be feared that, beyond keeping the troops interested, the excellently intentioned education scheme accomplished little.

Christmas Day, the last which these vast assemblages of men in arms were to celebrate, passed off happily. The 36th Division's good organization provided luxuries

Map VII.

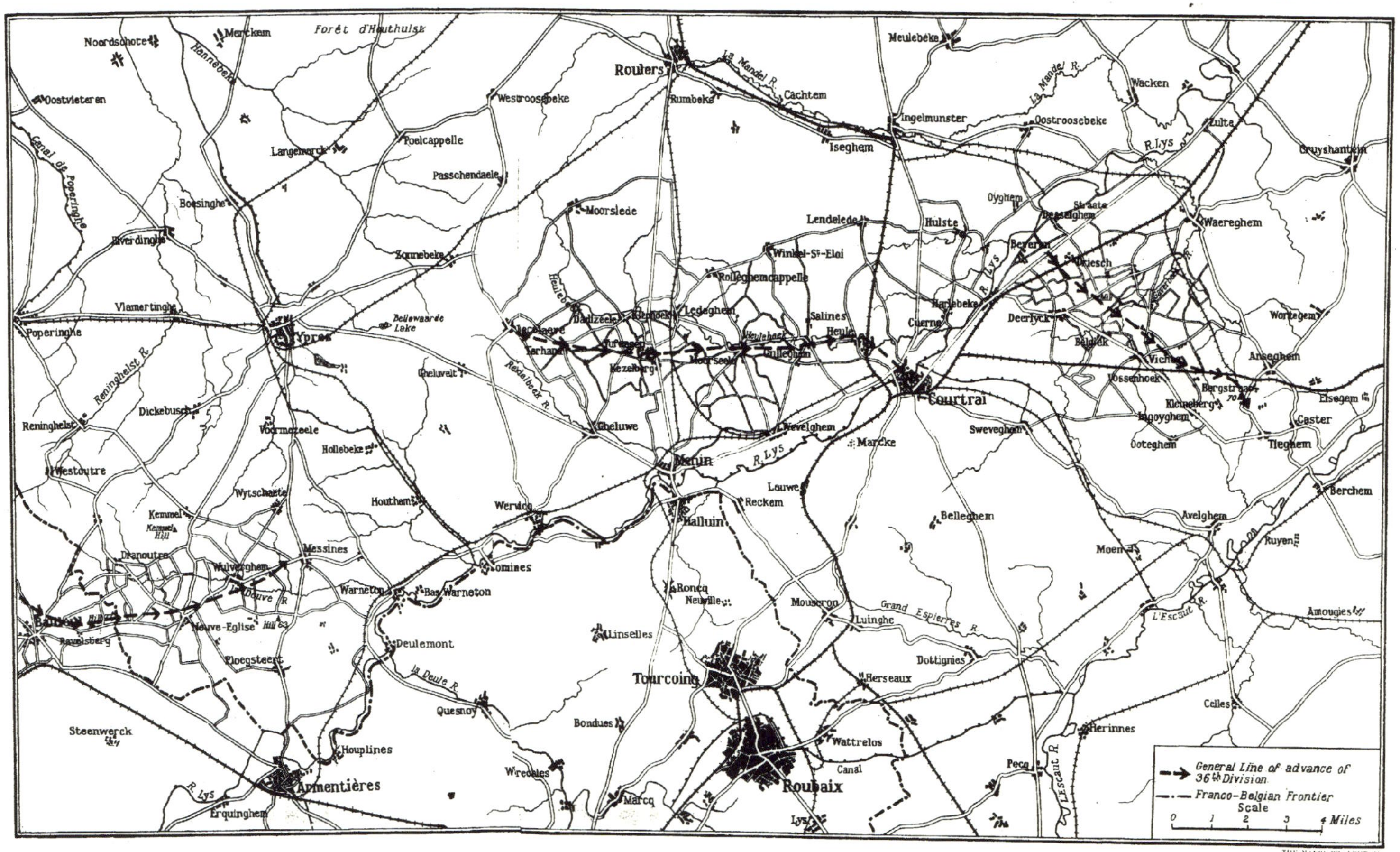

The Final Advances, 1918.

in abundance, while other troops in the neighbourhood found themselves unable to bring up the festal fare they had ordered across the still abominable roads of the Ypres battlefields. The following message was received by both battalions of the Royal Irish Rifles from the Regiment's Colonel, General Sir Henry Wilson, Chief of the Imperial General Staff :—

" OFFICERS, WARRANT OFFICERS, NON-COMMISSIONED OFFICERS AND MEN OF THE ROYAL IRISH RIFLES.

" Since last I sent you a Christmas greeting, the British Army has emerged triumphantly from the supreme crisis of the War. It has never been put to a more searching test, and it has never responded more magnificently.

" As your Colonel, I have always watched with interest the doings of all the Battalions of the Royal Irish Rifles, and I am proud of the distinguished part they have played. They have maintained the fighting tradition of Irish soldiers.

" Some of you will shortly be returning to civil life. To these I wish God-speed, and hope that the lesson of comradeship that you have learned in a great regiment in time of war will serve you in good stead all through life.

" To those who remain in the Army I send warm greetings, and hope that you will maintain in peace time the high standard you have attained in war.

" Officers, Warrant Officers, Non-commissioned Officers and Men, I wish you all happiness in the coming year on the conclusion of your great task and the return of peace.

" HENRY WILSON, *General,*
" *Colonel of the Royal Irish Rifles.*"

From the beginning of January, as has been said, men returned home for demobilization. During the month the 1st Battalion sent 105, and the 2nd 92. At the beginning of February the Prince of Wales visited both battalions, the officers of which were presented to him. There was, as may be imagined, plenty of amusement to help while away the weeks of waiting : sport of all kinds, visits from Miss Ashwell's Concert Parties. To enable men to see Lille, a regular bus service was established.

Orders were received in February that one service battalion of the Royal Irish Rifles was to be sent to the Rhine, to form part of the newly created Light Division. The 12th Battalion was selected. All men who did not desire to volunteer for the service or who were shortly due for demobilization were demobilized or transferred as quickly as possible, and the strength made up from volunteers and men not due to go for some time of the three other battalions of the Regiment in the 36th Division. From the 1st Battalion 155 rank and file, from the 2nd 3 officers and 123 other ranks, were sent toward the end of the month. That marked the end of the battalions as such, so far as this war was concerned. The cadre of the 2nd Battalion, which was due first for foreign service, left Mouscron on March 1st for Dunkirk, and, after a delay of three weeks in camp there, returned to England. It was another two months before the cadre of the 1st Battalion, 3 officers and 34 other ranks, with the band, which had come out in February, entrained at Mouscron for the journey home. It sailed from Dunkirk on May 29th.

That marks the end of the story of the Regiment's troops on active service in the war. A few words must suffice to complete the record of the Reserve battalions. As has been stated, the 3rd Battalion moved to Belfast in May, 1916, after the Rebellion. A detachment, consisting of one company, was sent to Newry. At Belfast the rapid training and despatch of reinforcements to the front continued, quickening, indeed, after the opening of the Battle of the Somme, with its heavy casualties. At the end of 1916 the 121st reinforcement was despatched. On July 17th, 1917, the Battalion, with other units in the Irish Northern District, was inspected by Field-Marshal Sir John French, who expressed himself as most pleased with the turn-out of the men, the march past, and the parade generally.

The 4th Battalion in 1917 transferred to the 5th all men under eighteen years and eight months. From the beginning of that year its band was removed from its establishment, and that of the 1st Battalion was thereafter attached to it. The 5th Battalion had been almost drafted away when it was reconstituted, in April, 1917, as one of the new "A4" battalions. This reconstruction, with youths under nineteen, at once raised the strength to over 1,000, and training began on a slightly changed plan. Men were now drafted on reaching nineteen years of age and becoming fully trained. In August, 1917, the Battalion returned to Belfast, and in April, 1918, to Ballykinlar Camp, where it remained a few weeks only.

In the spring of 1918 the War Office determined, in view of the disturbed state of the country, to move all the Irish troops out of Ireland. The 3rd, 4th, 5th, 17th, 18th, 19th and 20th Battalions of the Royal Irish Rifles all found themselves at Salisbury Plain together at the end of April. The 17th, 18th and 19th were at once broken up. There were no longer anything like the number of Irish recruits to fill the ranks of so many battalions.

There was here a rather extraordinary incident, orders being actually issued that the 4th Battalion was to be disbanded also, and the 20th—created comparatively late in the war—retained. Upon representations being made in the proper quarter, these orders were swiftly cancelled. The 20th was now broken up, and the 4th became in its place an "A4" battalion. Its establishment was now 6 companies and 1,553 all ranks. This huge figure was almost reached in August, 1918, but the resumption of the offensive by the British Army on the Western Front soon lowered the figure. The 3rd, 4th and 5th Battalions were now, and till the end, in what was known as the Irish Brigade.

Their existence continued without great incident, save for the many "mobilization schemes" with which they were kept alert. Sport furnished a relief from monotony. The 5th Battalion particularly distinguished itself. One of its boys won the Lightweight Boxing Championship of the Command, which contained 200,000 troops, while it also won outright the Irish Brigade Cross-Country Running Challenge Cup.

In early 1919, came the order for general demobilization. These three humbler sisters of the combatant battalions then brought their work to an end. It had been finely accomplished. It may be said that they have no war history, for the events are limited to half a dozen moves and the single incident of the Irish Rebellion. But much valuable endeavour, achieved quietly and outside the limelight, stands to their credit.

It is fitting to add a note with regard to an organization which was throughout the war in close touch with the Regiment—the Ulster Women's Gift Fund. This was formed in August, 1914, for the purpose of supplying comforts to the men of the three Ulster

CONCLUSION

Regiments—Royal Inniskilling Fusiliers, Royal Irish Fusiliers, Royal Irish Rifles—on active service, as well as to the North Irish Horse and to Ulster soldiers in other units.

The beginnings were small, but as more and more battalions entered the field, the work and the staff steadily increased. All the work of packing and administration was carried out by voluntary helpers, of whom a number, during the last two years of the war, devoted the whole of their time to the work. At the end of the war there were over four hundred such voluntary helpers. The people of Ulster supported the enterprise well, over £120,000 being raised in the Province for this Fund alone, which thus had no need to look to the British Red Cross or any other society for assistance.

When the first news of prisoners arrived, it was realized that a new and most important branch of work would devolve upon the Fund. As names and addresses came through, they were entered on the lists, and each man thenceforward received a fortnightly parcel till the end of the war. When, late in 1916, the Central Prisoners of War Committee in London reorganized the despatch of parcels, the two Regular battalions were taken over by that committee. The Ulster Women's Fund continued to supply the prisoners of other battalions and the other Ulster regiments. That it had plenty of work upon its hands is shown by the fact that, at the date of the Armistice, the Fund was packing and despatching six hundred parcels a day. It also continued to send comforts to the 1st and 2nd Battalions, as well as the rest.

APPENDICES

APPENDIX I

LIST OF HONOURS AND REWARDS ISSUED TO OFFICERS BELONGING TO THE FIRST SEVEN BATTALIONS OF THE ROYAL IRISH RIFLES FOR SERVICES IN THE GREAT WAR, 1914-19.

NOTE.—This list is as accurate as possible from data available. Omissions or errors may have occurred. It is hoped that notification of same will be sent to the publishers with a view to corrections being made should a second impression become necessary.

RANK AND NAME.	NO. OF BATTALION, ETC.	AWARDED.	"LONDON GAZETTE," ETC.
Adams, T./2nd-Lieut. Frank	Attached 2nd Bn.	M.C.	15/2/19
Allatt, Col. H. T. W.	3rd Bn.	Mentioned in Despatches	25/1/17
Allen, Bt. Lieut.-Col. Edward	Retired Pay, late R. Irish Rifles	C.M.G.	14/1/16
		Mentioned in Despatches	1/1/16
Alston, Major J. W. (killed)	2nd Bn.	Mentioned in Despatches	22/6/15
Anderson, T./Lieut. (A./Capt.) Andrew Millar	2nd Bn.	M.C.	3/6/19
		French Croix de Guerre avec etoile en Bronze	19/6/19
Barnett, T./Lieut. Alexander	7th Bn.	M.C.	1/1/17
Barrington, Lieut.-Col. (T./Br. Gen.) T. P.	2nd Bn.	Mentioned in Despatches	15/6/16
Barrows, Lieut. W. P.	5th Bn., attached King's African Rifles	Mentioned in Despatches	5/6/19
Becher, Major (T./Lieut.-Col.) Cecil Morgan Ley	2nd Bn.	D.S.O.	1/1/17
		Mentioned in Despatches	9/12/14
		Mentioned in Despatches	6/12/16
	Attached Leicester R.	Belgian Ordre de Leopold avec Croix de Guerre (Officier)	24/10/19
Bellingham, Capt. (A./Major) Alan Mure	1st or 2nd Bns., attached 25th Bn. Machine Gun Corps	M.C.	16/9/18
		Russian Order of St. Vladimir, 4th Class, with swords and ribbon	War Office confidential list, 16/7/21
Bird, Lieut.-Col. (T./Brig.-Gen.) Wilkinson Dent, D.S.O.	2nd Bn.	Extra A.D.C. to King and Bt. Col.	18/2/15
		C.B.	3/6/16
		C.M.G.	1/1/18
		Mentioned in Despatches	9/12/14
		Mentioned in Despatches	12/2/18
		French Legion d'Honneur, Croix d'Officier	3/11/14
		French Croix de Guerre	21/4/17
Biscoe, Capt. A. J.	1st Bn.	Mentioned in Despatches	22/6/15
Boyle, T./2nd-Lieut. John Kemmy	7th Bn., attd. 1st Bn.	M.C.	26/9/17
Bradford, Lieut.-Col. E. C.	6th Bn.	Mentioned in Despatches	27/3/16
Bridcutt, Capt. (A./Lieut.-Col.) John Henry (killed in action)	1st or 2nd Bns., attached 7th Bn Bedfordshire Regt.	D.S.O.	4/6/17
		Mentioned in Despatches	4/1/17
		Mentioned in Despatches	23/7/17
Broomfield, 2nd-Lieut. Arthur Allen	5th Bn., attd. 2nd Bn.	M.C.	15/3/16
Brown, T./2nd-Lieut. Archibald	7th Bn., attd. 48th Light Trench Mortar Battery	M.C.	18/10/17
Browne, Lieut. Lindsay	4th Bn., attd 2nd Bn.	M.C.	18/2/15
		Mentioned in Despatches	17/2/15
Burges, Lieut. W. A. (killed in action)	1st Bn.	Mentioned in Despatches	22/6/15
Calverley, Lieut. (T./Capt.) Geoffry Walter	2nd Bn.	D.S.O.	25/8/16
		Mentioned in Despatches	4/1/17
Campbell, T./Lieut. (T./Capt.) David	6th Bn.	M.C.	4/6/17
		Mentioned in Despatches	21/7/17
Carstairs, Major (A./Lieut.-Col.) A. J. H.	R. of O., R. Irish Rifles	Mentioned in Despatches	28/12/18
		Mentioned in Despatches	9/7/19
		O.B.E.	3/6/19

RANK AND NAME.	NO. OF BATTALION, ETC.	AWARDED.	"LONDON GAZETTE," ETC.
Castello, Lieut. (T./Capt.) Leon Benham	5th Bn.	Mentioned in Despatches	4/1/17
		Mentioned in Despatches	9/7/19
		French Legion d'Honneur, Croix de Chevalier	17/12/17
		French Croix de Guerre	6/11/18
Clapham, T./2nd-Lieut. Frederick Horace	6th Bn.	M.C.	4/6/17
		Mentioned in Despatches	21/7/17
Cole-Hamilton, Capt. (T./Lieut.-Col.) Claude George	15th Bn., R. of O., late R. Irish Rifles	C.M.G.	4/6/17
		Bar to D.S.O.	30/1/20
		Mentioned in Despatches	25/5/17
		Mentioned in Despatches	24/5/18
		Mentioned in Despatches	9/7/19
Condon, 2nd-Lieut. (T./Lieut. and A./Capt.) James Edmund Smith	3rd Bn., attd. 15th Bn.	M.C.	18/2/18
		Bar to M.C.	30/1/20
		Mentioned in Despatches	9/7/19
Cooke, 2nd-Lieut. C. E.	3rd Bn., attd. 1st Bn.	Mentioned in Despatches	17/2/15
Cooke-Collis, Major and Bt. Lieut.-Col. (T./Br.-Gen.) William James Norman	1st or 2nd Bns.	D.S.O.	3/6/18
		Brevet Lieut.-Col.	23/11/16
		C.M.G.	3/6/19
		C.B.	10/6/19
		Mentioned in Despatches	28/1/16
		Mentioned in Despatches	13/7/16
		Mentioned in Despatches	6/12/16
		Mentioned in Despatches	25/9/16
		Mentioned in Despatches	28/11/17
		Mentioned in Despatches	11/6/18
		Mentioned in Despatches	5/6/19
		Mentioned in Despatches	20/5/20
		Mentioned in Despatches	14/1/21
		French Legion d'Honneur, Croix d'Officier	1/5/17
		Russian Order of St. Stanislaus, 3rd Class, with Sword	15/2/17
Cowley, Capt. (A./Major) Victor Leopold Spencer	2nd Bn., attd. 31st Bn. Machine Gun Corps	M.C.	1/1/18
		D.S.O.	3/6/19
		Mentioned in Despatches	9/12/14
		Mentioned in Despatches	28/12/18
		Mentioned in Despatches	10/7/19
Craig, T./Lieut. J.	7th Bn.	Mentioned in Despatches	4/1/17
Crawford, Lieut. (A./Capt.) F.	2nd Bn.	Mentioned in Despatches	14/6/18
Curran, Capt. J. P. C.	3rd Bn.	Mentioned in Despatches	30/1/19
Currey, Capt. H. P.	1st or 2nd Bns.	Brevet Major	3/6/18
Curzon, Lieut.-Col. Fitzroy Edmond Penn (killed)	R.P., R. Irish Rifles, attd. 6th R. Irish Regt.	Mentioned in Despatches	4/1/17
Daunt, Lieut.-Col. R. A. C., D.S.O.	2nd Bn.	Mentioned in Despatches	15/6/16
Davis, 2nd-Lieut. Edmund Frank	2nd Bn.	M.C.	10/8/21
Dobbin, 2nd-Lieut. William Leonard Price (deceased)	2nd Bn.	M.C.	1/1/18
Dowling, Qr.Mr. and Capt. J. J. E.	1st or 2nd Bns., attd. 1st Bn. Leinster Regt.	Mentioned in Despatches	22/1/19
Doyle, Lieut. (A./Capt.) C. S.	3rd Bn., attd. 108th Light Trench Mortar Battery	Mentioned in Despatches	9/7/19
Drought, 2nd-Lieut. Robert Victor (deceased)	3rd Bn., attd. 7th Bn.	M.C.	16/8/17
Duffield, Major James	1st or 2nd Bns.	Hon. Lieut.-Col.	12/12/19
Dunn, Major Ernest George	1st or 2nd Bns.	D.S.O.	23/10/19
		French Croix de Guerre	6/2/22
		Mentioned in Despatches	5/4/16
		Mentioned in Despatches	13/7/16
		Mentioned in Despatches	19/10/17
Eastwood, Capt. H. J., M.C.	2nd Bn. R. Ulster Rifles	Mentioned in Despatches (M.C. awarded whilst belonging to Rifle Brigade.)	9/9/21
Eastwood, Capt. (T./Major) W., (killed)	6th Bn.	Mentioned in Despatches	27/3/16

APPENDICES

RANK AND NAME.	NO. OF BATTALION, ETC.	AWARDED.	"LONDON GAZETTE," ETC.
Edwards, Qr.Mr. and Capt. George William	1st Bn.	Promoted to Hon. Major	3/6/19
		Mentioned in Despatches	22/6/15
		Mentioned in Despatches	1/1/16
		Mentioned in Despatches	25/5/17
		Mentioned in Despatches	24/5/18
		Belgian Croix de Guerre	4/9/19
Faber, Lieut. (A./Capt.) L. E., M.C.	5th Bn.	Mentioned in Despatches	21/12/17
		(M.C. awarded whilst belonging to Royal Fusiliers)	
Ffrench-Mullen, Capt. Ernest	3rd Bn., attd. 1/10th Bn. London Regiment	M.C.	12/12/19
		Mentioned in Despatches	12/1/20
		Egyptian Order of the Nile, 4th Class	16/1/20
Forbes, Major Hon. Bertram Aloysius	1st or 2nd Bns.	O.B.E.	3/6/19
		Mentioned in Despatches	25/10/16
		Mentioned in Despatches	5/6/19
Forbes, Lieut. (A./Capt.) R. H.	3rd Bn., attd. Machine Gun Corps	Mentioned in Despatches	25/5/17
Foster, Qr.Mr. and Hon. Capt. Harry William	2nd Bn.	M.C.	1/1/18
		Mentioned in Despatches	4/1/17
		Mentioned in Despatches	25/5/17
Francis, Major (T./Lieut.-Col.) Sidney Goodall, D.S.O.	West Yorks Regt. Comdg. 7th Bn. R. Irish Rifles	Bt. Lieut.-Col.	*1/1/17
		Bar to D.S.O.	*1/1/18
		Brevet Colonel	1/1/19
		Mentioned in Despatches	23/5/15
		Mentioned in Despatches	*4/1/17
		Mentioned in Despatches	*18/5/17
		Mentioned in Despatches	*18/12/17
		Mentioned in Despatches	20/12/18
		Mentioned in Despatches	5/7/19
		French Legion d'Honneur, Chevalier	15/12/19
Gartlan, Lieut. (now Capt.) Gerald Ian	1st or 2nd Bns.	M.C.	23/6/15
		Brevet Major	1/1/18
		D.S.O.	1/1/19
		Mentioned in Despatches	22/6/15
		Mentioned in Despatches	11/12/17
		Mentioned in Despatches	20/12/18
Gifford, Major Herbert Llewellyn	1st or 2nd Bns.	O.B.E.	12/12/19
Goodman, Major (A./Lieut.-Col.) Harry Russell	2nd Bn.	Mentioned in Despatches	9/12/14
		Mentioned in Despatches	25/5/17
		D.S.O.	17/9/17
		Mentioned in Despatches	12/12/17
Graham, Capt. Fergis Reginald Winsford	1st Bn.	M.C.	23/6/15
		Brevet Major	4/6/17
		D.S.O.	8/3/19
		Mentioned in Despatches	22/6/15
		Mentioned in Despatches	6/12/16
		Mentioned in Despatches	21/7/17
		Mentioned in Despatches	14/6/18
		Mentioned in Despatches	11/6/20
		French Croix de Guerre	17/8/18
Gribben, Lieut. Edward	3rd Bn., and No. 70 Sqdn. Royal Flying Corps	M.C.	26/9/17
Grove-White, T./Lieut. (A./Capt.) Ion Alexander	2nd Bn., attd. 107th Light Trench Mortar Battery	M.C.	8/3/19
		Mentioned in Despatches	21/12/17
		French Croix de Guerre	19/6/19
Harding, 2nd-Lieut. (T./Capt.) Christopher	1st or 2nd Bns., attd. 9th Bn.	M.C.	26/9/16
		Bar to M.C.	17/9/17
Hart, Lieut. John James	1st or 2nd Bns., attd. Nigeria Regt.	M.C.	4/3/18
Hartery, T./2nd-Lieut. M. J.	7th Bn.	Mentioned in Despatches	4/1/17
Haslett, T./2nd-Lieut. John	1st Bn.	M.C.	11/1/19
Hayward, Lieut. R. B.	3rd Bn.	Mentioned in Despatches	25/1/17
Hill, T./Lieut. William Carlile (deceased)	2nd Bn., attd. 74th Trench Mortar Battery	M.C.	12/3/17

* For service with Royal Irish Rifles.

RANK AND NAME.	NO. OF BATTALION, ETC.	AWARDED.	"LONDON GAZETTE," ETC.
Hill-Dillon, Capt. and Bt. Major Stephen Searle	1st or 2nd Bns.	D.S.O.	18/2/15
		Brevet Major	1/1/18
		Bt. Lieut.-Col.	1/1/23
		Mentioned in Despatches	9/12/14
		Mentioned in Despatches	15/5/17
		Mentioned in Despatches	11/12/17
Hoare, Capt. Edward James	2nd Bn. R. Ulster Rifles	M.C.	10/8/21
Hogg, Lieut. William Frederick	3rd Bn., attd. 14th Bn.	M.C.	14/11/16
Hume, Capt. G. C.	5th Bn., attd. 12th Bn.	Mentioned in Despatches	9/7/19
Hussey, T./Lieut. P. W.	6th Bn.	Mentioned in Despatches	28/11/17
Hutcheson, Capt. (T./Lieut.-Col.) Robert Barrett	1st or 2nd Bns., attd. Labour Corps	Mentioned in Despatches	30/5/18
		Italian Croce di Guerra	21/8/19
		French Croix de Guerre (Silver Star)	17/8/18
Ivey, Capt. (A./Major) Thomas H.	1st Bn.	D.S.O.	3/6/18
		Mentioned in Despatches	*9/12/14
		Mentioned in Despatches	24/5/18
Jeffares, Capt. R. T.	4th Bn., attd. 2nd Bn.	Mentioned in Despatches	21/12/17
Kearne, 2nd-Lieut. M. C.	2nd Bn.	Mentioned in Despatches	17/2/15
Keating, Capt. P. W.	1st Bn.	Mentioned in Despatches	3/2/20
Kemp, Lieut. (T./Capt.) Albert Edward, D.C.M.	2nd Bn.	M.C. (D.C.M. awarded whilst in the ranks of the Worcester Regt.)	15/2/19
Kerr, T./Lieut. T.	7th Bn.	Mentioned in Despatches	25/5/17
King-Harman, T./Major Wentworth Alexander	Special List (Ret. List, late R. Irish Rifles)	D.S.O.	1/1/18
		Bt. Lieut.-Col.	3/6/19
		Mentioned in Despatches	11/12/17
		Mentioned in Despatches	20/12/18
		Mentioned in Despatches	5/7/19
Kingston, T./Lieut. W.	7th Bn.	Mentioned in Despatches	25/5/17
Laurie, Lieut.-Col. G. B.	1st Bn.	Mentioned in Despatches	17/2/15
		Mentioned in Despatches	22/6/15
Leach, Lieut. E. W. V.	3rd Bn.	Mentioned in Despatches	4/1/17
Leader, Capt. (T./Lieut.-Col.) J.	R. of O., R. Irish Rifles	Mentioned in Despatches	15/6/16
Leathes, Major Carterel de Mussenden	5th Bn.	O.B.E., Class IV	1/1/19
Lee, Capt. G. B.	1st or 2nd Bns.	Mentioned in Despatches	15/8/17
		Mentioned in Despatches	12/3/18
Leeper, Lieut. (A./Capt.). J. C.	1st Bn.	Mentioned in Despatches	28/12/18
		Belgian Croix de Guerre	4/9/19
Loyd, T./2nd-Lieut. E. B. K.	2nd Bn.	Mentioned in Despatches	25/5/17
Ludlow-Hewitt, Capt. (T./Major) Edgar Rainey	1st or 2nd Bns., and Royal Flying Corps	M.C.	14/1/16
		Brevet Major	1/1/17
		D.S.O.	1/1/18
		Mentioned in Despatches	22/6/15
		Mentioned in Despatches	1/1/16
		Mentioned in Despatches	4/1/17
		Mentioned in Despatches	11/12/17
		Mentioned in Despatches	31/12/18
		Mentioned in Despatches	11/7/19
		French Legion d'Honneur, Chevalier	14/7/17
McAlindon, 2nd-Lieut. Thomas (died)	2nd Bn.	M.C.	26/9/17
McArevey, Lieut. (A./Capt.) Joseph Bertrand	3rd Bn. attd. 2nd Bn.	M.C.	26/9/17
MacCartney, Lieut. G. N. C. H. A.	2nd Bn. R. Ulster Rifles	Mentioned in Despatches	9/9/21
McCabe, T./2nd-Lieut. S .T.	6th Bn.	Mentioned in Despatches	6/12/16
McCammond, Lieut.-Col. Walter Edward Carson	3rd Bn.	Bt. Col.	3/6/18
McCammon, Lieut.-Col. T. V. P.	5th Bn.	Mentioned in Despatches	25/1/17
McCaull, T./Lieut. C. N.	2nd Bn., attd. 107th Light Trench Mortar Battery	Mentioned in Despatches	9/7/19
McCullough, 2nd-Lieut. David John	1st or 2nd Bns., attd. 36th Divn. Headquarters	M.C.	1/1/18
MacFarren, T./2nd-Lieut. Ernest	7th Bn.	Serbian Order of St. Sava, 5th Class	3/10/17
		Serbian Order of the White Eagle, 5th Class	15/2/17
McFerran, Lieut.-Col. Edwin Millar Gilliland	4th Bn., Comdg.	C.B.E.	3/6/19

* Granted while serving with Coldstream Guards.

APPENDICES

RANK AND NAME.	NO. OF BATTALION, ETC.	AWARDED.	"LONDON GAZETTE," ETC.
McFerran, 2nd-Lieut. Maurice Anderdon (deceased)	4th Bn., attd. 2nd Bn.	M.C.	4/2/18
McGavin, Lieut. (A./Capt.) Nathan	1st or 2nd Bns., attd. 1/10th Bn. London R. (T.F.)	M.C.	12/12/19
		Mentioned in Despatches	5/6/19
McHugh, 2nd-Lieut. Denis	1st or 2nd Bns., attd. 14th Bn.	M.C.	17/9/17
McIntosh, 2nd-Lieut. Henry	1st Bn.	M.C.	8/3/19
Macnamara, Major (T./Lieut.-Col.) C. C. (died of wounds)	1st or 2nd Bns., attd. Egyptian Army	Mentioned in Despatches	25/10/16
		Egyptian Order of the Nile, 4th Class	25/7/16
MacPherson, T./2nd-Lieut. William Angus Smily	1st Bn.	M.C.	2/12/18
McWhinnie, Major William John	Retired Pay, late R. Irish Rifles	Italian Order of St. Maurice and St. Lazarus, Cavalier	29/10/20
Maitland, 2nd-Lieut. William Samuel	5th Bn., attd. 1st Bn.	M.C.	22/9/16
Malone, T./Capt. William Adolphe	7th Bn., attd. 2nd Bn.	M.C.	26/7/18
Marriott-Watson, 2nd-Lieut. Richard Brereton (killed)	2nd Bn.	M.C.	1/1/17
Marshall, Lieut. H.	5th Bn., attd. 2nd Bn.	Mentioned in Despatches	9/7/19
Martin, 2nd-Lieut. Joseph	1st Bn.	Promotion to Captain	18/2/15
		Mentioned in Despatches	17/2/15
Martin, Capt. Richard Ross	2nd Bn. R. Ulster Rifles	O.B.E., Class IV	9/9/21
		Mentioned in Despatches	9/9/21
Master, Capt. C. L.	2nd Bn.	Mentioned in Despatches	9/12/14
Maynard, Major Percy Guy Wolfe	1st or 2nd Bns., attd. Egyptian Army	D.S.O.	1/1/19
		Mentioned in Despatches	22/1/19
		Hedjaz Order of El Nahda, 4th Class	8/3/20
Merriman, Major Arthur Drummond Nairne	1st Bn.	D.S.O.	3/6/16
		Mentioned in Despatches	1/1/16
		Mentioned in Despatches	15/6/16
		Mentioned in Despatches	9/9/21
Mogridge, Lieut. E. C.	3rd Bn., attd. Machine Gun Corps	Mentioned in Despatches	25/5/17
Moreland, 2nd-Lieut. James Alexander	3rd Bn., attd. 2nd Bn.	M.C.	4/2/18
Moss, Lieut. William Philipson	3rd Bn., attd. 2nd Bn.	M.C.	1/1/17
Moyles, 2nd-Lieut. David Arthur	1st or 2nd Bns., attd. 8th Bn.	M.C.	17/9/17
Muir, 2nd-Lieut. James Lennon	4th Bn., attd. 1st Bn.	M.C.	24/6/16
		Bar to M.C.	10/8/21
Munn, T./2nd-Lieut. Norman Barry	2nd Bn.	M.C.	16/9/18
Murphy, Lieut. (A./Capt.) Edmund Victor Burke	1st Bn.	M.C.	1/1/17
		Mentioned in Despatches	*3/2/20
Murphy, 2nd-Lieut. P.	2nd Bn.	Mentioned in Despatches	21/12/17
Murphy, Lieut. (A./Major) Patrick	2nd Bn., Comdt. 66th Div. Recp. Camp	M.C.	3/6/19
Murphy, 2nd-Lieut. P. J.	2nd Bn.	Mentioned in Despatches	25/5/17
Newport, Capt. C. J.	1st or 2nd Bns.	Mentioned in Despatches	1/1/16
Noblett, Major L. H.	R. of O., R. Irish Rifles	Brevet Lieut.-Col.	1/1/18
		C.B.E.	3/6/19
		Belgian Ordre de la Couronne, Chevalier	9/4/20
Norman, Capt. Geoffrey Schuyler	2nd Bn.	M.C.	1/1/17
		Mentioned in Despatches	22/6/15
Ogier, T./Capt. Cyril Alfred	7th Bn. (Lieut. 3rd Royal Jersey Militia)	M.C.	16/9/18
		Panamanian La Solidaridad, 3rd Class	17/2/20
O'Halloran, T./Lieut. H.	6th Bn.	Mentioned in Despatches	28/11/17
O'Lone, T./Lieut. (T./Capt.) R. J.	1st or 2nd Bns.	Mentioned in Despatches	1/1/16
O'Sullivan, Capt. A. M. (killed)	1st Bn.	Mentioned in Despatches	22/6/15
Panter, Lieut. (A./Capt.) George William	1st or 2nd Bns. (and Royal Air Force)	M.B.E.	3/6/19
		Mentioned in Despatches	1/6/16
Parsons, T./Lieut. K.	6th Bn.	Mentioned in Despatches	21/7/17
Patton, Capt. John Henry Alexander	5th Bn., attd. 15th Bn.	M.C.	1/1/19
		Bar to M.C.	8/3/19
Pollock, T./Capt. J. H. H.	6th Bn., attd. H.Q. 54th Division	Mentioned in Despatches	12/1/20

* Attd. 46th Bn. Royal Fusiliers.

RANK AND NAME.	NO. OF BATTALION, ETC.	AWARDED.	"LONDON GAZETTE," ETC.
Poore, T./Lieut. A. T. M.	6th Bn.	Mentioned in Despatches	6/12/16
Reilly, Lieut. (A./Capt.) John Edwin	2nd Bn., seconded to 8th Bn. Tank Corps	M.C.	8/3/19
Rigby, Capt. Walter	5th Bn., R. of O., late R. Irish Rifles, and Egyptian Army Police Service Bn.	D.S.O.	4/5/17
Rigg, T./Major William Trevor	6th Bn.	French Croix de Guerre	14/7/17
	7th Bn.	Mentioned in Despatches	21/12/17
Rodwell, Capt. R. M.	1st or 2nd Bns. and 3rd Nigeria Regiment	Mentioned in Despatches	30/1/20
Rogers, Capt. Henry Waters Lyttleton	4th Bn.	O.B.E., Class IV	3/6/19
		Mentioned in Despatches	30/12/18
		Mentioned in Despatches	9/7/19
Rose, Capt. Richard De Ras	2nd Bn.	M.C.	26/9/17
		Bar to M.C.	16/9/18
		Mentioned in Despatches	21/12/17
Rule, 2nd-Lieut. Clifford	3rd Bn., attd. 2nd Bn.	French Croix de Guerre	19/6/19
Salmon, Lieut. Cyril Sebastian	4th Bn. and 25th Bn. Machine Gun Corps	M.C.	3/6/19
Scollard, Capt. David (deceased)	1st or 2nd Bns., attd. 7th Bn.	M.C.	12/3/17
Scott, T./Lieut. Robert Clement	2nd Bn.	M.C.	1/2/19
Seth-Smith, Capt. Hugh Eric Seth	4th Bn., attd. 7th Bn.	M.C.	1/1/18
Smyth, T./Lieut. (A./Capt.) G. B. J.	7th Bn., attd. 2nd Bn.	Mentioned in Despatches	28/12/18
Soutry, Major Trevor Lloyd Blunden	1st or 2nd Bns.	D.S.O.	1/1/17
		Brevet Lieut.-Col.	3/6/18
		Mentioned in Despatches	22/6/15
		Mentioned in Despatches	4/1/17
		Mentioned in Despatches	15/5/17
		Mentioned in Despatches	11/12/17
		Mentioned in Despatches	30/5/18
		French Croix de Guerre (Silver Star)	17/8/18
		Italian Order of St. Maurice and St. Lazarus, Cavalier	12/9/18
Spedding, Major C. R., D.S.O.	2nd Bn.	Mentioned in Despatches	9/12/14
Steele, 2nd-Lieut. (T./Capt.) James Stuart	1st or 2nd Bns., attd. 7th Bn.	M.C.	18/10/17
		Mentioned in Despatches	25/5/17
		Mentioned in Despatches	10/6/21
Stevens, Capt. R. W. M.	1st or 2nd Bns.	Mentioned in Despatches	9/12/14
Steventon, Lieut. R. W.	4th Bn., attd. 7th Bn. R. Dublin Fus.	Mentioned in Despatches	14/6/18
Stewart, 2nd-Lieut. James Noel Greer	3rd Bn., attd. 2nd Bn.	M.C.	15/10/18
Swettenham, Lieut.-Col. Geo. Kilmer, D.S.O.	5th Bn., late Ret. Pay, R. of O.	C.B.E.	3/6/19
Tate, Lieut. Thomas Marshall	1st Bn.	French Croix de Guerre	19/6/19
Taylor, Lieut. (A./Capt.) A. C.	1st Bn.	Mentioned in Despatches	4/1/17
		Mentioned in Despatches	21/12/17
Tayler, Capt. Harry	4th Bn., attd. 1st Bn.	M.C.	15/2/19
		Mentioned in Despatches	15/6/19
Tee, Capt. (A./Major) Charles Clifford (died)	1st or 2nd Bns. and Machine Gun Corps	M.C.	3/6/18
		O.B.E., Class IV	3/2/20
		Mentioned in Despatches	28/11/17
		Mentioned in Despatches	3/2/20
		Russian Order of St. Stanislaus, 2nd Class	16/7/21
Teele, Capt. William Beaconsfield	2nd Bn.	M.C.	1/2/19
Thomas, Capt. E. M.	2nd Bn.	Mentioned in Despatches	9/7/19
Tod, Lieut. William	3rd Bn., attd. 2nd Bn.	M.C.	15/2/19
Varwell, Capt. Ralph Peter	1st or 2nd Bns.	M.C.	4/6/17
		Brevet Major	1/1/19
		Mentioned in Despatches	22/6/15
		Mentioned in Despatches	20/5/18
		Mentioned in Despatches	30/12/18
		French Croix de Guerre	26/11/19

APPENDICES

RANK AND NAME.	NO. OF BATTALION, ETC.	AWARDED.	"LONDON GAZETTE," ETC.
Wakefield, Capt. C. J.	1st or 2nd Bns., and King's African Rifles, West African Frontier Force	Mentioned in Despatches	1/1/16
		Mentioned in Despatches	5/6/19
		Mentioned in Despatches	29/11/20
Walkington, T./Lieut. Dolway Bell	2nd Bn.	M.C.	15/10/18
Wallace, T./Capt. Alexander	2nd Bn.	French Croix de Guerre	19/6/19
Wallace, Lieut. (T./Capt.) Frederic Campbell	5th Bn.	M.C.	1/1/18
		Bar to M.C.	24/9/18
		D.S.O.	1/1/19
		Mentioned in Despatches	15/6/16
		Mentioned in Despatches	4/1/17
		Mentioned in Despatches	20/5/18
		Mentioned in Despatches	20/12/18
Watson, Lieut. Charles Sidney Waller	3rd Bn., attd. 6th Bn. R. Innis. Fusiliers	M.C.	8/3/19
		Mentioned in Despatches	14/6/18
Welman, Major H. L.	R.P., late R. Irish Rifles	Brevet Lieut.-Col.	1/1/18
Whitfeld, Lieut. A. N.	2nd Bn.	Mentioned in Despatches	9/12/14
Whitfeld, Lieut. Gerald Herbert Penn	1st Bn.	M.C.	1/1/18
		Mentioned in Despatches	25/5/17
Wilkins, Lieut. (T./Capt.) Cyril Francis	2nd Bn.	M.C.	1/1/17
		D.S.O.	1/1/18
		French Croix de Guerre	19/6/19
		Mentioned in Despatches	21/12/17
		Mentioned in Despatches	20/12/18
Wilson, Major-Gen. Henry Hughes, C.B., D.S.O. (deceased)	Colonel, R. Irish Rifles	Temp. Lieut.-Gen.	18/2/15
		K.C.B.	23/6/15
		Prom. Lieut.-General	17/3/17
		Prom. to General	4/9/18
		G.C.B.	17/12/18
		Field-Marshal	31/7/19
		Mentioned in Despatches	9/9/14
		Mentioned in Despatches	19/10/14
		Mentioned in Despatches	1/1/16
		Mentioned in Despatches	4/1/17
		French Legion d'Honneur, Grand Officier	24/2/16
		Italian Order of St. Maurice and St. Lazarus, Grand Officier	25/3/18
		Japanese Order of the Rising Sun, Grand Cordon	9/11/18
		American Distinguished Service Medal	12/7/19
		Greek Order of the Redeemer, Grand Cross	24/10/19
		Siamese Order of the White Elephant, 1st Class	26/11/19
		Chinese Order of Chia-Ho, 1st Class "Ta Shou Pao-Knang"	17/2/20
		Serbian White Eagle with Swords, 1st Class	15/10/20
		Belgian Ordre de Leopold, Grand Officier	21/1/21
		French Legion d'Honneur, Grand Cross	11/10/21
		Japanese Grand Cordon of the Order of the Rising Sun with flowers of the Paulownia	24/1/22
		Belgian Croix de Guerre	29/3/22
Wilson, Lieut. (A./Capt.) W. J. B.	7th Bn.	Mentioned in Despatches	21/12/17
Workman, Lieut. Edward	5th Bn., attd. 2nd Bn.	M.C.	15/3/16
Workman, 2nd-Lieut. Franz	5th Bn., attd. 10th Bn.	M.C.	14/1/16
		Mentioned in Despatches	1/1/16
Wright, Lieut. (T./Capt.) A. O'H. (killed)	1st Bn.	Mentioned in Despatches	22/6/15
Young, Lieut. Roy Allen	4th Bn., attd. 2nd Bn.	M.C.	16/8/17
Young, 2nd/Lieut. V. C.	7th Bn.	Mentioned in Despatches	21/12/17

APPENDIX II

LIST OF DECORATIONS AWARDED TO WARRANT OFFICERS, NON-COMMISSIONED OFFICERS AND MEN OF THE FIRST SEVEN BATTALIONS OF THE ROYAL IRISH RIFLES FOR SERVICES IN THE GREAT WAR, 1914-19.

	RANK AND NAME.	NO. OF BATTALION, ETC.	AWARDED.	"LONDON GAZETTE," ETC.
13956	Anderson, Cpl. H.	2nd Bn.	M.S.M.	3/6/19
4942	Arnopp, Rfn. W.	1st Bn.	M.M.	28/9/17
2254	Ashe, Rfn. E.	1st Bn.	M.M.	17/6/19
7795	Atkinson, Rfn. J.	2nd Bn.	M.M.	18/10/17
40202	Atcheson, Rfn. (A./L./Cpl.) A.	2nd Bn.	Mentioned in Despatches	9/7/19
9335	Bacon, Sergt. J.	1st Bn.	M.M.	28/9/17
16213	Bailey, Rfn. J.	1st Bn.	M.M.	14/5/19
43492	Bain, Rfn. J.	2nd Bn.	M.M.	11/2/19
9661	Baines, C.S.M. J.	1st Bn.	D.C.M.	3/9/18
79	Bankhead, Rfn. W. J.	1st Bn.	M.M.	17/6/19
6433	Bannon, Sergt. J.	4th Bn., attd. 1/4th Bn. King's African Rifles	D.C.M.	3/6/19
8178	Barr, L./Cpl. T.	1st Bn.	M.M.	13/3/18
8222	Barrett, Sergt. J.	2nd Bn.	Belgian Croix de Guerre	4/9/19
4948	Bartaby, L./Cpl. E.	2nd Bn.	M.M.	18/10/17
6985	Baxter, Rfn. (A./L./Cpl.) W. R.	2nd Bn.	Mentioned in Despatches	9/7/19
40855	Baxter, Rfn. W.	1st Bn.	M.M.	14/5/19
13990	Beattie, L./Cpl. B.	2nd Bn.	M.M.	29/8/18
6876	Beckett, A./Cpl. W.	2nd Bn.	D.C.M.	26/7/17
8651	Behan, L./Cpl. J.	2nd Bn.	Mentioned in Despatches	9/12/14
41951	Bellis, Sergt. J. H.	2nd Bn.	D.C.M.	22/10/17
4953	Bevan, Sergt. R.	2nd Bn.	M.M.	18/10/17
3/9100	Blain, Cpl. J.	6th Bn.	M.M.	22/1/17
9921	Blakey, Cpl. Wray	3rd Bn.	Serbian Silver Medal for Valour	20/9/19
7473	Booth, Q.M.S. (A./S.M.) B.	2nd Bn.	M.S.M.	1/1/17
			Mentioned in Despatches	21/12/17
41809	Boothway, Rfn. E. A.	7th Bn.	M.M.	19/11/17
47277	Bow, Rfn. J.	1st Bn.	D.C.M.	12/3/19
9348	Bowers, Rfn. A.	1st Bn.	D.C.M.	5/8/15
9/14140	Bowers, Sergt. R. B.	2nd Bn.	M.S.M.	3/6/19
		2nd Bn., attd. 117th Inf. Bde.	Belgian Croix de Guerre	4/9/19
902	Boyd, Rfn. P.	2nd Bn.	M.M.	11/2/19
9073	Bradshaw, L./Cpl. J.	1st Bn.	D.C.M.	3/6/15
8164	Breen, Sergt. P. A.	1st Bn.	Mentioned in Despatches	22/6/15
4239	Brissett, Rfn. P.	7th Bn.	M.M.	19/11/17
9314	Brock, Sergt. S.	1st Bn.	M.M.	9/11/16
1660	Brock, Cpl. J. H.	1st Bn.	M.M.	9/11/16
2360	Brown, Rfn. D.	1st Bn.	Mentioned in Despatches	22/6/15
40664	Brown, Rfn. A.	1st Bn.	M.M.	17/6/19
4964	Bullock, Rfn. A. J.	1st Bn.	M.M.	13/3/18
5/22496	Burgess, Sergt. F. H.	5th Bn.	Mentioned in Despatches	14/6/18
4647	Burney, Sergt. T.	2nd Bn.	M.S.M.	18/1/19
6858	Byers, C.S.M. J. A.	2nd Bn.	M.C.	27/7/16
9249	Cairns, L./Cpl. H.	1st Bn.	D.C.M.	30/6/15
40949	Caithness, Rfn. J.	2nd Bn.	M.M.	21/8/17
5111	Caldwell, Rfn. J.	2nd Bn.	M.M.	21/8/17
6223	Campbell, Rfn. J.	6th Bn.	Mentioned in Despatches	6/12/16
7436	Campbell, Rfn. W. J. A.	1st Bn.	D.C.M.	5/8/15
			Bar to D.C.M.	15/3/16
7007125	Carlisle, Rfn. F. (A./Cpl.)	2nd Bn. R. Ulster Rifles (now Tank Corps)	M.M.	28/9/21
			Mentioned in Despatches	9/9/21
10736	Carolan, Sergt. A. J.	1st Bn.	M.M.	14/5/19
			Bar to M.M.	23/7/19

174

APPENDICES

No.	RANK AND NAME.	NO. OF BATTALION, ETC.	AWARDED.	"LONDON GAZETTE," ETC.
9975	Carolan, Rfn. L.	2nd Bn.	Mentioned in Despatches	17/2/15
7991	Carroll, Rfn. J.	2nd Bn.	Mentioned in Despatches	22/6/15
			Mentioned in Despatches	1/1/16
5710	Carroll, Sergt.-Major William (deceased)	1st Bn.	M.C.	23/6/15
			Mentioned in Despatches	22/6/15
			Russian Medal of St. George, 1st Class	25/8/15
7991	Carroll, C.S.M. J.	2nd Bn.	M.S.M.	17/12/17
11049	Carroll, Rfn. M.	2nd Bn.	M.M.	11/2/19
7752	Carthy, Sergt. M.	2nd Bn.	D.C.M.	15/3/16
			M.S.M.	1/3/19
47469	Carton, Rfn. J.	1st Bn.	D.C.M.	4/3/18
			Belgian Croix de Guerre	4/9/19
40029	Carton, L./Cpl. J.	7th Bn.	M.M.	11/5/17
47168	Chambers, Cpl. J.	1st Bn.	D.C.M.	3/6/19
43448	Christie, Sergt. H.	2nd Bn.	M.M.	11/2/19
8519	Clarke, C.S.M. W.	1st Bn.	D.C.M.	3/6/18
			Belgian Croix de Guerre	12/7/18
4981	Clarke, A./Cpl. L.	2nd Bn.	M.M.	18/10/17
5164	Clarke, Sergt. J.	2nd Bn.	M.M.	14/5/19
9346	Clarke, Sergt. W. H.	1st Bn.	M.S.M.	18/1/19
5390	Coey, Rfn. J.	7th Bn.	D.C.M.	20/10/16
8078	Coleman, A./Sergt. J.	2nd Bn.	Mentioned in Despatches	1/1/16
8082	Coleman, L./Cpl. P.	1st Bn.	M.M.	2/11/17
3956	Condron, Rfn. A.	1st Bn.	M.M.	9/11/16
40049	Condy, Rfn. J.	3rd Bn.	M.M.	26/3/17
9397	Conlan, Cpl. (A./Sergt.) P.	2nd Bn.	D.C.M.	16/8/17
10659	Connolly, Sergt. N.	7th Bn.	M.M.	19/11/17
8497	Copeland, Rfn. A.	1st Bn.	D.C.M.	30/6/15
8229	Corr, Sergt. M.	2nd Bn.	M.S.M.	17/6/18
7146	Corrigan, R.Q.M.S. L.	1st Bn.	Mentioned in Despatches	25/5/17
			Mentioned in Despatches	21/12/17
			M.S.M.	17/6/18
			French Croix de Guerre	19/6/19
5717	Costello, Rfn. R.	2nd Bn.	M.M.	18/10/17
14319	Courtney, Sergt. W. R.	1st Bn.	M.M.	17/6/19
43023	Courtney, Rfn. T.	2nd Bn.	M.M.	18/10/17
6427	Coyle, Sergt. J.	1st Bn.	D.C.M.	30/6/15
2329	Cromie, Sergt. J.	1st Bn.	D.C.M.	3/6/19
7165	Crozier, Sergt. J. J.	2nd Bn.	M.M.	21/8/17
5/8232	Crutchley, L./Cpl. S. C.	7th Bn.	M.M.	26/3/17
3383	Cullen, Sergt. A.	2nd Bn.	M.M.	11/2/19
7/1228	Cullen, Rfn. J.	6th Bn.	M.M.	14/9/16
7759	Curtin, Rfn. J.	2nd Bn.	D.C.M.	16/8/17
8223	Darcy, L./Cpl. M.	1st Bn.	D.C.M.	30/6/15
			Russian Medal of St. George, 4th Class	25/8/15
7/4091	D'Authreau, C.S.M. C. H.	7th Bn.	Mentioned in Despatches	25/5/17
			French Medaille Militaire	14/7/17
7214	Davis, Sergt. G.	2nd Bn.	M.M.	1/9/16
5228	Day, Rfn. J.	1st Bn.	D.C.M.	22/10/17
1/8959	Deeds, Rfn. T.	6th Bn.	D.C.M.	3/9/18
16397	De Lacy, R.S.M. Jas. Christopher	7th Bn.	M.C.	4/6/17
			Bar to M.C.	16/9/18
7603	Delevey, Sergt. C.	1st Bn.	M.M.	9/11/16
8998	Devine, Sergt. P.	1st Bn.	D.C.M.	22/10/17
6550	Dickson, Rfn. J.	1st Bn.	M.M.	6/1/17
20/156	Doherty, Sergt. J. A.	1st Bn.	D.C.M.	3/9/18
8383	Donnelly, L./Cpl. J.	1st Bn.	D.C.M.	3/6/15
			Russian Cross of Order of St. George, 3rd Class	25/8/15
25322	Doherty, Rfn. J.	1st Bn.	M.M.	14/5/19
16445	Douglas, L./Cpl. Gordon	2nd Bn.	Belgian Croix de Guerre	4/9/19
4653	Downey, Rfn. J.	1st Bn.	M.M.	2/11/17
5420	Driscoll, C.S.M. J.	1st Bn.	D.C.M.	14/1/16
4094	Drowyn, Cpl. F. T.	7th Bn.	M.M.	19/11/17
6222	Duffy, Sergt. H. J.	2nd Bn.	Mentioned in Despatches	9/7/19
4525	Duffy, L./Cpl. C.	7th Bn.	M.M.	11/5/17

No.	RANK AND NAME.	NO. OF BATTALION, ETC.	AWARDED.	"LONDON GAZETTE," ETC.
5495	Dunlop, L./Cpl. D.	1st Bn.	M.M.	13/3/18
8725	Elliott, Cpl. (A./Sergt.) Frank	2nd Bn.	French Croix de Guerre	1/5/17
6/9665	Elliott, L./Cpl. William	6th Bn.	Italian Bronze Medal for Military Valour	31/8/17
14538	Ervine, Q.M.S. A. G.	1st Bn.	M.S.M.	18/1/19
6/5822	Fagan, R.Q.M.S. J.	6th Bn.	Mentioned in Despatches	21/7/17
			M.S.M.	17/12/17
8526	Farrell, L./Cpl. A.	2nd Bn.	M.M.	28/7/17
5937	Fay, Rfn. T.	2nd Bn.	M.M.	18/10/17
9493	Fee, Sergt. W. J.	1st Bn.	Mentioned in Despatches	4/1/17
85	Ferguson, Cpl. J.	1st Bn.	M.M.	17/6/19
4849	Ferris, C.S.M. D.	2nd Bn.	Mentioned in Despatches	24/5/18
8368	Flanagan, Rfn. William	1st Bn.	French Medaille d'Honneur avec Glaives en Bronze	17/3/20
3510	Flynn, L./Sergt. Patrick	7th Bn.	French Medaille Militaire	14/7/17
G/21297	Folan, Rfn. J.	1st Bn.	Silver N.C.O's. Order of the Karageorges Star with Swords	24/4/17
3835	Fowles, C.S.M. S.	1st Bn.	D.C.M.	14/1/16
			M.S.M.	22/2/19
41894	Freeman, Rfn. N. W.	7th Bn.	M.M.	19/11/17
1124	Freeney, Rfn. J.	7th Bn.	M.M.	19/11/17
3/25226	Fuller, C.S.M. R.	3rd Bn.	D.C.M.	18/2/19
			Ordre de Leopold	5/4/19
8721	Galloway, L./Cpl. T.	2nd Bn.	M.M.	28/7/17
6770	Gamble, Rfn. T.	2nd Bn.	M.M.	28/7/17
9213	Gardiner, Sergt. T.	2nd Bn.	Mentioned in Despatches	28/12/18
			Mentioned in Despatches	9/11/19
6959	Gare, Rfn. A.	2nd Bn.	Mentioned in Despatches	17/2/15
8695	Gaskin, Rfn. J.	1st Bn.	M.M.	21/12/16
7/4112	Gibbons, Rfn. F. W.	7th Bn.	M.M.	14/11/16
4231	Gifford, Rfn. E. P.	7th Bn.	M.M.	19/11/17
41145	Gillman, Rfn. W. C.	2nd Bn.	M.M.	19/3/18
			Bar to M.M.	17/6/19
			D.C.M.	1/1/19
17744	Gowdy, A./Sergt. J.	2nd Bn.	M.S.M.	17/6/18
			M.M.	29/8/18
8796	Graham, L./Cpl. J.	1st Bn.	M.M.	1/9/16
7127	Gray, Rfn. W.	2nd Bn.	French Medaille Militaire	1/12/14
22007	Gray, Rfn. W.	1st Bn.	M.M.	29/3/19
8719	Greene, C.S.M. J.	1st Bn.	M.M.	13/3/19
			*Bar to M.M.	6/12/20
8185	Greene, Sergt. J.	7th Bn.	D.C.M.	19/11/17
9461	Griffiths, Rfn. D.	2nd Bn.	M.M.	30/1/20
8207	Gudgeon, Rfn. W.	2nd Bn.	D.C.M.	12/3/19
4536	Hall, Rfn. T.	2nd Bn.	M.M.	18/10/17
7/1252	Halpenny, Cpl. J.	7th Bn.	M.M.	16/11/16
5740	Harbinson, L./Cpl. S.	2nd Bn.	Mentioned in Despatches	1/1/16
7081	Harris, C.S.M. William James	2nd Bn.	Belgian Croix de Guerre	12/7/18
7/6558	Henley, Sergt. H. T.	7th Bn.	M.M.	16/11/16
9562	Henneker, Sergt. Charles Henry David	1st Bn.	French Medaille Militaire	15/12/19
7648	Henry, Sergt. Edward	2nd Bn.	Mentioned in Despatches	9/12/14
			Russian Medal of St. George, 2nd Class	25/8/15
12895	Henry, L./Cpl. W.	6th Bn.	Italian Bronze Medal	2/5/17
8264	Herrington, L./Sergt. G.	5th Bn.	M.M.	24/1/19
16549	Herdman, L./Cpl. R.	1st Bn.	D.C.M.	5/12/18
			Belgian Croix de Guerre	4/9/19
1226	Higgins, Sergt. H.	2nd Bn.	M.M. and Bar	13/8/18
			D.C.M.	16/1/19
5043	Highman, Sergt. A. J.	2nd Bn.	M.M.	29/8/18
			M.S.M.	13/6/19
16138	Hill, C.S.M. W.	1st Bn.	Mentioned in Despatches	9/7/19
9/14927	Hooks, Sergt. Joshua	1st Bn.	French Croix de Guerre	19/6/19
47489	Hodgen, Rfn. J.	2nd Bn.	M.M.	11/2/19
42617	Hoffman, Rfn. S.	2nd Bn.	M.M.	18/10/17

* Gazetted as *Green*.

	RANK AND NAME.	NO. OF BATTALION, ETC.	AWARDED.	"LONDON GAZETTE," ETC.
14924	Holmes, Sergt. J.	1st Bn.	M.S.M.	17/6/18
40010	House, Rfn. A.	7th Bn.	M.M.	19/11/17
47307	House, Rfn. W. R.	1st Bn.	M.M.	17/6/19
7006359	Houston, Sergt. R. A.	2nd Bn. Royal Ulster Rifles	Mentioned in Despatches	9/9/21
7254	Houston, Sergt. R.	1st Bn.	M.M.	13/3/18
7574	Houston, Sergt. J.	7th Bn.	M.M.	19/11/17
			Bar to M.M.	21/3/19
9525	Hugheston, Rfn. G.	3rd Bn.	M.M.	29/8/18
2260	Humphreys, Rfn. R.	1st Bn.	M.M.	17/6/19
9114	Humpson, Cpl. P.	2nd Bn.	Mentioned in Despatches	1/1/16
8982	Hunter, Rfn. W.	1st Bn.	D.C.M.	3/6/15
8235	Hutchinson, Rfn. G. (killed)	2nd Bn.	Mentioned in Despatches	24/5/18
10365	Hutchinson, Rfn. S.	2nd Bn.	M.M.	14/5/19
9790	Hyland, L./Cpl. P.	1st Bn.	M.M.	9/11/16
24053	Irvine, Rfn. James	2nd Bn.	Belgian Croix de Guerre	26/11/19
43894	James, Rfn. J. W.	1st Bn.	M.M.	2/11/17
41052	Jeacock, Rfn. E.	1st Bn.	M.M.	29/8/18
43893	Jeffcott, Sergt. L. T.	1st Bn.	M.M.	20/8/19
8027	Johnston, Rfn. E.	2nd Bn.	M.M.	28/7/17
40880	Johnston, Rfn. A.	1st Bn.	M.M.	2/11/17
8666	Johnston, Rfn. J.	2nd Bn.	D.C.M.	1/4/15
6/11347	Johnston, Rfn. S.	6th Bn.	Mentioned in Despatches	28/11/17
1516	Johnstone, Rfn. R.	1st Bn.	D.C.M.	5/8/15
4133	Journeaux, Cpl. H. F.	7th Bn.	M.M.	19/11/17
5980	Kane, Rfn. T.	2nd Bn.	Mentioned in Despatches	9/7/19
7/4163	Kangeard, Sergt. L. J.	7th Bn.	D.C.M.	1/1/17
5915	Kavanagh, Rfn. J.	2nd Bn.	M.M.	16/8/17
6824	Kavanagh, Rfn. (A./Cpl.) B.	1st Bn.	Mentioned in Despatches	21/12/17
10856	Kearney, Rfn. J.	1st Bn.	M.M.	13/3/18
10225	Keeling, L./Cpl. G.	1st Bn.	M.M.	13/9/18
5606	Kelly, Rfn. D.	7th Bn.	M.M.	19/11/17
8716	Kelly, Bdsmn. C. R.	1st Bn.	Mentioned in Despatches	22/6/15
9394	Kelly, C.S.M. M.	6th Bn.	Mentioned in Despatches	6/12/16
8716	Kennedy, Rfn. A.	1st Bn.	M.M.	9/11/16
9010	Kennedy, Sergt. J.	6th Bn.	M.M.	9/12/16
7264	Kennedy, Rfn. John	1st Bn.	French Croix de Guerre	1/5/17
G/154	Kenny, R.S.M. J.	1st Bn.	M.S.M.	3/6/19
8842	Kenny, Sergt. (O.R.S.) C.	1st Bn.	Promotion to Colour-Sergeant (O.R.S.), with effect from 23/10/18.	Authority:— W.O. File 18/Misc/95.
			Mentioned in Despatches	9/7/19
5357	Kernoghan, Rfn. H.	2nd Bn.	M.M.	21/8/19
9867	Kierans, Rfn. T. K.	2nd Bn.	M.M.	11/2/19
6782	Killeen, Rfn. P.	2nd Bn.	M.M.	19/11/17
2255	Kirk, R.S.M. J.	3rd Bn.	M.S.M.	22/2/19
7006050	Kirk, Rfn. A.	2nd Bn.	M.M.	28/9/21
103	Lanigan, Sergt. J.	1st Bn.	Mentioned in Despatches	28/12/18
			M.M.	17/6/19
8976	Lawrence, Sergt. C.	1st Bn.	M.M.	11/8/19
9646	Lawrence, Sergt. V. J. F.	7th Bn.	D.C.M.	19/11/17
6/10617	Lawson, Sergt. A.	6th Bn.	M.S.M.	2/11/17
4/9335	Leary, C.S.M. S. J.	6th Bn.	Mentioned in Despatches	28/11/17
6177	Leatham, Cpl. J.	1st Bn.	M.M.	17/6/19
4145	Le Breton, C.S.M. J. D.	7th Bn.	D.C.M.	25/8/17
			French Medaille Militaire	1/5/17
6/10674	Ledlie, Rfn. Thomas	6th Bn.	French Medaille Militaire	17/8/18
9550	Lees, L./Cpl. W. R.	1st Bn.	D.C.M.	3/6/16
5041	Leggett, Rfn. J.	2nd Bn.	M.M.	11/2/19
7007394	Leitch, Rfn. P.	2nd Bn.	M.M.	28/9/21
4872	Lennon, L./Cpl. J.	1st Bn.	Mentioned in Despatches	22/6/15
7007237	Le Rue, A./Cpl. H. F.	2nd Bn.	M.M.	28/9/21
5707	Leverett, A./C.Q.M.S. J.	1st Bn.	D.C.M.	22/10/17
5067	Lewis, Rfn. T.	2nd Bn.	M.M.	30/1/20
5070	Lloyd, Rfn. G. H.	7th Bn.	M.M.	19/11/17

	RANK AND NAME.	NO. OF BATTALION, ETC.	AWARDED.	"LONDON GAZETTE," ETC.
2662	Lockett, Rfn. A.	2nd Bn.	M.M.	16/7/18
41157	Longhurst, L./Cpl. J.	2nd Bn.	M.M.	11/2/19
8066	Lorimer, L./Cpl. D.	2nd Bn.	Mentioned in Despatches	1/1/16
4463	Loughrey, L./Cpl. J.	7th Bn.	D.C.M.	1/4/20
8887	Love, L./Cpl. D.	1st Bn.	M.M.	11/11/16
			Bar to M.M.	17/9/17
16800	Lucas, Cpl. G.	1st Bn.	M.M.	13/3/18
4152	Luce, L./Cpl. J. A.	7th Bn.	M.M.	19/11/17
43917	Ludkin, L./Cpl. P. T.	1st Bn.	Mentioned in Despatches	28/12/18
8447	Lunn, C.S.M. T.	1st Bn.	D.C.M.	20/12/16
7428	Lynsky, Rfn. J.	2nd Bn.	Mentioned in Despatches	1/1/16
9876	McBratney, Rfn. W.	1st Bn.	M.M.	14/5/19
10791	McCabe, Rfn. W.	2nd Bn.	M.M.	21/8/17
40089	McCabe, Rfn. J.	7th Bn.	M.M.	26/3/17
47356	McCabe, Rfn. P.	2nd Bn.	D.C.M.	12/3/19
			French Croix de Guerre	19/6/18
9362	McCambey, Sergt. J.	2nd Bn.	M.M.	21/12/16
9367	McCamley, A./C.Q.M.S. J.	2nd Bn.	M.S.M.	17/6/18
8890	McCann, Rfn. J.	1st Bn.	M.M.	9/11/16
8619	McCarthy, Rfn. T.	1st Bn.	M.M.	7/10/18
16692	McCaughan, L./Cpl. G.	1st Bn.	M.M.	2/11/17
9133	McClarnon, Rfn. H.	7th Bn.	M.M.	18/7/17
7006255	McCormick, Cpl. W.	2nd Bn.	M.M.	29/3/22
9405	McCourt, Sergt. D.	1st Bn.	M.M.	9/11/16
8729	McCoughey, L./Cpl. C.	1st Bn., attd. 197th Light Trench Mortar Battery	D.C.M.	3/6/19
8985	McCrea, C.S.M. S.	2nd Bn.	D.C.M.	25/8/17
15244	McCullough, Sergt. R.	2nd Bn.	D.C.M.	16/1/19
13177	McCullough, L./Cpl. W.	1st Bn. attd. "H.Q.," 36th Division	Mentioned in Despatches	9/7/19
3/8841	McDermott, Rfn. M.	2nd Bn.	M.M.	29/7/16
10411	McDermott, Rfn. F.	2nd Bn.	M.M.	18/10/17
8773	McDonnell, Rfn. C.	1st Bn.	M.M.	2/11/17
5399	McDowell, Sergt. John	1st Bn.	Belgian Croix de Guerre	4/9/19
7674	McFarland, A./Sergt. A.	2nd Bn.	M.M.	18/10/17
7359	McFarlane, L./Cpl. W.	1st Bn.	Mentioned in Despatches	17/2/15
9280	McFaull, C.Q.M.S. William	1st Bn.	French Croix de Guerre	19/6/19
7973	McGibney, C.S.M. J. J.	2nd Bn.	Mentioned in Despatches	22/6/15
9732	McGrath, Rfn. A.	2nd Bn.	Mentioned in Despatches	17/2/15
15414	McGuigan, Cpl. A. C.	1st Bn.	M.S.M.	18/1/19
936	McHarg, Rfn. R.	2nd Bn.	M.M.	20/10/19
3/9060	McIlvenny, Rfn. J. G.	6th Bn.	M.M.	22/1/17
25697	McIlwaine, Rfn. W. J.	2nd Bn.	M.M.	11/2/19
8848	McIlwrath, Rfn. W.	2nd Bn.	M.M.	21/8/17
2/16801	McKee, A./Cpl. R.	2nd Bn.	M.M.	21/9/16
9604	McKeown, Cpl. J.	1st Bn.	M.M.	29/8/18
9362	McNulty, L./Cpl. M.	2nd Bn.	M.M.	28/7/17
8722	McTeague, L./Cpl. P.	2nd Bn.	D.C.M.	22/10/17
18393	Mackey, C.S.M. J. J.	1st Bn.	D.C.M.	12/3/19
9577	Magee, C.S.M. J.	1st Bn.	D.C.M.	4/6/17
5256	Magill, Cpl. J.	1st Bn.	M.M.	13/3/18
5994	Magill, Sergt. T.	2nd Bn.	D.C.M.	3/6/19
4530	Maguire, Rfn. J.	7th Bn.	M.M.	19/11/17
7265	Maguire, Sergt. J. P.	1st Bn.	Mentioned in Despatches	21/12/17
			Belgian Croix de Guerre	12/7/18
10404	Malone, Cpl. J.	1st Bn.	M.M.	13/3/18
5320	Manderson, Sergt. E. A.	1st Bn.	M.M.	7/10/18
7007030	Marshall, Sergt. I.	2nd Bn.	Mentioned in Despatches	9/9/21
7/4447	Martin, Rfn. F.	7th Bn.	M.M.	16/11/16
9006	Martin, Rfn. W. J.	1st Bn.	M.S.M.	1/7/18
9222	Massey, A./Sergt. S. J.	1st Bn.	M.M.	25/5/17
5077	Matthews, L./Cpl. H. T.	1st Bn.	M.M.	6/1/17
5/5266	Maxwell, Cpl. (A./L./Sergt.) D.	6th Bn.	D.C.M.	16/8/17
8708	Meneilly, Rfn. H.	2nd Bn.	M.S.M.	17/6/18
7737	Meredith, Sergt. John	1st Bn.	Belgian Decoration Militaire avec Croix de Guerre	24/10/19
43100	Millar, Rfn. A.	2nd Bn.	M.M.	14/5/19

APPENDICES

	RANK AND NAME.	NO. OF BATTALION, ETC.	AWARDED.	"LONDON GAZETTE," ETC.
10064	Miller, R.S.M. D.	2nd Bn.	D.C.M.	3/6/18
			Bar to D.C.M.	16/1/19
			M.S.M.	24/9/21
5/5822	Mills, Rfn. Alexander	2nd (now 5th) Bn.	Russian Medal of St. George, 3rd Class	15/2/17
6798	Miskimmin, Sergt. G.	1st Bn.	M.M.	13/3/18
4184	Mitchell, Rfn. T. J.	2nd Bn.	Mentioned in Despatches	1/1/16
54110	Mitchen, Rfn. J.	2nd Bn.	M.M.	13/3/19
1224	Montgomery, Rfn. J.	1st Bn.	M.M.	29/3/19
7/2684	Moore, Rfn. Daniel	7th Bn.	Italian Bronze Medal	26/5/17
25311	Morgan, Rfn. J.	1st Bn.	D.C.M.	11/3/19
7332	Morley, L./Cpl. C.	2nd Bn.	Mentioned in Despatches	17/2/15
			Mentioned in Despatches	1/1/16
4744	Mulholland, S.M. P.	6th Bn.	Mentioned in Despatches	27/3/16
			Mentioned in Despatches	6/12/16
			M.S.M.	13/2/17
			D.C.M.	26/7/17
6/11563	Mulligan, Sergt. S.	6th Bn.	M.M.	22/1/17
			French Medaille Militaire	1/5/17
45899	Murphy, C.S.M. F.	1st Bn.	M.S.M.	3/6/19
5820	Murphy, Rfn. S.	1st Bn.	D.C.M.	3/6/16
7453	Murray, L./Cpl. H.	2nd Bn.	Mentioned in Despatches	9/12/14
7750	Murray, C.S.M. J.	1st Bn.	D.C.M.	1/1/19
7006371	Naughton, Rfn. J.	2nd Bn. Royal Ulster Rifles	Mentioned in Despatches	9/9/21
7274	Ness, Sergt. R.	1st Bn.	M.S.M.	17/6/18
43318	Nichols, Rfn. A.	2nd Bn.	M.M.	11/2/19
2/7374	Nicholson, C.S.M. J.	7th Bn.	D.C.M.	1/1/18
			M.S.M.	18/1/19
9479	Noone, L./Cpl. E.	1st Bn.	M.M.	13/11/18
1284	Nunn, Rfn. J.	1st Bn.	M.M.	21/10/16
			Serbian Gold Medal	21/10/16
9558	O'Connor, Cpl. J.	2nd Bn.	D.C.M.	17/12/14
			Mentioned in Despatches	9/12/14
			Russian Cross of the Order of St. George, 4th Class	25/8/15
40022	O'Donnell, Rfn. D.	7th Bn.	M.M.	26/3/17
10353	O'Donnell, L./Cpl. P.	6th Bn.	Mentioned in Despatches	21/7/17
6781	O'Gara, Rfn. M.	2nd Bn.	M.M.	18/10/17
10298	O'Hare, L./Cpl. P. J.	2nd Bn.	Mentioned in Despatches	25/5/17
7511	O'Lone, Sergt. W.	2nd Bn.	D.C.M.	1/4/15
			Bar to D.C.M.	1/4/15
7954	O'Rawe, Rfn. J.	2nd Bn.	M.S.M.	18/1/19
7/7861	O'Reilly, Rfn. P.	7th Bn., attd. 48th Light Trench Mortar Battery	D.C.M.	1/1/17
8003	O'Shea, Sergt. J.	2nd Bn.	M.M.	28/7/17
43952	Oatway, Rfn. W.	2nd Bn.	M.M.	18/10/17
7284	Osbaldeston, L./Cpl. A.	1st Bn.	D.C.M.	1/4/15
5644	Owens, Cpl. J.	2nd Bn.	M.M.	13/3/18
			*Bar to M.M.	13/11/18
9132	Palmer, Bdsmn. H.	2nd Bn.	Mentioned in Despatches	22/6/15
4071	Parks, Rfn. S.	2nd Bn.	M.M.	20/8/19
6543	Patterson, Cpl. W. J.	1st Bn.	M.M.	2/11/17
7048	Paterson, Rfn. T.	2nd Bn.	M.M.	13/3/18
9027	Pedlow, Sergt. S. J.	2nd Bn.	M.S.M.	17/6/18
4236	Perks, Cpl. H.	7th Bn.	M.M.	19/11/17
6308	Phelan, Clr.-Sergt. R.	1st Bn., attd. Gold Coast Regt.	Mentioned in Despatches	6/8/18
9401	Pitman, L./Cpl. W.	2nd Bn.	M.M.	11/2/19
			Italian Bronze Medal	12/9/18
5099	Poole, A./Sergt. W. S.	1st Bn.	D.C.M.	22/10/17
43957	Potter, L./Cpl. E. C.	1st Bn.	M.M.	28/9/17
8160	Poulton, L./Cpl. E. C.	1st Bn.	M.M.	11/5/17
11129	Preston, Rfn. T.	2nd Bn.	M.M.	18/10/17
5249	Purcell, Rfn. Arthur Woodward	3rd Bn.	Serbian Silver Medal for Valour	20/9/19
44135	Quarterman, Rfn. H.	2nd Bn.	M.M.	18/10/17

* Gazetted as *Patrick, Owen S.*

	RANK AND NAME.	NO. OF BATTALION, ETC.	AWARDED.	"LONDON GAZETTE," ETC.
8556	Quee, Sergt. H. F.	2nd Bn.	D.C.M.	16/1/19
18645	Quigg, Cpl. R.	2nd Bn.	V.C.	9/9/16
			Russian Order of St. George, 4th Class	15/2/17
9583	Quigley, Rfn. N.	2nd Bn.	M.M.	18/10/17
			Bar to M.M.	13/3/18
12405	Quinn, Sergt. D.	2nd Bn.	M.M.	15/2/19
8175	Quinlan, Cpl. J.	1st Bn.	Mentioned in Despatches	22/6/15
9285	Quinn, Sergt. J.	2nd Bn.	Mentioned in Despatches	1/1/16
44265	Ray, Rfn. A. W.	1st Bn.	M.M.	7/10/18
9641	Reading, A./Cpl. J.	2nd Bn.	M.M.	1/9/16
6346	Rees, Sergt. H.	1st Bn.	D.C.M.	30/6/15
			Russian Cross of the Order of St. George, 4th Class	25/8/15
7036	Reilly, Sergt. J.	2nd Bn.	M.M.	29/8/17
20428	Riley, Rfn. J.	1st Bn.	M.M.	13/9/18
5121	Roberts, L./Cpl. J.	2nd Bn.	M.M.	18/10/17
5219	Roberts, Cpl. J.	2nd Bn.	M.M.	18/10/17
14447	Roberts, Cpl. J.	1st Bn.	M.M.	13/3/18
43978	Robertson, Cpl. F.	1st Bn.	M.M.	11/2/19
40839	Robinson, L./Cpl. W. J.	1st Bn.	D.C.M.	22/10/17
8690	Rodger, Rfn. William Herbert	2nd Bn.	Russian Medal of St. George, 4th Class.	25/8/15
3284	Roy, R.S.M. T.	5th Bn.	M.S.M.	22/2/19
6955	Russell, Rfn. D.	2nd Bn.	Mentioned in Despatches	22/6/15
7982	Salinger, L./Cpl. F.	2nd Bn.	M.M.	13/3/18
3/1525	Salt, Rfn. W.	2nd Bn.	M.M.	18/10/17
20229	Savage, Rfn. W.	1st Bn.	M.M.	17/6/19
9763	Scott, Rfn. W.	2nd Bn.	M.M.	13/3/18
10803	Scott, Cpl. J.	2nd Bn.	Mentioned in Despatches	14/6/18
8097	Seavers, Rfn. W.	7th Bn.	M.M.	11/5/17
44009	Seibert, Rfn. W.	1st Bn.	M.M.	14/5/19
8914	Sexton, Cpl. C.	1st Bn.	Mentioned in Despatches	22/6/15
605	Shearer, Rfn. W.	2nd Bn.	D.C.M.	1/4/15
9996	Sheridan, Rfn. M.	2nd Bn.	M.M.	18/10/17
9672	Shields, Rfn. P.	1st Bn.	M.M.	6/1/17
7095	Simner, C.S.M. W. H.	1st Bn.	D.C.M.	5/8/15
			M.M.	1/9/16
12366	Simpson, Sergt. A. J.	1st Bn.	M.M.	2/11/17
8593	Sinclair, L./Cpl. G.	2nd Bn.	M.M.	18/10/17
6928	Smith, Rfn. J.	2nd Bn	M.M.	18/10/17
7876	Smith, Rfn. A.	7th Bn.	M.M.	18/7/17
8487	Smyth, Rfn. W.	1st Bn.	M.M.	11/11/16
			Bar to M.M.	2/11/17
3/8582	Smyth, Sergt. J.	2nd Bn.	M.M.	18/10/17
18800	Smyth, Rfn. J.	1st Bn.	M.M.	20/10/19
7104	Smythe, A./Cpl. J.	2nd Bn.	M.M.	18/10/17
8551	Somers, C.Q.M.S. R. G.	2nd Bn.	D.C.M.	3/9/18
8794	Spence, Rfn. W. R.	1st Bn.	M.M.	28/9/17
8900	Spence, Rfn. J.	1st Bn.	M.M.	13/3/18
10/13508	Stafford, R.Q.M.S. T. H.	2nd Bn.	M.S.M.	17/6/18
6775	Stanley, L./Cpl. J. A. W.	1st Bn.	M.M.	13/11/18
5952	Steele, Sergt. J.	1st Bn.	M.M.	29/8/18
8875	Stevenson, L./Cpl. James	1st Bn.	French Croix de Guerre	19/6/19
7323	Stovin, C.S.M. C. E.	1st Bn.	Mentioned in Despatches	22/6/15
			D.C.M.	1/1/17
44037	Tait, L./Cpl. A. R.	2nd Bn.	D.C.M.	12/3/19
9746	Taplin, Cpl. W.	2nd Bn.	M.M.	14/5/19
5/22289	Taylor, C.Q.M.S. G. S.	5th Bn.	Mentioned in Despatches	14/6/18
8380	Taylor, Sergt. W. H.	2nd Bn.	D.C.M.	14/1/16
6030	Thompson, Cpl. R. A.	7th Bn.	M.M.	19/11/17
9759	Thompson, L./Cpl. J.	2nd Bn.	Mentioned in Despatches	1/1/16
8965	Thompson, C.S.M. R.	7th Bn.	D.C.M.	19/11/17
8722	Traynor, Rfn. J.	1st Bn.	Mentioned in Despatches	15/6/16
7174	Trueman, Rfn. T.	Attd. 2nd Bn.	D.C.M.	15/3/16
41928	Truss, Rfn. T. H.	7th Bn.	M.M.	19/11/17
9258	Tumelty, Rfn. H.	1st Bn.	M.M.	2/11/17
7/7804	Turkington, Sergt. S.	6th Bn.	M.S.M.	17/12/17

APPENDICES

	RANK AND NAME.	NO. OF BATTALION, ETC.	AWARDED.	"LONDON GAZETTE," ETC.
9647	Turner, A./R.Q.M.S. J.	2nd Bn.	M.M.	18/10/17
			M.S.M.	18/1/19
4212	Vickers, Rfn. J. C.	7th Bn.	M.M.	19/11/17
42448	Vile, Rfn. F. A.	1st Bn.	M.M.	17/9/17
3753	Walker, Rfn. E. M.	2nd Bn.	M.M.	13/11/18
G/150	Walsh, T./R.S.M. J.	1st Bn.	M.S.M.	3/6/19
9889	Walsh, Sergt. J.	1st Bn.	M.M.	21/9/16
9927	Walsh, Sergt. J.	2nd Bn.	M.M.	18/10/17
10733	Ward, R.S.M. W.	1st Bn.	Mentioned in Despatches	21/12/17
			French Medaille d'Honneur avec Glaives (en vermeil)	29/1/19
13817	Warnock, Rfn. J.	1st Bn.	M.M.	17/6/19
4883	Weldon, Cpl. James	2nd Bn.	Belgian Croix de Guerre	26/11/19
9970	Welsh, L./Cpl. James	2nd Bn.	Serbian Gold Medal	15/2/17
8185	Wharton, Rfn. J.	6th Bn.	M.M.	9/12/16
6720	Whelan, Cpl. J.	2nd Bn.	M.M.	18/10/17
7859	White, A./Sergt. W.	6th Bn.	M.M.	27/6/18
8193	Willott, Cpl. J.	1st Bn.	M.M.	17/6/19
40032	Williams, Cpl. H.	2nd Bn.	M.M.	11/2/19
41772	Willson, Rfn. T. S. U.	7th Bn.	M.M.	19/11/17
40923	Wilson, A./Sergt. A. J.	1st Bn.	M.M.	20/10/19
10485	Wilson, Rfn. R.	2nd Bn.	D.C.M.	15/3/16
6436	Wright, L./Cpl. J. A.	2nd Bn.	D.C.M.	22/10/17
9098	Wood, Cpl. W. H.	2nd Bn.	M.M.	28/7/17
			Bar to M.M.	23/7/19
10564	Woodside, Rfn. S.	2nd Bn.	M.M.	11/2/19
40615	Yardley, Rfn. (L./Cpl.) W.	1st Bn.	M.M.	29/9/18
			D.C.M.	12/3/19
			Belgian Croix de Guerre	4/9/19

APPENDIX III

ROLL OF HONOUR.
OFFICERS.

The names of Officers on this Roll have been extracted from the official publication, "Officers Died in the Great War, 1914—1919."

Only the Officers who belonged to one of the First Seven Battalions of the Regiment are included in this Roll.

The total number of Officers belonging to the Regiment killed during the Great War is shown separately at the end of this Appendix.

Adrian, William Kearns, 2/Lt., k. in a., 24/8/16 (attd. 1st Bn.).
Allgood, Bertram, Capt., k. in a., 6/12/14.
Allison, Hazlett Samuel, Major, k. in a., 9/8/17.
Alston, James William, Major (T./Lt.-Col.), k. in a., 15/4/15.
Andrews, Robert H., 2/Lt. (Tp.), k. in a., 25/9/15.
Andrews, William Ernest, Lt. (T./Capt.), k. in a., 2/8/15.
Baker, Osbert Clinton, Lt.-Col., k. in a., 9/5/15.
Barrington, Noel Scott, Lt., k. in a., 10/3/15.
Barton, Charles Erskine, Capt., d. of w., 23/8/18.
Barton, Thomas Eyre, 2/Lt., k. in a., 16/7/16 (att. 2nd).
Bayly, Launcelot Myles, M.C., Lt. (A./Capt.), d. of w., 22/10/18.
Biscoe, Arthur John, Capt., d. of w., 12/3/15.
Bland, John George, 2/Lt., d. of w., 9/7/15.
Boas, Ernest George, 2/Lt., k. in a., 1/7/16 (att. 13th Bn.).
Boyhan, Thomas Francis, 2/Lt., d. of w., 12/9/16 (att. 7th Bn.).
Boyle, John K., M.C., Lt., d. of w. (P. of W.).
Bridcutt, John Henry, D.S.O., Capt. (A./Lt.-Col.), k. in a., 1/10/18.
Brown, Hugh, 2/Lt. (Tp.), k. in a., 31/7/17.
Browne, Dominick Augustus, Capt., k. in a., 1/7/16.
Browne, Maximilian Herbert, M.C., T./Lt. (A./Capt.), killed, 21/6/18.
Burges, William Armstrong, Lt., k. in a., 10/3/15.
Byrne, Vincent Cornel, 2/Lt., k. in a., 31/7/17 (att. 1st Bn.).
Cairnes, Alfred Bellingham, Major (Tp.), k. in a., 9/9/16.
Calverley, Geoffrey Walter, D.S.O., Lt., killed, 7/1/18 (att. R.F.C.).
Calvert, James Howard, 2/Lt. (Tp.), killed, 24/4/16.
Calwell, Walter Henry, Lt., d. of w., 27/8/18 (att. 2nd Bn.).
Campbell, Lawford Bwine, Lt. (Tp.), k. in a., 1/7/16.
Clancy, George David Louis, 2/Lt., drowned, 4/5/17 (att. 1st Leins. Rgt.).
Cliff-McCuloch, Walter Alexander, Lt. (Tp.), k. in a., 27/2/18.
Coffee, Francis Warren, 2/Lt., k. in a., 16/8/17 (att. 14th R. Ir. Rfs.).
Daniel, Ernest, Lt., k. in a., 21/10/18 (att. 1st Bn.).
Darling, Claude Henry Whish, 2/Lt., k. in a., 12/12/15 (att. 2nd Bn.).
Darling, William Oliver Fortesque, Lt., k. in a., 16/10/15 (att. 1st Bn.).
Davis, Henry Ouseley, Capt., k. in a., 27/10/14 (att. 2nd Bn.).
Davy, Howard Samuel, 2/Lt., k. in a., 15/2/15.
Dean, William, 2/Lt., k. in a., 1/7/16 (att. 10th Bn.).
Dobbie, William, 2/Lt., k. in a., 7/6/17.
Dobbin, William Leonard Price, M.C., Lt., k. in a., 21/3/18.
Doherty, Patrick, 2/Lt. (Tp.), d. of w., 1/8/17.
Drage, George T., Major, died, 19/10/18.

THE ROYAL ULSTER RIFLES

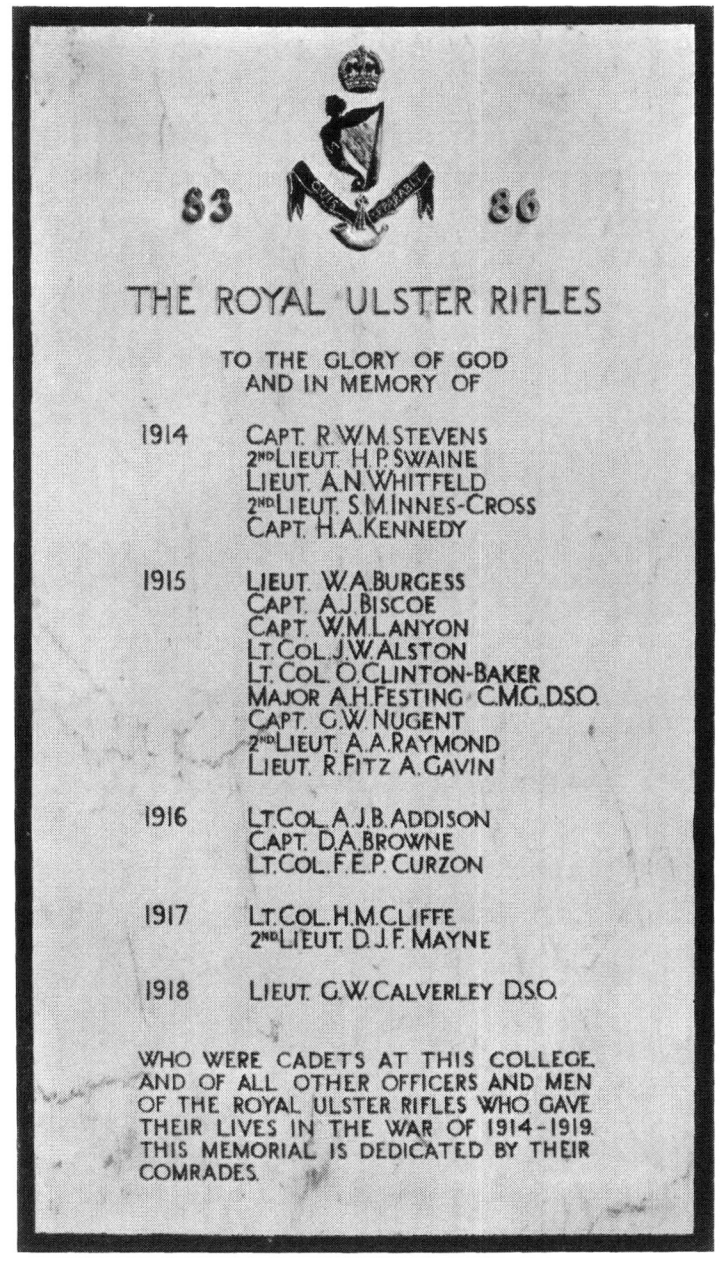

83   86

TO THE GLORY OF GOD
AND IN MEMORY OF

1914
- Capt. R.W.M. Stevens
- 2nd Lieut. H.P. Swaine
- Lieut. A.N. Whitfeld
- 2nd Lieut. S.M. Innes-Cross
- Capt. H.A. Kennedy

1915
- Lieut. W.A. Burgess
- Capt. A.J. Biscoe
- Capt. W.M. Lanyon
- Lt. Col. J.W. Alston
- Lt. Col. O. Clinton-Baker
- Major A.H. Festing C.M.G., D.S.O.
- Capt. G.W. Nugent
- 2nd Lieut. A.A. Raymond
- Lieut. R. Fitz A. Gavin

1916
- Lt. Col. A.J.B. Addison
- Capt. D.A. Browne
- Lt. Col. F.E.P. Curzon

1917
- Lt. Col. H.M. Cliffe
- 2nd Lieut. D.J.F. Mayne

1918
- Lieut. G.W. Calverley D.S.O.

WHO WERE CADETS AT THIS COLLEGE, AND OF ALL OTHER OFFICERS AND MEN OF THE ROYAL ULSTER RIFLES WHO GAVE THEIR LIVES IN THE WAR OF 1914-1919. THIS MEMORIAL IS DEDICATED BY THEIR COMRADES.

Photo by]   [*Gale & Polden, Ltd.*

MEMORIAL TABLET IN THE ROYAL MILITARY COLLEGE CHAPEL, SANDHURST.

Drought, Robert Victor, M.C., 2/Lt., d. of w., 9/6/17 (att. 14th Bn.).
Eastwood, William, Major (Tp.), k. in a., 11/8/15 (att. 6th Bn.).
Ellison, Frederick John Gwynn, 2/Lt., k. in a., 16/8/17 (att. 13th Bn.).
Elmitt, George Carleton Brooksley, 2/Lt., k. in a., 16/8/17.
Elphick, Kevin, 2/Lt., d. of w., 28/9/16 (att. 2nd Bn.).
Empey, Simeon, Robert Franks, 2/Lt., died, 17/8/16.
Ennis, Reginald Joseph, 2/Lt., k. in a., 16/8/17.
Enright, Thomas, 2/Lt., d. of w., 20/4/18.
Farran, Edmond Chomley Lambert, Capt., k. in a., 16/6/15.
Festing, Arthur Hoskyns, C.M.G., D.S.O., Major, k. in a., 9/5/15.
Field, John William, 2/Lt. (T./Capt.), k. in a., 20/9/15.
Furniss, James, 2/Lt., k. in a., 31/7/17.
Gardiner, James Totton, 2/Lt., d. of w., 1/11/18 (P. of W.).
Gavin, Robert Fitzaustin, Lt., k. in a., 25/9/15.
Gault, John Victor, 2/Lt., k. in a., 23/10/16 (att. 1st Bn.).
Gibson, Matthew Henry, M.C., T./Lt. (A./Capt.), d. of w., 28/10/18 (att. 12th Bn.).
Giles, Victor Marshall, 2/Lt. (Tp.), k. in a., 28/6/16.
Gilliland, Valentine Knox, Capt., k. in a., 8/5/15 (att. 2nd Bn.).
Gilmore, Andrew, 2/Lt., k. in a., 11/3/15.
Glastonbury, Harold Mynett, 2/Lt., d. of w., 1/7/16 (att. 1st Bn.).
Goulding, Frederick Ernest, 2/Lt. (Tp.), died, 5/8/18.
Gregg, William Henry, 2/Lt., k. in a., 1/7/16
Hamilton, Douglas, 2/Lt., k. in a., 9/5/15 (att. 1st Bn.).
Hannah, Robert, 2/Lt., k. in a., 16/8/17.
Harpur, Edward Percival H., Lt. (Tp.), d. of w., 11/9/16.
Hatte, Edward Stokes, 2/Lt. (Tp.), k. in a., 16/8/17.
Healy, John Frederick, Lt., k. in a., 1/7/16 (att. 9th Bn.).
Hellmers, Alfred, 2/Lt., d. of w., 11/5/15.
Henderson, George York, M.C., Lt., k. in a., 22/11/17 (att. 10th Bn.).
Henley, Henry Thomas, 2/Lt. (Tp.), k. in a., 8/3/17.
Hill, Oldham Cyril Darley, 2/Lt., k. in a., 16/8/17 (att. 7th Bn.).
Hill, William Carlisle, M.C., Lt. (Tp.), k. in a., 7/6/17 (and 74th T.M.B.)
Hutcheson, Norman Heber, Lt., k. in a., 12/3/15.
Innes-Cross, Sydney Maxwell, 2/Lt., k. in a., 27/10/14.
Irwin, William James, 2/Lt., k. in a., 16/8/17 (att. 7th Bn.).
Jackson, Patrick Arthur Dudley, 2/Lt., k. in a., 4/1/17.
Jeffares, Richard Thorpe, Capt., d. of w., 6/10/17 (att. 2nd Bn.).
Johnston, Rowland Ivan, 2/Lt., d. of w., 28/8/18.
Jones, Hubert Victor Edward, 2/Lt. (Tp.), k. in a., 25/10/18.
Joy, Frederick Charles Patrick, 2/Lt., k. in a., 16/6/15 (att. 2nd Bn.).
Kennedy, Herbert Alexander, Capt., d. of w., 28/10/14.
Kerr, James, Lt., k. in a., 21/3/18.
Kingston, William, Lt. (Tp.), k. in a., 16/8/17.
Laing, Gilbert James, 2/Lt., k. in a., 12/3/15.
La Nauze, George Mansfield, Lt., k. in a., 9/5/15.
La Nauze, William, Lt., k. in a., 16/5/15.
Lane, Charles Henry, 2/Lt., d. of w., 21/8/18 (att. 10th Bn.).
Lanyon, William Mortimer, Capt., k. in a., 5/4/15.
Lash, Augustus Oliver, Major, d. of w., 11/9/16.
La Touche, Averell Digges, Lt., k. in a., 25/9/15 (att. 2nd Bn.).
Laurie, George Brenton, Lt.-Col., k. in a., 12/3/15.
Leach, Ernest Walter Vindin, Capt. (Acting), k. in a., 2/1/17 (att. 2nd Bn.).
Lennard, Edward Wood, 2/Lt., k. in a., 30/11/17 (att. 1st Bn.).
Lennox, Alfred James, 2/Lt. (Tp.), k. in a., 20/1/17.
Levis, James Henry Bruce, 2/Lt. (Tp.), k. in a., 12/8/15.
Lucas, Norman Carey, 2/Lt. (Tp.), d. of w., 2/10/16.

McAlidon, Thomas, M.C., 2/Lt. (A./Capt.), died, 17/9/18.
McCammon, Thomas Valentine Plaisted, Lt.-Col., d. of w., 28/4/17 (att. 20th Bn.).
McCann, Bertie Joseph, 2/Lt. (Tp.), k. in a., 12/11/16.
McClelland, Alfred, 2/Lt., d. of w., 13/10/17.
McConnell, Harold Jeffrey, 2/Lt., died, 31/5/18.
McConnell, William Clark, Lt., k. in a., 9/7/16 (att. 2nd Bn.).
McDonnell, Martin Joseph, 2/Lt., d. of w., 24/1/17.
MacFarren, Ernest, 2/Lt. (Tp.), d. of w., 8/11/16.
McFerran, Maurice Anderdon, M.C., 2/Lt., k. in a., 21/3/18.
McGusty, George Ross, Lt. (Tp.), d. of w., 14/6/16.
MacIlwaine, Julian M., Capt., k. in a., 22/3/18 (att. R.F.C., 12 Sqd.).
McIntosh, James Marshall, 2/Lt., k. in a., 16/6/15.
McKee, Patrick Joseph, 2/Lt., k. in a., 10/8/17 (att. 2nd Bn.).
McLaughlin, Arthur, Lt., k. in a., 9/5/15 (att. 1st Bn.).
McMahon, Patrick, 2/Lt., d. of w., 11/6/17.
McMaster, Charles, M.C., T./Lt. (A./Capt.), k. in a., 16/8/17 (att. T.M.B.).
Macnamara, Charles Carroll, Major, d. of w., 15/7/16.
Magenis, R. H. C., 2/Lt., k. in a., 15/9/14.
Mahony, Edward Archibald, Lt., k. in a., 16/8/17.
Marriott-Watson, Richard Brereton, M.C., Lt., k. in a., 24/3/18.
Martin, John Sinclair, Lt., k. in a., 9/5/15.
Martyr, John Francis, Capt., d. of w., 11/8/15.
Master, Charles Lionel, Capt., k. in a., 12/10/14.
Masterman, Frederick Michel, 2/Lt., k. in a., 1/7/16.
Mayne, Denis John Heriot, 2/Lt., killed, 12/10/17 (and R.F.C.).
Mercier, H. B., 2/Lt., died, 3/11/18 (and R.A.F.).
Millar, Ian Arthur, 2/Lt. (Tp.), d. of w., 30/9/16.
Millar, James Lytton, 2/Lt., k. in a., 29/7/16 (att. 15th Bn.).
Miller, Joseph Ewing Bruce, Lt., d. of w., 24/5/15 (att. 1st Bn.).
Mitchell, Arthur Gorman, 2/Lt., k. in a., 13/5/16 (att. 2nd Bn.).
Moore, Morgan Edward Jellett, M.C., Lt., d. of w., 27/3/18 (P. of W.).
Morgan, Samuel Valentine, Capt., k. in a., 10/8/17.
Motherwell, John Ernest, 2/Lt. (A./Capt.), k. in a., 21/10/16 (att. 1st Bn.).
Morton, William, Lt., k. in a., 5/9/15 (att. 2nd Bn.).
Mulcahy-Morgan, Edward Spread, Lt., k. in a., 27/10/14.
Mulcahy-Morgan, Francis Campion, Lt. (Tp.), k. in a., 6/9/16.
Murphy, Johnston, Lt., k. in a., 2/7/16.
Murphy, Robert, 2/Lt., (Tp.) d. of w., 1/10/18.
Neill, Robert Larmour, Lt., k. in a., 9/5/15 (att. 1st Bn.).
Nicholson, Alfred Francis James Steele, 2/Lt. (A./Capt.), k. in a., 16/8/17.
Oakshott, Albert Neville, Lt. (Tp.), k. in a., 16/8/17.
O'Kane, Paul, Lt., k. in a., 21/3/18 (att. 1st Bn.).
O'Lone, Robert James, 2/Lt. (T/Capt.), k. in a., 11/11/15.
O'Lone, Walter Percy, 2/Lt., k. in a., 25/9/15.
O'Reilly, Herbert Wilson, 2/Lt., d. of w., 20/1/16 (att. 2nd Bn.).
Orr, Walter Leslie, 2/Lt., k. in a., 25/9/15 (att. 2nd Bn.).
O'Sullivan, Arthur Moore, Capt., k. in a., 9/5/15.
Owens, William, 2/Lt., k. in a., 16/8/17.
Parsons, Kenneth Templeton Jerrard, Capt. (Tp.), died, 14/8/17
Paull, Bryan Dolphin, 2/Lt., k. in a., 30/9/16.
Pollin, Robert Kelly, 2/Lt., k. in a., 31/7/17.
Popplewell, Harry Bury, Capt., k. in a., 22/7/18 (att. 3rd King's Afr. Rfs.).
Power, Henry Richard, Lt., k. in a., 22/8/17 (att. R.F.C., 48th Sqd.).
Pryor, Ferdinand William, Lt., d. of w., 12/9/16 (att. 6th Innis. Fus.).
Rainey, William, 2/Lt., k. in a., 23/11/17.
Raymond, Arthur Augustus, Lt., k. in a., 1/8/15.

APPENDICES

Rea, Vivian Trevor Tighe, Lt., k. in a., 25/10/14 (att. 2nd Bn.).
Reid, Alexander Daniel, D.S.O., Major (A./Lt.-Col.), k. in a., 31/7/17.
Reynolds, Thomas James, Capt., k. in a., 25/10/14.
Richardson, Allan William, Lt. (Tp.), k. in a., 11/8/15.
Ross, Arthur J., Capt., k. in a., 16/8/17 (att. 1st Bn.).
Ross, Kenneth, 2/Lt., k. in a., 20/6/16.
Ross, Melbourne, 2/Lt., k. in a., 25/9/15 (att. 2nd Bn.).
Scollard, David, M.C., Capt., k. in a., 20/4/17 (att. 7th Bn.)
Sheen, George Edward Hayes, Capt., died, 19/2/15.
Shorland-Ball, Leslie, 2/Lt., k. in a., 6/9/16.
Sinclair, George Stanley, 2/Lt., died, 28/5/17 (att. 1st Bn.).
Smiles, William Alan, Capt. (Tp.), k. in a., 9/7/16.
Smith, Samuel Douard Irvine, Lt., k. in a., 1/7/16 (att. 1st Bn.).
Smyth, George Bostall Jenkinson, Lt. (Tp.) (A./Capt.), k. in a., 22/10/18.
Spedding, Charles Rodney, D.S.O., Major, k. in a., 19/9/14.
Stanley, John Joseph, 2/Lt., k. in a., 9/12/17.
Stein, John Francis, 2/Lt., k. in a., 28/9/16.
Stevens, Reginald Walter Morton, Capt., d. of w., 29/8/14.
Stoker, Edward Alexander, M.C., Lt., d. of w., 12/9/16 (att. 6th Bn.).
Strange, William Hilbert Charles, 2/Lt. (Tp.), k. in a., 31/10/16.
Swaine, Henry Poyntz, 2/Lt., k. in a., 15/9/14.
Thompson, John Crawford, 2/Lt., k. in a., 21/3/18.
Wale, Clifford Hardwicke, 2/Lt. (Tp.), k. in a., 19/1/16.
Walkington, Charles Edward, Capt., k. in a., 14/10/18.
Watson, James, 2/Lt., k. in a., 7/7/16 (att. 2nd Bn.).
Webb, Gilbert Watson, Capt., died, 1/7/16 (and R.F.C.).
Whelan, John Percy, Capt., k. in a., 11/12/14 (att. R. Ir. Regt.).
Whitfeld, Arthur Noel, Lt., k. in a., 14/10/14.
Whitford, Myles, 2/Lt. (Tp.), k. in a., 29/4/16.
Wilkie, Alexander Buchan, 2/Lt., d. of w., 30/11/17.
Williams, Charles Beasley, Capt. (Tp.), k. in a., 28/8/15.
Williams, Ernest Joseph, Lt., k. in a., 15/10/18 (att. 2nd Bn.).
Windus, Charles Eric, 2/Lt., k. in a., 9/5/15.
Witherow, John Thomas, 2/Lt. (Tp.), d. of w., 5/8/17.
Workman, Edward, Lt., d. of w., 26/1/16 (att. 2nd Bn.).
Wright, Allan O'Halloran, Capt., k. in a., 13/3/15.

TOTAL : **188.**

Total number of Officers in the Regiment (a) Killed in Action, (b) Died of Wounds, (c) Killed, other than in action, (d) Died from natural causes, etc. :—

361.

ROLL OF HONOUR.
OTHER RANKS.

Total number of Warrant Officers, Non-commissioned Officers and Men in Battalions 1 to 7 (a) Killed in Action, (b) Died of Wounds, (c) Killed, other than in action, (d) Died, from natural causes, etc. :—

3,118.

A complete Roll of Soldiers of The Royal Irish Rifles who were killed in action or died as the result of wounds, etc., can be found in " Part 67," The Royal Irish Rifles, published by H.M. Stationery Office, at Imperial House, Kingsway, London, W.C. 2, or 23, Forth Street, Edinburgh, or from Eason & Sons, Ltd., 41 & 42, Lower Sackville Street, Dublin. Price 5/-.

APPENDIX IV

NUMBER OF OTHER RANKS WHO PROCEEDED AS REINFORCEMENTS FROM THE SPECIAL RESERVE BATTALIONS—3RD, 4TH, 5TH BATTALIONS ROYAL IRISH RIFLES—DURING THE GREAT WAR, 1914-18.

	3rd Battalion.	4th Battalion.	5th Battalion.
1914	1098	153	380
1915	2469	577	582
1916	1878	439	569
1917	1243	561	206
1918	1381	458	197
Totals	8069	2188	1934
Grand Total	12,191.		

Note.—The above figures are taken from Part II Battalion Orders of the Units. It has not been found practicable to include the number of officers in each case. In addition to the above a large number of Other Ranks were transferred, at home, from each of the three battalions to other Infantry units, and the Labour Corps. Most probably a considerable proportion of these transfers proceeded overseas with their new units.

APPENDIX V

TITLE OF THE REGIMENT.

In accordance with instructions contained in A.O. 509 of 1920 the title of the Regiment has changed to that of the ROYAL ULSTER RIFLES, with effect from January 1st, 1921.

APPENDIX VI

LIST OF BATTLE HONOURS.

1914. *Battle Honours.*	Battalion.
Mons	
Le Cateau	
Retreat from Mons	
Marne	
Aisne	2nd.
La Bassée	
Messines	
Armentières	
Ypres	
Nonne Bosschen	
France and Flanders, 1914–1918	1st, 2nd, 7th, 8th, 9th, 10th, 11th, 12th, 13th, 14th, 15th, 16th.
1915.	
Neuve Chapelle	1st.
Aubers	
Ypres	2nd.
Frezenberg	
Suvla	
Sari Bair	
Gallipoli	6th.
Kosturino	
Macedonia, 1915–1917	
1916.	
Somme	1st, 2nd, 7th, 8th, 9th, 10th, 11th, 12th, 13th, 14th, 15th, 16th.
Albert	1st, 2nd, 8th, 9th, 10th, 11th, 12th, 13th, 14th, 15th, 16th.
Bazentin	
Pozières	2nd.
Ancre Heights	
Guillemont	7th.
Ginchy	
Struma	6th.
1917.	
Messines	2nd, 7th, 8th, 9th, 10th, 11th, 12th, 13th, 14th, 15th, 16th.
Ypres	1st, 2nd, 7th, 8th, 9th, 10th, 11th, 12th, 13th, 14th, 15th, 16th.
Pilckem	1st, 2nd, 7th, 8th, 9th, 10th, 11th.
Langemarck	1st, 2nd, 8th, 9th, 10th, 11th, 12th, 13th, 14th, 15th, 16th.
Gaza	6th.
Cambrai	2nd, 8/9th, 10th, 11/13th, 12th, 14th, 15th, 16th.
Jerusalem	
Tell 'Asur	6th.
Palestine, 1917–1918	
1918.	
Somme	1st, 2nd, 12th, 15th, 16th.
St. Quentin	1st, 2nd, 12th, 15th, 16th.
Rosières	1st, 2nd, 15th.
Lys	
Kemmel	
Messines	12th.
Bailleul	
Ypres	1st, 2nd, 12th, 15th, 16th.
Courtrai	1st, 2nd, 12th, 15th, 16th.

APPENDIX VII

REGIMENTAL COMMITTEE ON BATTLE HONOURS FOR THE GREAT WAR.

Battalion.

1st	...	Lieut.-Colonel H. R. Charley, C.B.E.
2nd	...	Major H. R. Goodman, D.S.O., and Lieut.-Colonel C. M. L. Becher, D.S.O.
3rd	...	Lieut.-Colonel W. E. C. McCammond.
4th	...	No answers to invitations.
5th	...	No answers to invitations.
6th	...	Lieut.-Colonel C. M. L. Becher, D.S.O.
7th	...	Lieut.-Colonel C. M. L. Stocker.
8th	...	Lieut.-Colonel C. J. Cole-Hamilton, C.M.G., D.S.O.
9th	...	Brigadier-General F. P. Crozier, C.B., C.M.G., D.S.O.
10th	...	Major E. R. A. May.
11th	...	Captain C. C. Craig, P.C.
12th	...	Lieut.-Colonel W. R. Goodwin, C.M.G., D.S.O.
13th	...	Major R. Workman.
14th	...	Lieut.-Colonel J. A. Mulholland.
15th	...	Captain F. T. Hill.
16th	...	Colonel Sir W. J. Allen, K.B.E., D.S.O.
17th	...	No representative could be found.
18th	...	Colonel R. G. Sharman Crawford, P.C., C.B.E.
19th	...	No representative could be found.
20th	...	No representative could be found.
21st	...	No representative could be found.

Chairman : Major-General Sir W. D. Bird, K.B.E., C.B., C.M.G., D.S.O., acting for the Colonel of the Regiment.

The following battalions served in the field :—1st, 2nd, 6th, 7th, 8th, 9th, 10th, 11th, 12th, 13th, 14th, 15th, 16th.

THE
ROYAL IRISH RIFLES

The Harp and Crown, with the motto, *"Quis Separabit."* The Sphinx, superscribed "Egypt."

BATTLE HONOURS

"India."
"Cape of Good Hope, 1806."
"Talavera."
"Bourbon."
"Busaco."

"Fuentes d'Onor."
"Ciudad Rodrigo."
"Badajoz."
"Salamanca."
"Vittoria."
"Nivelle."

"Orthes."
"Toulouse."
"Peninsula."
"Central India."
"South Africa, 1899-1902."

THE GREAT WAR

"Mons."
"Le Cateau."
"Retreat from Mons."
"Marne, 1914."
"Aisne, 1914."
"La Bassée, 1914."
"Messines, 1914, '17, '18."
"Armentières, 1914."
"Ypres, 1914, '15, '17, '18."
"Nonne Bosschen."
"Neuve Chapelle."
"Frezenberg."
"Aubers."

"Somme, 1916, '18."
"Albert, 1916."
"Bazentin."
"Pozières."
"Guillemont."
"Ginchy."
"Ancre Heights."
"Pilckem."
"Langemarck, 1917."
"Cambrai, 1917."
"St. Quentin."
"Rosières."
"Lys."

"Bailleul."
"Kemmel."
"Courtrai."
"France and Flanders, 1914-18."
"Kosturino."
"Struma."
"Macedonia, 1915-17."
"Suvla."
"Sari Bair."
"Gallipoli, 1915."
"Gaza."
"Jerusalem."
"Tell 'Asur."
"Palestine, 1917-18."

Printed in Great Britain
by Amazon